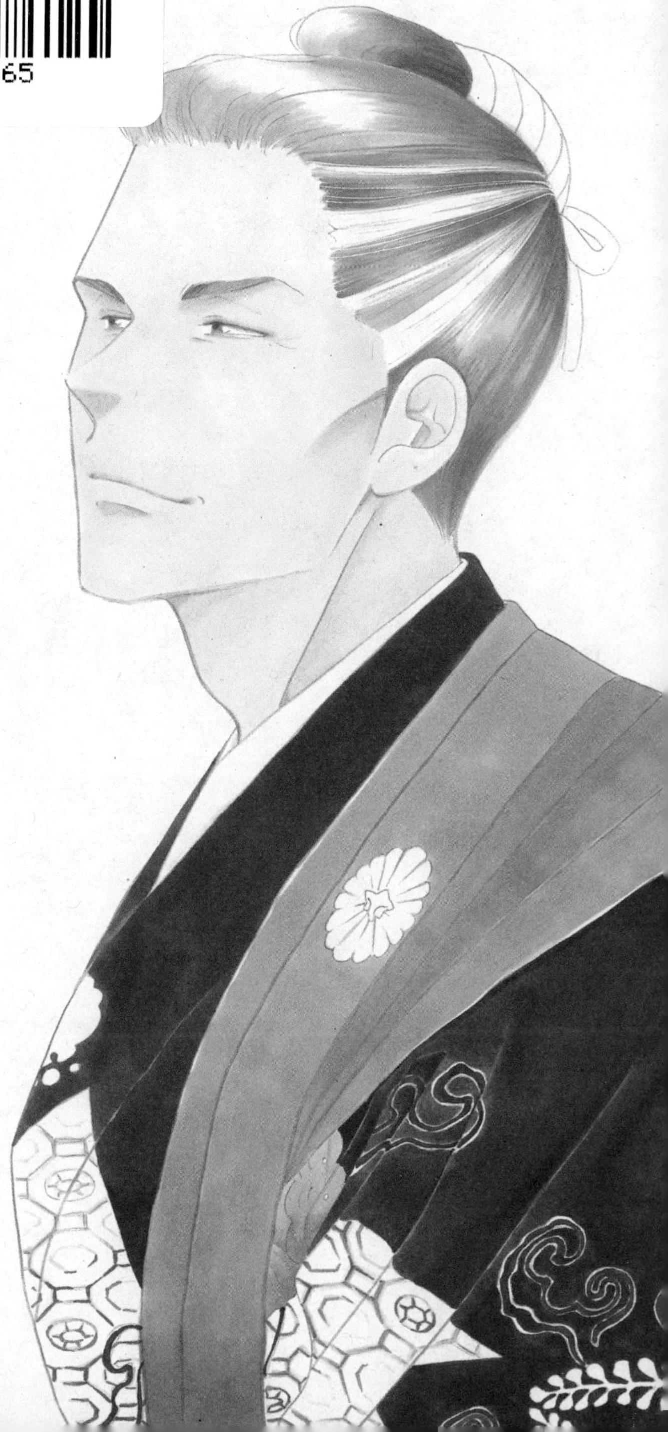

TABLE *of* CONTENTS

Ōoku

THE INNER CHAMBERS

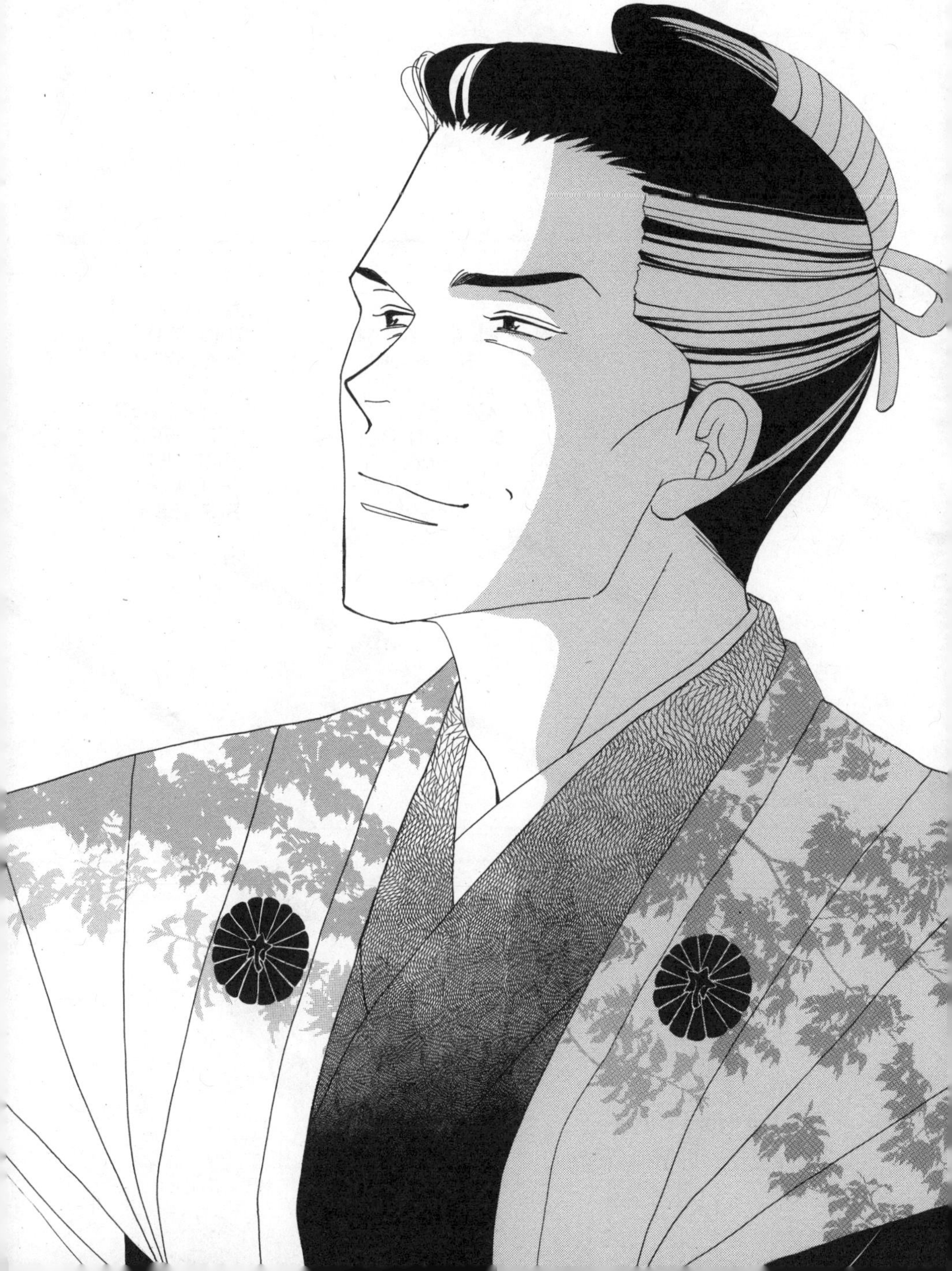

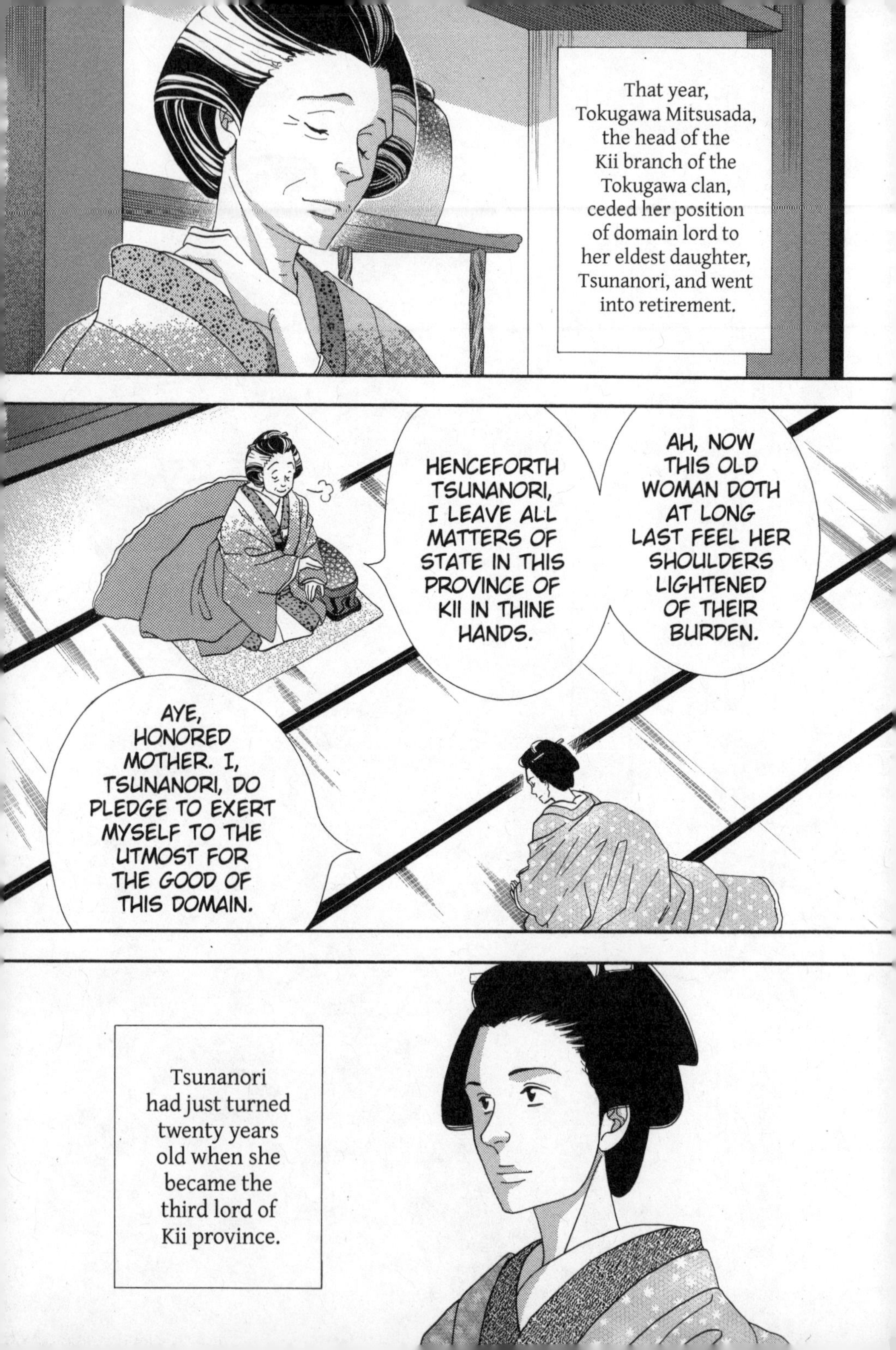
That year, Tokugawa Mitsusada, the head of the Kii branch of the Tokugawa clan, ceded her position of domain lord to her eldest daughter, Tsunanori, and went into retirement.
AH, NOW THIS OLD WOMAN DOTH AT LONG LAST FEEL HER SHOULDERS LIGHTENED OF THEIR BURDEN.
HENCEFORTH TSUNANORI, I LEAVE ALL MATTERS OF STATE IN THIS PROVINCE OF KII IN THINE HANDS.
AYE, HONORED MOTHER. I, TSUNANORI, DO PLEDGE TO EXERT MYSELF TO THE UTMOST FOR THE GOOD OF THIS DOMAIN.
Tsunanori had just turned twenty years old when she became the third lord of Kii province.

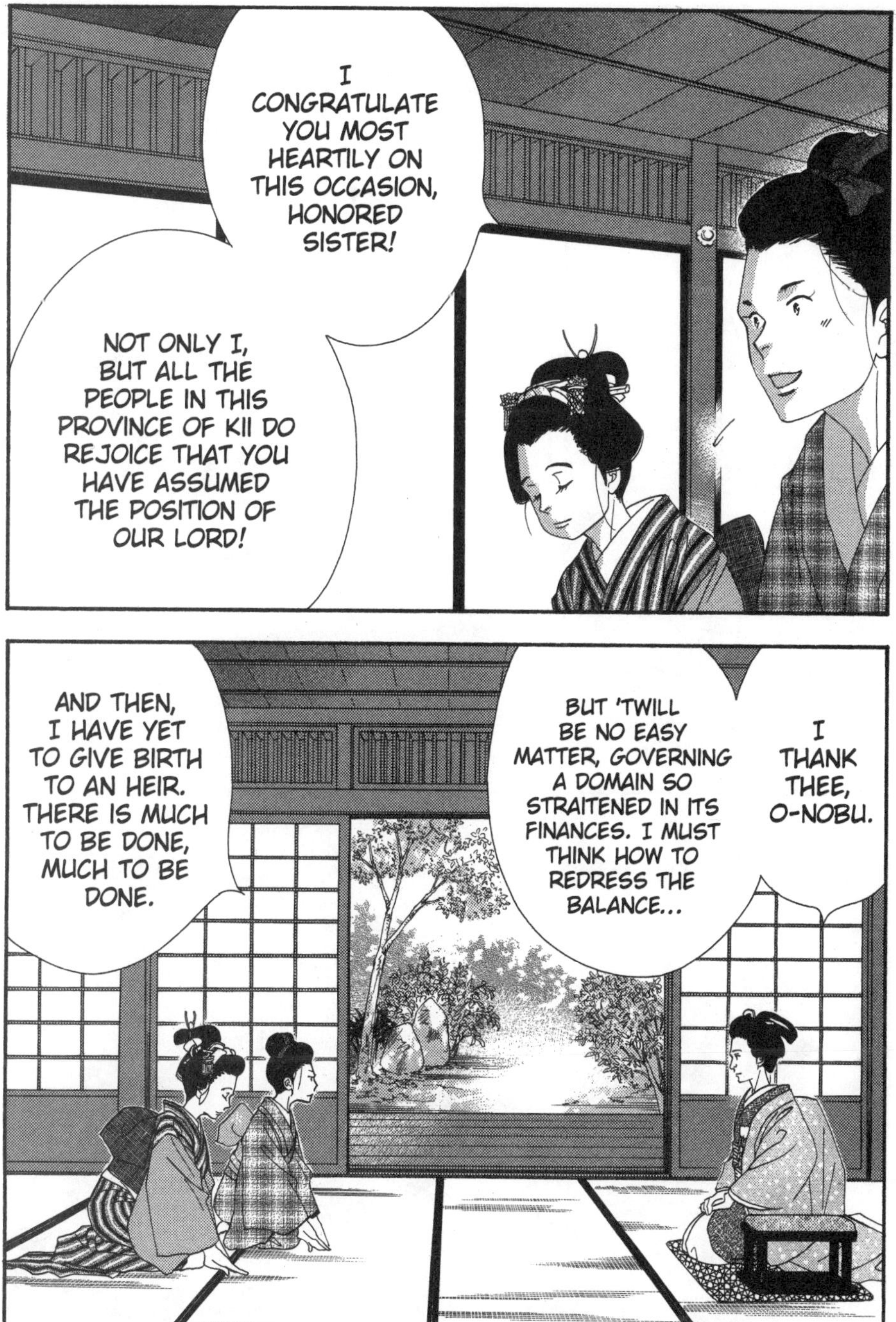
I CONGRATULATE YOU MOST HEARTILY ON THIS OCCASION, HONORED SISTER!
NOT ONLY I, BUT ALL THE PEOPLE IN THIS PROVINCE OF KII DO REJOICE THAT YOU HAVE ASSUMED THE POSITION OF OUR LORD!
I THANK THEE, O-NOBU.
BUT 'TWILL BE NO EASY MATTER, GOVERNING A DOMAIN SO STRAITENED IN ITS FINANCES. I MUST THINK HOW TO REDRESS THE BALANCE...
AND THEN, I HAVE YET TO GIVE BIRTH TO AN HEIR. THERE IS MUCH TO BE DONE, MUCH TO BE DONE.

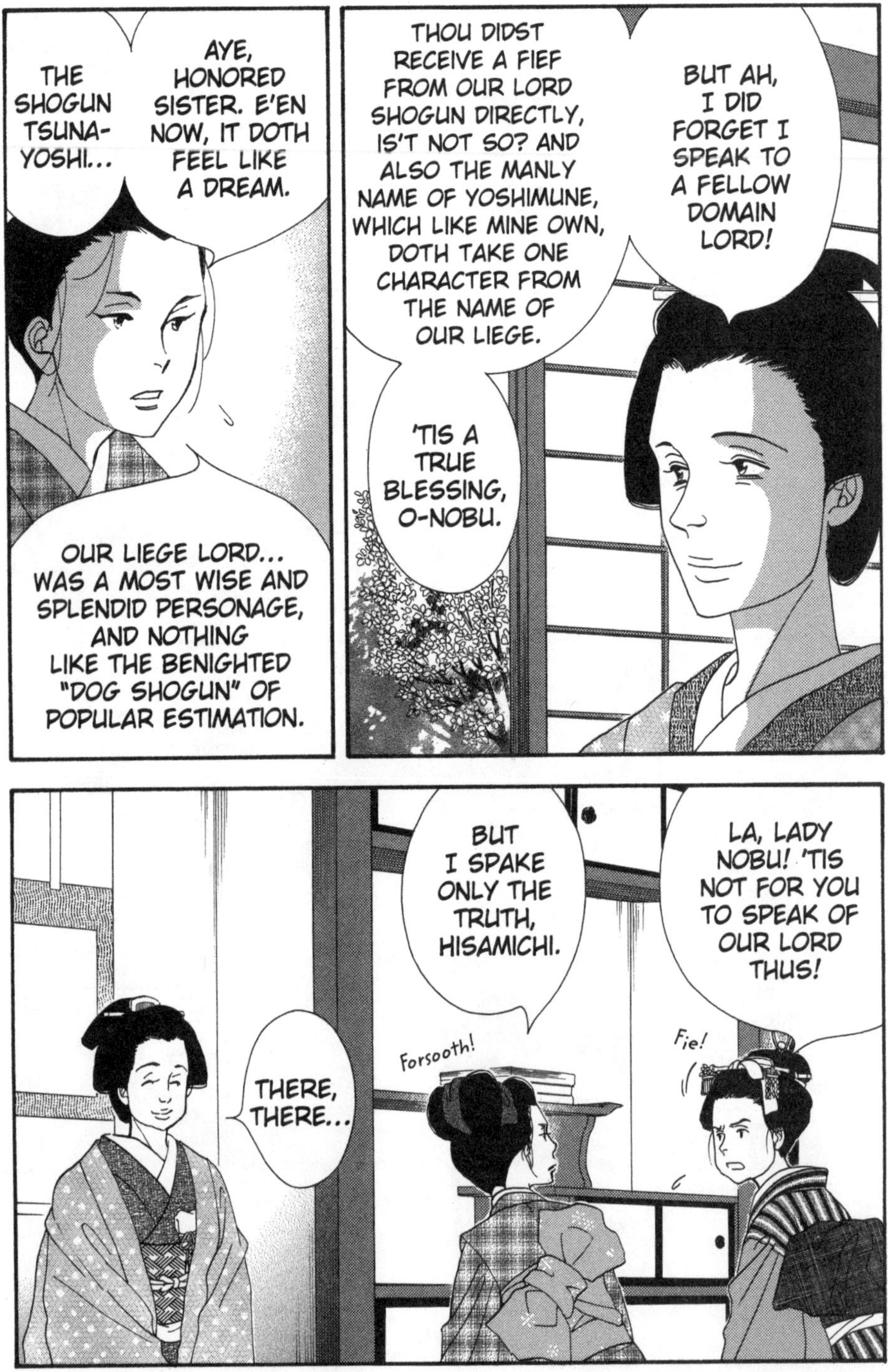

BUT AH, I DID FORGET I SPEAK TO A FELLOW DOMAIN LORD!
THOU DIDST RECEIVE A FIEF FROM OUR LORD SHOGUN DIRECTLY, IS'T NOT SO? AND ALSO THE MANLY NAME OF YOSHIMUNE, WHICH LIKE MINE OWN, DOTH TAKE ONE CHARACTER FROM THE NAME OF OUR LIEGE.
'TIS A TRUE BLESSING, O-NOBU.
AYE, HONORED SISTER. E'EN NOW, IT DOTH FEEL LIKE A DREAM.
THE SHOGUN TSUNA-YOSHI...
OUR LIEGE LORD... WAS A MOST WISE AND SPLENDID PERSONAGE, AND NOTHING LIKE THE BENIGHTED "DOG SHOGUN" OF POPULAR ESTIMATION.
LA, LADY NOBU! 'TIS NOT FOR YOU TO SPEAK OF OUR LORD THUS!
Fie!
BUT I SPAKE ONLY THE TRUTH, HISAMICHI.
Forsooth!
THERE, THERE...

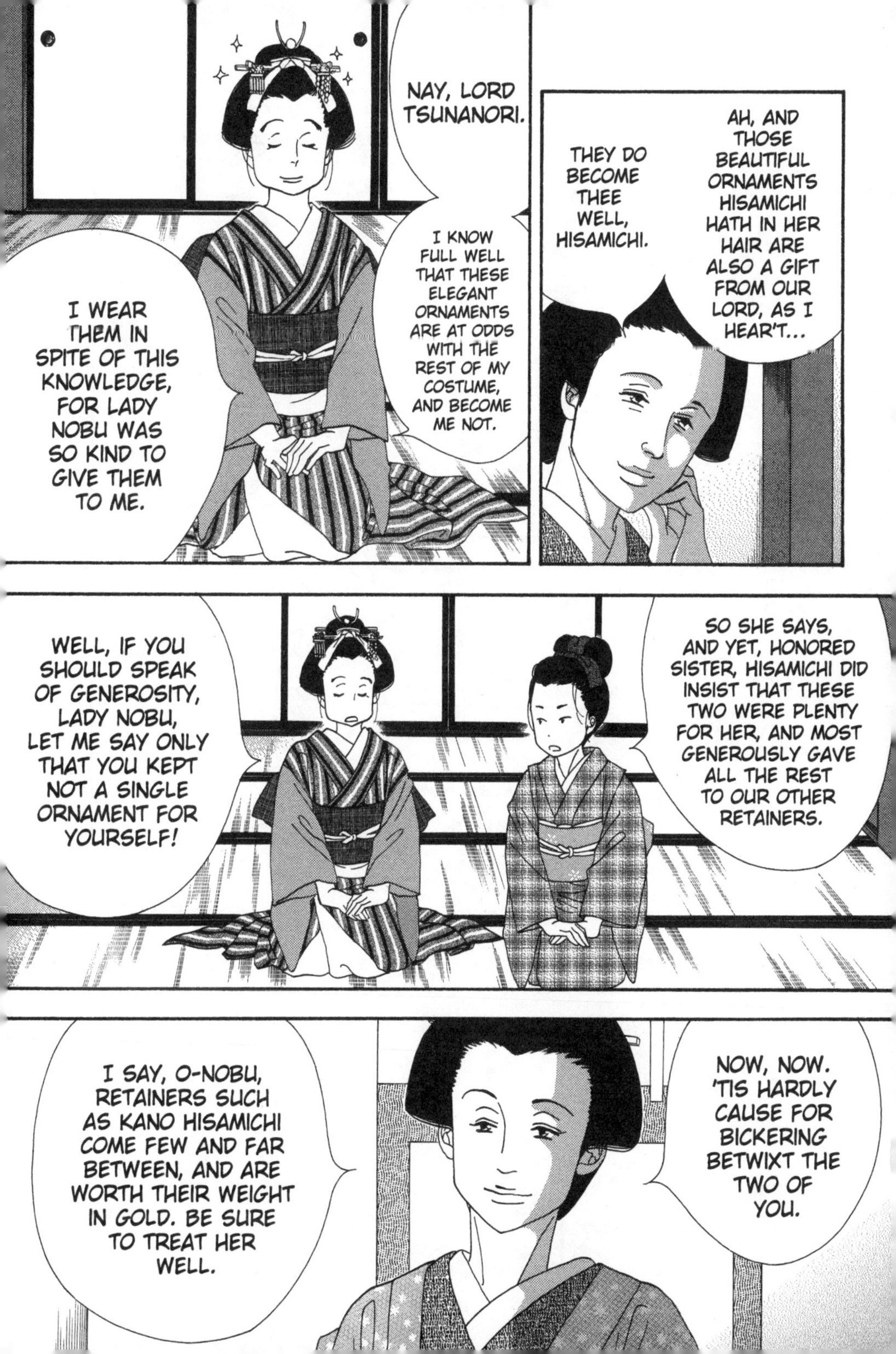
AH, AND THOSE BEAUTIFUL ORNAMENTS HISAMICHI HATH IN HER HAIR ARE ALSO A GIFT FROM OUR LORD, AS I HEAR'T...
THEY DO BECOME THEE WELL, HISAMICHI.
NAY, LORD TSUNANORI.
I KNOW FULL WELL THAT THESE ELEGANT ORNAMENTS ARE AT ODDS WITH THE REST OF MY COSTUME, AND BECOME ME NOT.
I WEAR THEM IN SPITE OF THIS KNOWLEDGE, FOR LADY NOBU WAS SO KIND TO GIVE THEM TO ME.
SO SHE SAYS, AND YET, HONORED SISTER, HISAMICHI DID INSIST THAT THESE TWO WERE PLENTY FOR HER, AND MOST GENEROUSLY GAVE ALL THE REST TO OUR OTHER RETAINERS.
WELL, IF YOU SHOULD SPEAK OF GENEROSITY, LADY NOBU, LET ME SAY ONLY THAT YOU KEPT NOT A SINGLE ORNAMENT FOR YOURSELF!
NOW, NOW. 'TIS HARDLY CAUSE FOR BICKERING BETWIXT THE TWO OF YOU.
I SAY, O-NOBU, RETAINERS SUCH AS KANO HISAMICHI COME FEW AND FAR BETWEEN, AND ARE WORTH THEIR WEIGHT IN GOLD. BE SURE TO TREAT HER WELL.

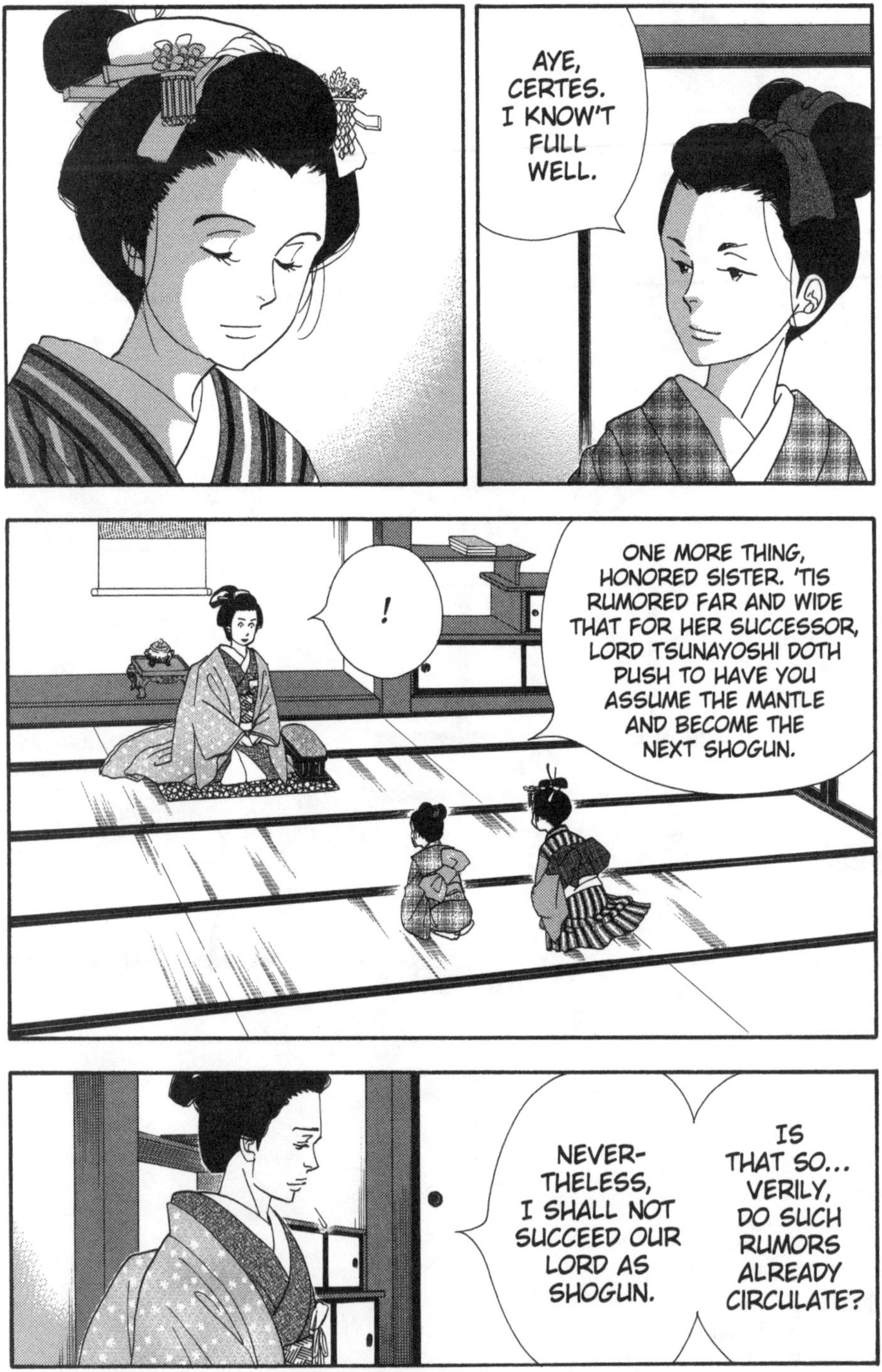
AYE, CERTES. I KNOW'T FULL WELL.
ONE MORE THING, HONORED SISTER. 'TIS RUMORED FAR AND WIDE THAT FOR HER SUCCESSOR, LORD TSUNAYOSHI DOTH PUSH TO HAVE YOU ASSUME THE MANTLE AND BECOME THE NEXT SHOGUN.
!
IS THAT SO... VERILY, DO SUCH RUMORS ALREADY CIRCULATE?
NEVER-THELESS, I SHALL NOT SUCCEED OUR LORD AS SHOGUN.

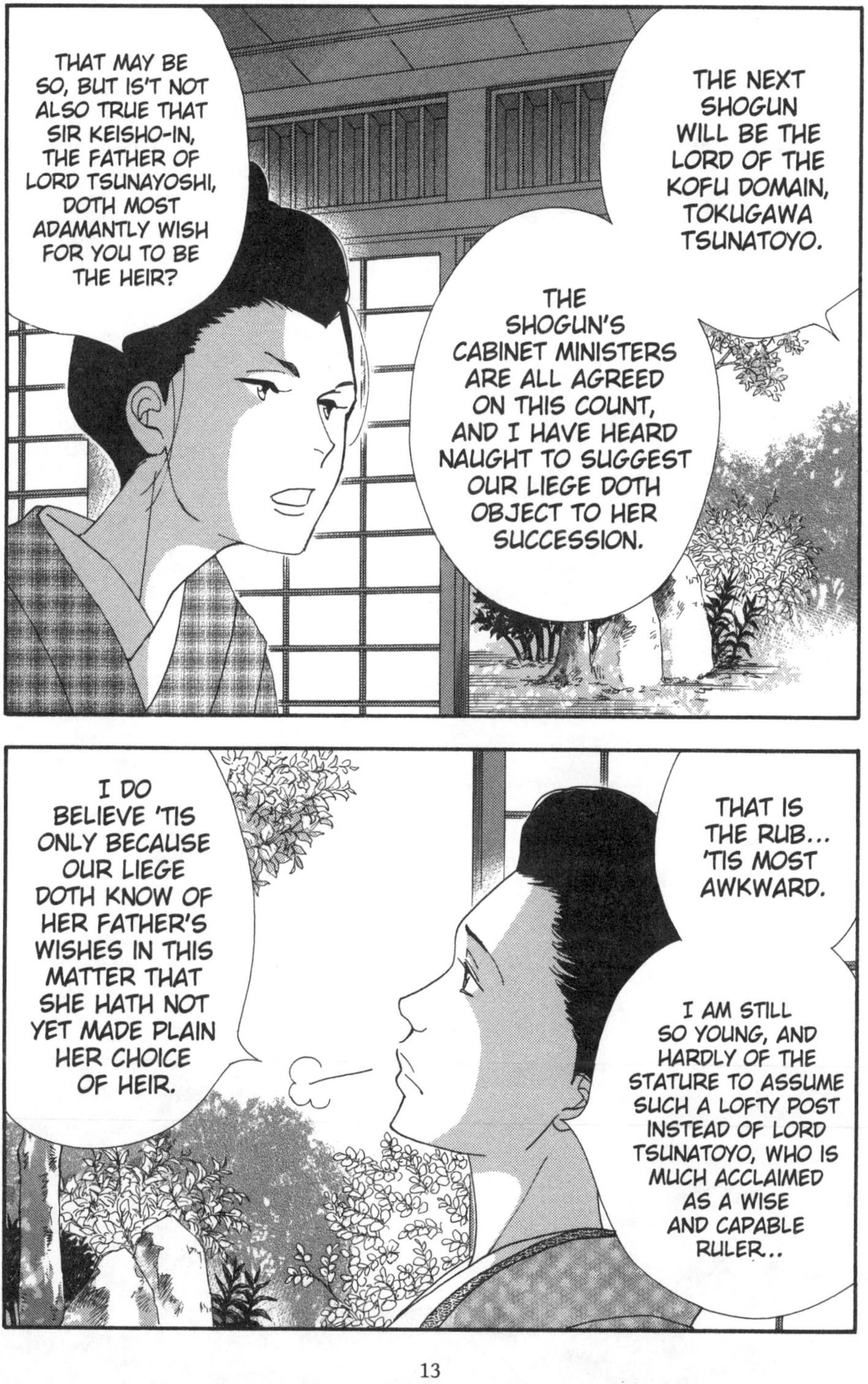
THE NEXT SHOGUN WILL BE THE LORD OF THE KOFU DOMAIN, TOKUGAWA TSUNATOYO.
THE SHOGUN'S CABINET MINISTERS ARE ALL AGREED ON THIS COUNT, AND I HAVE HEARD NAUGHT TO SUGGEST OUR LIEGE DOTH OBJECT TO HER SUCCESSION.
THAT MAY BE SO, BUT IS'T NOT ALSO TRUE THAT SIR KEISHO-IN, THE FATHER OF LORD TSUNAYOSHI, DOTH MOST ADAMANTLY WISH FOR YOU TO BE THE HEIR?
THAT IS THE RUB... 'TIS MOST AWKWARD.
I AM STILL SO YOUNG, AND HARDLY OF THE STATURE TO ASSUME SUCH A LOFTY POST INSTEAD OF LORD TSUNATOYO, WHO IS MUCH ACCLAIMED AS A WISE AND CAPABLE RULER..
I DO BELIEVE 'TIS ONLY BECAUSE OUR LIEGE DOTH KNOW OF HER FATHER'S WISHES IN THIS MATTER THAT SHE HATH NOT YET MADE PLAIN HER CHOICE OF HEIR.

AND ABOVE ALL, WHAT MUST BE, MUST BE!

WE OF THE KII DOMAIN, LIKE OUR KIN IN OWARI AND MITO, ARE NOTHING MORE THAN BRANCHES OF THE TOKU-GAWA FAMILY, TO STEP INTO THE BREACH SHOULD THE MAIN LINE FAIL TO PRODUCE AN HEIR. SO LONG AS LORD TSUNATOYO, AS THE NIECE OF THE PRESENT SHOGUN, BE THERE TO ASSUME THE SUCCESSION, OUR PLACE IS HERE IN KII, NOT EDO.

DOST THOU UNDER-STAND?

...AYE, M'LORD.

Meanwhile, in Tokugawa Tsunatoyo's Edo mansion, her Valet of the Chamber, Manabe Akifusa, was airing her disgruntlement.

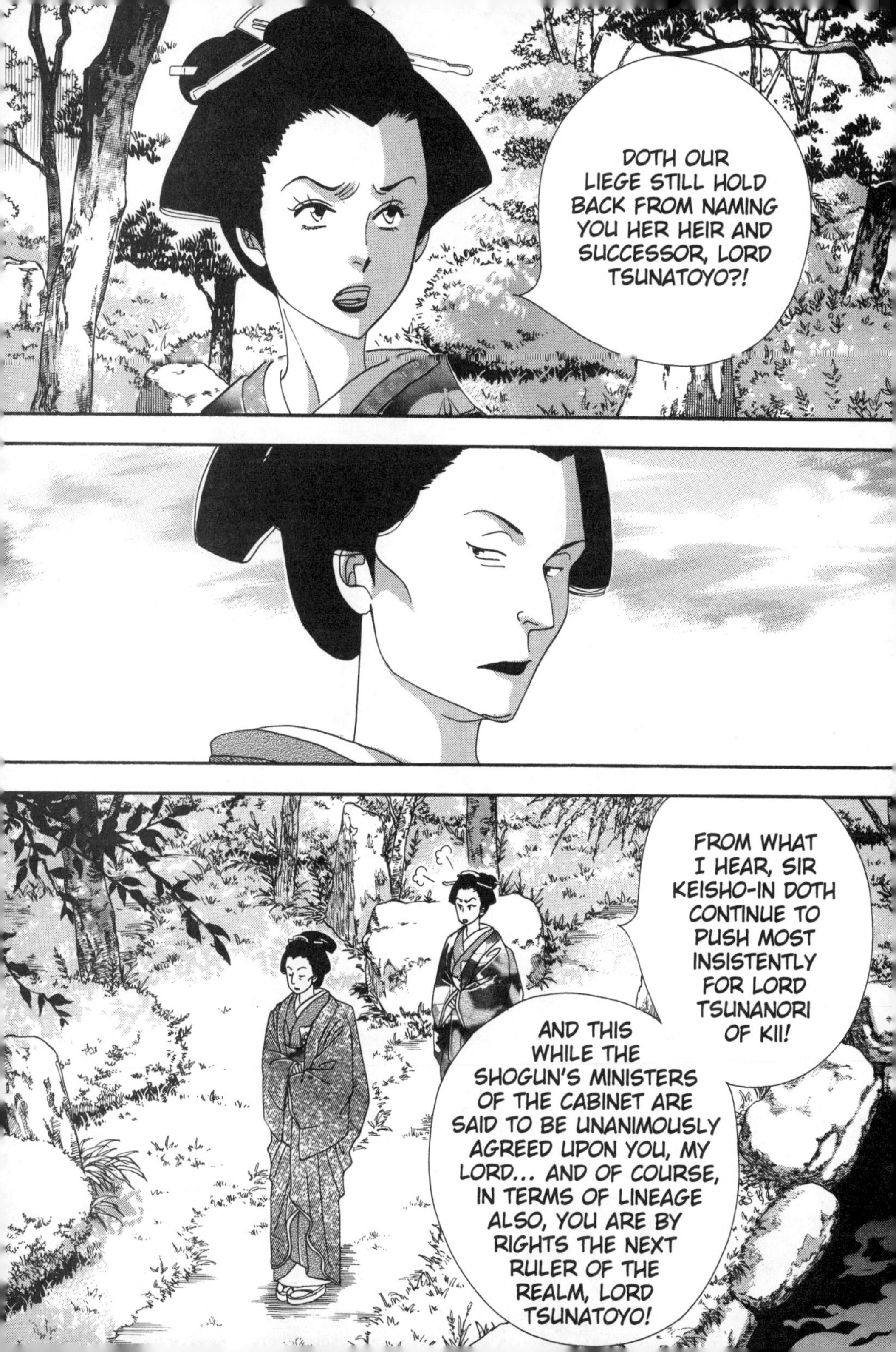
DOTH OUR LIEGE STILL HOLD BACK FROM NAMING YOU HER HEIR AND SUCCESSOR, LORD TSUNATOYO?!
FROM WHAT I HEAR, SIR KEISHO-IN DOTH CONTINUE TO PUSH MOST INSISTENTLY FOR LORD TSUNANORI OF KII!
AND THIS WHILE THE SHOGUN'S MINISTERS OF THE CABINET ARE SAID TO BE UNANIMOUSLY AGREED UPON YOU, MY LORD... AND OF COURSE, IN TERMS OF LINEAGE ALSO, YOU ARE BY RIGHTS THE NEXT RULER OF THE REALM, LORD TSUNATOYO!

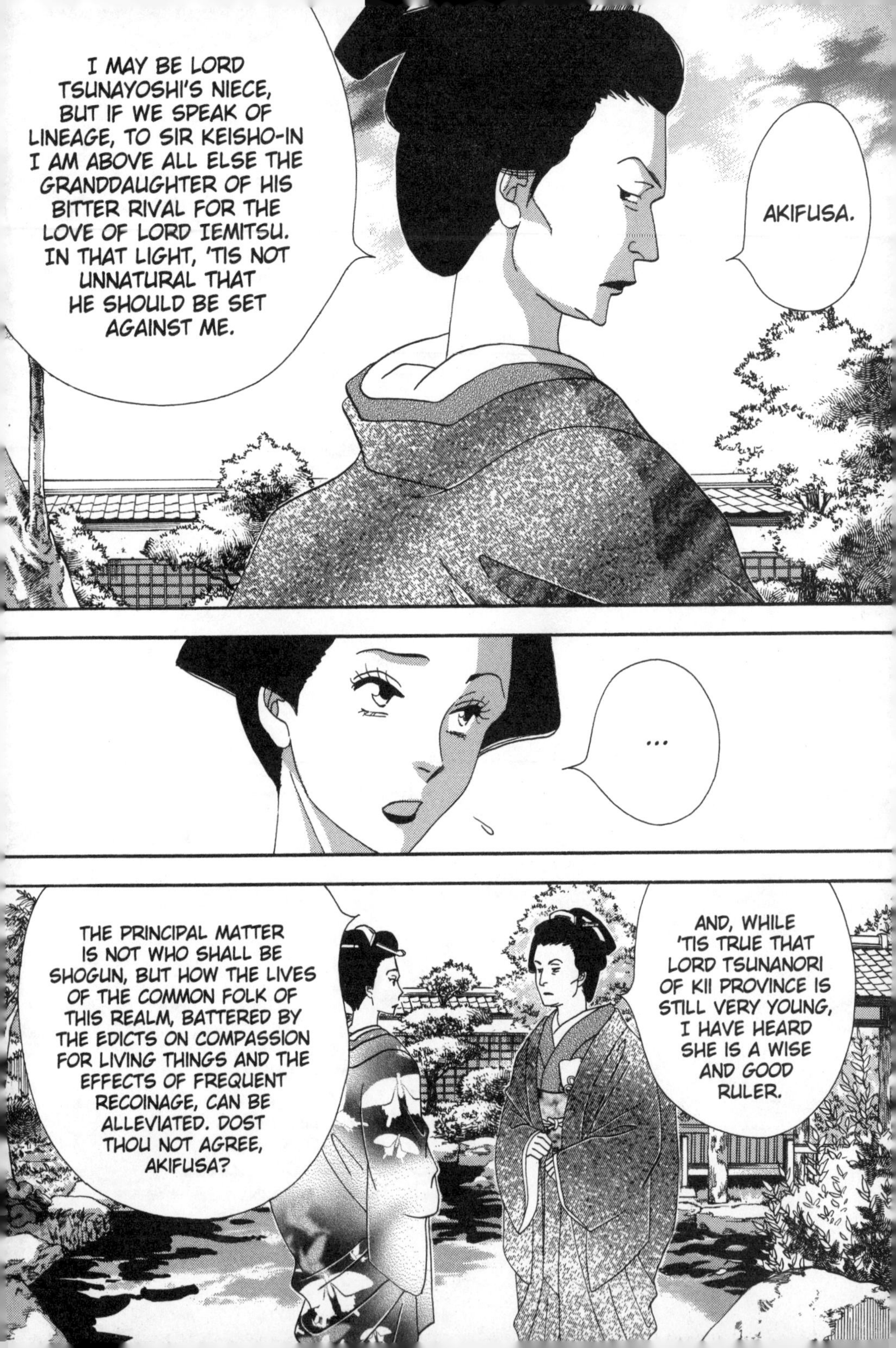
AKIFUSA.
I MAY BE LORD TSUNAYOSHI'S NIECE, BUT IF WE SPEAK OF LINEAGE, TO SIR KEISHO-IN I AM ABOVE ALL ELSE THE GRANDDAUGHTER OF HIS BITTER RIVAL FOR THE LOVE OF LORD IEMITSU. IN THAT LIGHT, 'TIS NOT UNNATURAL THAT HE SHOULD BE SET AGAINST ME.
...
AND, WHILE 'TIS TRUE THAT LORD TSUNANORI OF KII PROVINCE IS STILL VERY YOUNG, I HAVE HEARD SHE IS A WISE AND GOOD RULER.
THE PRINCIPAL MATTER IS NOT WHO SHALL BE SHOGUN, BUT HOW THE LIVES OF THE COMMON FOLK OF THIS REALM, BATTERED BY THE EDICTS ON COMPASSION FOR LIVING THINGS AND THE EFFECTS OF FREQUENT RECOINAGE, CAN BE ALLEVIATED. DOST THOU NOT AGREE, AKIFUSA?

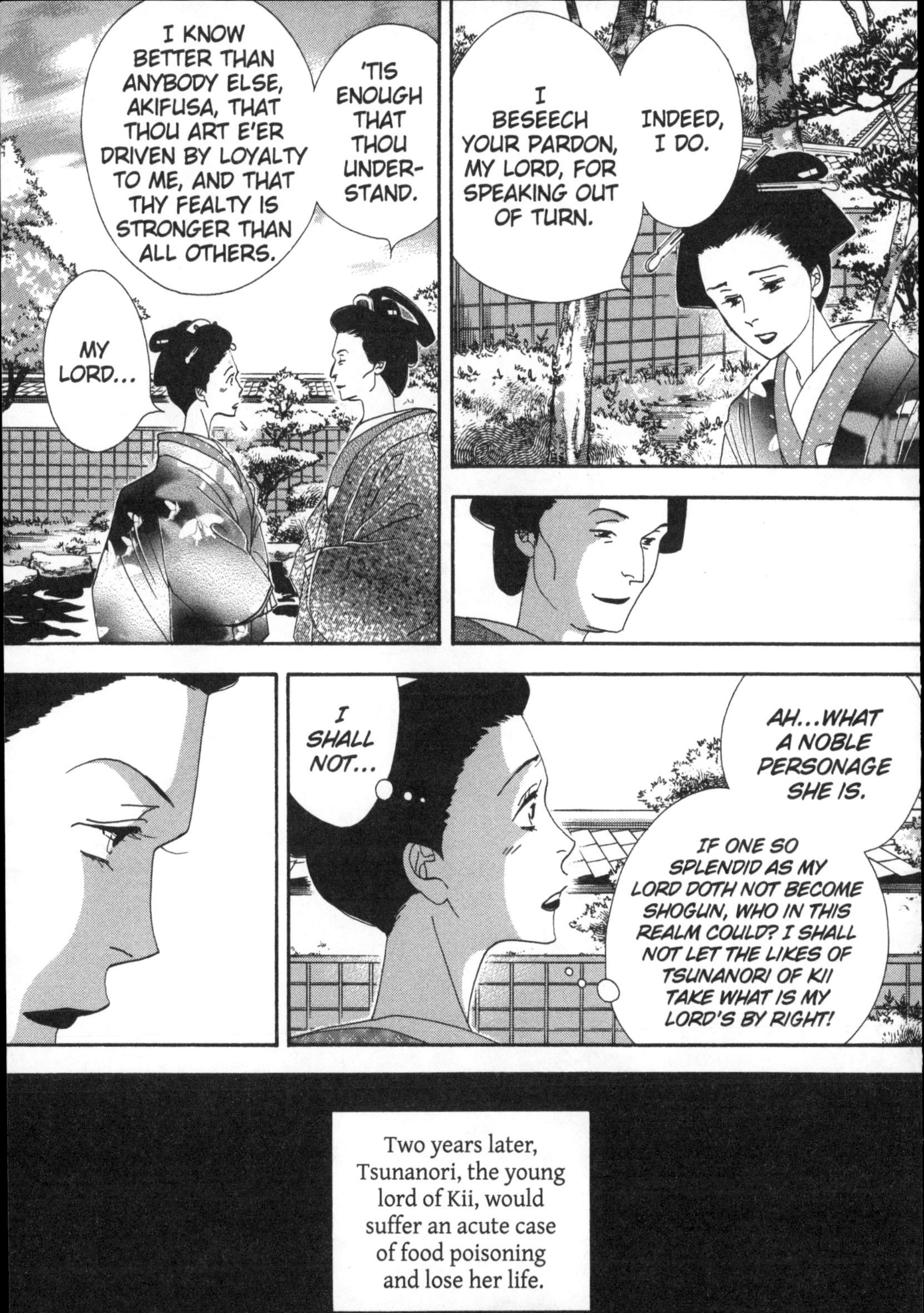
INDEED, I DO.
I BESEECH YOUR PARDON, MY LORD, FOR SPEAKING OUT OF TURN.
'TIS ENOUGH THAT THOU UNDER-STAND.
I KNOW BETTER THAN ANYBODY ELSE, AKIFUSA, THAT THOU ART E'ER DRIVEN BY LOYALTY TO ME, AND THAT THY FEALTY IS STRONGER THAN ALL OTHERS.
MY LORD...
AH...WHAT A NOBLE PERSONAGE SHE IS.
IF ONE SO SPLENDID AS MY LORD DOTH NOT BECOME SHOGUN, WHO IN THIS REALM COULD? I SHALL NOT LET THE LIKES OF TSUNANORI OF KII TAKE WHAT IS MY LORD'S BY RIGHT!
I SHALL NOT...
Two years later, Tsunanori, the young lord of Kii, would suffer an acute case of food poisoning and lose her life.

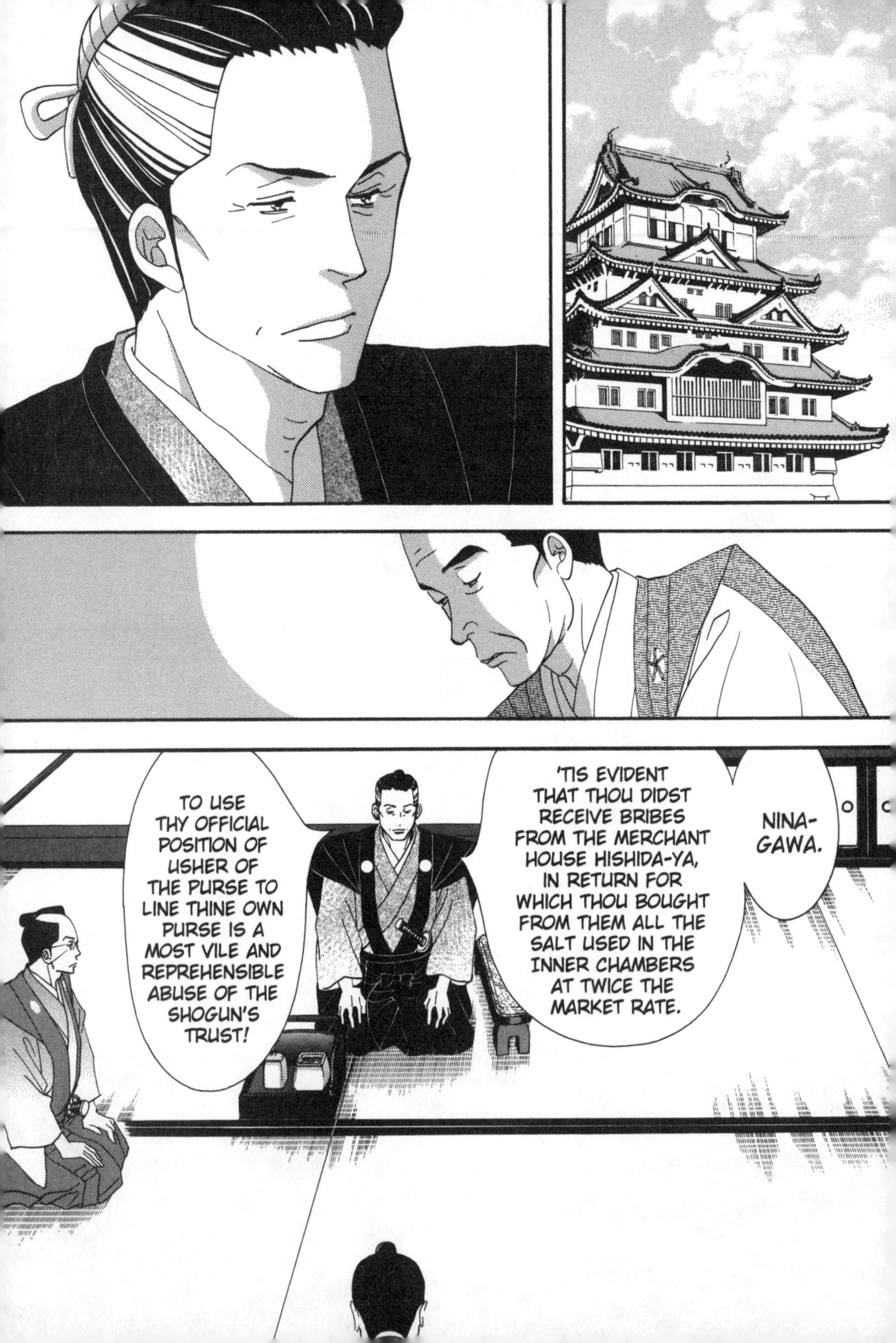
NINA-GAWA.
'TIS EVIDENT THAT THOU DIDST RECEIVE BRIBES FROM THE MERCHANT HOUSE HISHIDA-YA, IN RETURN FOR WHICH THOU BOUGHT FROM THEM ALL THE SALT USED IN THE INNER CHAMBERS AT TWICE THE MARKET RATE.
TO USE THY OFFICIAL POSITION OF USHER OF THE PURSE TO LINE THINE OWN PURSE IS A MOST VILE AND REPREHENSIBLE ABUSE OF THE SHOGUN'S TRUST!

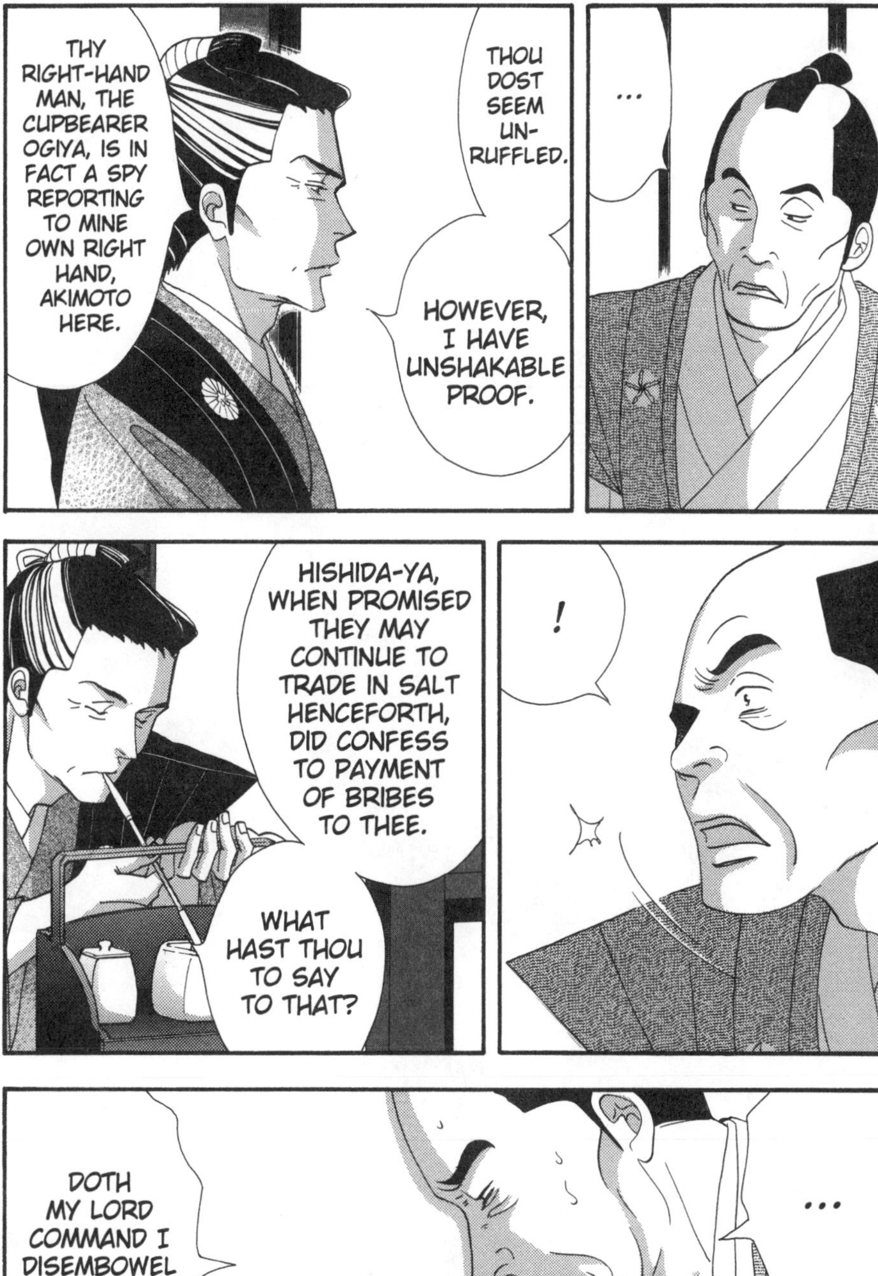
...
THOU DOST SEEM UN-RUFFLED.
THY RIGHT-HAND MAN, THE CUPBEARER OGIYA, IS IN FACT A SPY REPORTING TO MINE OWN RIGHT HAND, AKIMOTO HERE.
HOWEVER, I HAVE UNSHAKABLE PROOF.
!
HISHIDA-YA, WHEN PROMISED THEY MAY CONTINUE TO TRADE IN SALT HENCEFORTH, DID CONFESS TO PAYMENT OF BRIBES TO THEE.
WHAT HAST THOU TO SAY TO THAT?
...
DOTH MY LORD COMMAND I DISEMBOWEL MYSELF...?

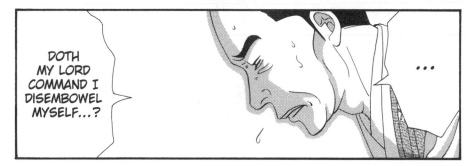

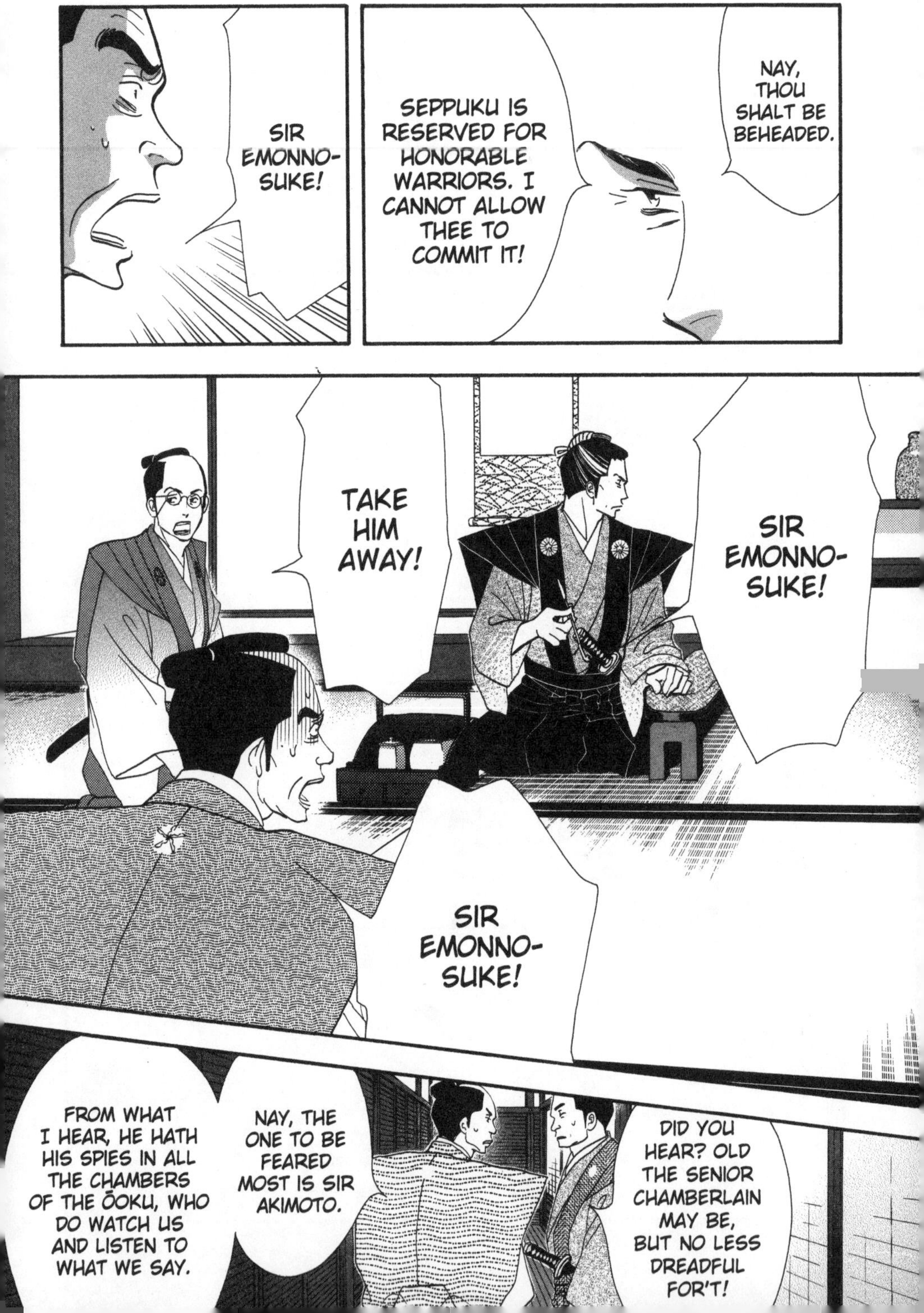
SEPPUKU IS RESERVED FOR HONORABLE WARRIORS. I CANNOT ALLOW THEE TO COMMIT IT!
NAY, THOU SHALT BE BEHEADED.
SIR EMONNO-SUKE!
SIR EMONNO-SUKE!
TAKE HIM AWAY!
SIR EMONNO-SUKE!
DID YOU HEAR? OLD THE SENIOR CHAMBERLAIN MAY BE, BUT NO LESS DREADFUL FOR'T!
NAY, THE ONE TO BE FEARED MOST IS SIR AKIMOTO.
FROM WHAT I HEAR, HE HATH HIS SPIES IN ALL THE CHAMBERS OF THE ŌOKU, WHO DO WATCH US AND LISTEN TO WHAT WE SAY.

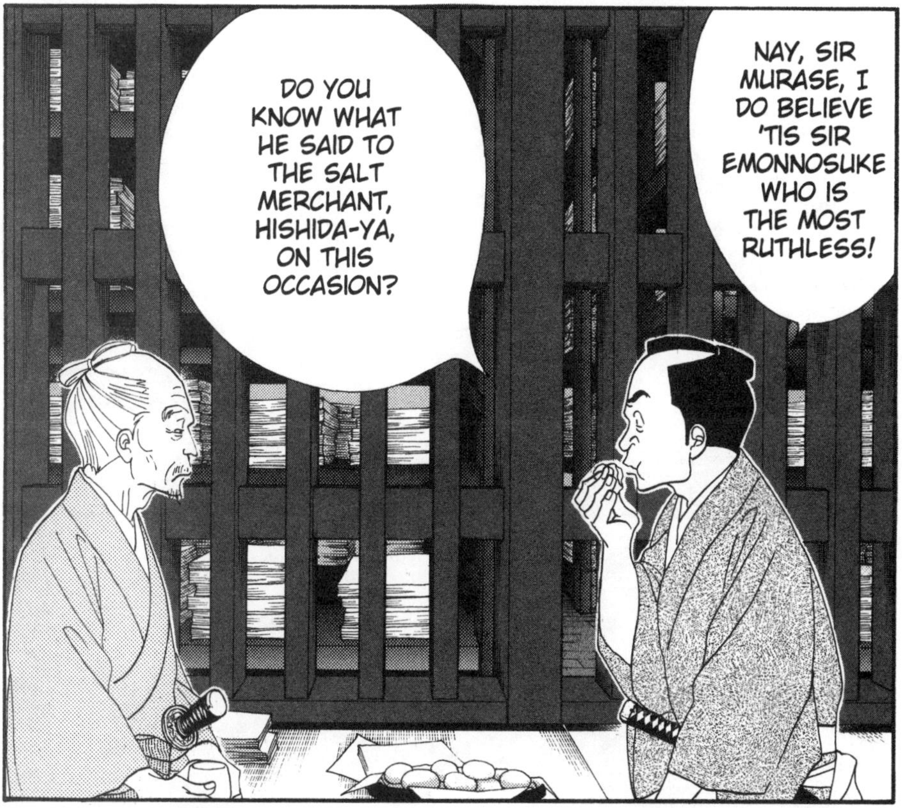
NAY, SIR MURASE, I DO BELIEVE 'TIS SIR EMONNOSUKE WHO IS THE MOST RUTHLESS!
DO YOU KNOW WHAT HE SAID TO THE SALT MERCHANT, HISHIDA-YA, ON THIS OCCASION?

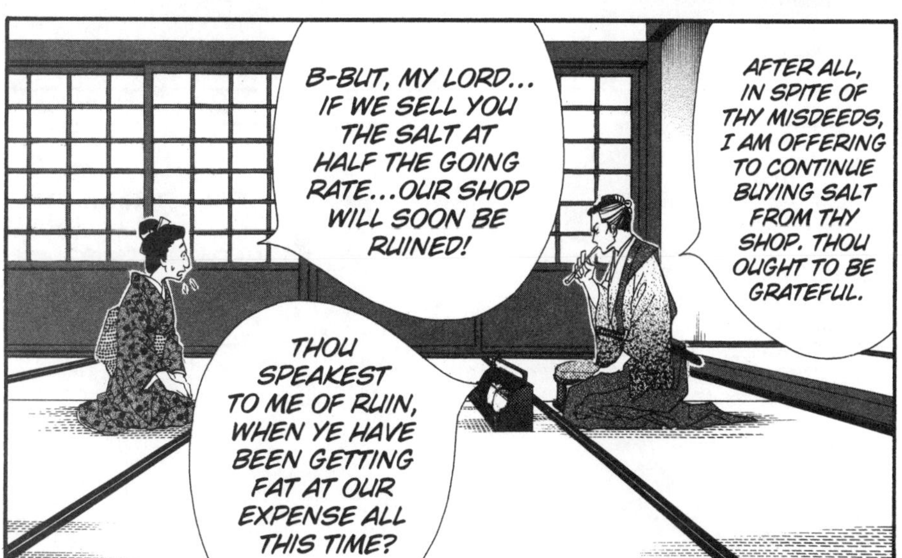
AFTER ALL, IN SPITE OF THY MISDEEDS, I AM OFFERING TO CONTINUE BUYING SALT FROM THY SHOP. THOU OUGHT TO BE GRATEFUL.
B-BUT, MY LORD... IF WE SELL YOU THE SALT AT HALF THE GOING RATE...OUR SHOP WILL SOON BE RUINED!
THOU SPEAKEST TO ME OF RUIN, WHEN YE HAVE BEEN GETTING FAT AT OUR EXPENSE ALL THIS TIME?

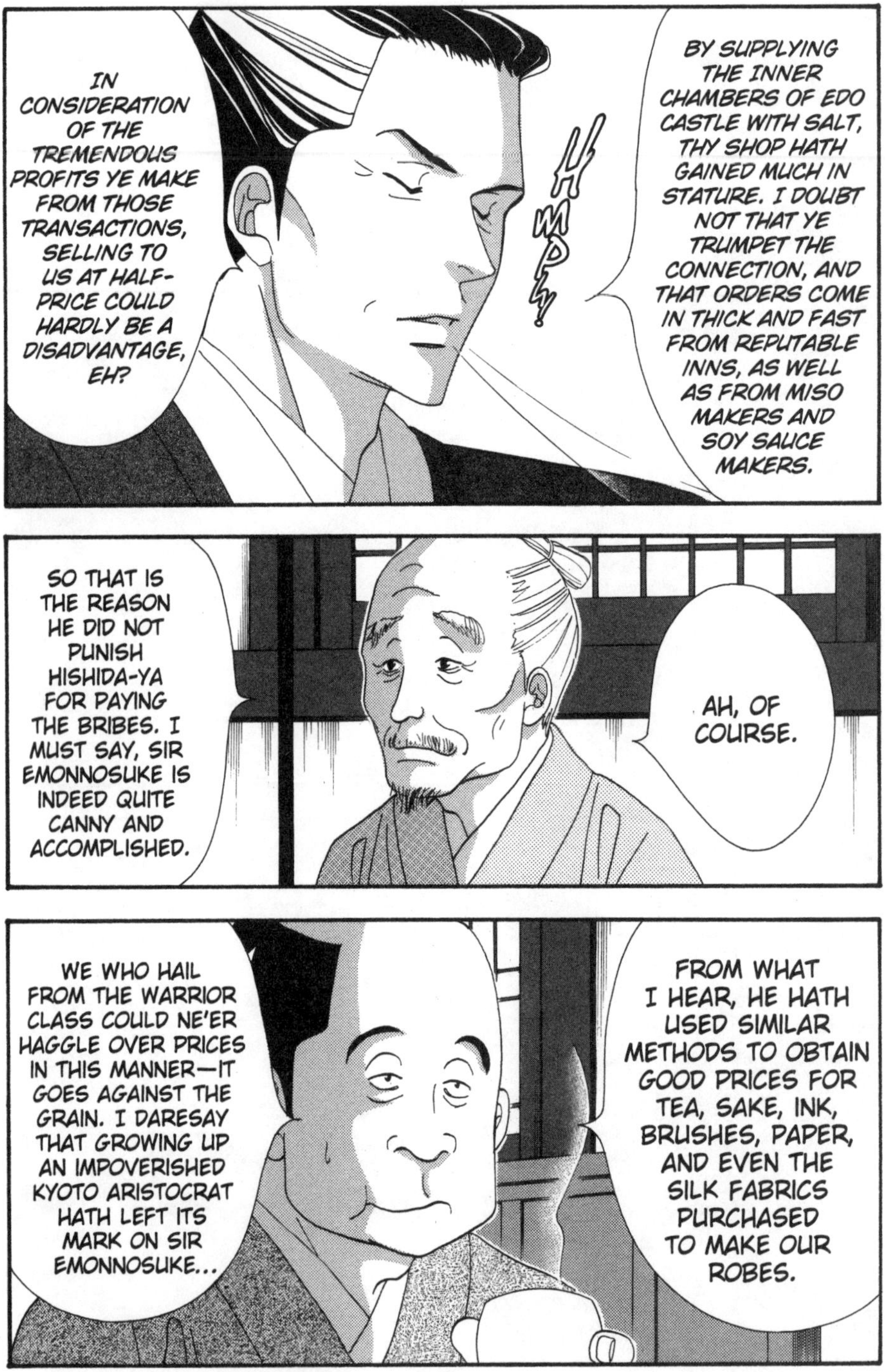
BY SUPPLYING THE INNER CHAMBERS OF EDO CASTLE WITH SALT, THY SHOP HATH GAINED MUCH IN STATURE. I DOUBT NOT THAT YE TRUMPET THE CONNECTION, AND THAT ORDERS COME IN THICK AND FAST FROM REPUTABLE INNS, AS WELL AS FROM MISO MAKERS AND SOY SAUCE MAKERS.
HMPH!
IN CONSIDERATION OF THE TREMENDOUS PROFITS YE MAKE FROM THOSE TRANSACTIONS, SELLING TO US AT HALF-PRICE COULD HARDLY BE A DISADVANTAGE, EH?
AH, OF COURSE.
SO THAT IS THE REASON HE DID NOT PUNISH HISHIDA-YA FOR PAYING THE BRIBES. I MUST SAY, SIR EMONNOSUKE IS INDEED QUITE CANNY AND ACCOMPLISHED.
FROM WHAT I HEAR, HE HATH USED SIMILAR METHODS TO OBTAIN GOOD PRICES FOR TEA, SAKE, INK, BRUSHES, PAPER, AND EVEN THE SILK FABRICS PURCHASED TO MAKE OUR ROBES.
WE WHO HAIL FROM THE WARRIOR CLASS COULD NE'ER HAGGLE OVER PRICES IN THIS MANNER—IT GOES AGAINST THE GRAIN. I DARESAY THAT GROWING UP AN IMPOVERISHED KYOTO ARISTOCRAT HATH LEFT ITS MARK ON SIR EMONNOSUKE...

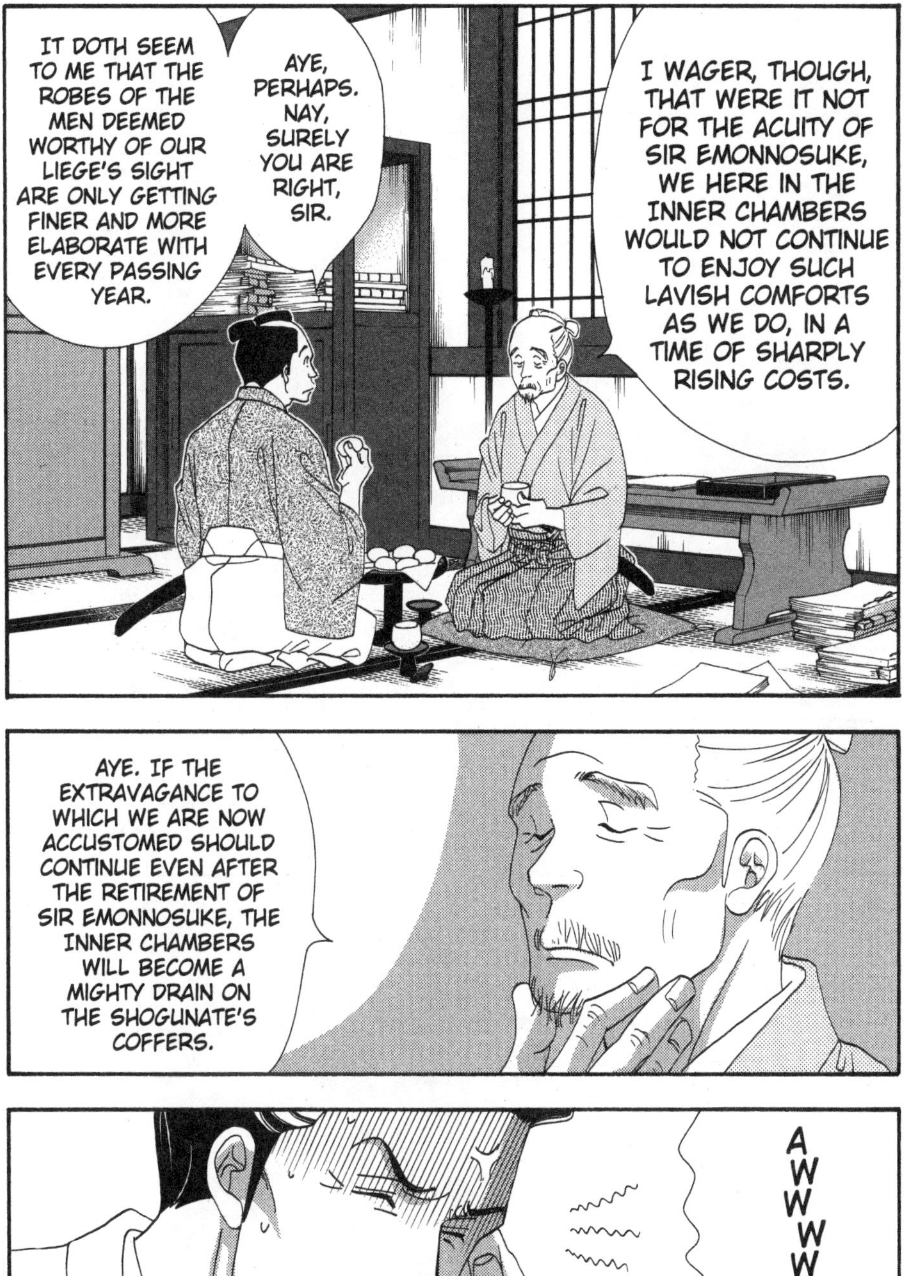
I WAGER, THOUGH, THAT WERE IT NOT FOR THE ACUITY OF SIR EMONNOSUKE, WE HERE IN THE INNER CHAMBERS WOULD NOT CONTINUE TO ENJOY SUCH LAVISH COMFORTS AS WE DO, IN A TIME OF SHARPLY RISING COSTS.
AYE, PERHAPS. NAY, SURELY YOU ARE RIGHT, SIR.
IT DOTH SEEM TO ME THAT THE ROBES OF THE MEN DEEMED WORTHY OF OUR LIEGE'S SIGHT ARE ONLY GETTING FINER AND MORE ELABORATE WITH EVERY PASSING YEAR.
AYE. IF THE EXTRAVAGANCE TO WHICH WE ARE NOW ACCUSTOMED SHOULD CONTINUE EVEN AFTER THE RETIREMENT OF SIR EMONNOSUKE, THE INNER CHAMBERS WILL BECOME A MIGHTY DRAIN ON THE SHOGUNATE'S COFFERS.
AWWWWGH!!

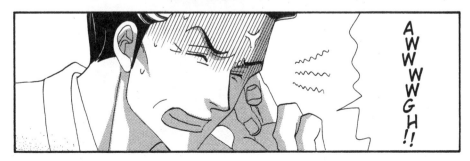

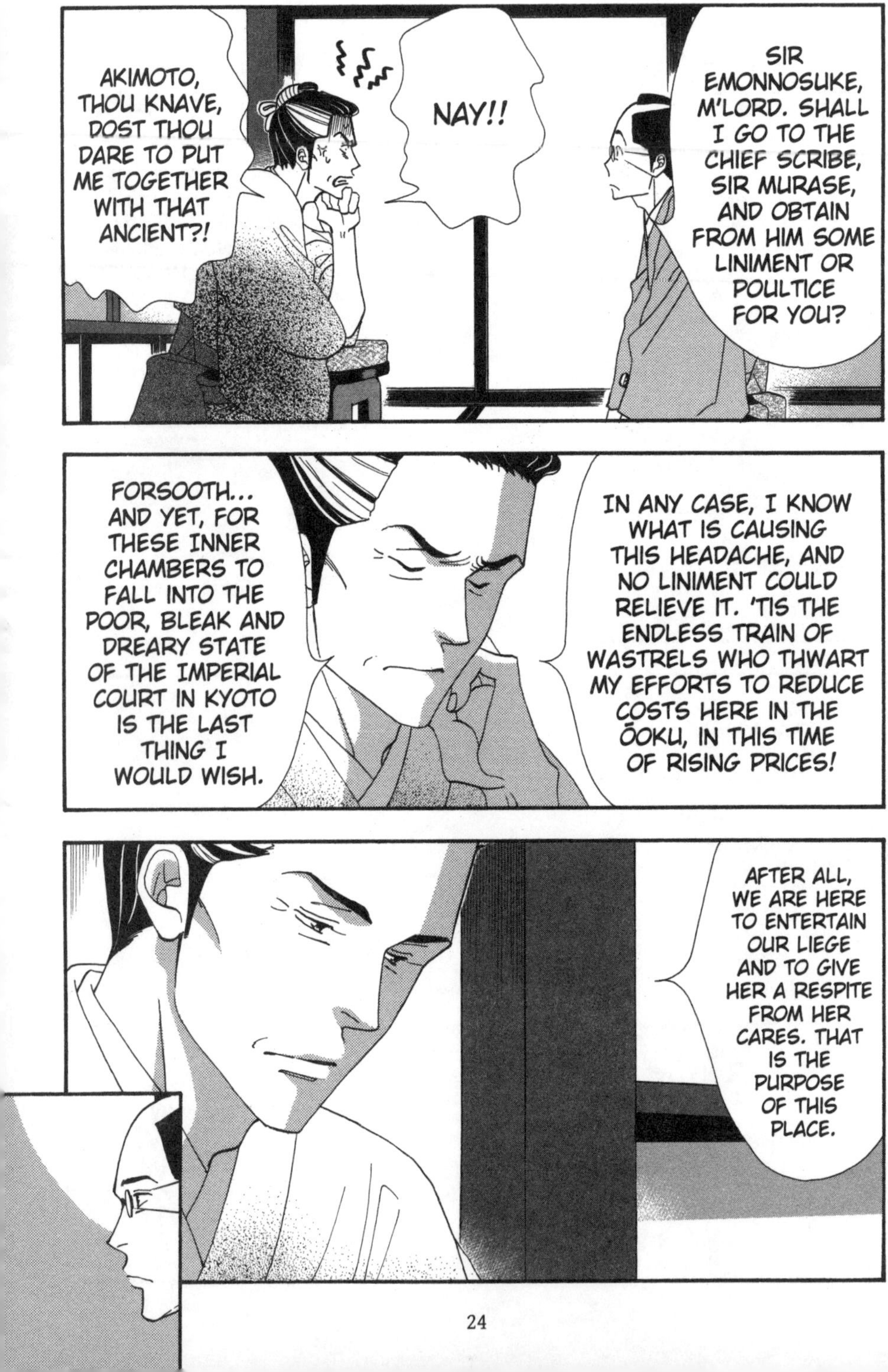
SIR EMONNOSUKE, M'LORD. SHALL I GO TO THE CHIEF SCRIBE, SIR MURASE, AND OBTAIN FROM HIM SOME LINIMENT OR POULTICE FOR YOU?
NAY!!
AKIMOTO, THOU KNAVE, DOST THOU DARE TO PUT ME TOGETHER WITH THAT ANCIENT?!
IN ANY CASE, I KNOW WHAT IS CAUSING THIS HEADACHE, AND NO LINIMENT COULD RELIEVE IT. 'TIS THE ENDLESS TRAIN OF WASTRELS WHO THWART MY EFFORTS TO REDUCE COSTS HERE IN THE ŌOKU, IN THIS TIME OF RISING PRICES!
FORSOOTH... AND YET, FOR THESE INNER CHAMBERS TO FALL INTO THE POOR, BLEAK AND DREARY STATE OF THE IMPERIAL COURT IN KYOTO IS THE LAST THING I WOULD WISH.
AFTER ALL, WE ARE HERE TO ENTERTAIN OUR LIEGE AND TO GIVE HER A RESPITE FROM HER CARES. THAT IS THE PURPOSE OF THIS PLACE.

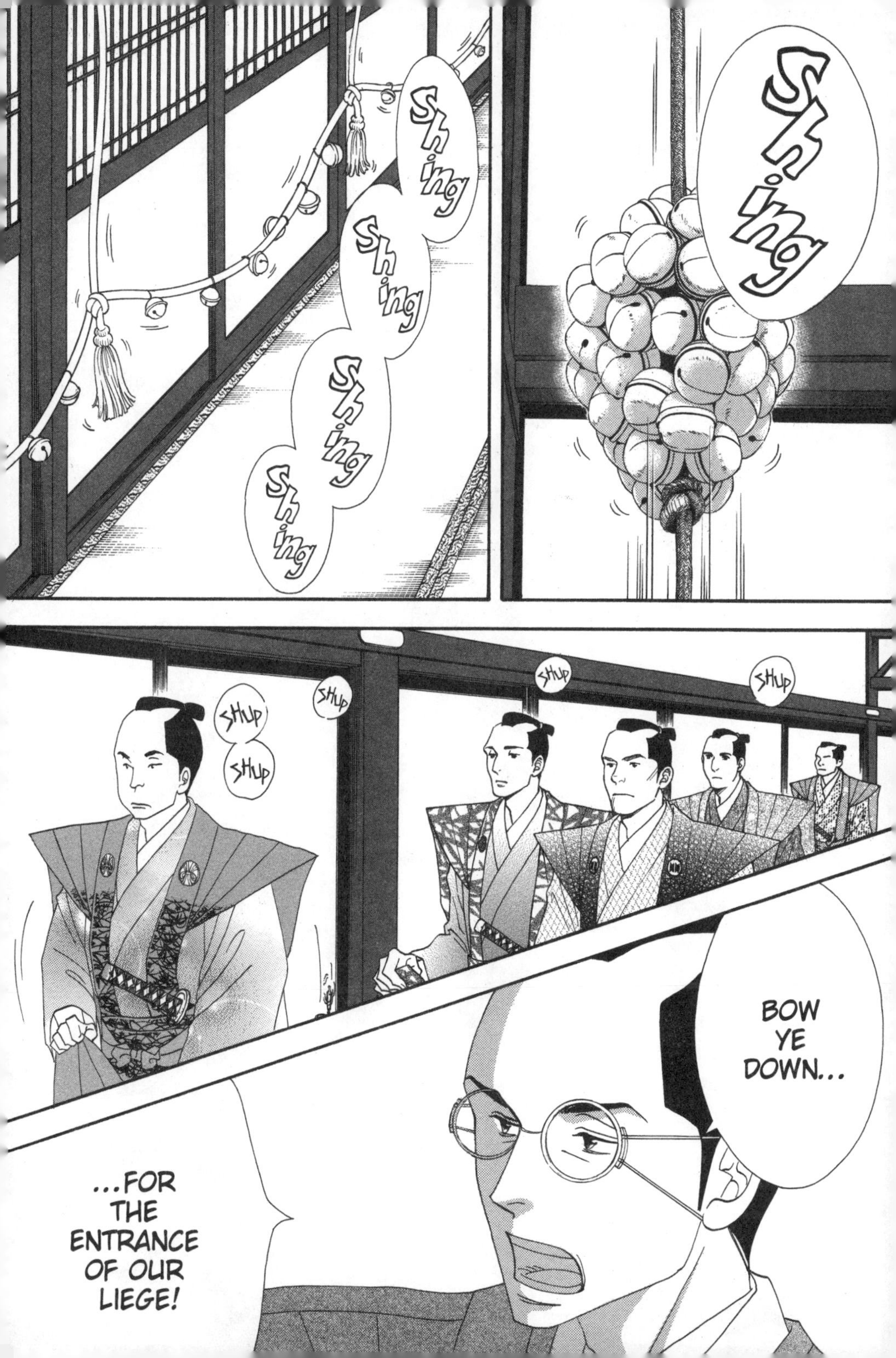
Shing
Shing
Shing
Shing
Shing
SHUP
SHUP
SHUP
SHUP
SHUP
BOW YE DOWN...
...FOR THE ENTRANCE OF OUR LIEGE!

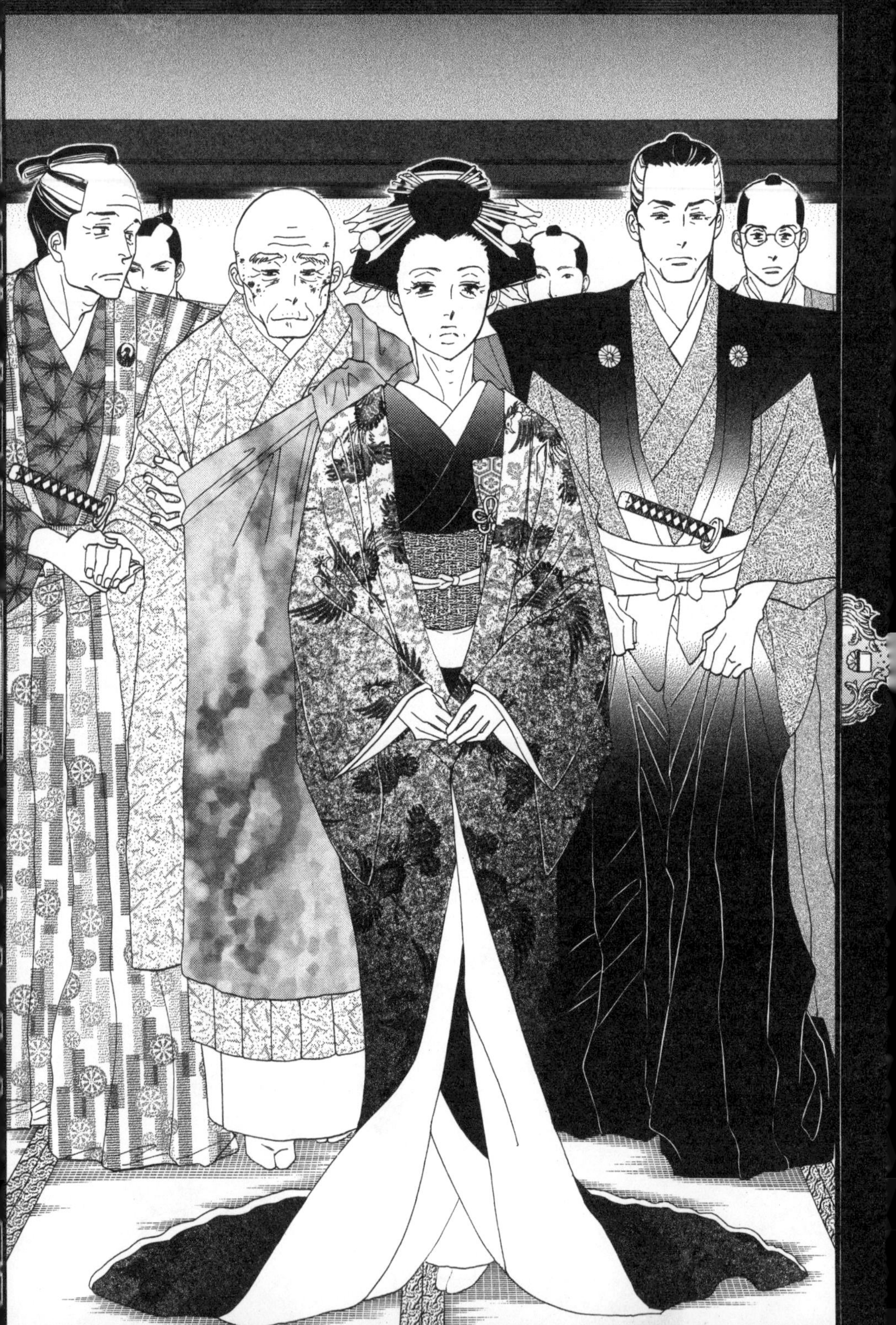

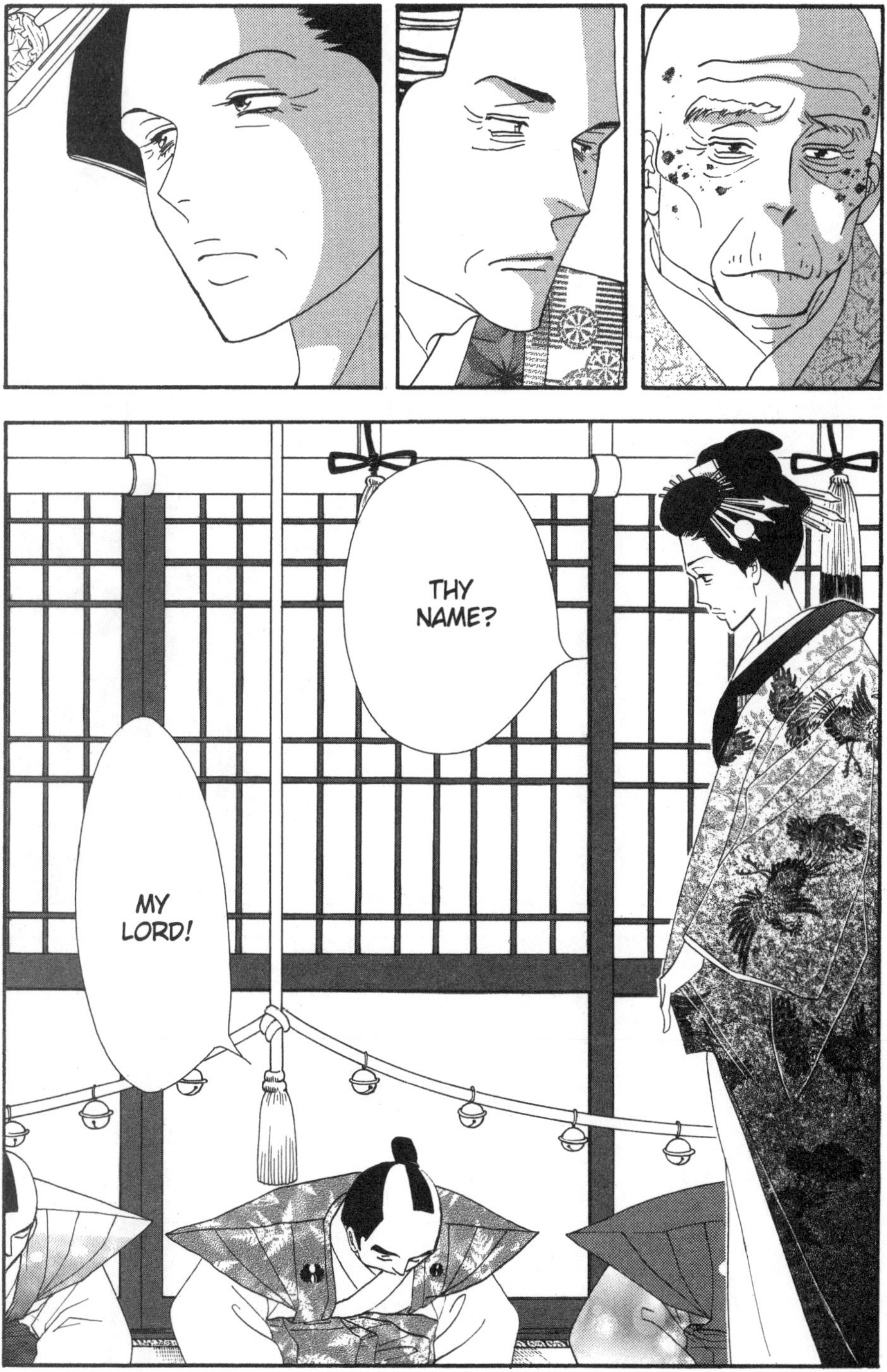
THY NAME?
MY LORD!

AYE.

MY NAME IS HIRAOKA, YOUR HIGHNESS.

THOU WERT NEVER WITH A WOMAN BEFORE, WERT THOU?

....!!

28

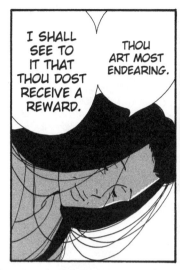

M-MY LORD! W-WAS MY PERFORMANCE NOT SATIS-FACTORY, YOUR HIGH-NESS?!
I-I WAS...
...QUITE RAPT, AND SO...!
THOU ART MOST ENDEARING.
I SHALL SEE TO IT THAT THOU DOST RECEIVE A REWARD.
LAST NIGHT AGAIN? HER HIGHNESS DOTH SPEND MORE TIME IN THE INNER CHAMBERS THAN IN HER OWN QUARTERS.
I MUST SAY, SHE DOTH REMAIN ABUNDANTLY LUSTFUL FOR ONE WHO HATH NO MORE HOPE OF BEARING AN HEIR, AT HER AGE...
THAT BEING SO, WHEREFORE DOTH SHE TARRY SO IN NAMING LORD TSUNATOYO AS HER SUCCESSOR?
AYE, BUT WHILE SIR KEISHO-IN DOTH SO STRONGLY PUSH FOR LORD TSUNANORI OF THE KII DOMAIN...
NOT ONLY IS SHE CLOSEST IN LINE BY BLOOD, BUT FROM THE VIEWPOINT OF ACCOMPLISHMENT AND CAPABILITY, SURELY LORD TSUNATOYO IS ALSO BY FAR THE MOST MEET.
I SAY 'TIS THE BARON OF MINO!

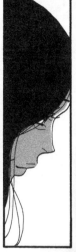

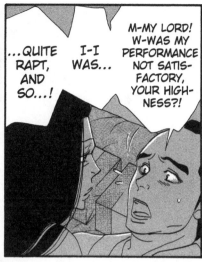

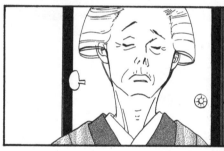

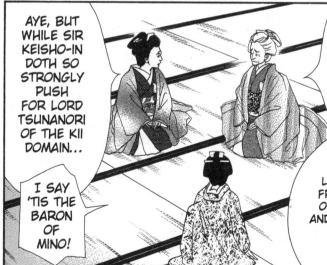

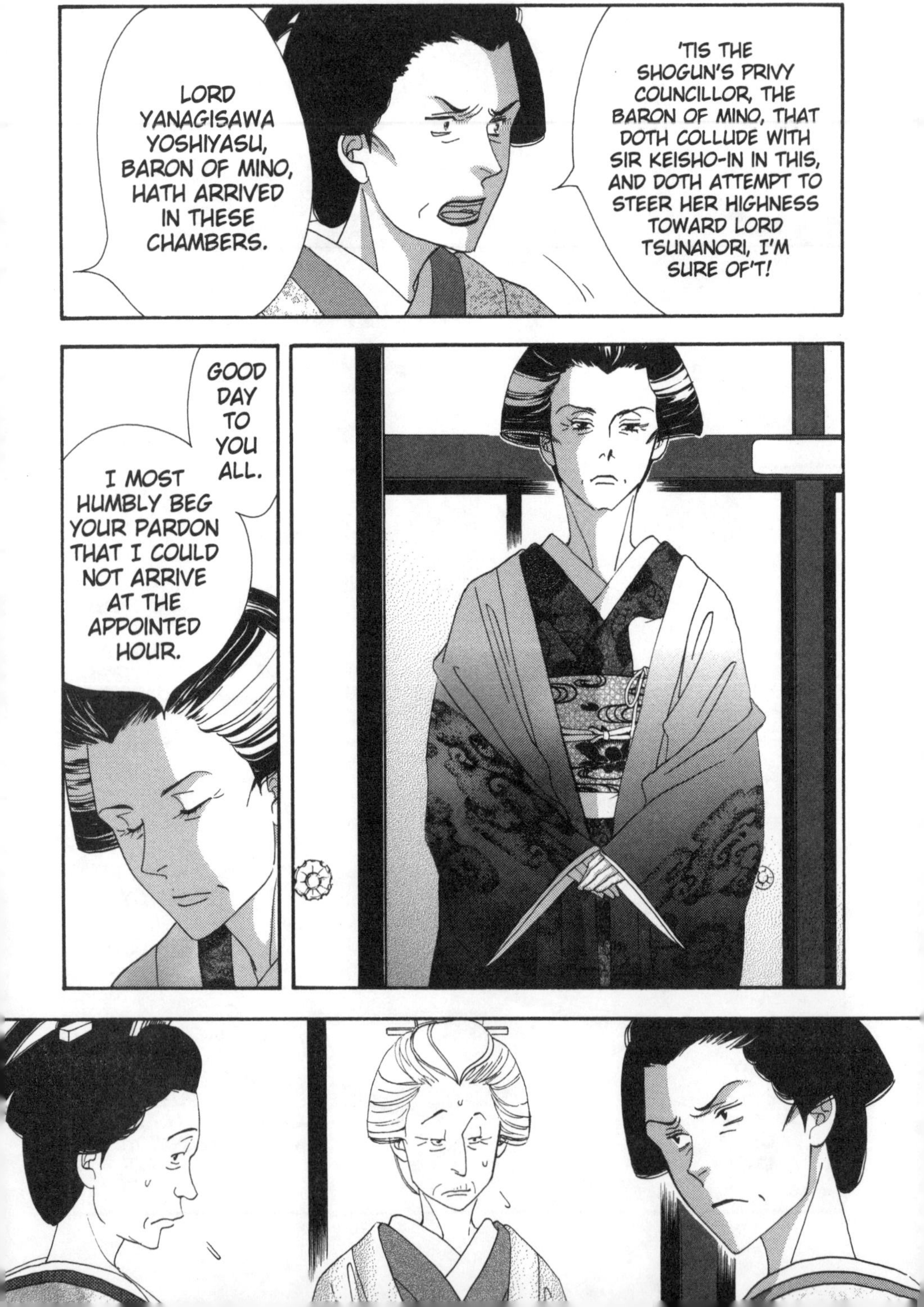
'TIS THE SHOGUN'S PRIVY COUNCILLOR, THE BARON OF MINO, THAT DOTH COLLUDE WITH SIR KEISHO-IN IN THIS, AND DOTH ATTEMPT TO STEER HER HIGHNESS TOWARD LORD TSUNANORI, I'M SURE OF'T!
LORD YANAGISAWA YOSHIYASU, BARON OF MINO, HATH ARRIVED IN THESE CHAMBERS.
GOOD DAY TO YOU ALL.
I MOST HUMBLY BEG YOUR PARDON THAT I COULD NOT ARRIVE AT THE APPOINTED HOUR.

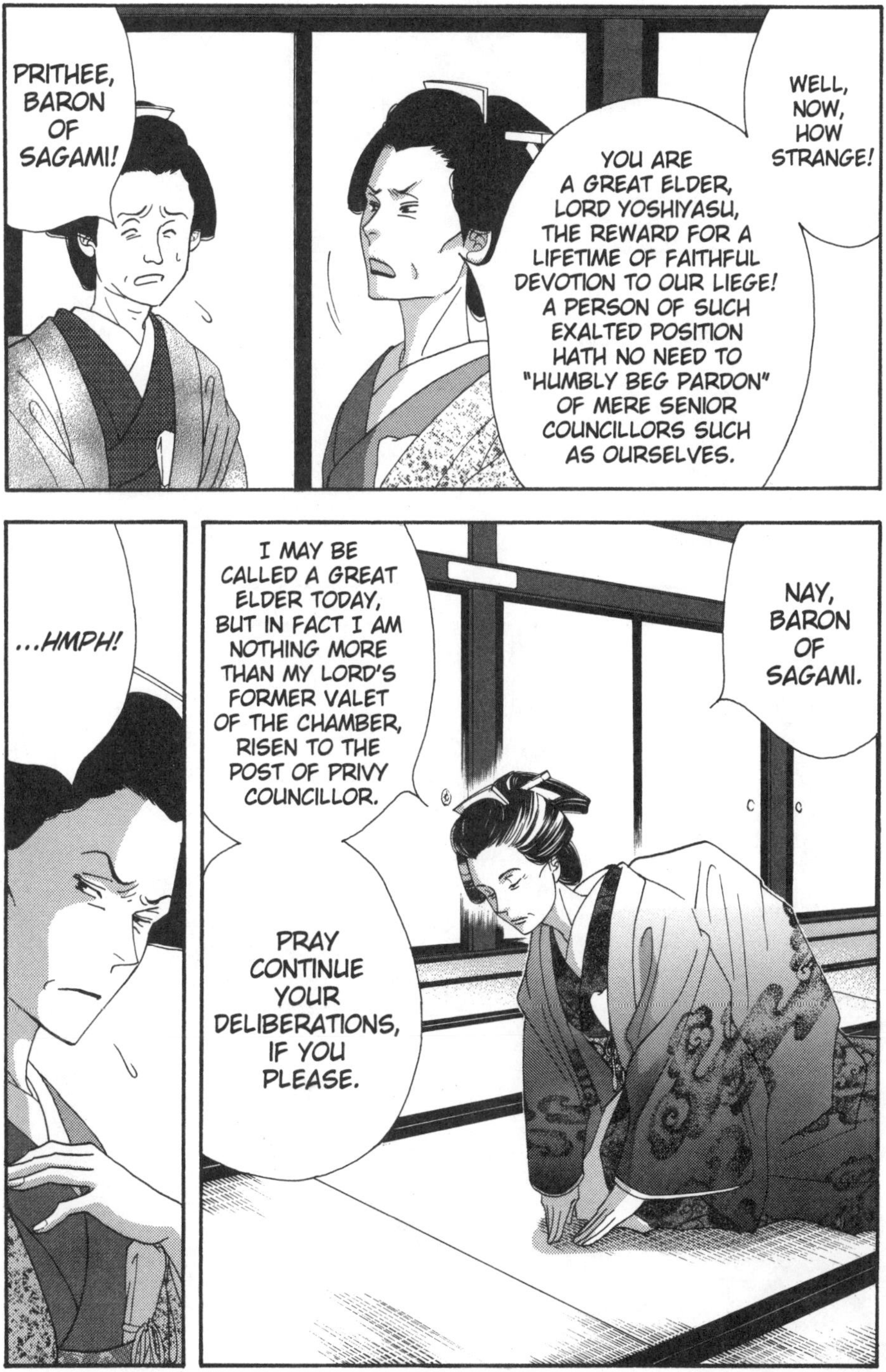
WELL, NOW, HOW STRANGE!
YOU ARE A GREAT ELDER, LORD YOSHIYASU, THE REWARD FOR A LIFETIME OF FAITHFUL DEVOTION TO OUR LIEGE! A PERSON OF SUCH EXALTED POSITION HATH NO NEED TO "HUMBLY BEG PARDON" OF MERE SENIOR COUNCILLORS SUCH AS OURSELVES.
PRITHEE, BARON OF SAGAMI!
NAY, BARON OF SAGAMI.
I MAY BE CALLED A GREAT ELDER TODAY, BUT IN FACT I AM NOTHING MORE THAN MY LORD'S FORMER VALET OF THE CHAMBER, RISEN TO THE POST OF PRIVY COUNCILLOR.
PRAY CONTINUE YOUR DELIBERATIONS, IF YOU PLEASE.
...HMPH!

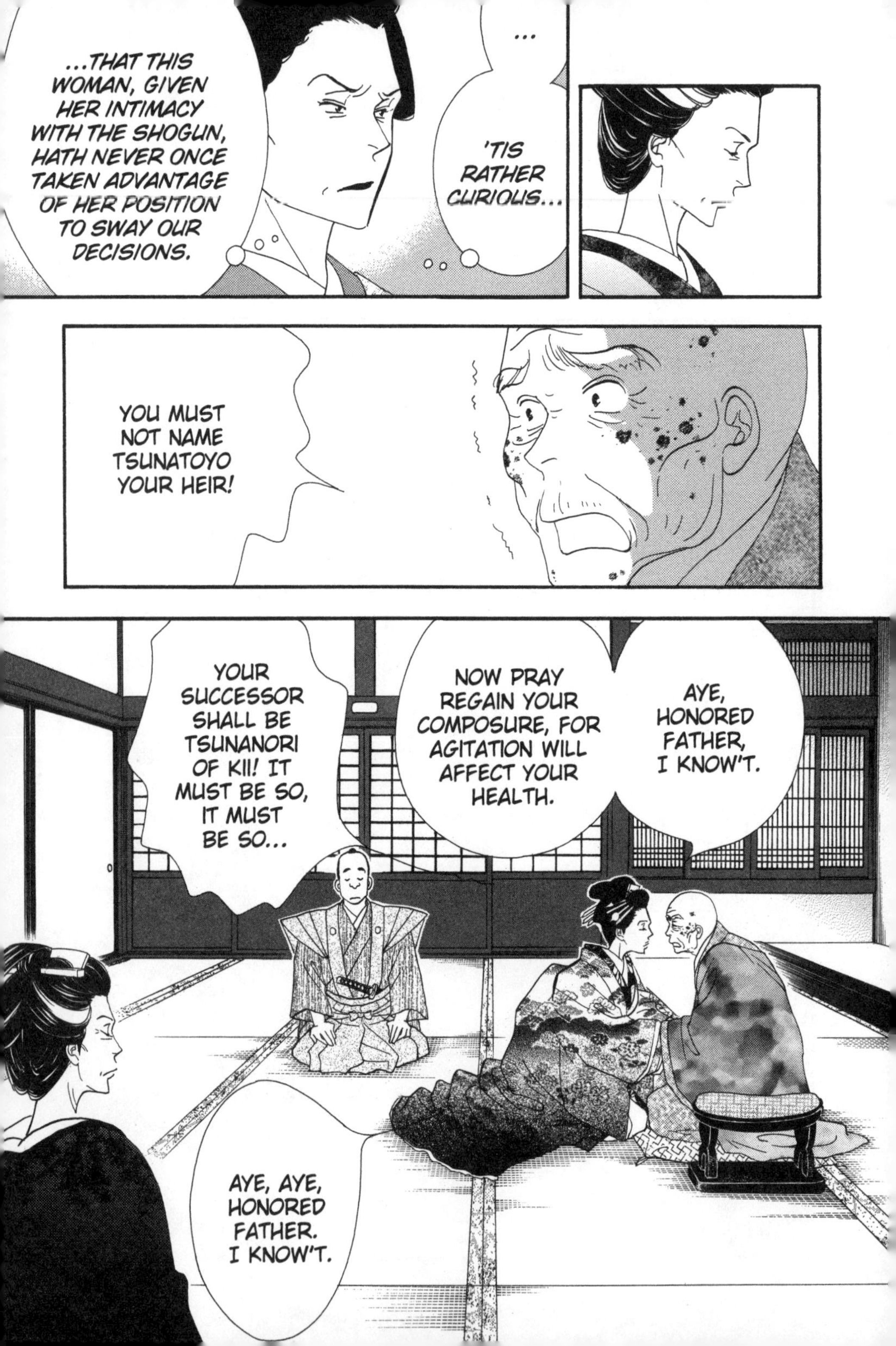
...
'TIS RATHER CURIOUS...
...THAT THIS WOMAN, GIVEN HER INTIMACY WITH THE SHOGUN, HATH NEVER ONCE TAKEN ADVANTAGE OF HER POSITION TO SWAY OUR DECISIONS.
YOU MUST NOT NAME TSUNATOYO YOUR HEIR!
AYE, HONORED FATHER, I KNOW'T.
NOW PRAY REGAIN YOUR COMPOSURE, FOR AGITATION WILL AFFECT YOUR HEALTH.
YOUR SUCCESSOR SHALL BE TSUNANORI OF KII! IT MUST BE SO, IT MUST BE SO...
AYE, AYE, HONORED FATHER. I KNOW'T.

...THOU!

SIR KEISHO-IN'S VALET OF THE CHAMBER! THY MASTER'S EARS ARE COVERED WITH SCALES AND GRIME. DO YE NOT BATHE THE SHOGUN'S FATHER?!

VALET!

I LIKE NOT TO BATHE.

BY YOUR LEAVE... WHEN WE DO TRY TO WASH HIS GRACE'S PERSON, HE DOTH FLAIL AND SHOUT THAT HE LIKETH NOT TO BATHE...

WE... THAT IS...

MY LORD!

...

I LIKE NOT TO BATHE.

33

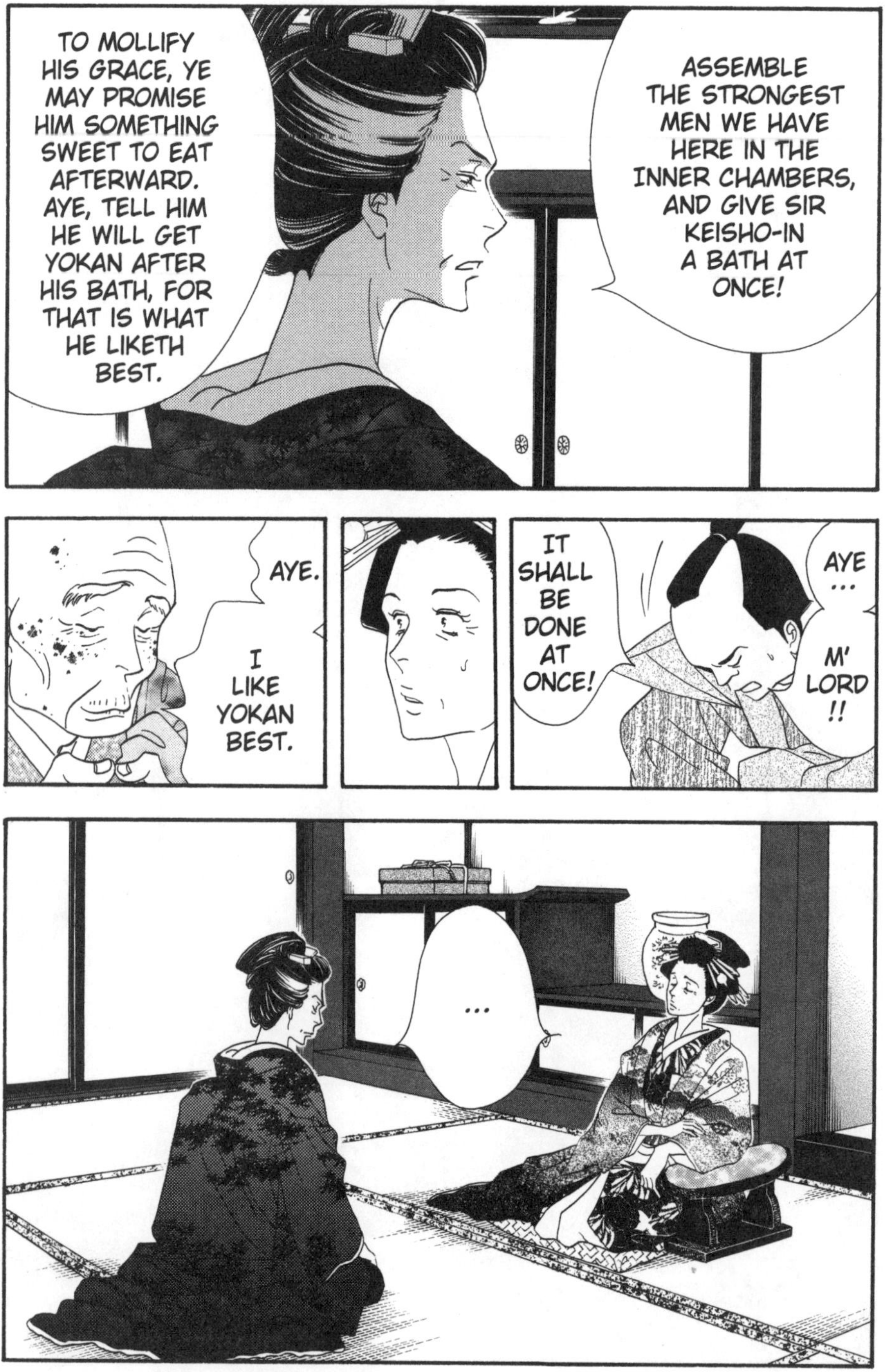
ASSEMBLE THE STRONGEST MEN WE HAVE HERE IN THE INNER CHAMBERS, AND GIVE SIR KEISHO-IN A BATH AT ONCE!
TO MOLLIFY HIS GRACE, YE MAY PROMISE HIM SOMETHING SWEET TO EAT AFTERWARD. AYE, TELL HIM HE WILL GET YOKAN AFTER HIS BATH, FOR THAT IS WHAT HE LIKETH BEST.
AYE... M' LORD!!
IT SHALL BE DONE AT ONCE!
AYE.
I LIKE YOKAN BEST.
...

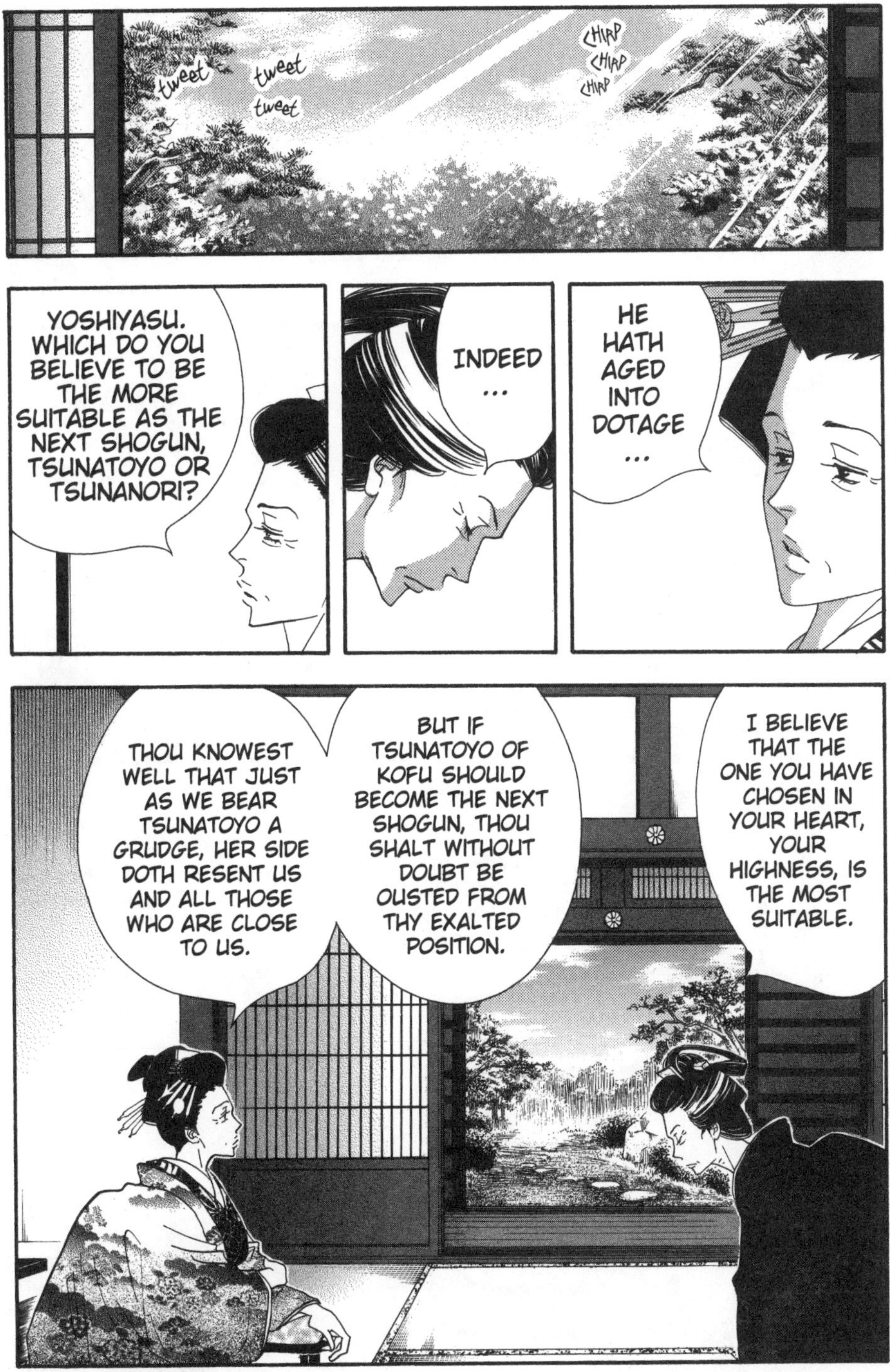
CHIRP
CHIRP
CHIRP
tweet
tweet
tweet
HE HATH AGED INTO DOTAGE ...
INDEED ...
YOSHIYASU. WHICH DO YOU BELIEVE TO BE THE MORE SUITABLE AS THE NEXT SHOGUN, TSUNATOYO OR TSUNANORI?
I BELIEVE THAT THE ONE YOU HAVE CHOSEN IN YOUR HEART, YOUR HIGHNESS, IS THE MOST SUITABLE.
BUT IF TSUNATOYO OF KOFU SHOULD BECOME THE NEXT SHOGUN, THOU SHALT WITHOUT DOUBT BE OUSTED FROM THY EXALTED POSITION.
THOU KNOWEST WELL THAT JUST AS WE BEAR TSUNATOYO A GRUDGE, HER SIDE DOTH RESENT US AND ALL THOSE WHO ARE CLOSE TO US.

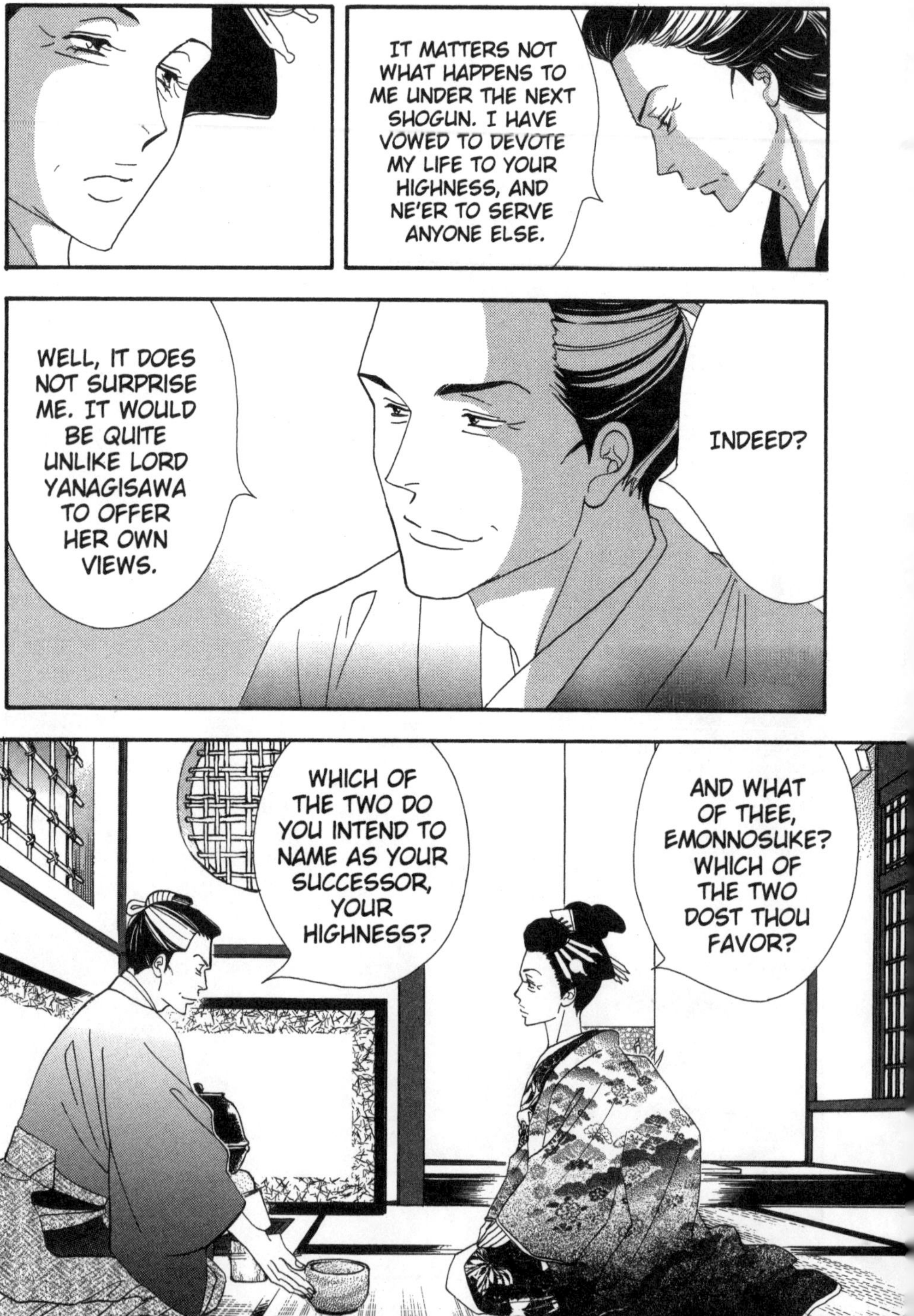
IT MATTERS NOT WHAT HAPPENS TO ME UNDER THE NEXT SHOGUN. I HAVE VOWED TO DEVOTE MY LIFE TO YOUR HIGHNESS, AND NE'ER TO SERVE ANYONE ELSE.
INDEED?
WELL, IT DOES NOT SURPRISE ME. IT WOULD BE QUITE UNLIKE LORD YANAGISAWA TO OFFER HER OWN VIEWS.
AND WHAT OF THEE, EMONNOSUKE? WHICH OF THE TWO DOST THOU FAVOR?
WHICH OF THE TWO DO YOU INTEND TO NAME AS YOUR SUCCESSOR, YOUR HIGHNESS?

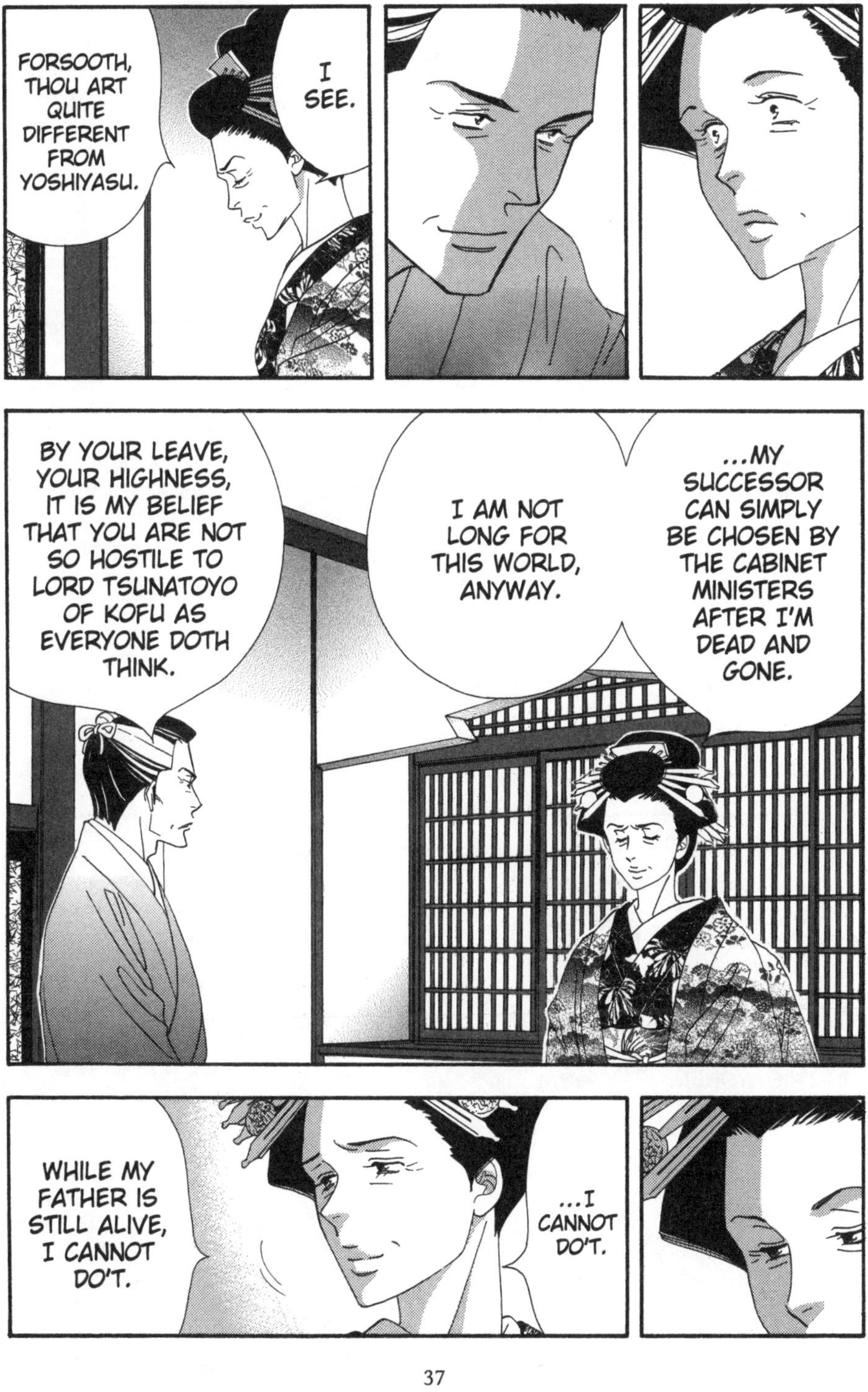
I SEE.
FORSOOTH, THOU ART QUITE DIFFERENT FROM YOSHIYASU.
...MY SUCCESSOR CAN SIMPLY BE CHOSEN BY THE CABINET MINISTERS AFTER I'M DEAD AND GONE.
I AM NOT LONG FOR THIS WORLD, ANYWAY.
BY YOUR LEAVE, YOUR HIGHNESS, IT IS MY BELIEF THAT YOU ARE NOT SO HOSTILE TO LORD TSUNATOYO OF KOFU AS EVERYONE DOTH THINK.
...I CANNOT DO'T.
WHILE MY FATHER IS STILL ALIVE, I CANNOT DO'T.

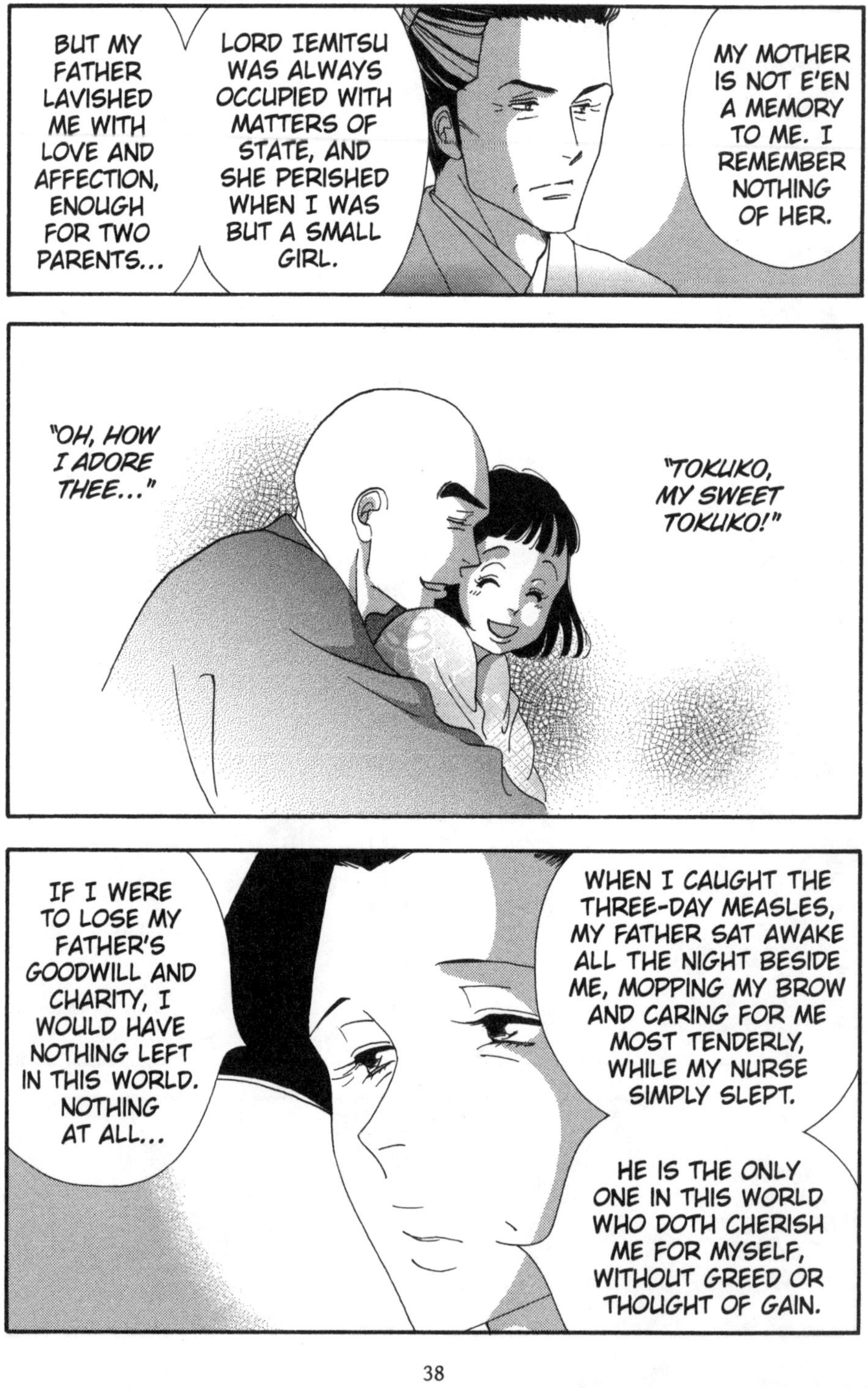
MY MOTHER IS NOT E'EN A MEMORY TO ME. I REMEMBER NOTHING OF HER.
LORD IEMITSU WAS ALWAYS OCCUPIED WITH MATTERS OF STATE, AND SHE PERISHED WHEN I WAS BUT A SMALL GIRL.
BUT MY FATHER LAVISHED ME WITH LOVE AND AFFECTION, ENOUGH FOR TWO PARENTS...
"TOKUKO, MY SWEET TOKUKO!"
"OH, HOW I ADORE THEE..."
WHEN I CAUGHT THE THREE-DAY MEASLES, MY FATHER SAT AWAKE ALL THE NIGHT BESIDE ME, MOPPING MY BROW AND CARING FOR ME MOST TENDERLY, WHILE MY NURSE SIMPLY SLEPT.
HE IS THE ONLY ONE IN THIS WORLD WHO DOTH CHERISH ME FOR MYSELF, WITHOUT GREED OR THOUGHT OF GAIN.
IF I WERE TO LOSE MY FATHER'S GOODWILL AND CHARITY, I WOULD HAVE NOTHING LEFT IN THIS WORLD. NOTHING AT ALL...

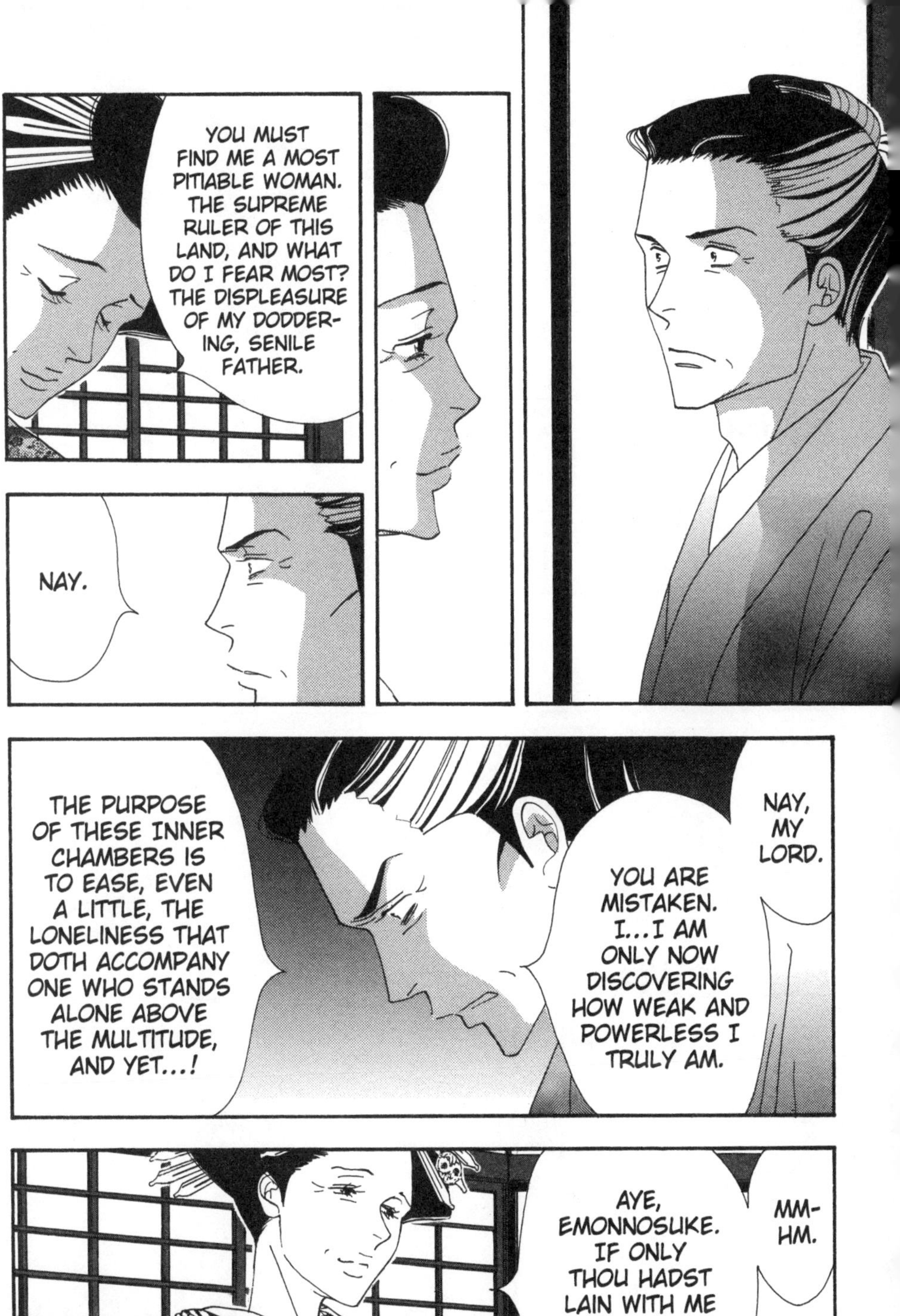
YOU MUST FIND ME A MOST PITIABLE WOMAN. THE SUPREME RULER OF THIS LAND, AND WHAT DO I FEAR MOST? THE DISPLEASURE OF MY DODDER-ING, SENILE FATHER.
NAY.
NAY, MY LORD.
YOU ARE MISTAKEN. I...I AM ONLY NOW DISCOVERING HOW WEAK AND POWERLESS I TRULY AM.
THE PURPOSE OF THESE INNER CHAMBERS IS TO EASE, EVEN A LITTLE, THE LONELINESS THAT DOTH ACCOMPANY ONE WHO STANDS ALONE ABOVE THE MULTITUDE, AND YET...!
MM-HM.
AYE, EMONNOSUKE. IF ONLY THOU HADST LAIN WITH ME THAT NIGHT...

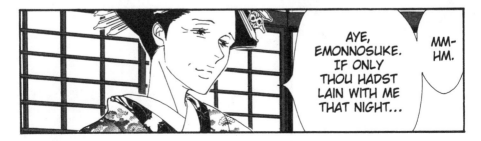

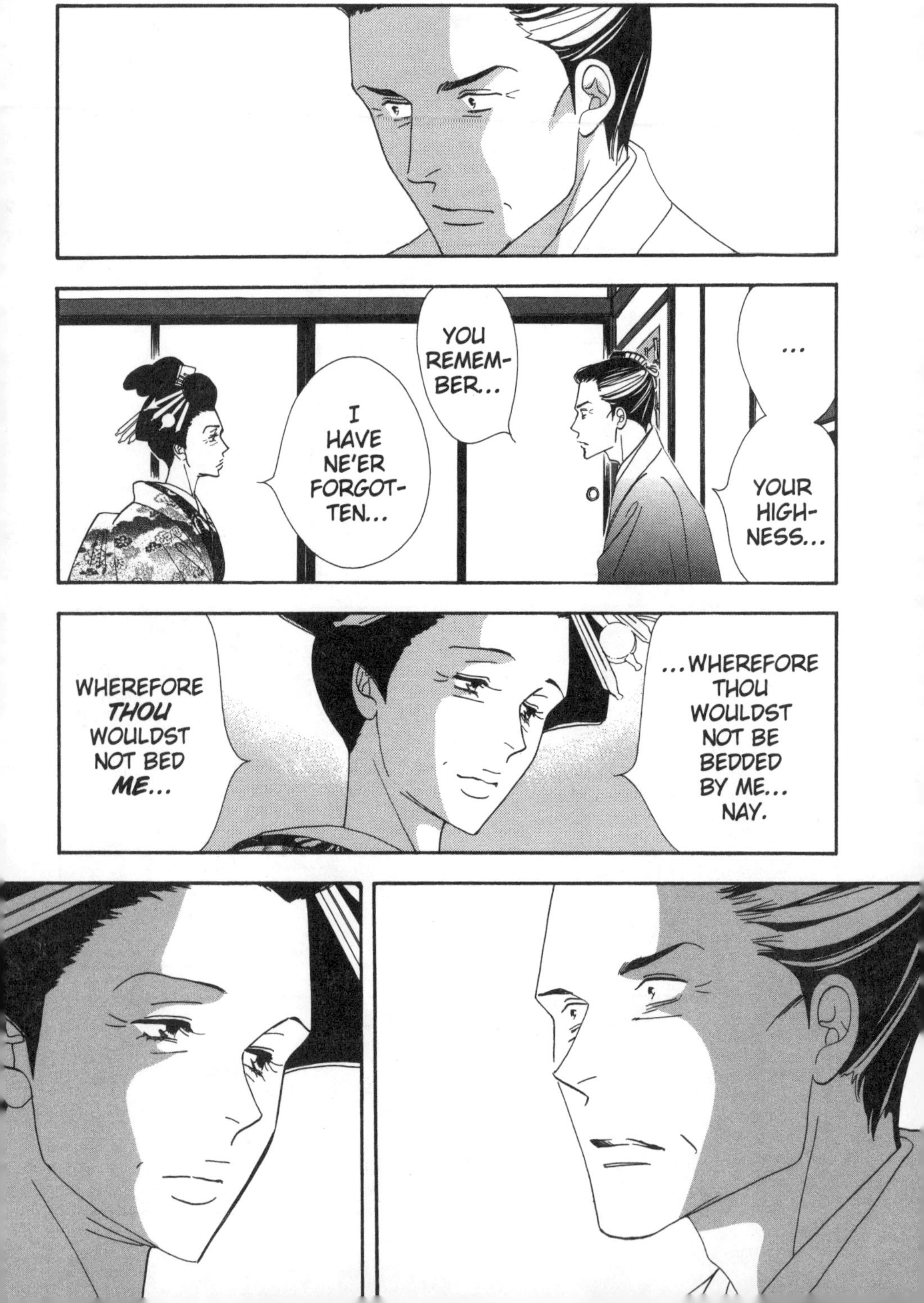
...
YOUR HIGHNESS...
YOU REMEMBER...
I HAVE NE'ER FORGOTTEN...
...WHEREFORE THOU WOULDST NOT BE BEDDED BY ME... NAY.
WHEREFORE *THOU* WOULDST NOT BED *ME*...

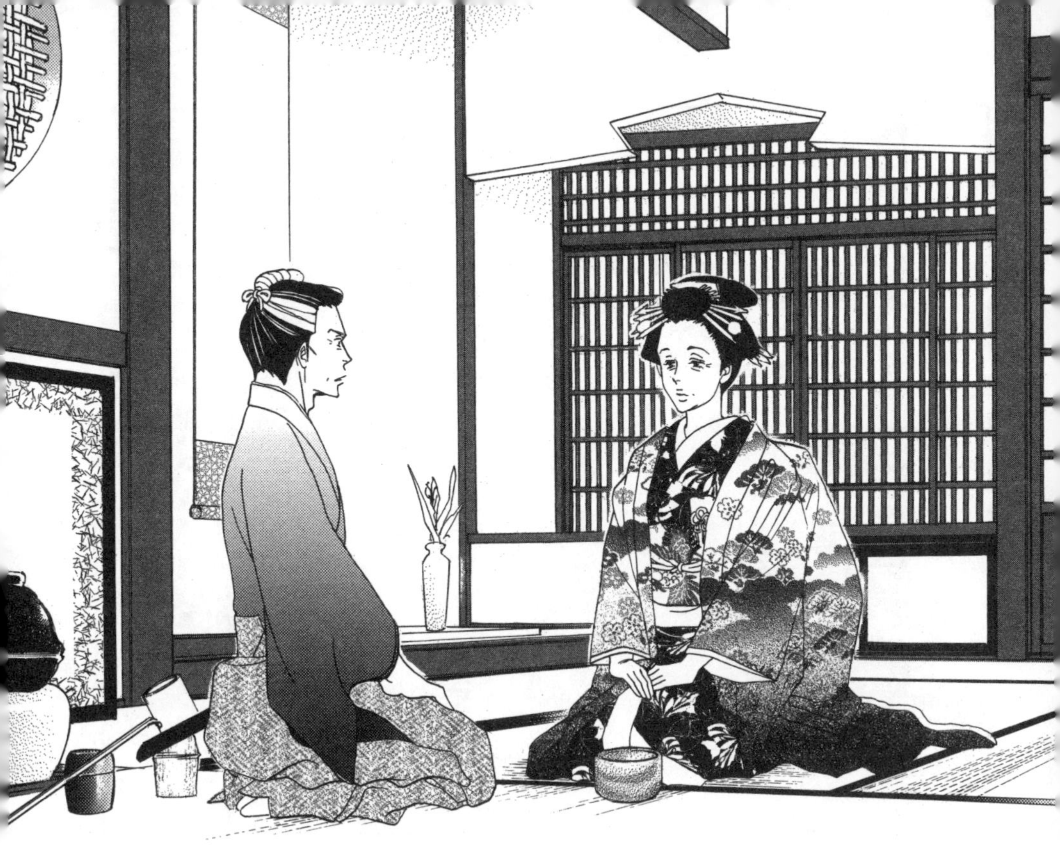

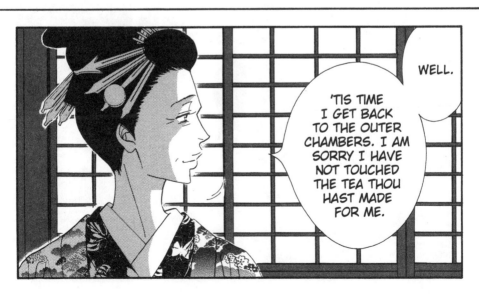

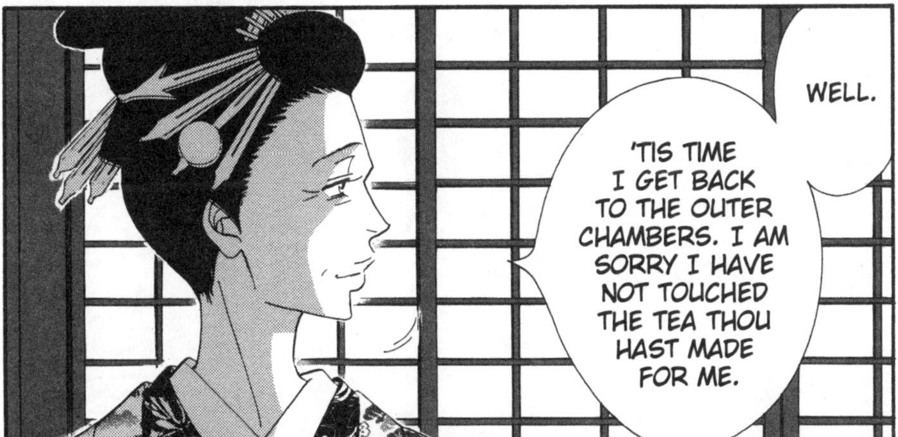
WELL.
'TIS TIME I GET BACK TO THE OUTER CHAMBERS. I AM SORRY I HAVE NOT TOUCHED THE TEA THOU HAST MADE FOR ME.

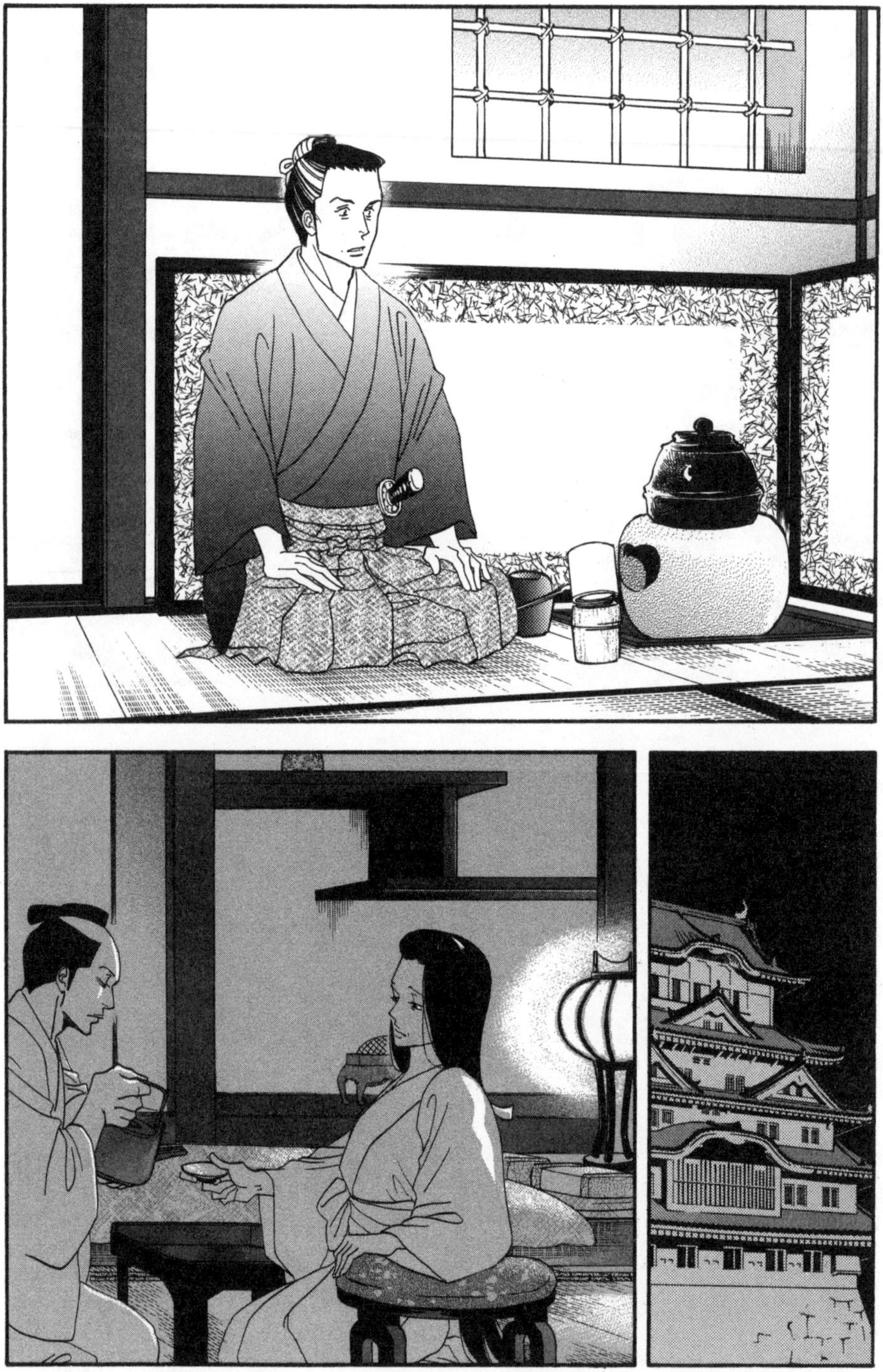

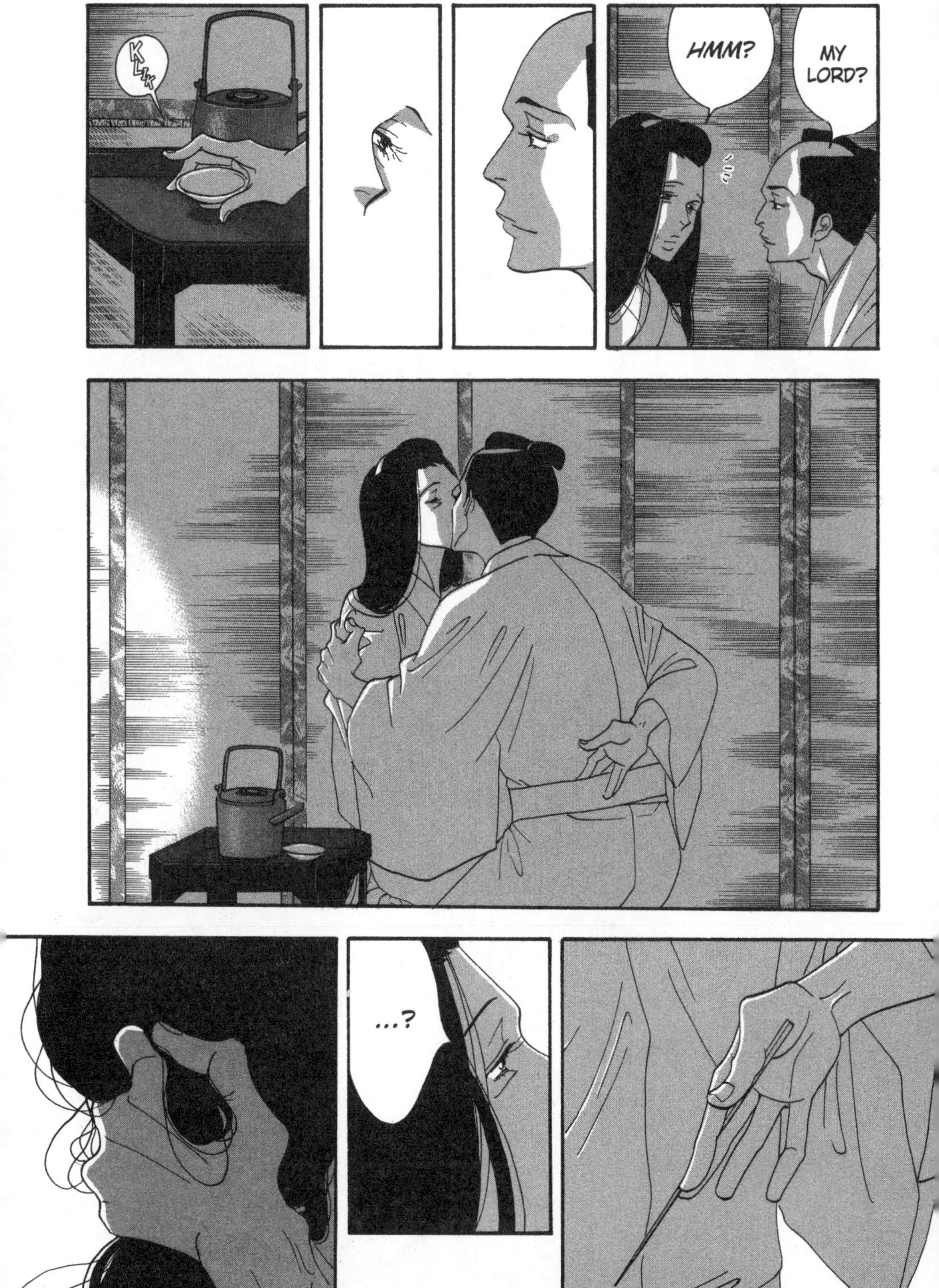
MY LORD?
HMM?
KLIK
...?

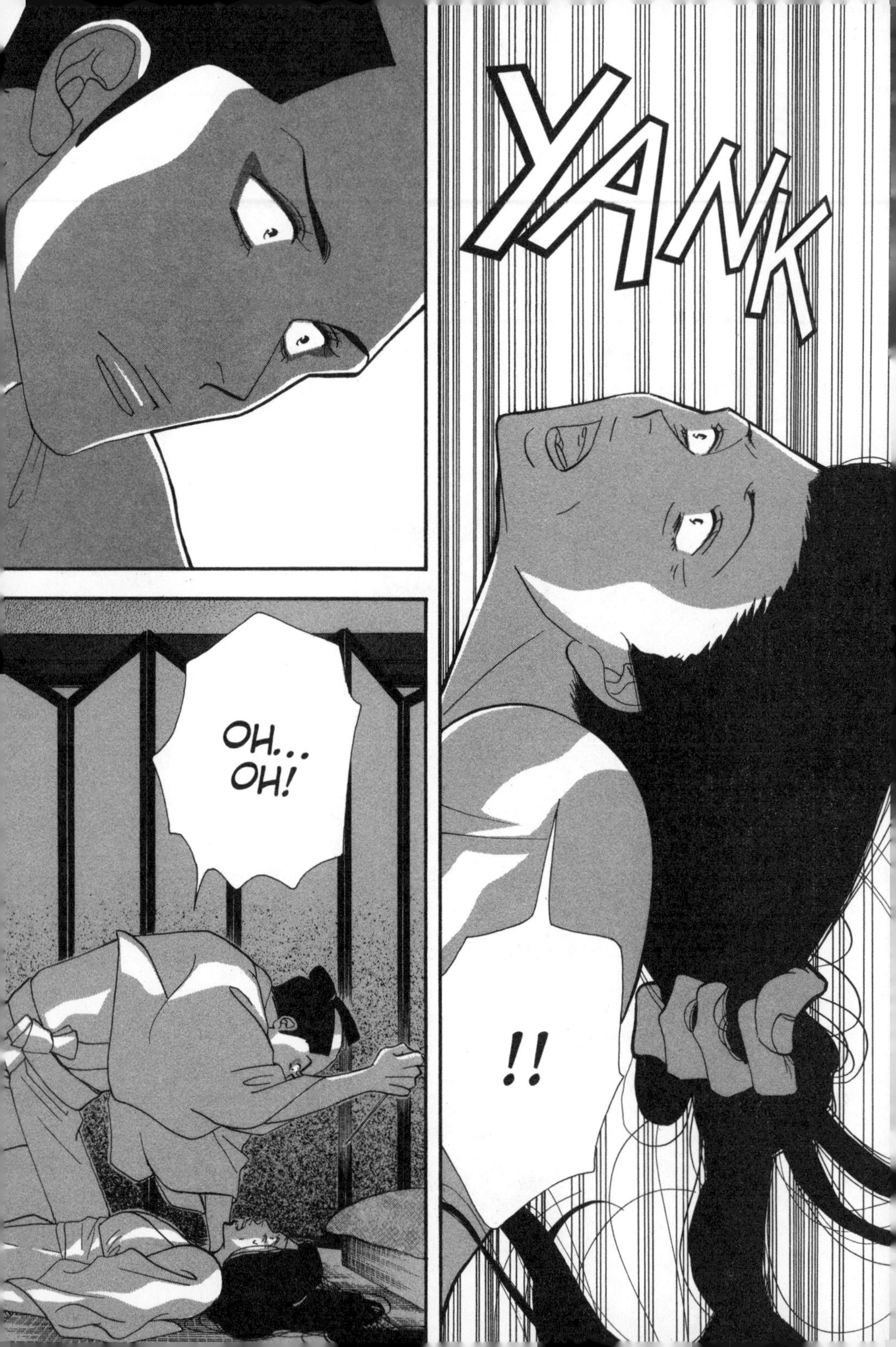
YANK
!!
OH...
OH!

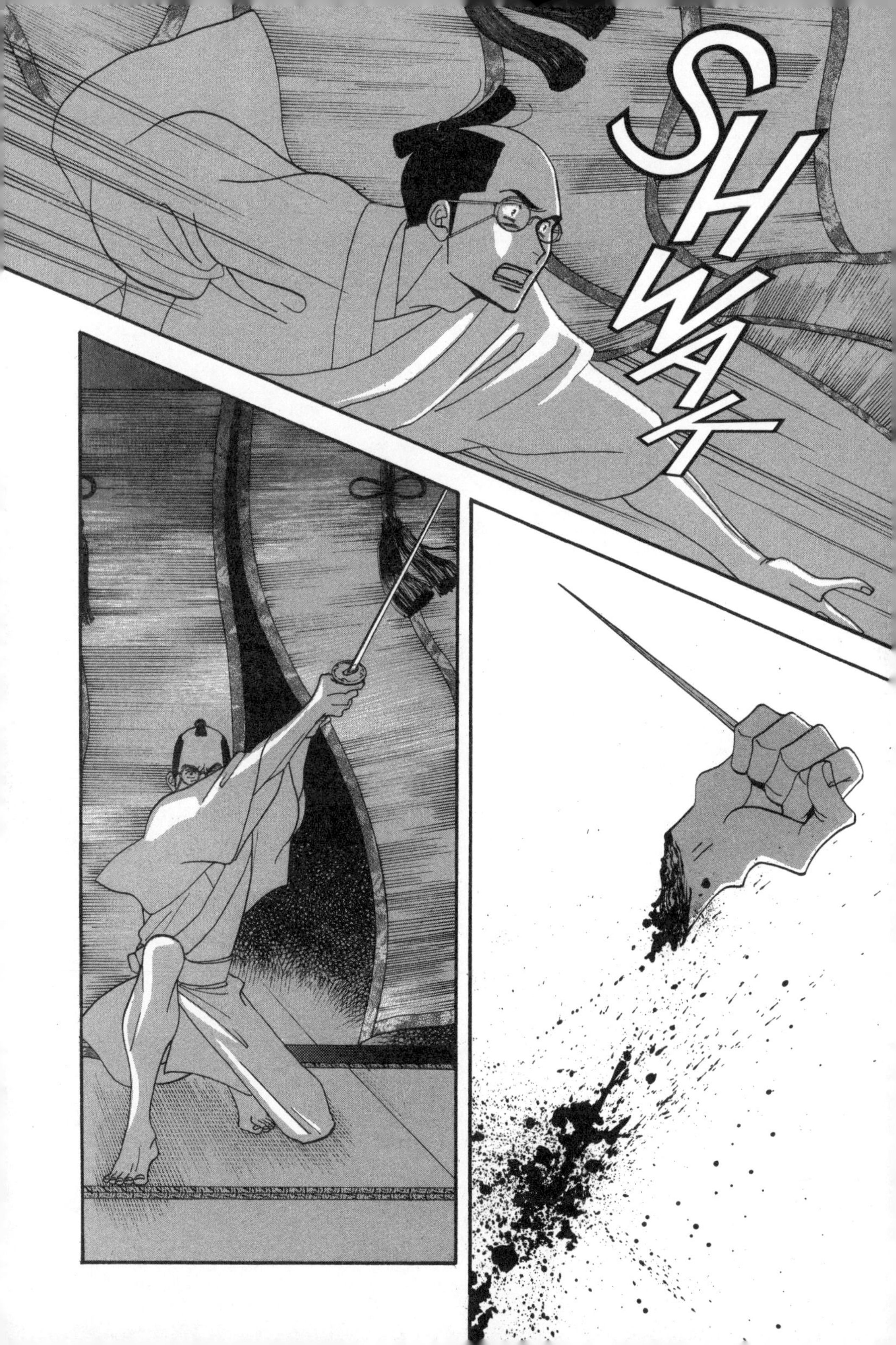
SHWAK

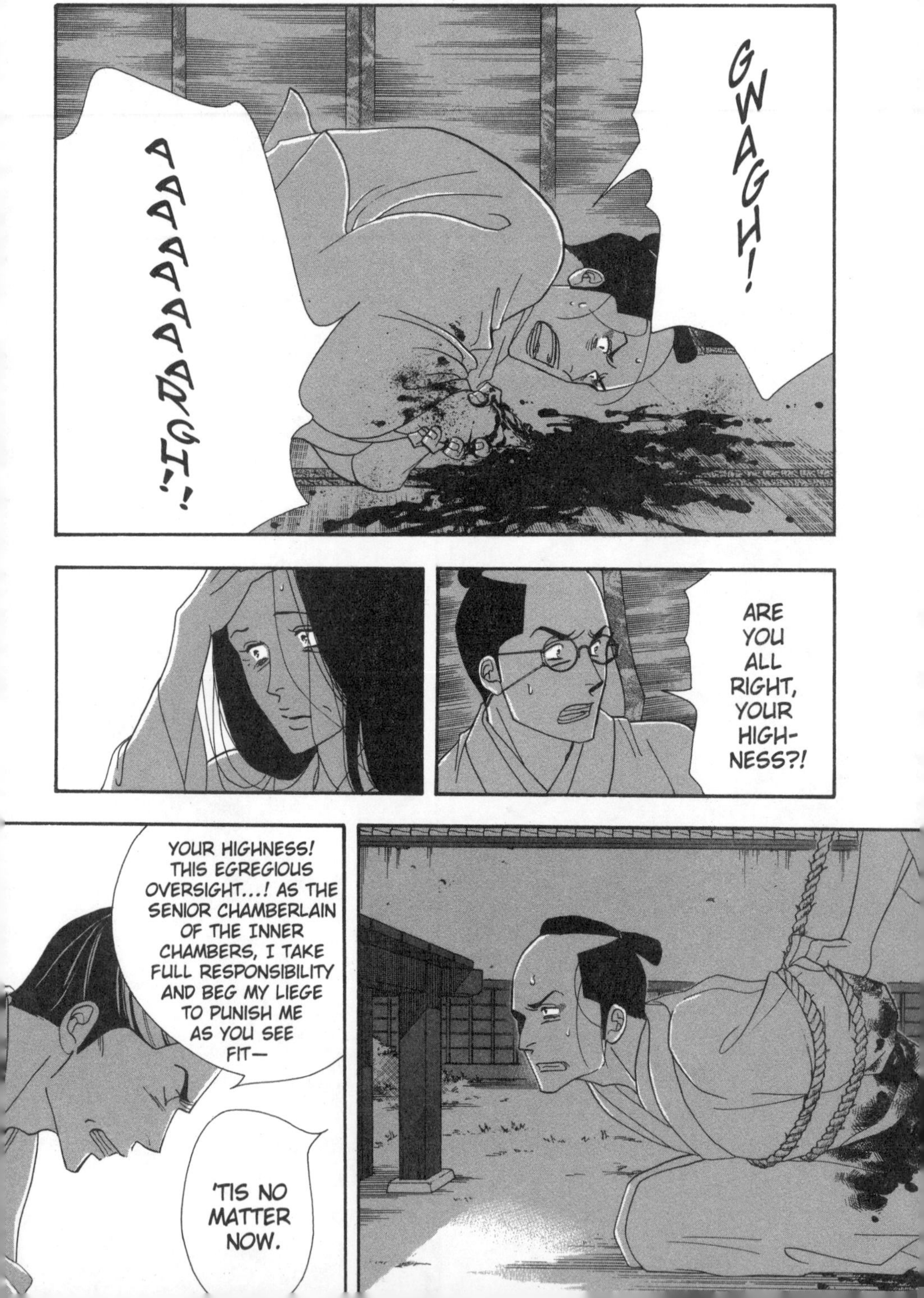
GWAGH!
AAAAAAAAARGH!!
ARE YOU ALL RIGHT, YOUR HIGHNESS?!
YOUR HIGHNESS! THIS EGREGIOUS OVERSIGHT...! AS THE SENIOR CHAMBERLAIN OF THE INNER CHAMBERS, I TAKE FULL RESPONSIBILITY AND BEG MY LIEGE TO PUNISH ME AS YOU SEE FIT—
'TIS NO MATTER NOW.

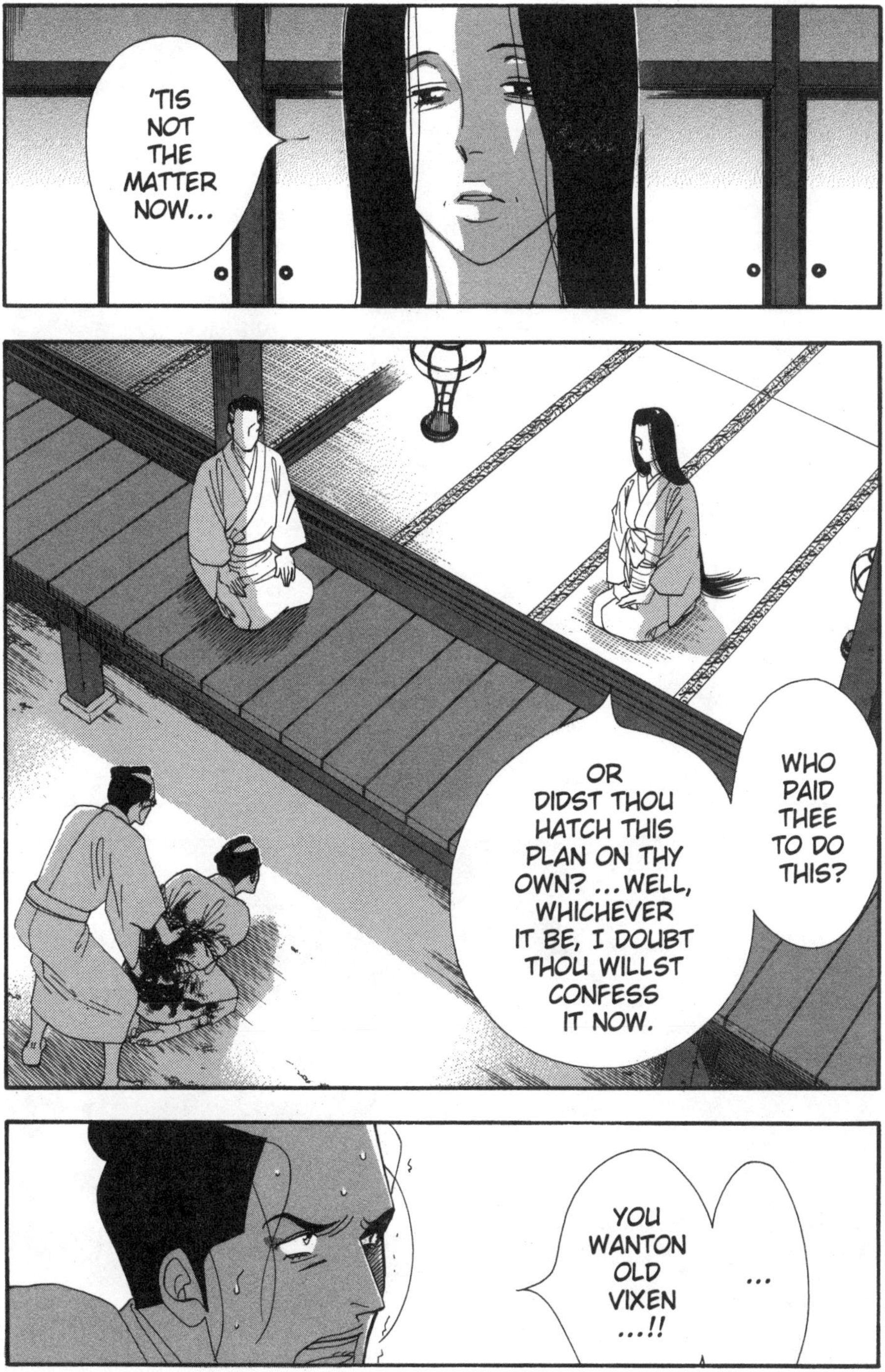
'TIS NOT THE MATTER NOW...
WHO PAID THEE TO DO THIS?
OR DIDST THOU HATCH THIS PLAN ON THY OWN? ...WELL, WHICHEVER IT BE, I DOUBT THOU WILLST CONFESS IT NOW.
...
YOU WANTON OLD VIXEN ...!!

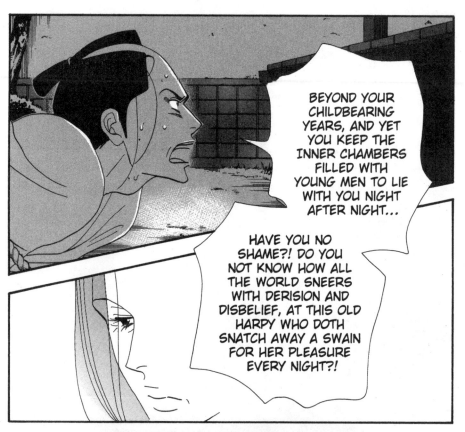

BEYOND YOUR CHILDBEARING YEARS, AND YET YOU KEEP THE INNER CHAMBERS FILLED WITH YOUNG MEN TO LIE WITH YOU NIGHT AFTER NIGHT...
HAVE YOU NO SHAME?! DO YOU NOT KNOW HOW ALL THE WORLD SNEERS WITH DERISION AND DISBELIEF, AT THIS OLD HARPY WHO DOTH SNATCH AWAY A SWAIN FOR HER PLEASURE EVERY NIGHT?!
ENOUGH! TAKE HIM AWAY.
NAY, LET HIM FINISH! I WILL HEAR IT ALL!
DOG SHOGUN!!

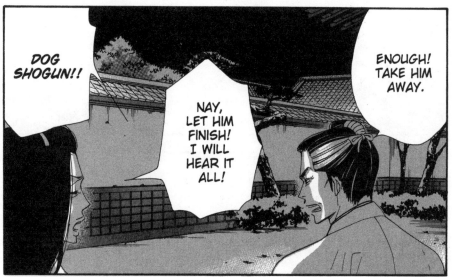

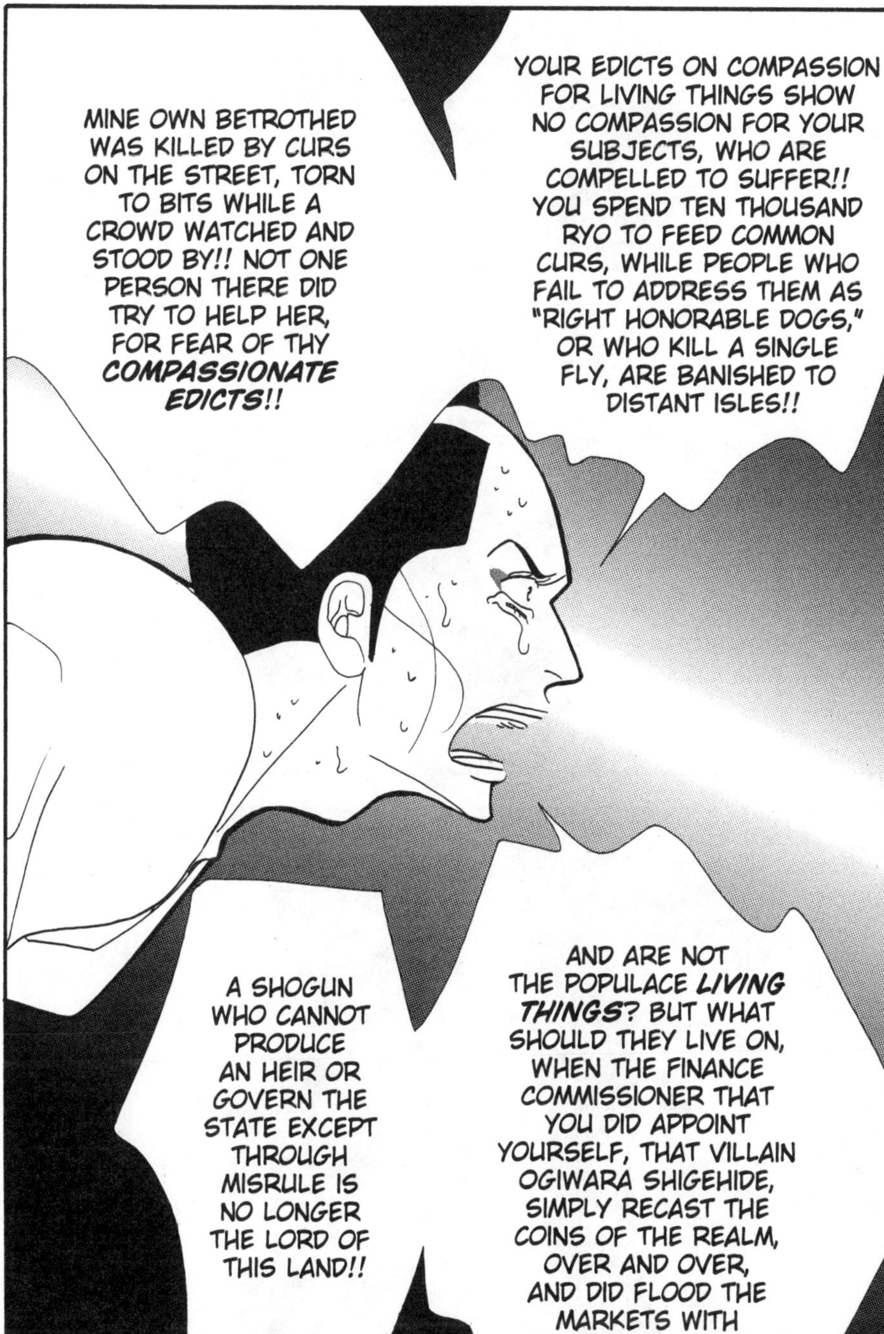
YOUR EDICTS ON COMPASSION FOR LIVING THINGS SHOW NO COMPASSION FOR YOUR SUBJECTS, WHO ARE COMPELLED TO SUFFER!! YOU SPEND TEN THOUSAND RYO TO FEED COMMON CURS, WHILE PEOPLE WHO FAIL TO ADDRESS THEM AS "RIGHT HONORABLE DOGS," OR WHO KILL A SINGLE FLY, ARE BANISHED TO DISTANT ISLES!!
MINE OWN BETROTHED WAS KILLED BY CURS ON THE STREET, TORN TO BITS WHILE A CROWD WATCHED AND STOOD BY!! NOT ONE PERSON THERE DID TRY TO HELP HER, FOR FEAR OF THY ***COMPASSIONATE EDICTS***!!
AND ARE NOT THE POPULACE ***LIVING THINGS***? BUT WHAT SHOULD THEY LIVE ON, WHEN THE FINANCE COMMISSIONER THAT YOU DID APPOINT YOURSELF, THAT VILLAIN OGIWARA SHIGEHIDE, SIMPLY RECAST THE COINS OF THE REALM, OVER AND OVER, AND DID FLOOD THE MARKETS WITH WORTHLESS MONEY?!
A SHOGUN WHO CANNOT PRODUCE AN HEIR OR GOVERN THE STATE EXCEPT THROUGH MISRULE IS NO LONGER THE LORD OF THIS LAND!!

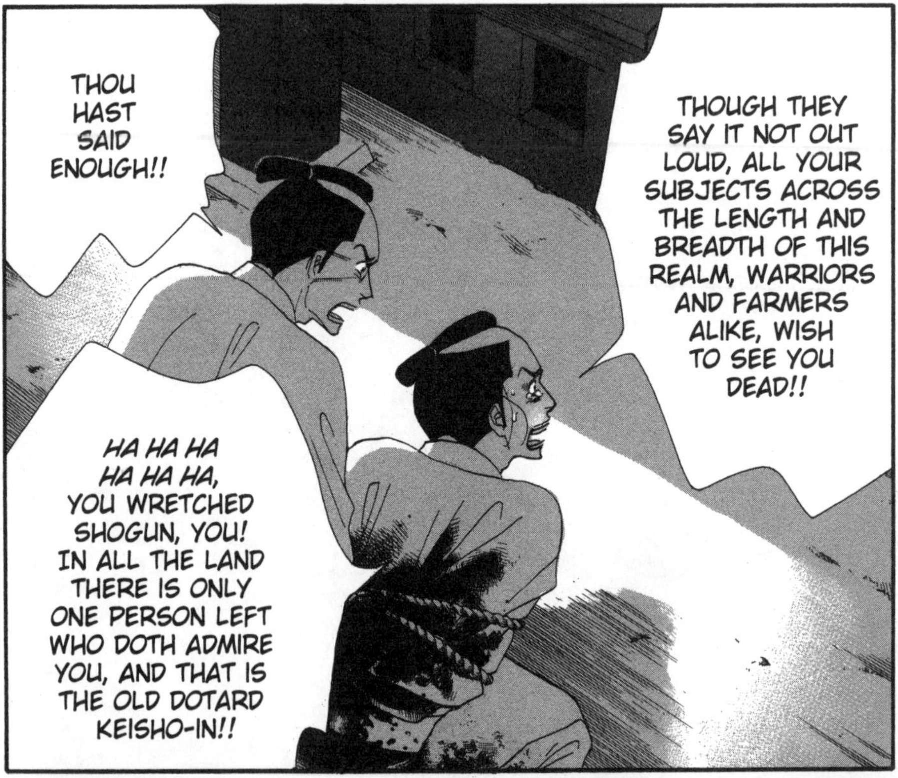
THOUGH THEY SAY IT NOT OUT LOUD, ALL YOUR SUBJECTS ACROSS THE LENGTH AND BREADTH OF THIS REALM, WARRIORS AND FARMERS ALIKE, WISH TO SEE YOU DEAD!!
THOU HAST SAID ENOUGH!!
HA HA HA HA HA HA, YOU WRETCHED SHOGUN, YOU! IN ALL THE LAND THERE IS ONLY ONE PERSON LEFT WHO DOTH ADMIRE YOU, AND THAT IS THE OLD DOTARD KEISHO-IN!!

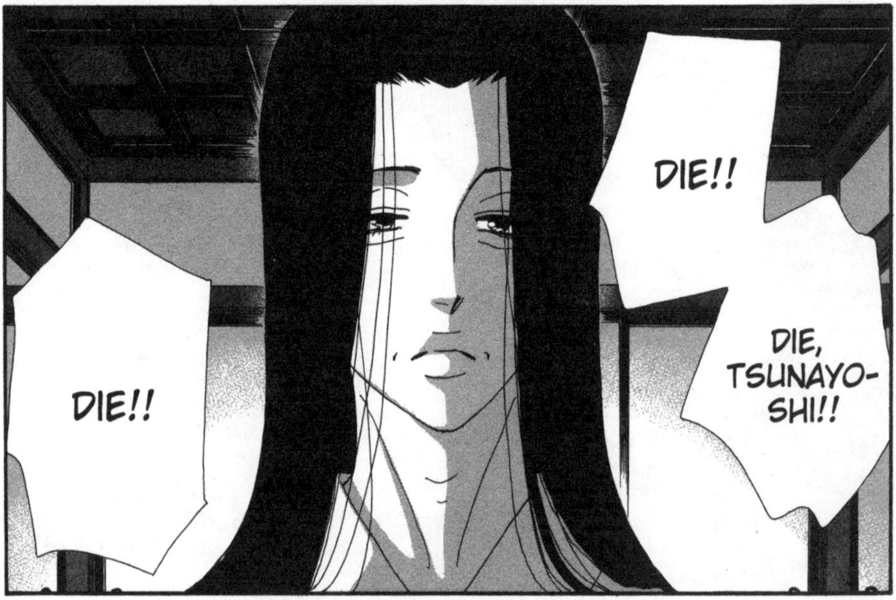
DIE!!
DIE, TSUNAYO-SHI!!
DIE!!

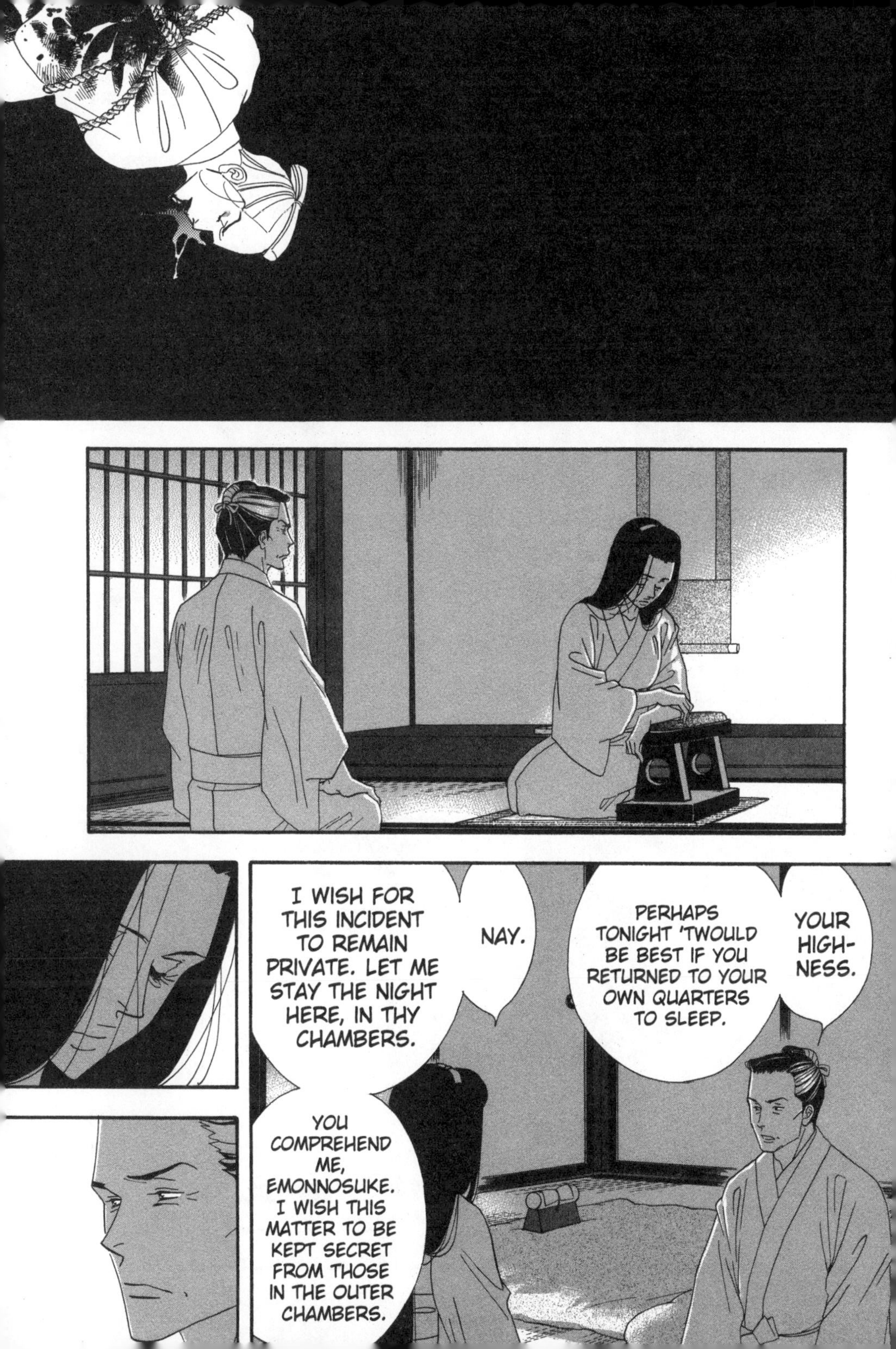
YOUR HIGH-NESS.
PERHAPS TONIGHT 'TWOULD BE BEST IF YOU RETURNED TO YOUR OWN QUARTERS TO SLEEP.
NAY.
I WISH FOR THIS INCIDENT TO REMAIN PRIVATE. LET ME STAY THE NIGHT HERE, IN THY CHAMBERS.
YOU COMPREHEND ME, EMONNOSUKE. I WISH THIS MATTER TO BE KEPT SECRET FROM THOSE IN THE OUTER CHAMBERS.

VERY WELL, MY LORD.
I SHALL COVERTLY INVESTIGATE ONCE MORE THE BACKGROUND OF THAT GROOM OF THE BEDCHAMBER WHO—
NO NEED FOR THAT.
'TIS EASY TO SURMISE HE WAS SENT BY TSUNATOYO OF KOFU.
AHH, FOR-SOOTH...
WHEREFORE DO I REMAIN ALIVE, EMONNOSUKE?
YOUR HIGH-NESS.
EVERYTHING THE ASSASSIN SAID WAS TRUE.
I WAS, FINALLY, UNABLE TO ACCOMPLISH EVEN ONE THING TO PASS DOWN FROM MY REIGN TO THE NEXT.
I WAS NOT A GOOD AND EFFECTIVE RULER, I COULD NOT PRODUCE AN HEIR AND THUS ENTRENCH TOKUGAWA HEGEMONY...

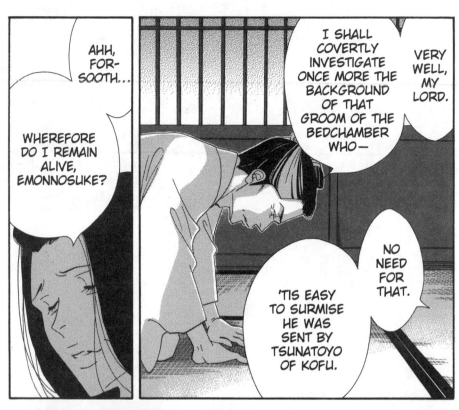

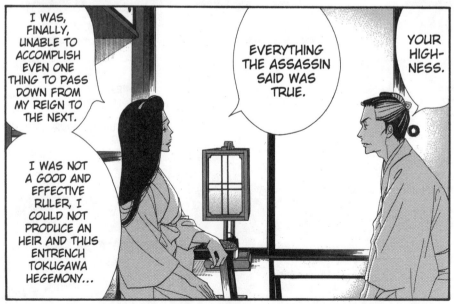

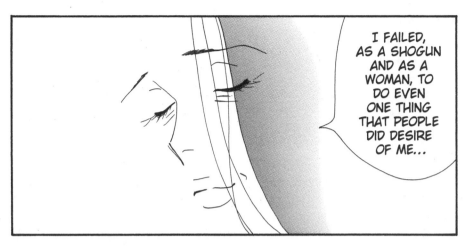

I FAILED, AS A SHOGUN AND AS A WOMAN, TO DO EVEN ONE THING THAT PEOPLE DID DESIRE OF ME...

NAY, MY LIEGE.

...

GO NOW.

THOU TOO HADST A MOST ARDUOUS NIGHT. REST NOW IN ANOTHER CHAMBER.

EMO-NNO-SUKE.

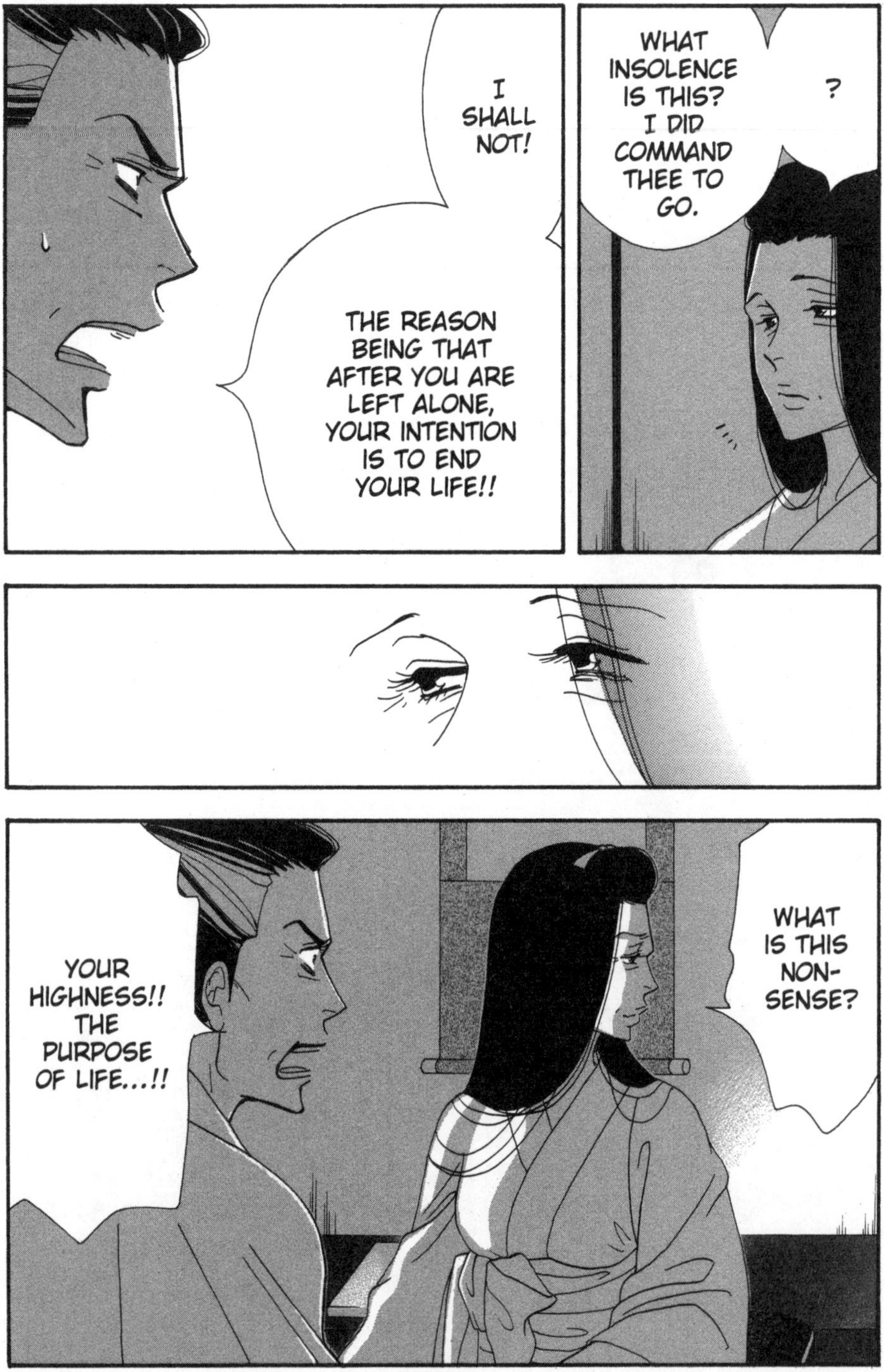
?
WHAT INSOLENCE IS THIS? I DID COMMAND THEE TO GO.
I SHALL NOT!
THE REASON BEING THAT AFTER YOU ARE LEFT ALONE, YOUR INTENTION IS TO END YOUR LIFE!!
WHAT IS THIS NON-SENSE?
YOUR HIGHNESS!! THE PURPOSE OF LIFE...!!

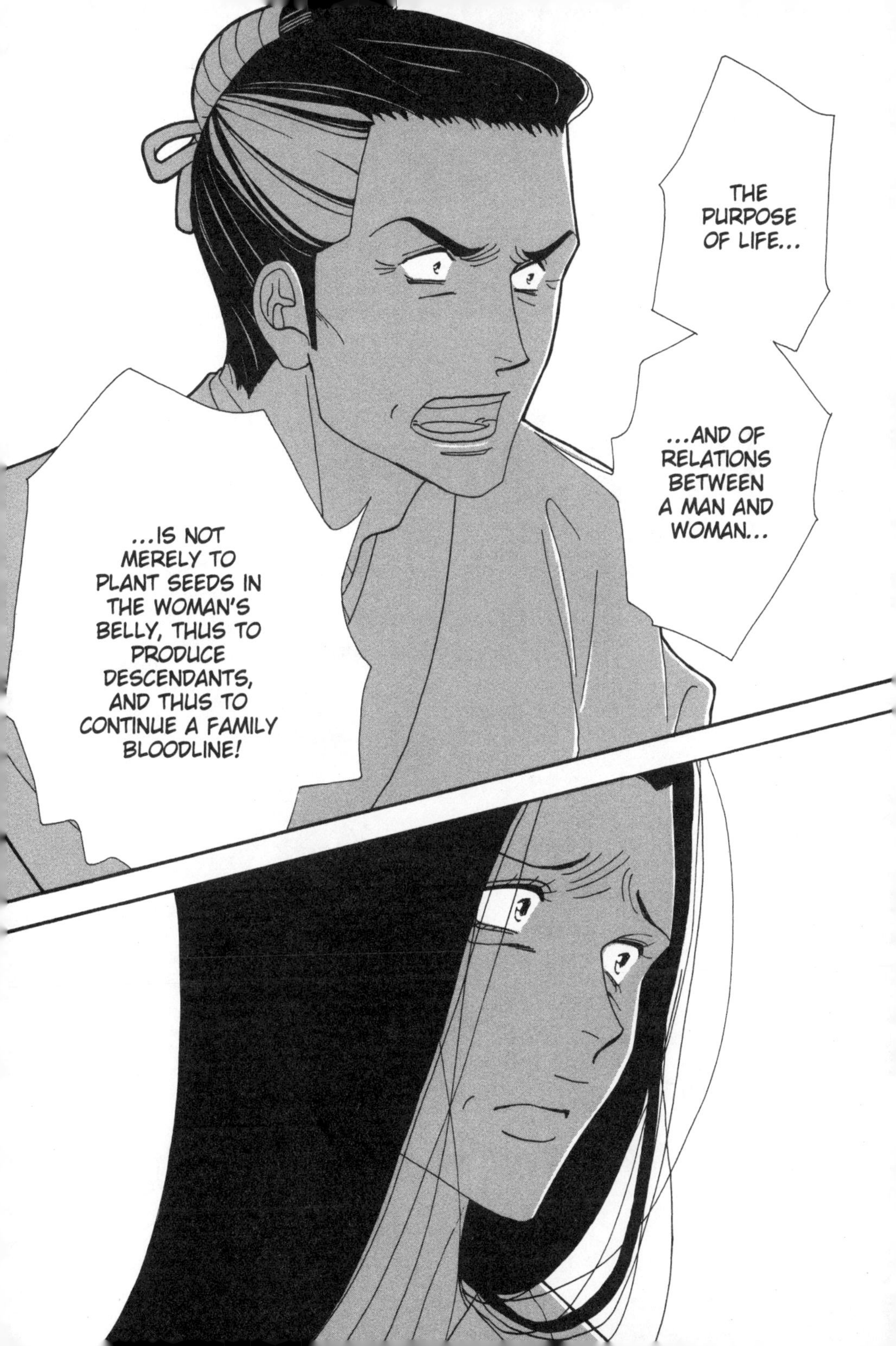
THE PURPOSE OF LIFE...
...AND OF RELATIONS BETWEEN A MAN AND WOMAN...
...IS NOT MERELY TO PLANT SEEDS IN THE WOMAN'S BELLY, THUS TO PRODUCE DESCENDANTS, AND THUS TO CONTINUE A FAMILY BLOODLINE!

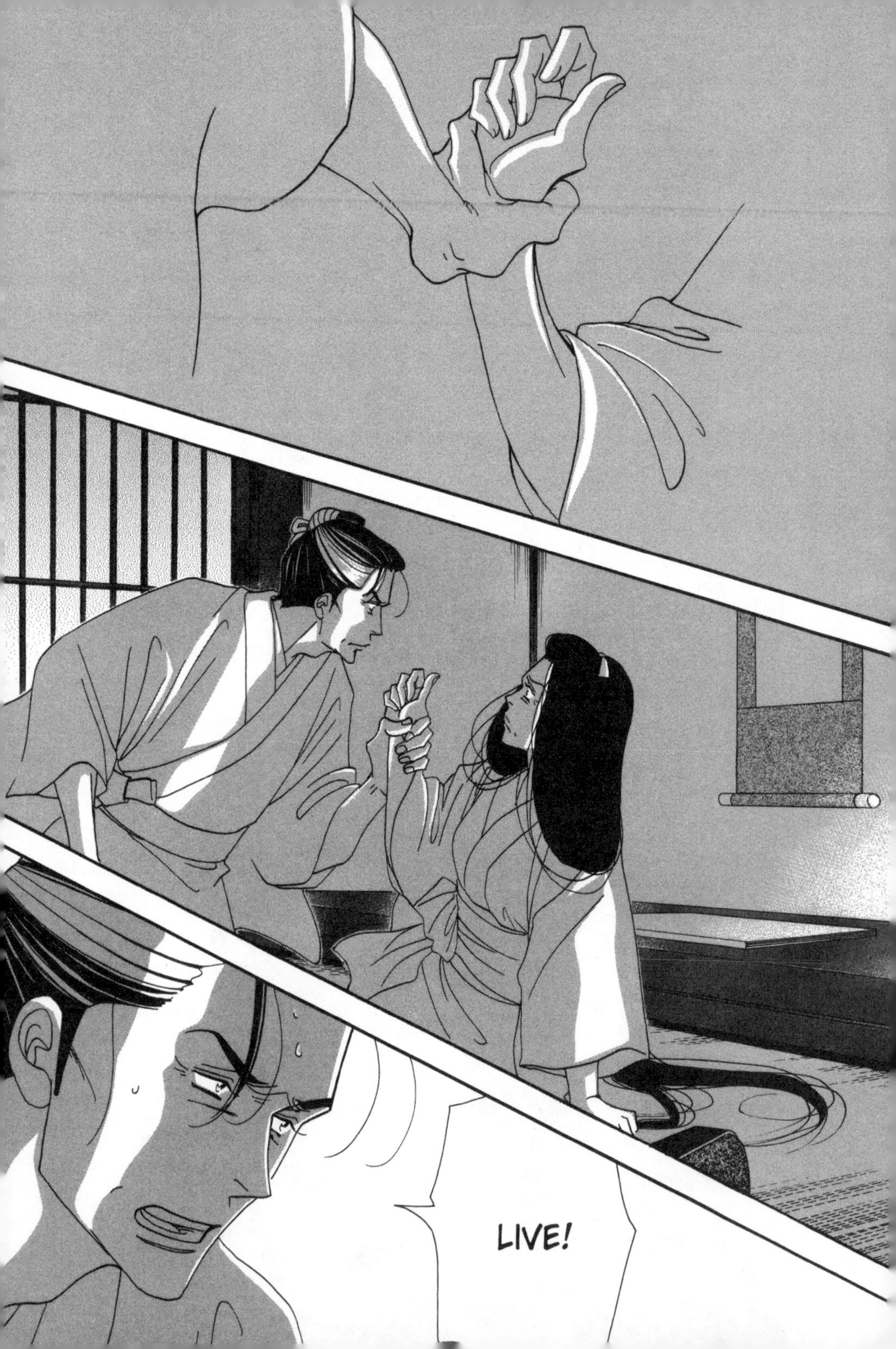
LIVE!

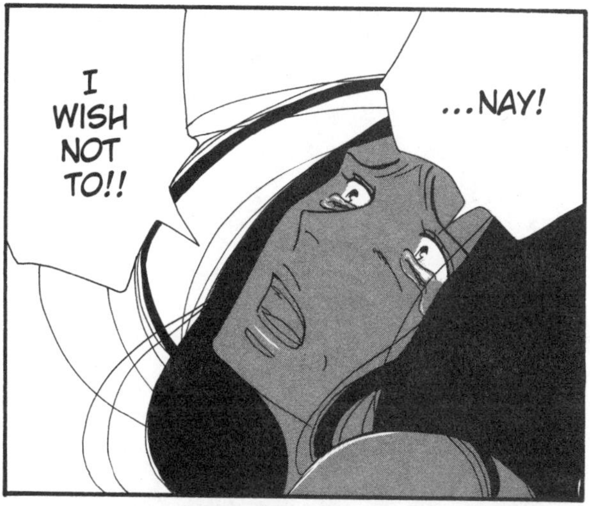
...NAY!
I WISH NOT TO!!

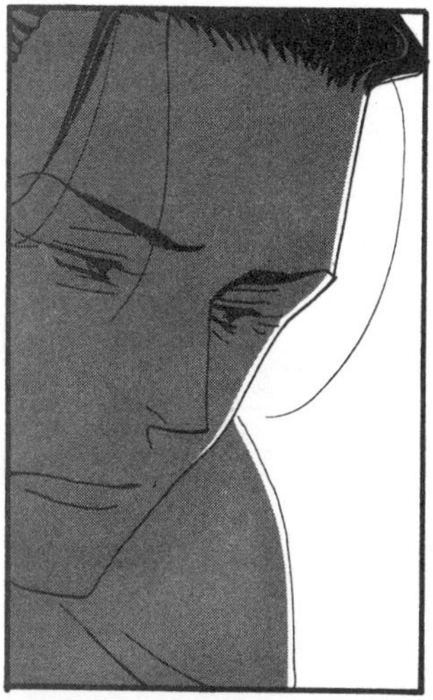

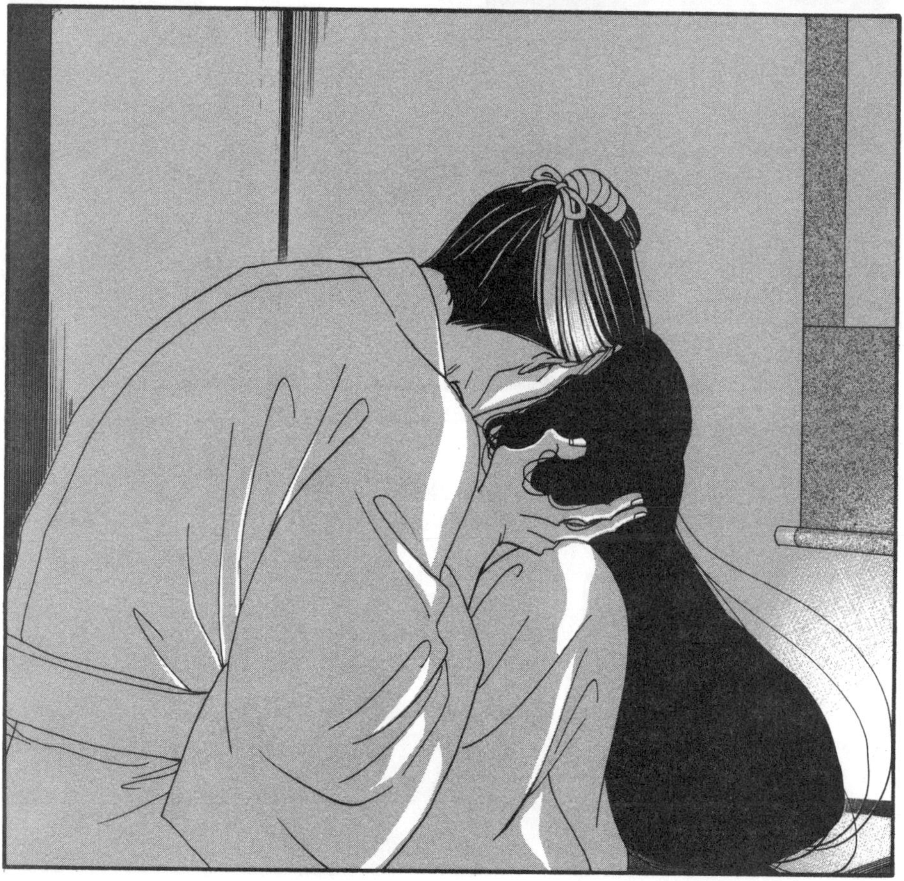

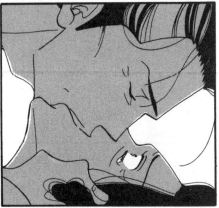
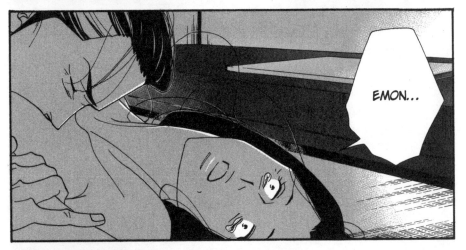

EMON...

I HAVE NOT LET A MAN SEE MY BARE SKIN IN YEARS! EMONNOSUKE, PRITHEE...!

NAY...

PRITHEE, STOP!

58

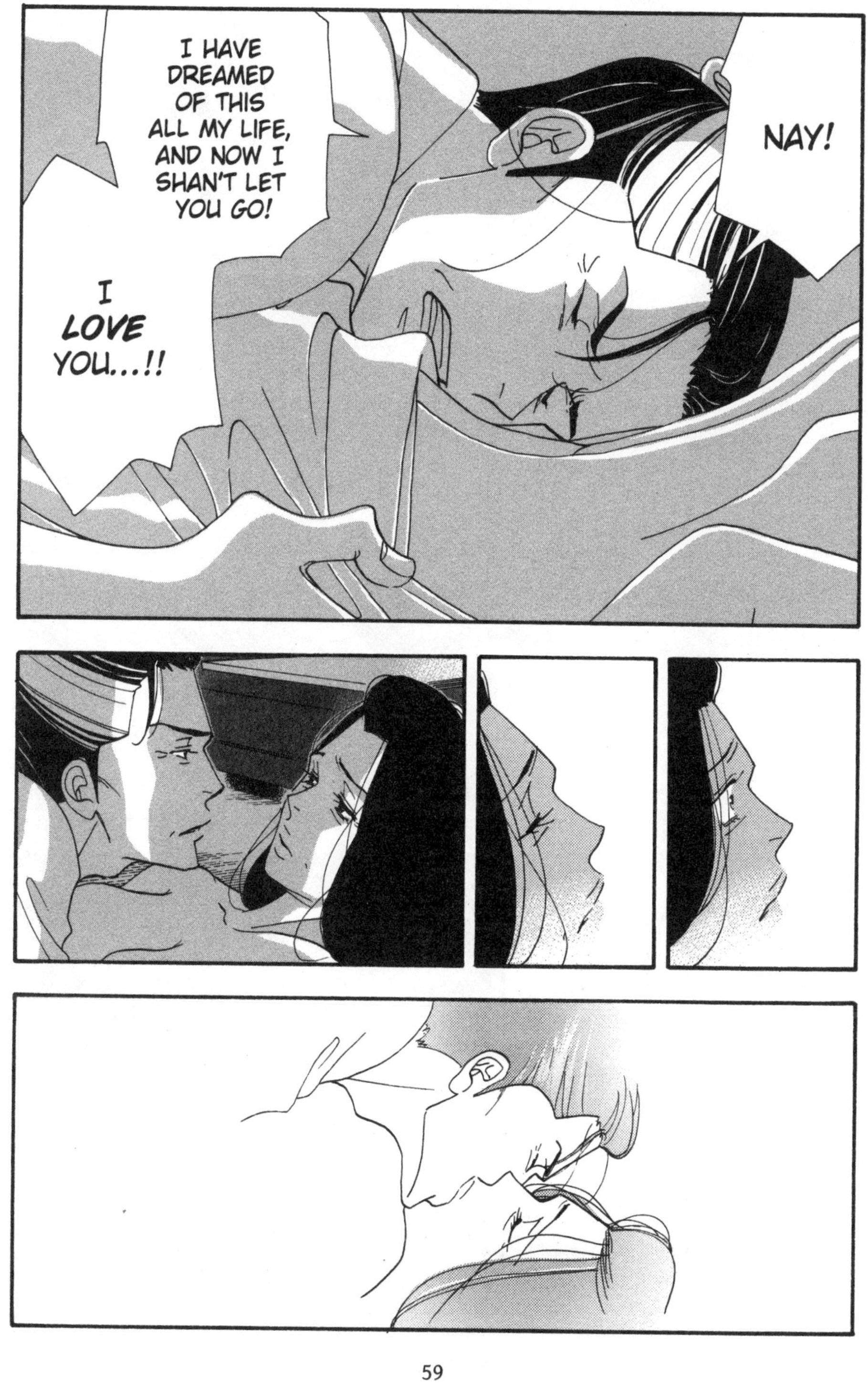
NAY!
I HAVE DREAMED OF THIS ALL MY LIFE, AND NOW I SHAN'T LET YOU GO!
I LOVE YOU...!!

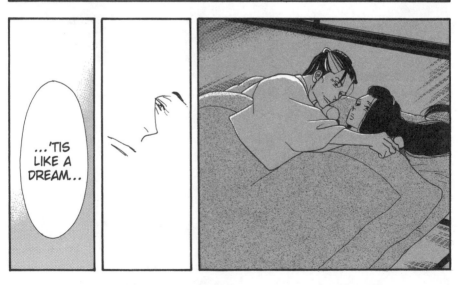

...'TIS LIKE A DREAM...

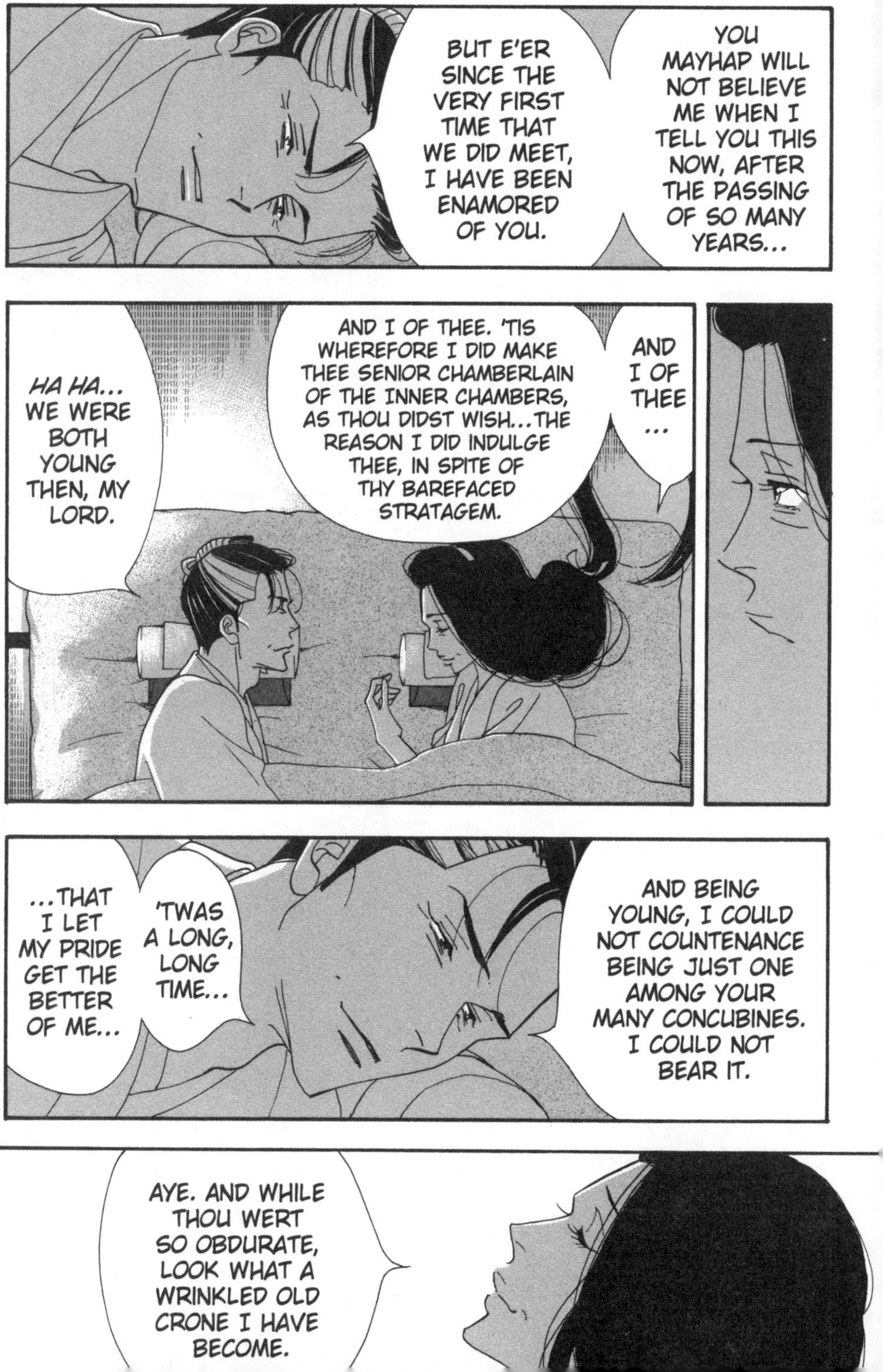
YOU MAYHAP WILL NOT BELIEVE ME WHEN I TELL YOU THIS NOW, AFTER THE PASSING OF SO MANY YEARS...
BUT E'ER SINCE THE VERY FIRST TIME THAT WE DID MEET, I HAVE BEEN ENAMORED OF YOU.
AND I OF THEE...
AND I OF THEE. 'TIS WHEREFORE I DID MAKE THEE SENIOR CHAMBERLAIN OF THE INNER CHAMBERS, AS THOU DIDST WISH...THE REASON I DID INDULGE THEE, IN SPITE OF THY BAREFACED STRATAGEM.
HA HA... WE WERE BOTH YOUNG THEN, MY LORD.
AND BEING YOUNG, I COULD NOT COUNTENANCE BEING JUST ONE AMONG YOUR MANY CONCUBINES. I COULD NOT BEAR IT.
'TWAS A LONG, LONG TIME...
...THAT I LET MY PRIDE GET THE BETTER OF ME...
AYE. AND WHILE THOU WERT SO OBDURATE, LOOK WHAT A WRINKLED OLD CRONE I HAVE BECOME.

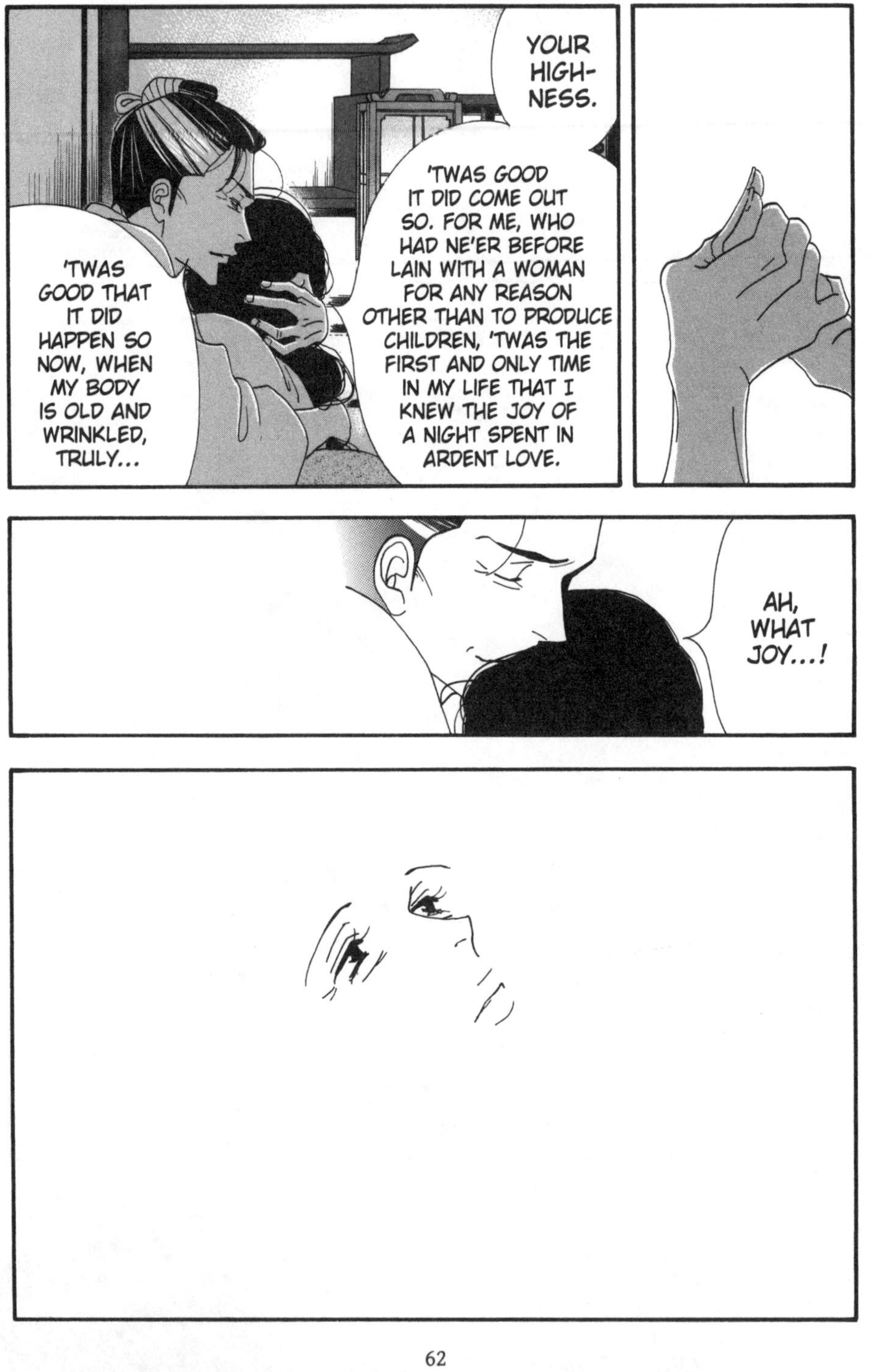
YOUR HIGH-NESS.
'TWAS GOOD IT DID COME OUT SO. FOR ME, WHO HAD NE'ER BEFORE LAIN WITH A WOMAN FOR ANY REASON OTHER THAN TO PRODUCE CHILDREN, 'TWAS THE FIRST AND ONLY TIME IN MY LIFE THAT I KNEW THE JOY OF A NIGHT SPENT IN ARDENT LOVE.
'TWAS GOOD THAT IT DID HAPPEN SO NOW, WHEN MY BODY IS OLD AND WRINKLED, TRULY...
AH, WHAT JOY...!

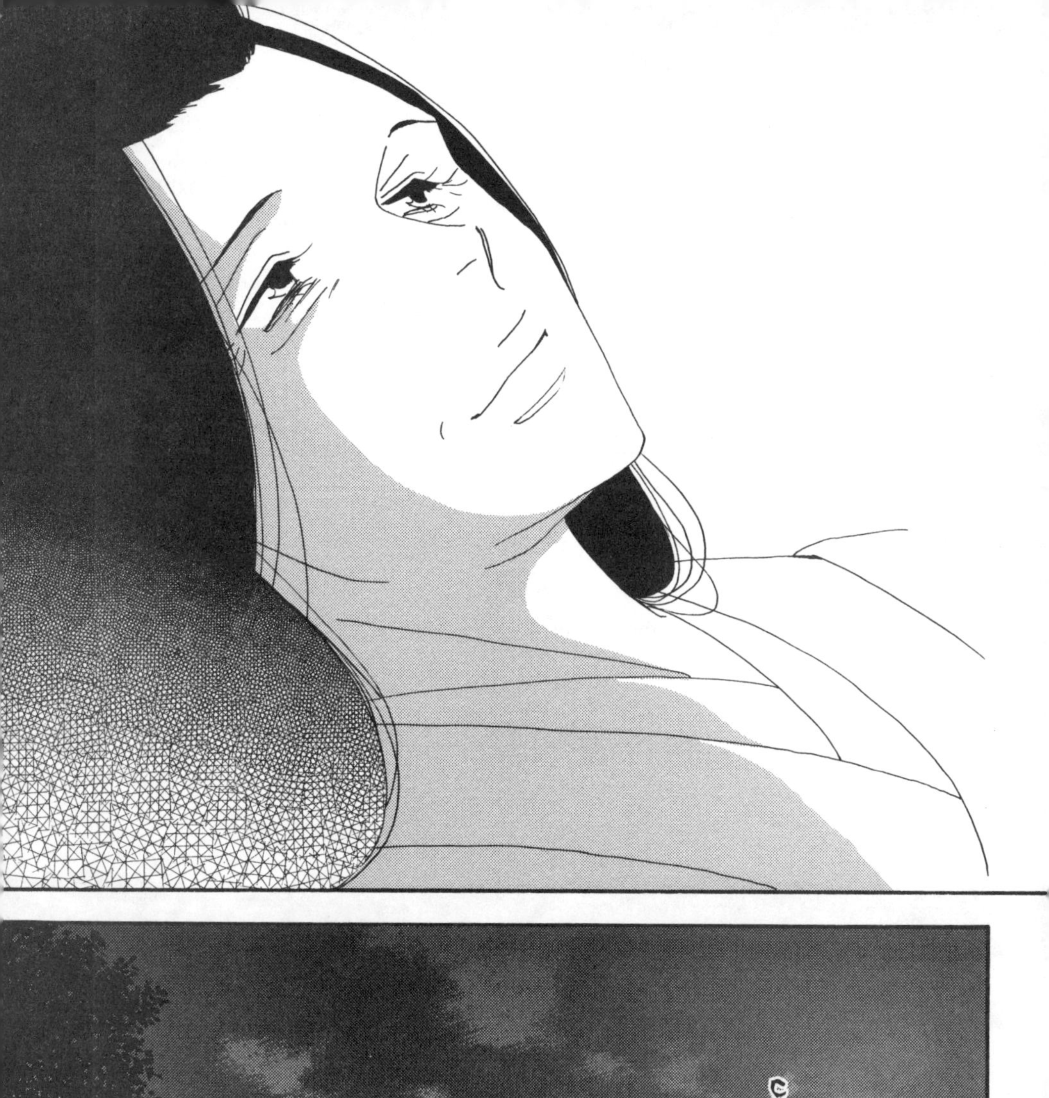

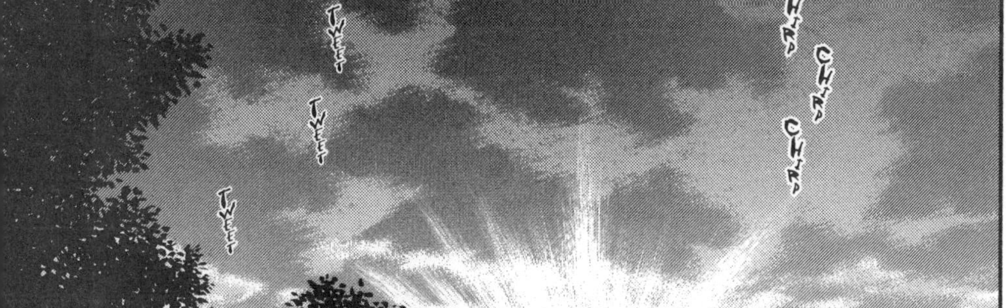
CHIRP
CHIRP
CHIRP
TWEET
TWEET
TWEET

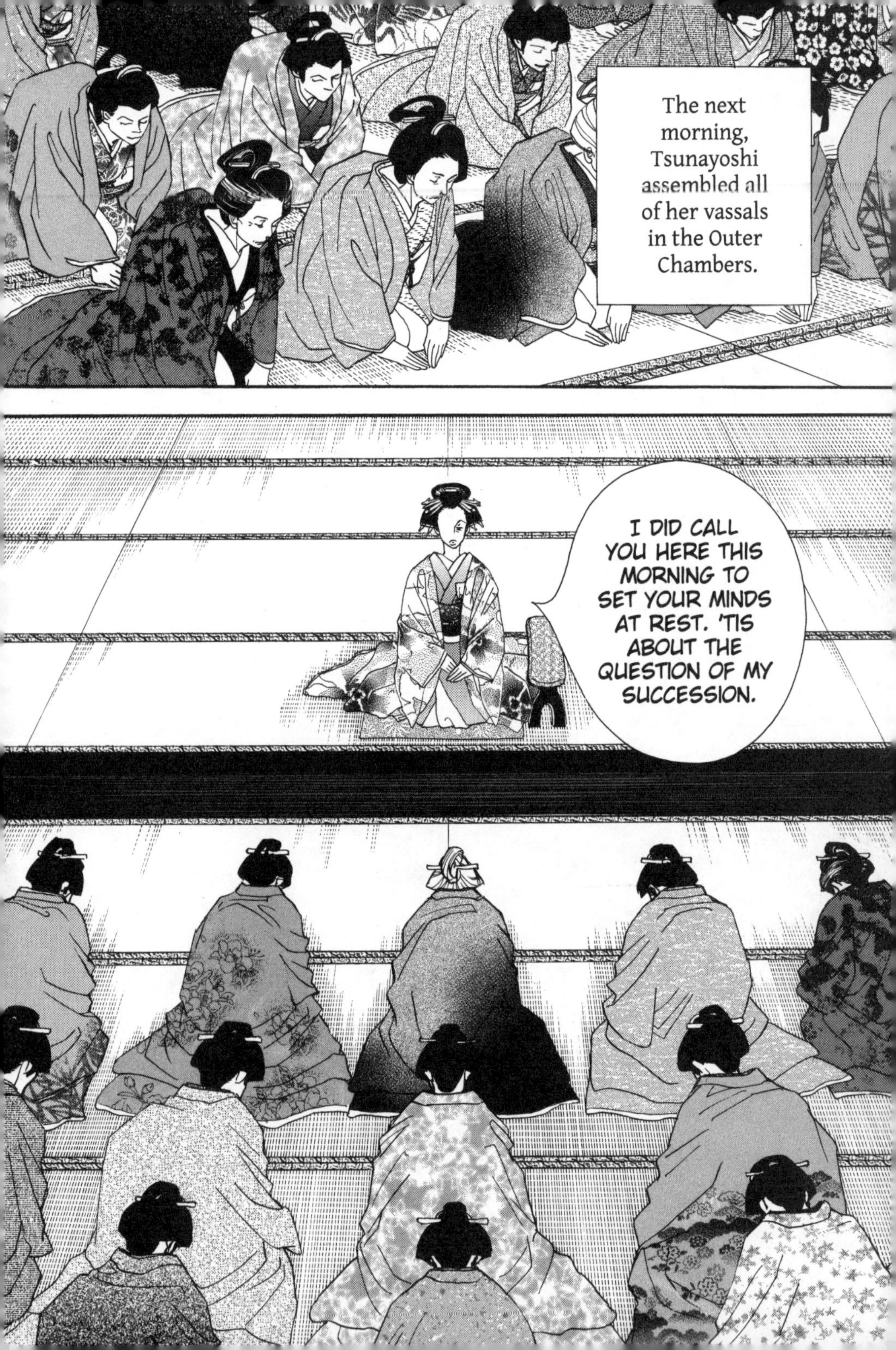
The next morning, Tsunayoshi assembled all of her vassals in the Outer Chambers.
I DID CALL YOU HERE THIS MORNING TO SET YOUR MINDS AT REST. 'TIS ABOUT THE QUESTION OF MY SUCCESSION.

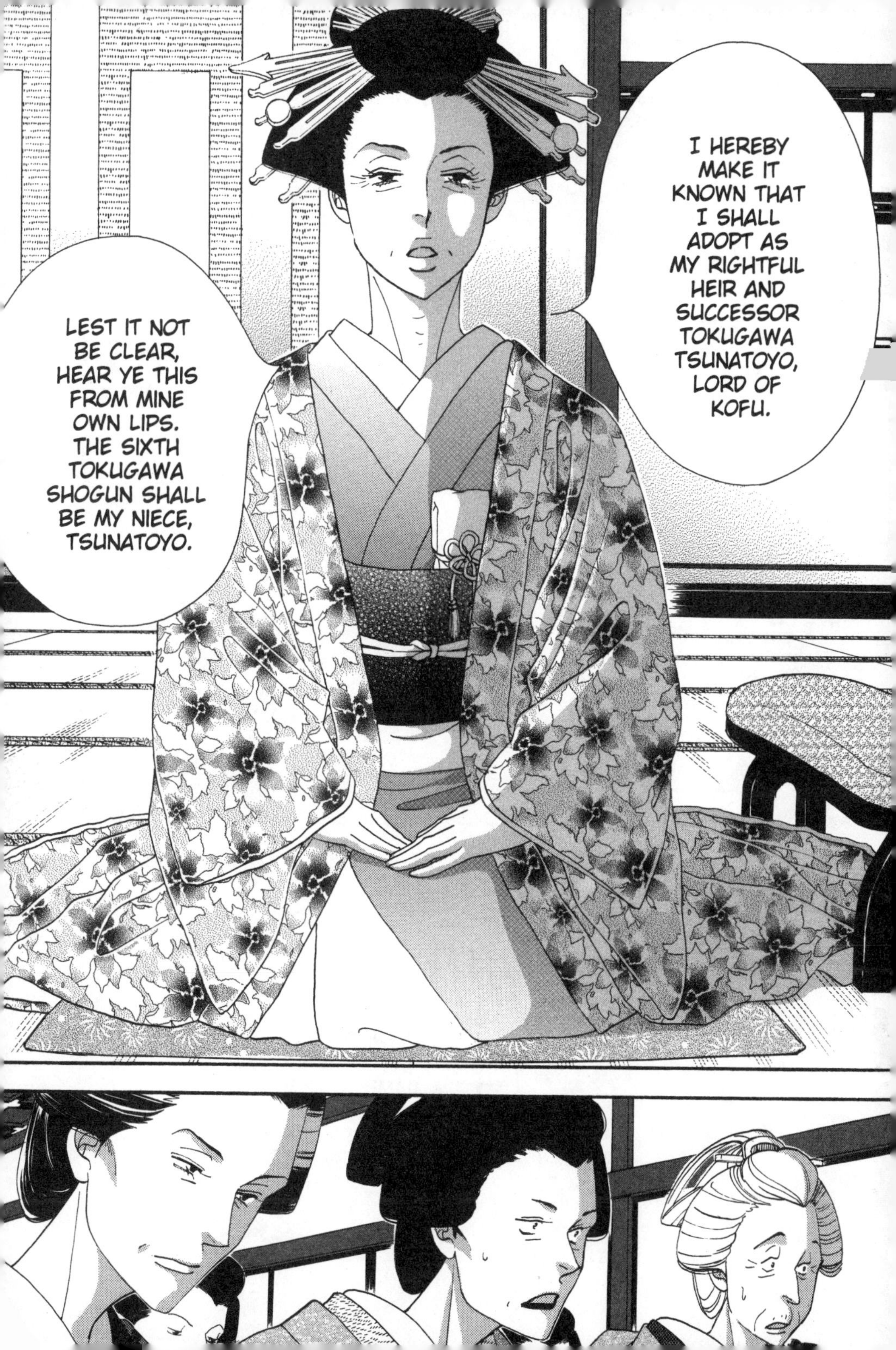
I HEREBY MAKE IT KNOWN THAT I SHALL ADOPT AS MY RIGHTFUL HEIR AND SUCCESSOR TOKUGAWA TSUNATOYO, LORD OF KOFU.
LEST IT NOT BE CLEAR, HEAR YE THIS FROM MINE OWN LIPS. THE SIXTH TOKUGAWA SHOGUN SHALL BE MY NIECE, TSUNATOYO.

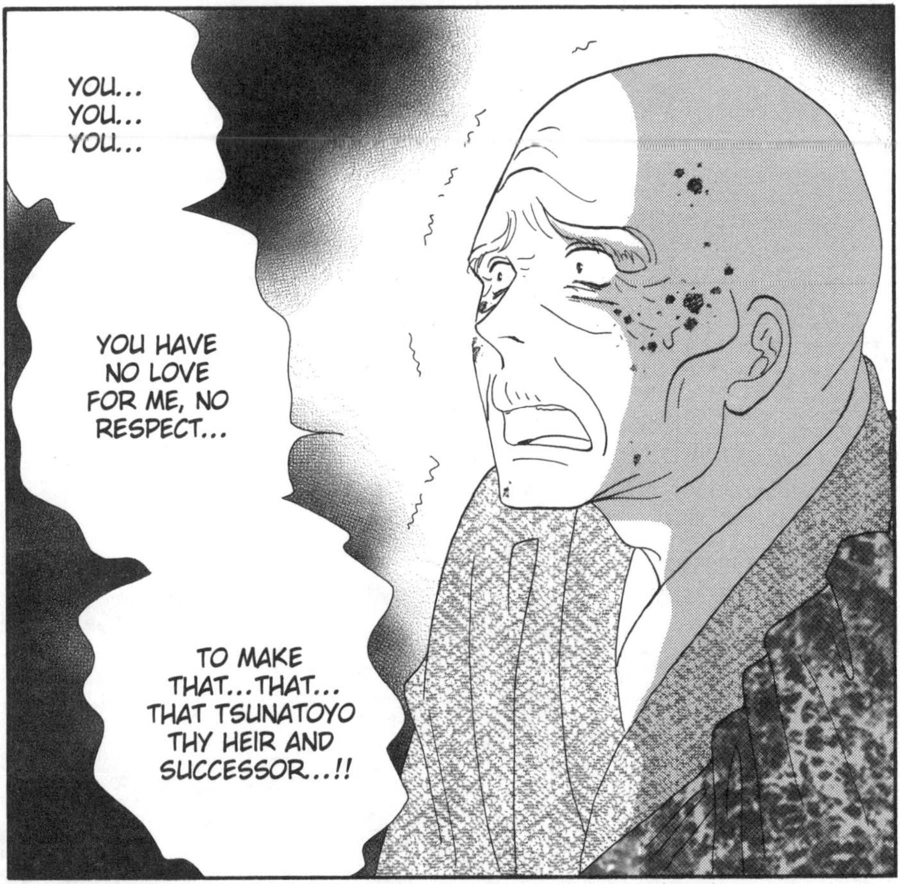
YOU... YOU... YOU...
YOU HAVE NO LOVE FOR ME, NO RESPECT...
TO MAKE THAT...THAT... THAT TSUNATOYO THY HEIR AND SUCCESSOR...!!
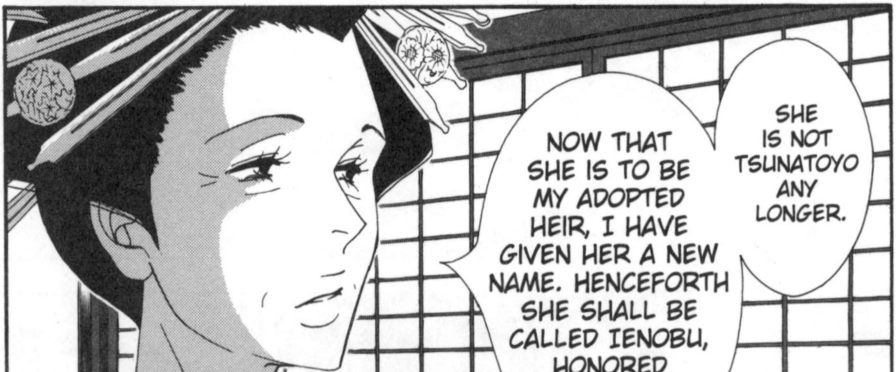
SHE IS NOT TSUNATOYO ANY LONGER.
NOW THAT SHE IS TO BE MY ADOPTED HEIR, I HAVE GIVEN HER A NEW NAME. HENCEFORTH SHE SHALL BE CALLED IENOBU, HONORED FATHER.

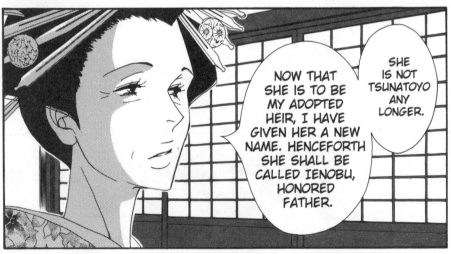

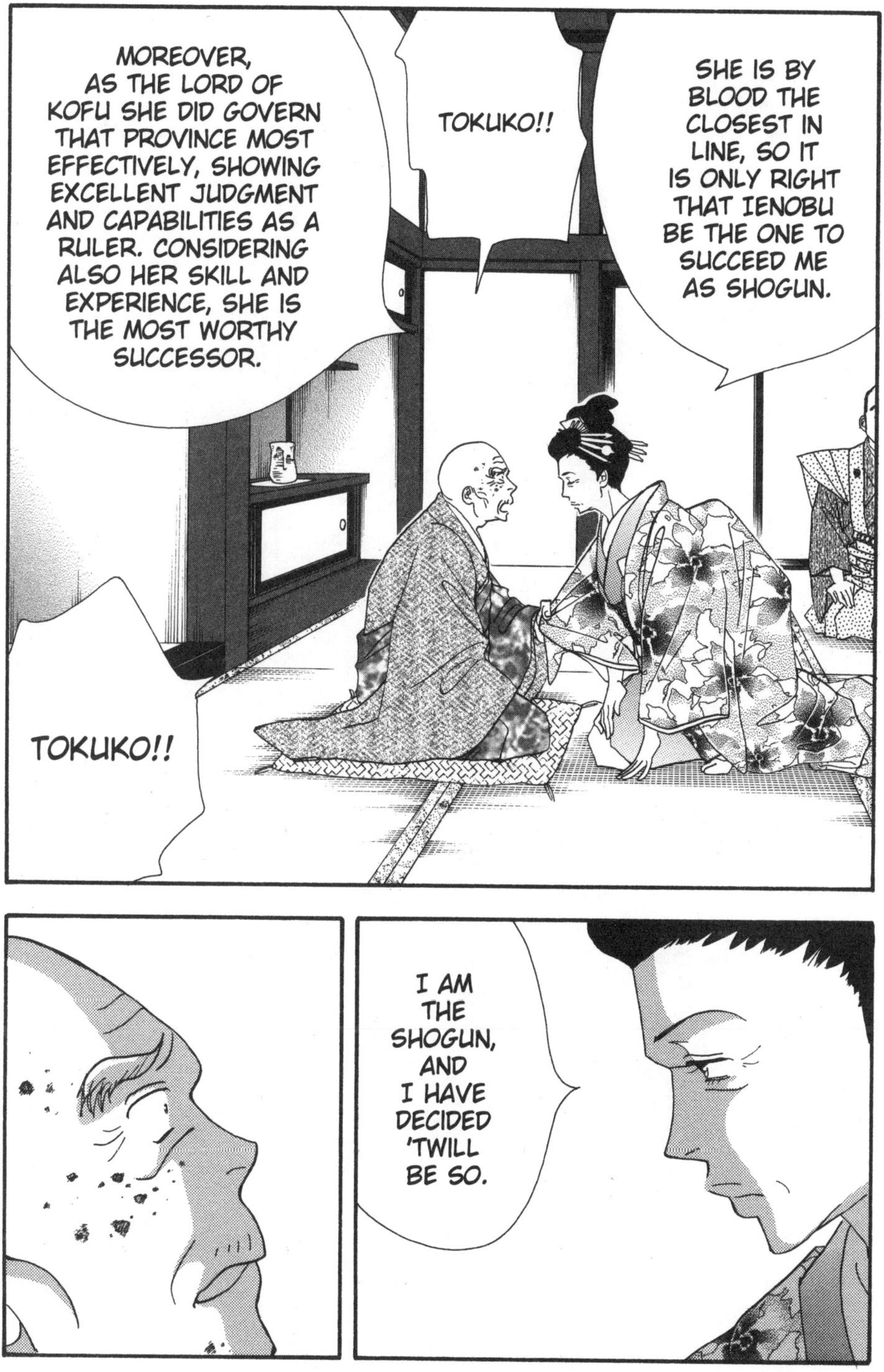
SHE IS BY BLOOD THE CLOSEST IN LINE, SO IT IS ONLY RIGHT THAT IENOBU BE THE ONE TO SUCCEED ME AS SHOGUN.
TOKUKO!!
MOREOVER, AS THE LORD OF KOFU SHE DID GOVERN THAT PROVINCE MOST EFFECTIVELY, SHOWING EXCELLENT JUDGMENT AND CAPABILITIES AS A RULER. CONSIDERING ALSO HER SKILL AND EXPERIENCE, SHE IS THE MOST WORTHY SUCCESSOR.
TOKUKO!!
I AM THE SHOGUN, AND I HAVE DECIDED 'TWILL BE SO.

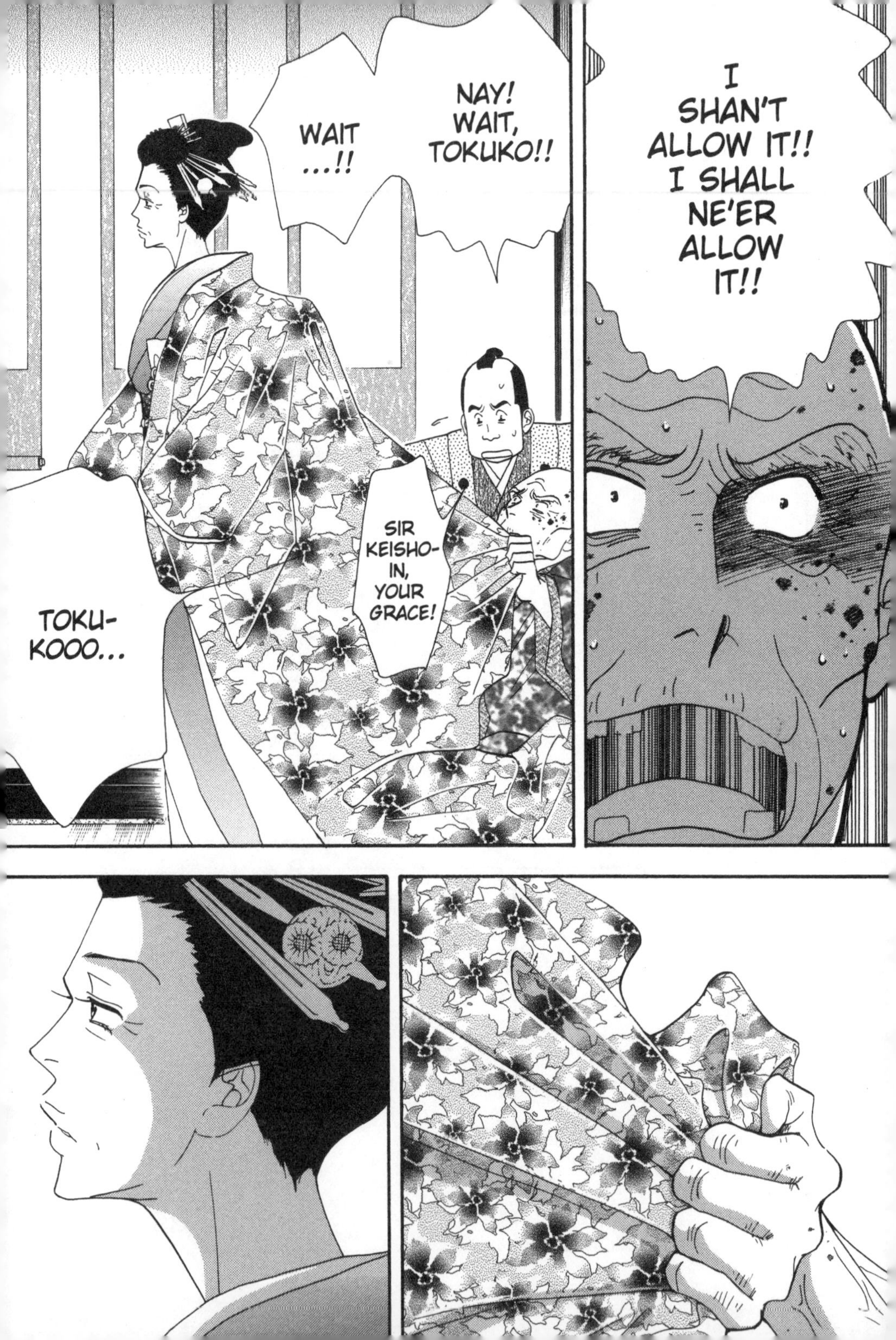
I SHAN'T ALLOW IT!! I SHALL NE'ER ALLOW IT!!
NAY! WAIT, TOKUKO!!
WAIT ...!!
SIR KEISHO-IN, YOUR GRACE!
TOKU-KOOO...

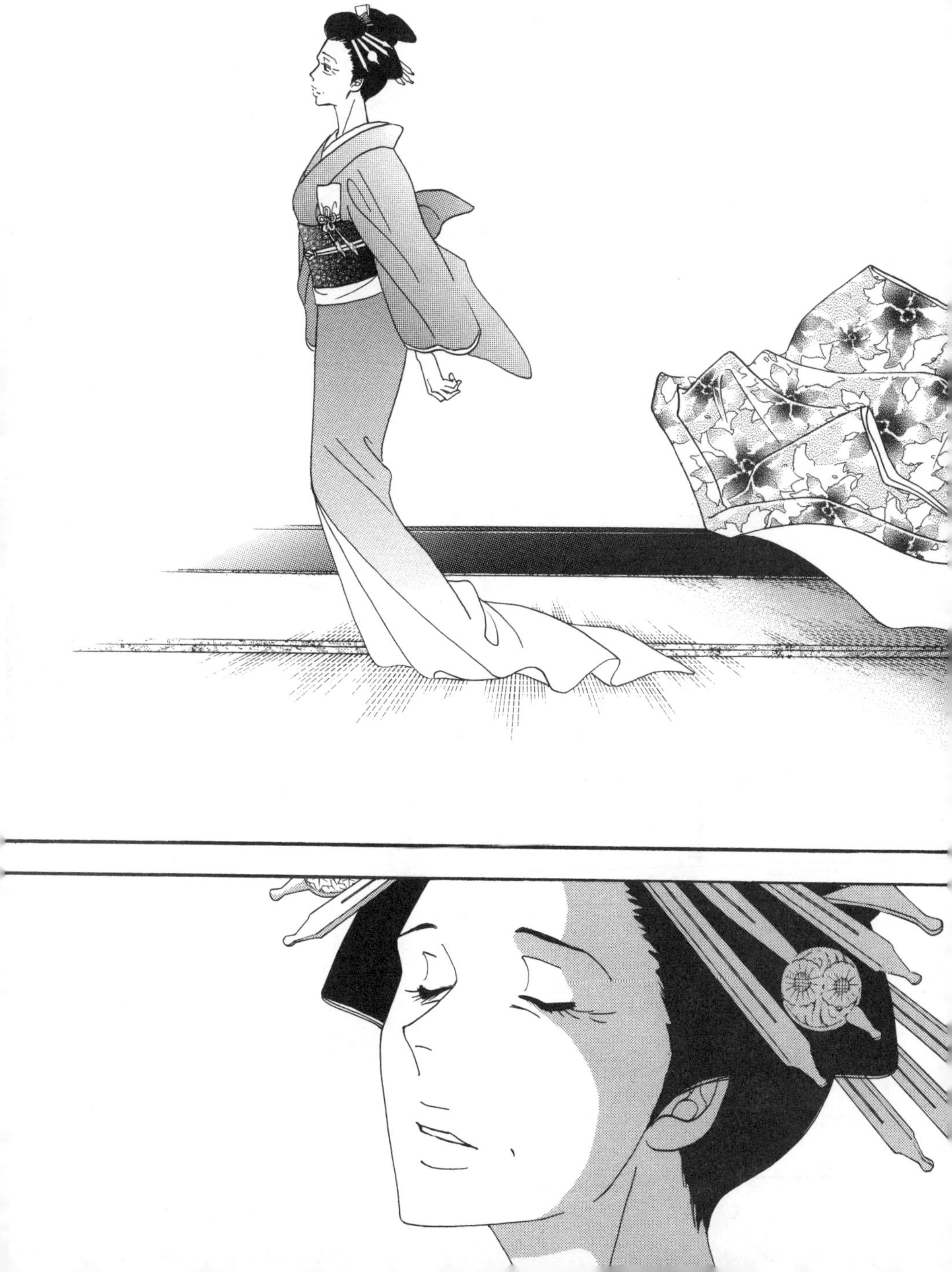

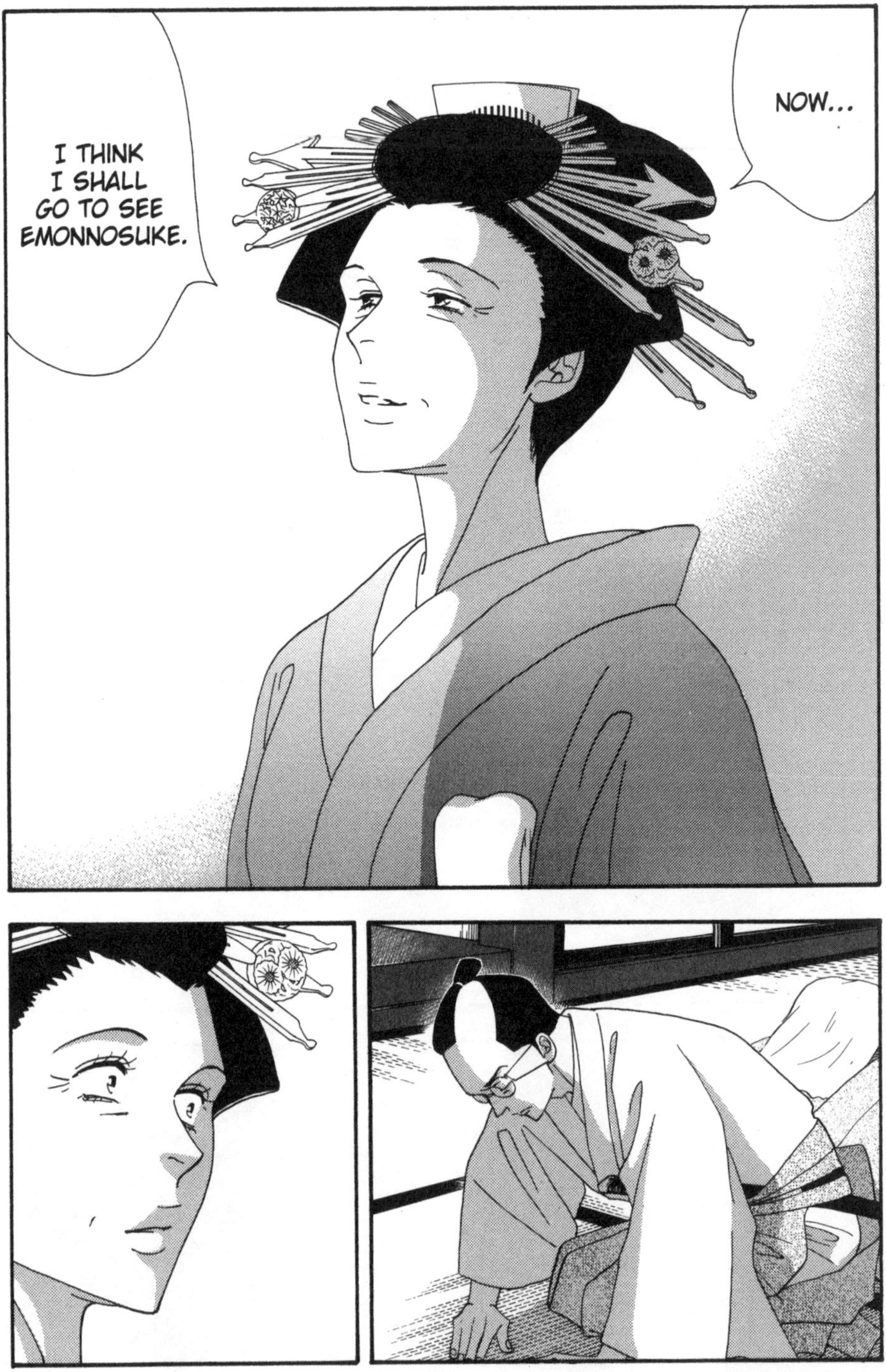
NOW...
I THINK I SHALL GO TO SEE EMONNOSUKE.

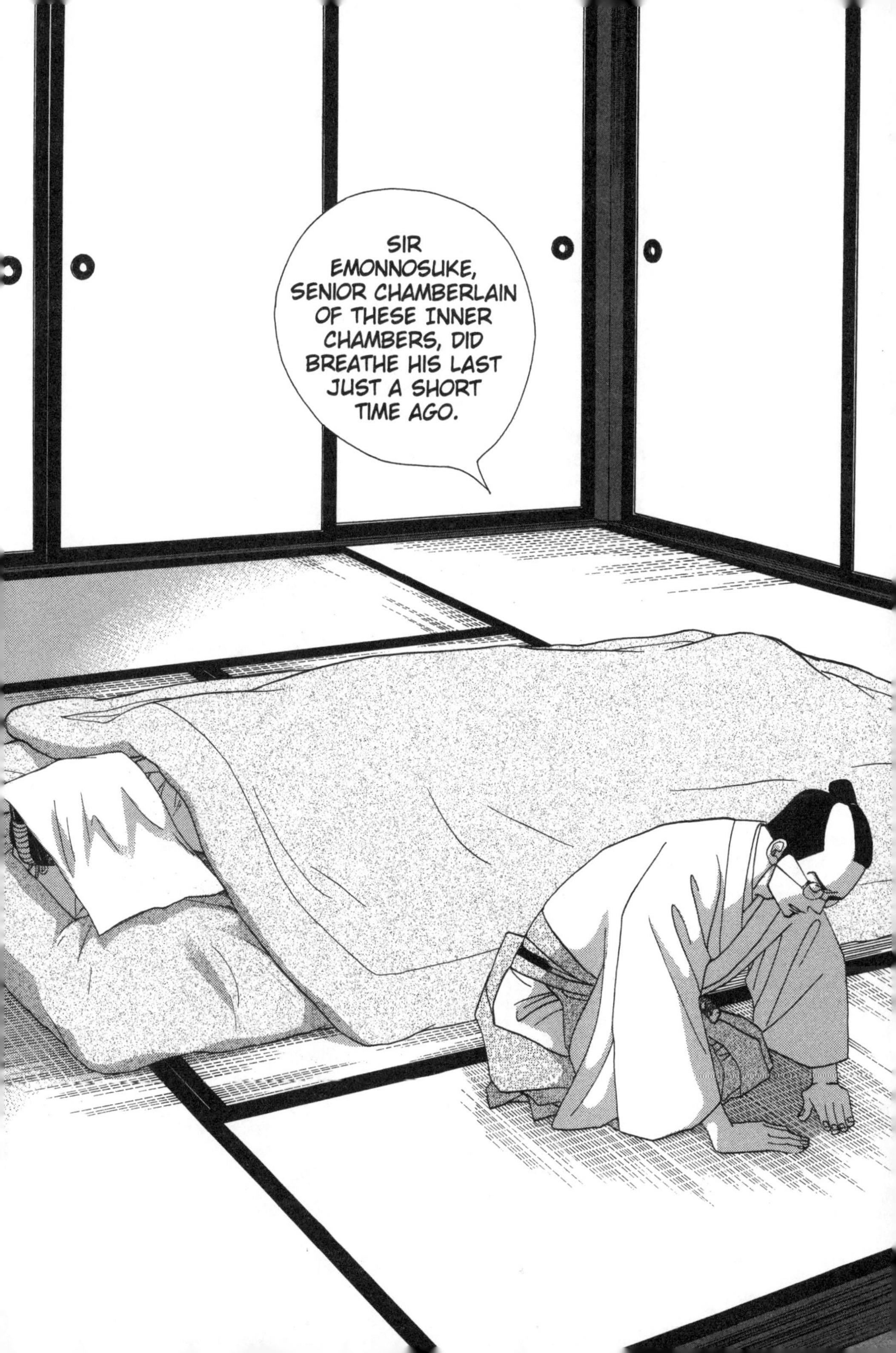
SIR EMONNOSUKE, SENIOR CHAMBERLAIN OF THESE INNER CHAMBERS, DID BREATHE HIS LAST JUST A SHORT TIME AGO.

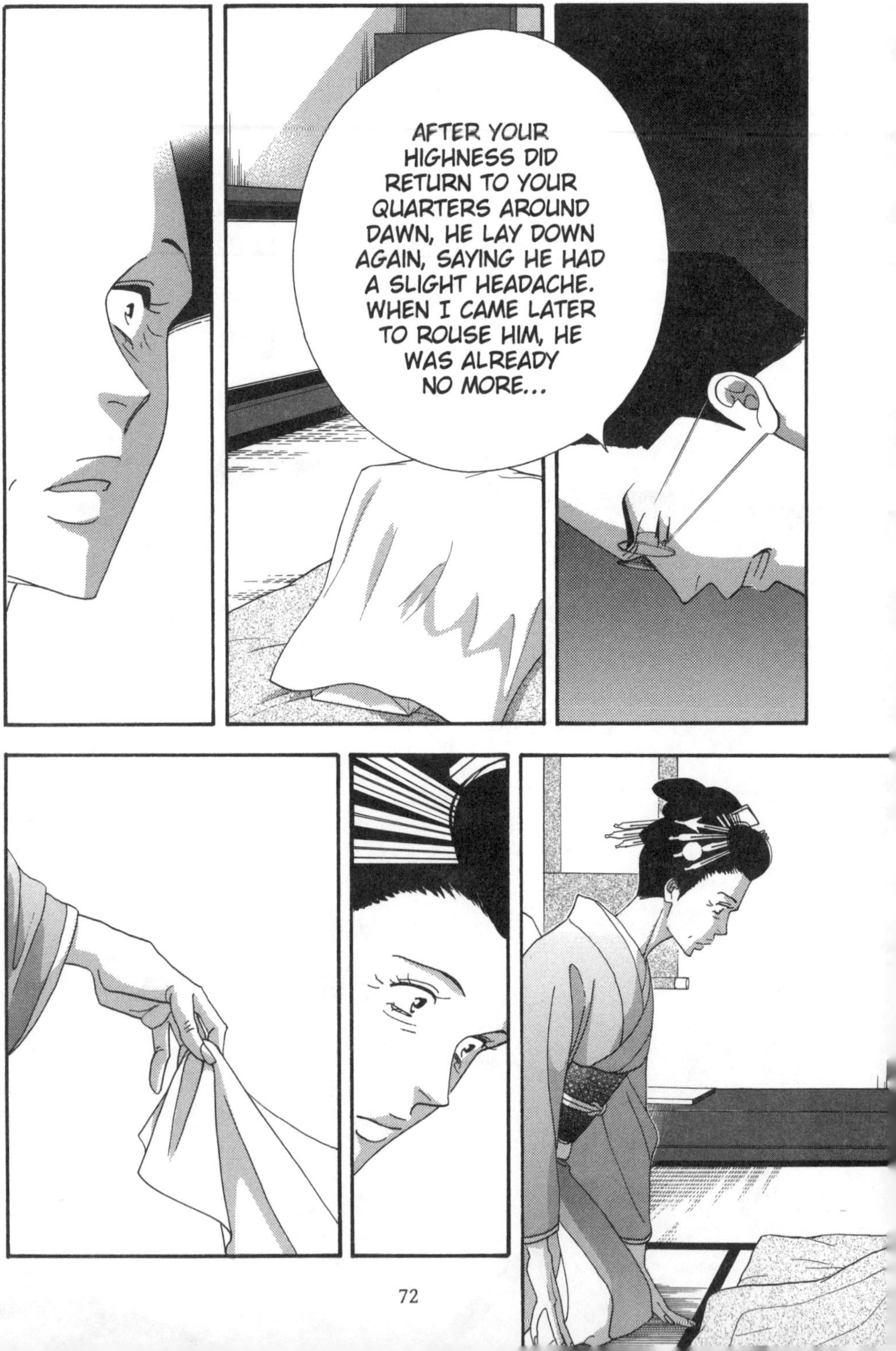
AFTER YOUR HIGHNESS DID RETURN TO YOUR QUARTERS AROUND DAWN, HE LAY DOWN AGAIN, SAYING HE HAD A SLIGHT HEADACHE. WHEN I CAME LATER TO ROUSE HIM, HE WAS ALREADY NO MORE...

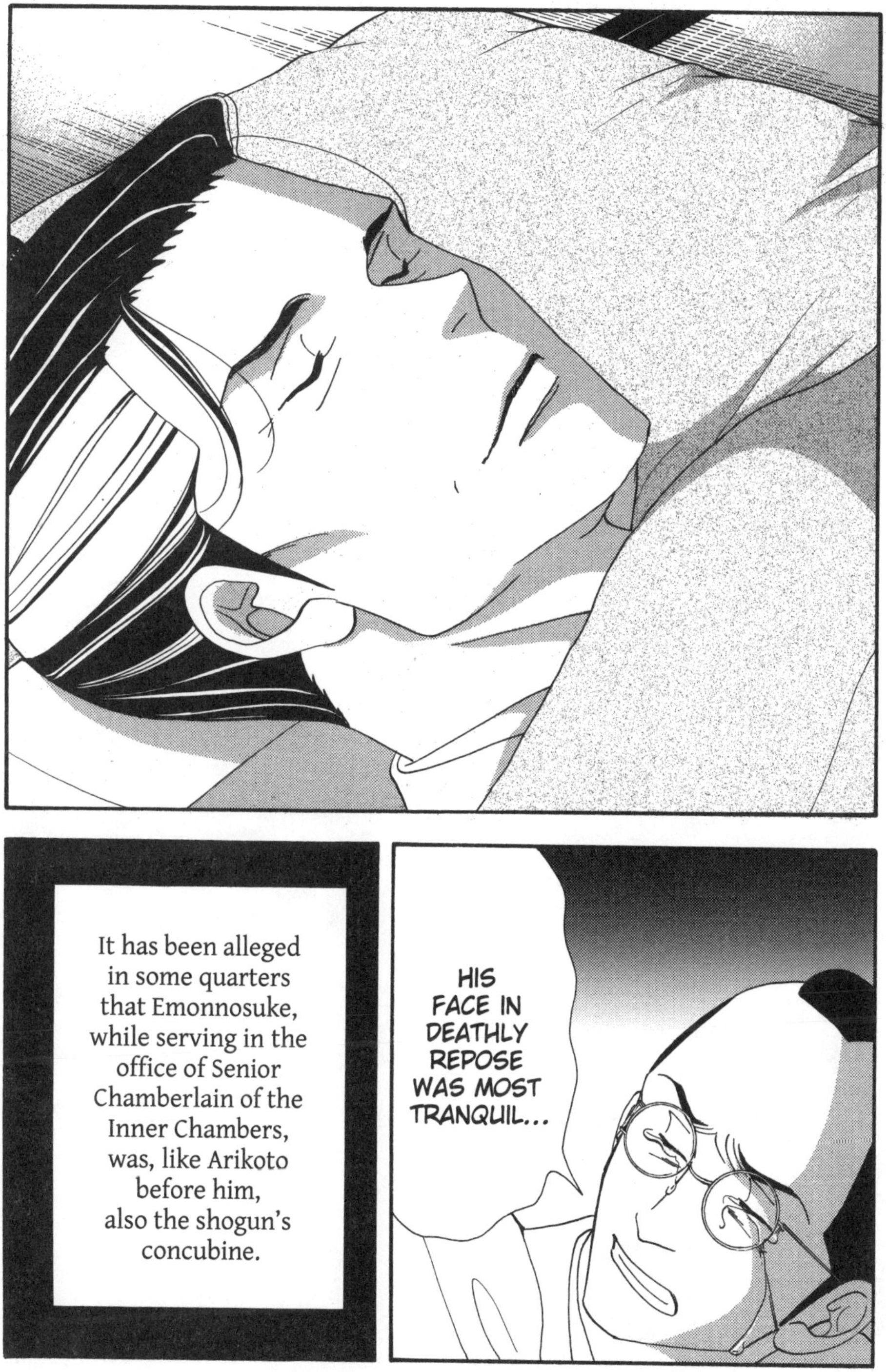
HIS FACE IN DEATHLY REPOSE WAS MOST TRANQUIL...
It has been alleged in some quarters that Emonnosuke, while serving in the office of Senior Chamberlain of the Inner Chambers, was, like Arikoto before him, also the shogun's concubine.

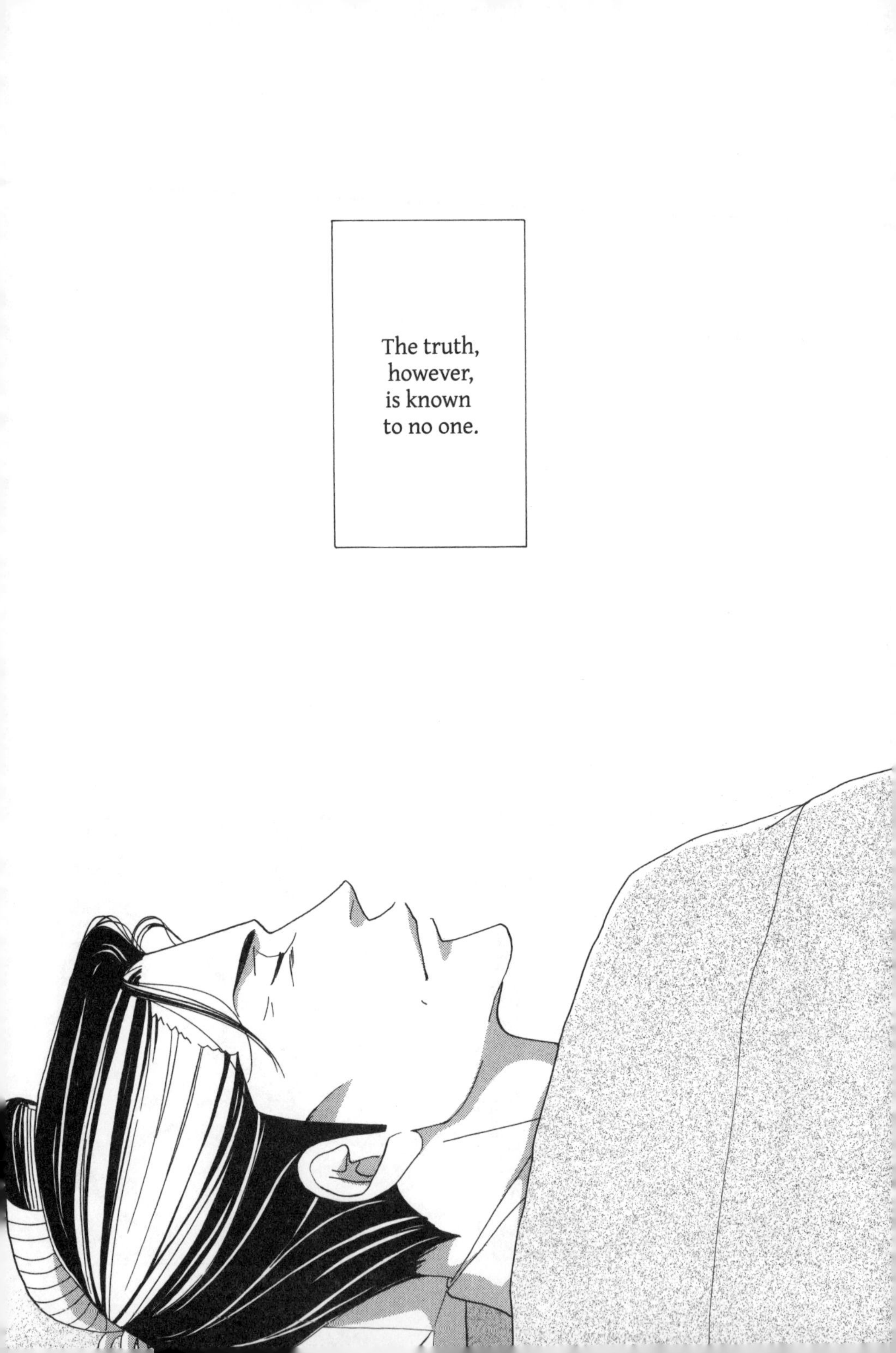
The truth, however, is known to no one.

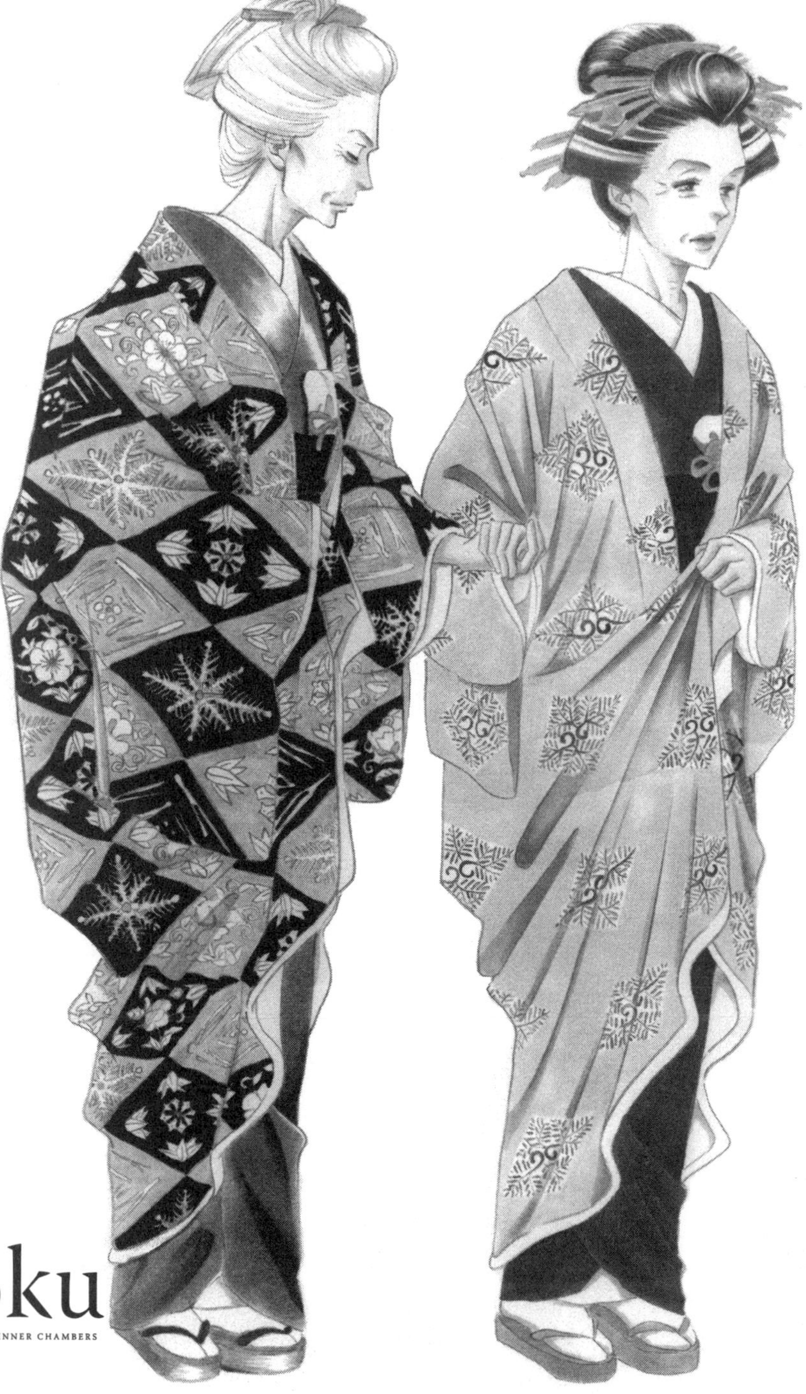

Ōoku

THE INNER CHAMBERS

Ōoku

THE INNER CHAMBERS

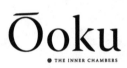

HEE HEE!

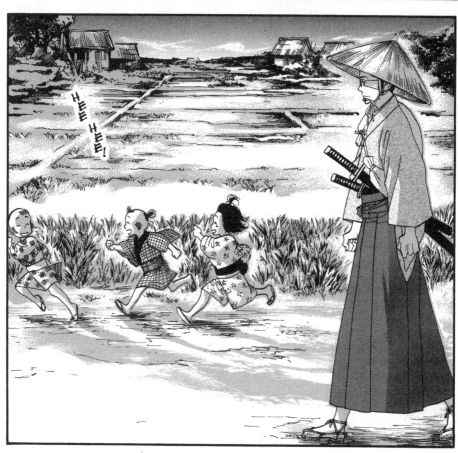

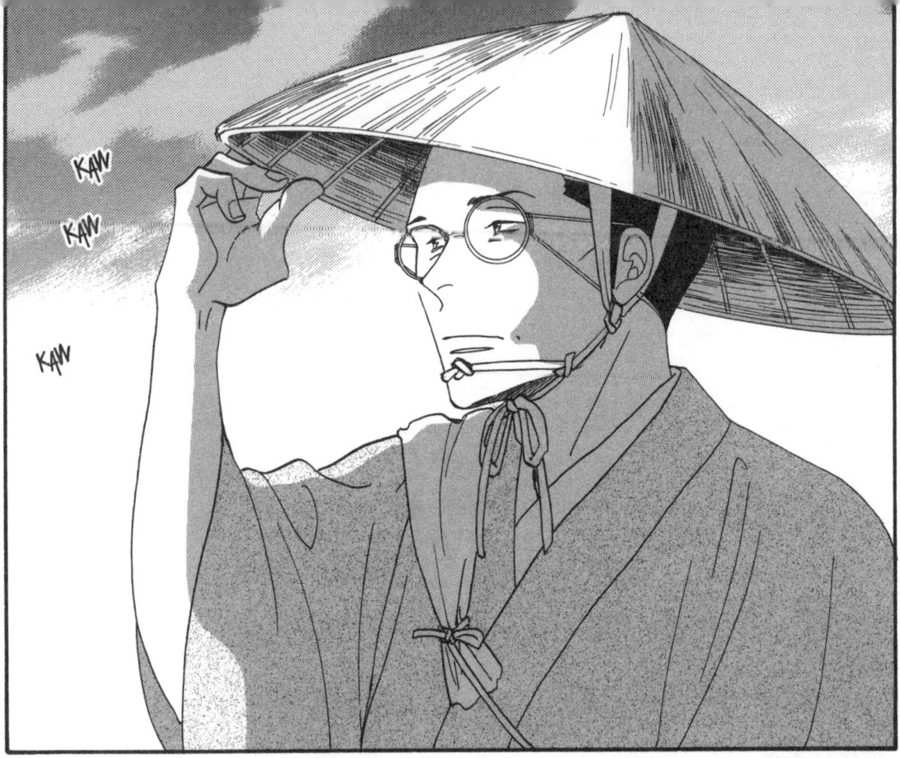
KAW
KAW
KAW

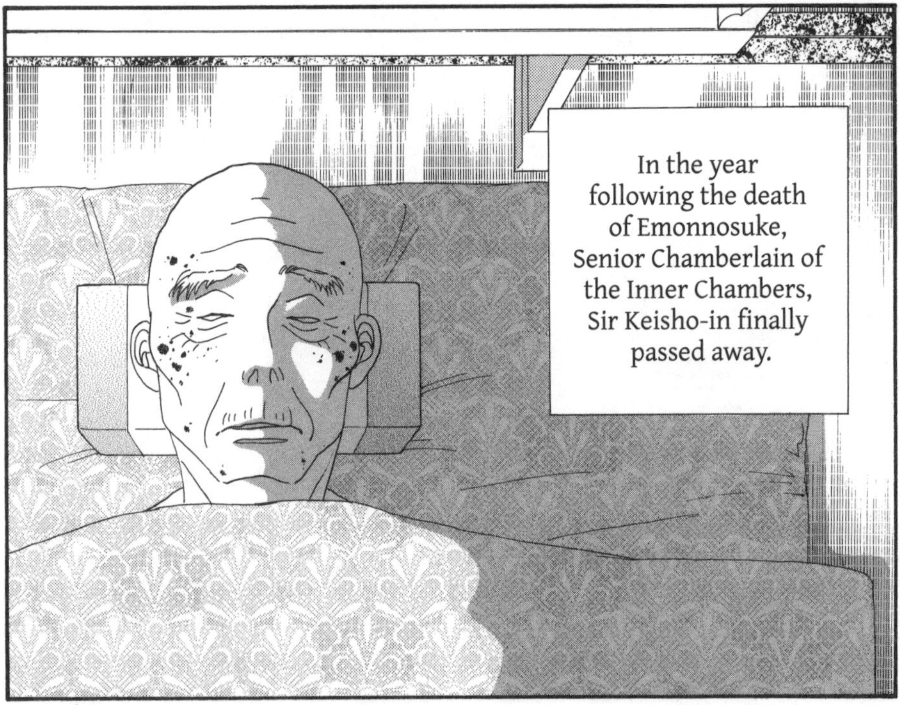
In the year following the death of Emonnosuke, Senior Chamberlain of the Inner Chambers, Sir Keisho-in finally passed away.

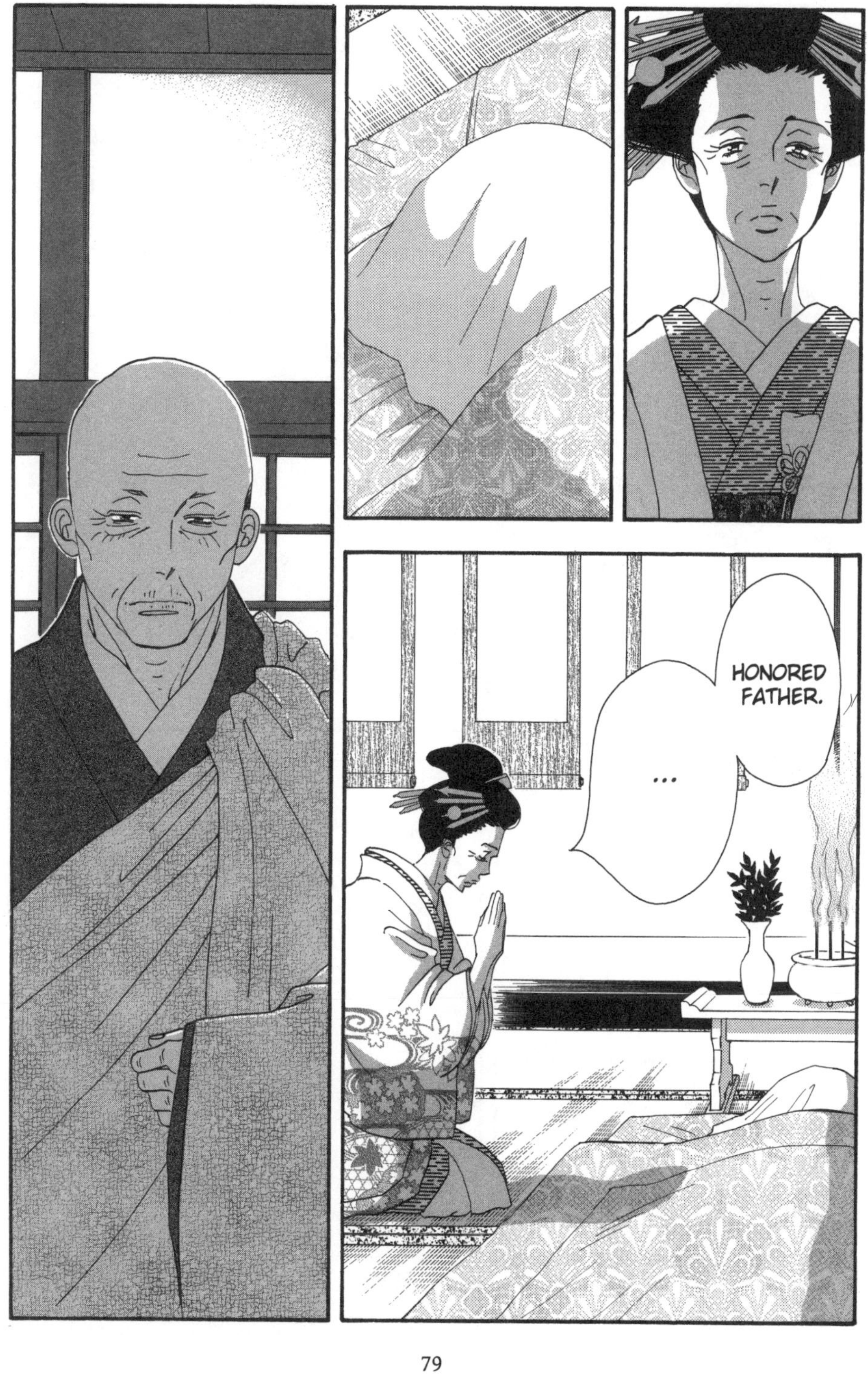
HONORED FATHER.
...

SIR EIKO-IN. WITH GREATEST RESPECT, MY NAME IS AKIMOTO AND I AM SERVING AS THE CURRENT SENIOR CHAMBERLAIN OF THE INNER CHAMBERS.

ON BEHALF OF ALL HERE IN THE ŌOKU, I WOULD LIKE TO EXPRESS MY GRATITUDE TO YOUR VENERABLE GRACE FOR TAKING THE TROUBLE TO COME HERE AT THIS TIME.

AND I THANK YOU FOR TAKING THE TROUBLE, AT SUCH A FLURRIED AND SORROWFUL JUNCTURE, OF NOTIFYING ME OF THIS DEMISE. I AM GRATEFUL TO YOU FOR'T, INDEED.

I DID ONLY CARRY OUT THE EXPRESS WISHES OF HIS GRACE SIR KEISHO-IN.

NOW I PRAY YOU TO BID A FINAL FAREWELL TO THE DEPARTED, WHO SPAKE OF YOU ALWAYS WITH SUCH LOVE.

I SHALL REMOVE MYSELF TO A SEPARATE CHAMBER...

80

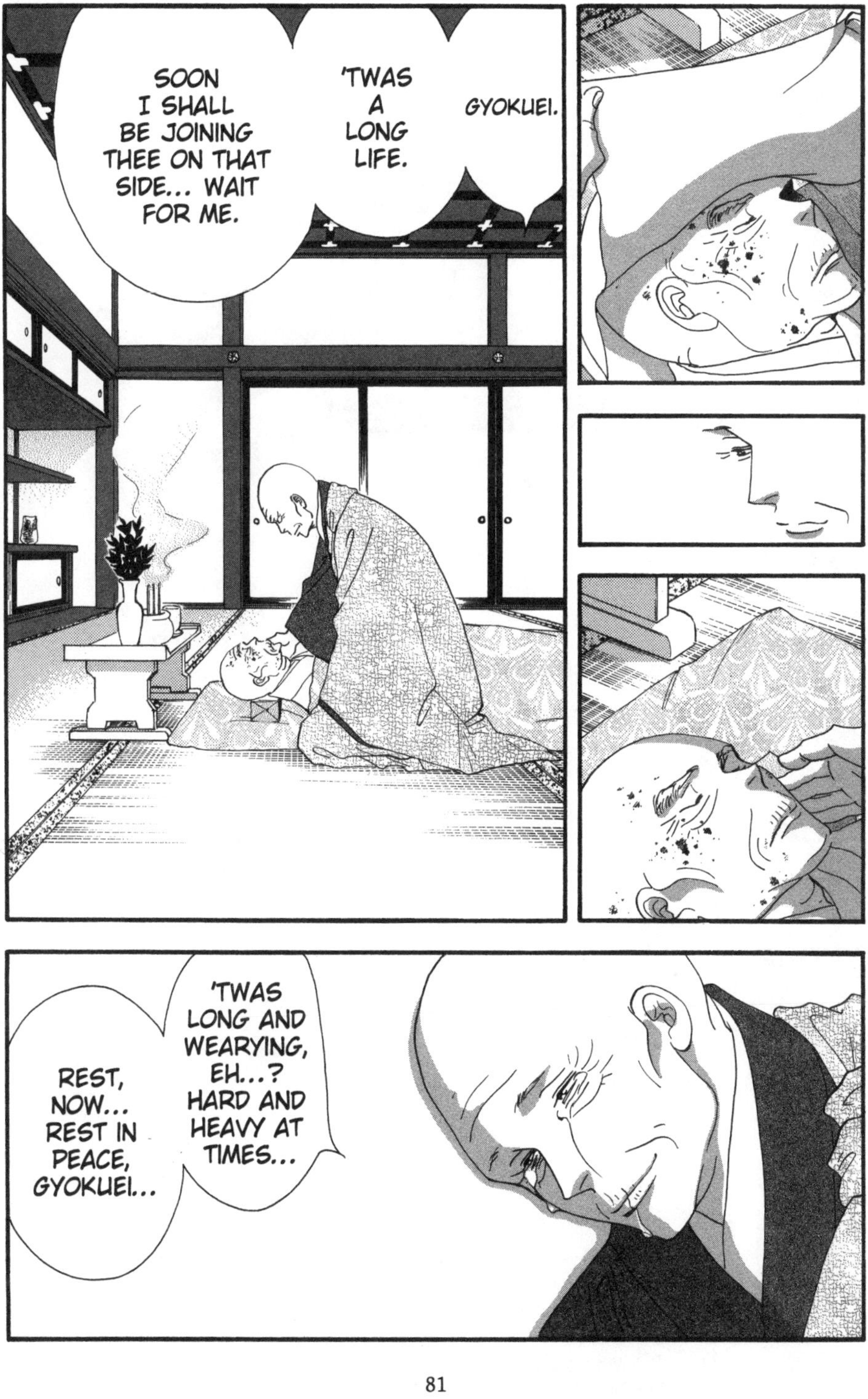
GYOKUEI.
'TWAS A LONG LIFE.
SOON I SHALL BE JOINING THEE ON THAT SIDE... WAIT FOR ME.
'TWAS LONG AND WEARYING, EH...? HARD AND HEAVY AT TIMES...
REST, NOW... REST IN PEACE, GYOKUEI...

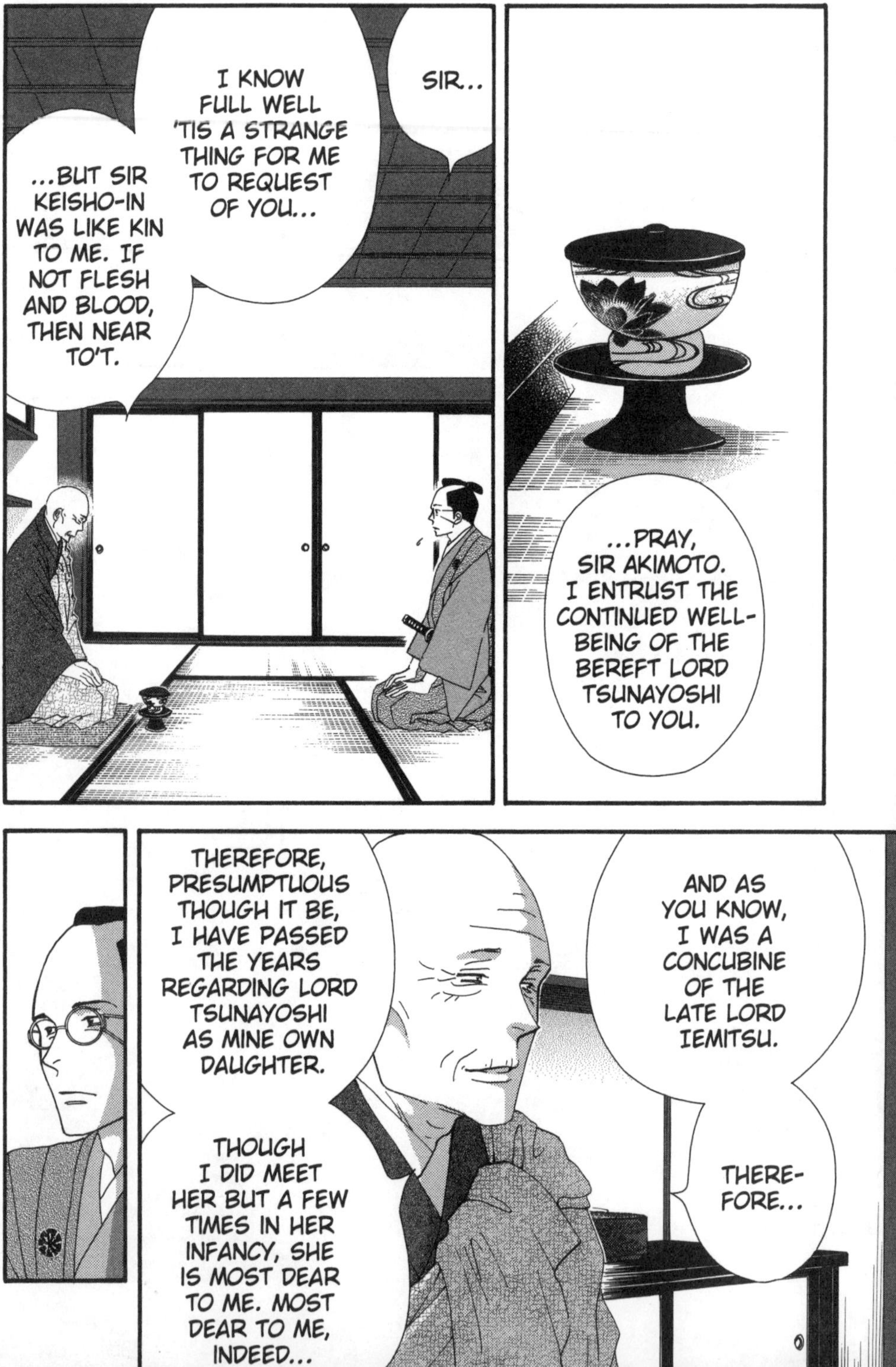
...PRAY, SIR AKIMOTO. I ENTRUST THE CONTINUED WELL-BEING OF THE BEREFT LORD TSUNAYOSHI TO YOU.
SIR...
I KNOW FULL WELL 'TIS A STRANGE THING FOR ME TO REQUEST OF YOU...
...BUT SIR KEISHO-IN WAS LIKE KIN TO ME. IF NOT FLESH AND BLOOD, THEN NEAR TO'T.
AND AS YOU KNOW, I WAS A CONCUBINE OF THE LATE LORD IEMITSU.
THERE-FORE...
THEREFORE, PRESUMPTUOUS THOUGH IT BE, I HAVE PASSED THE YEARS REGARDING LORD TSUNAYOSHI AS MINE OWN DAUGHTER.
THOUGH I DID MEET HER BUT A FEW TIMES IN HER INFANCY, SHE IS MOST DEAR TO ME. MOST DEAR TO ME, INDEED...

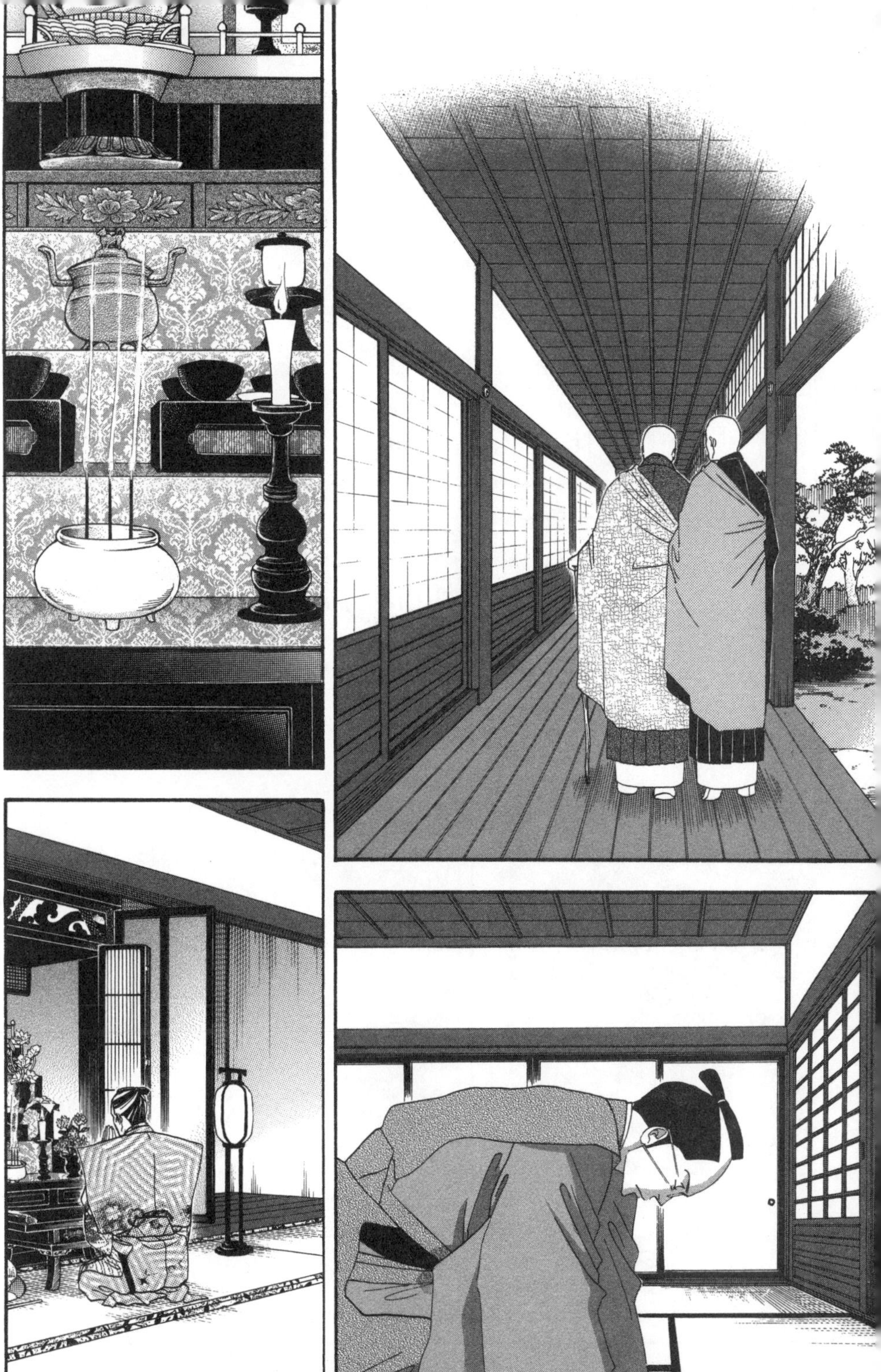

O-DEN.

DENBE.

YOUR HIGH-NESS!!

SHUP

84

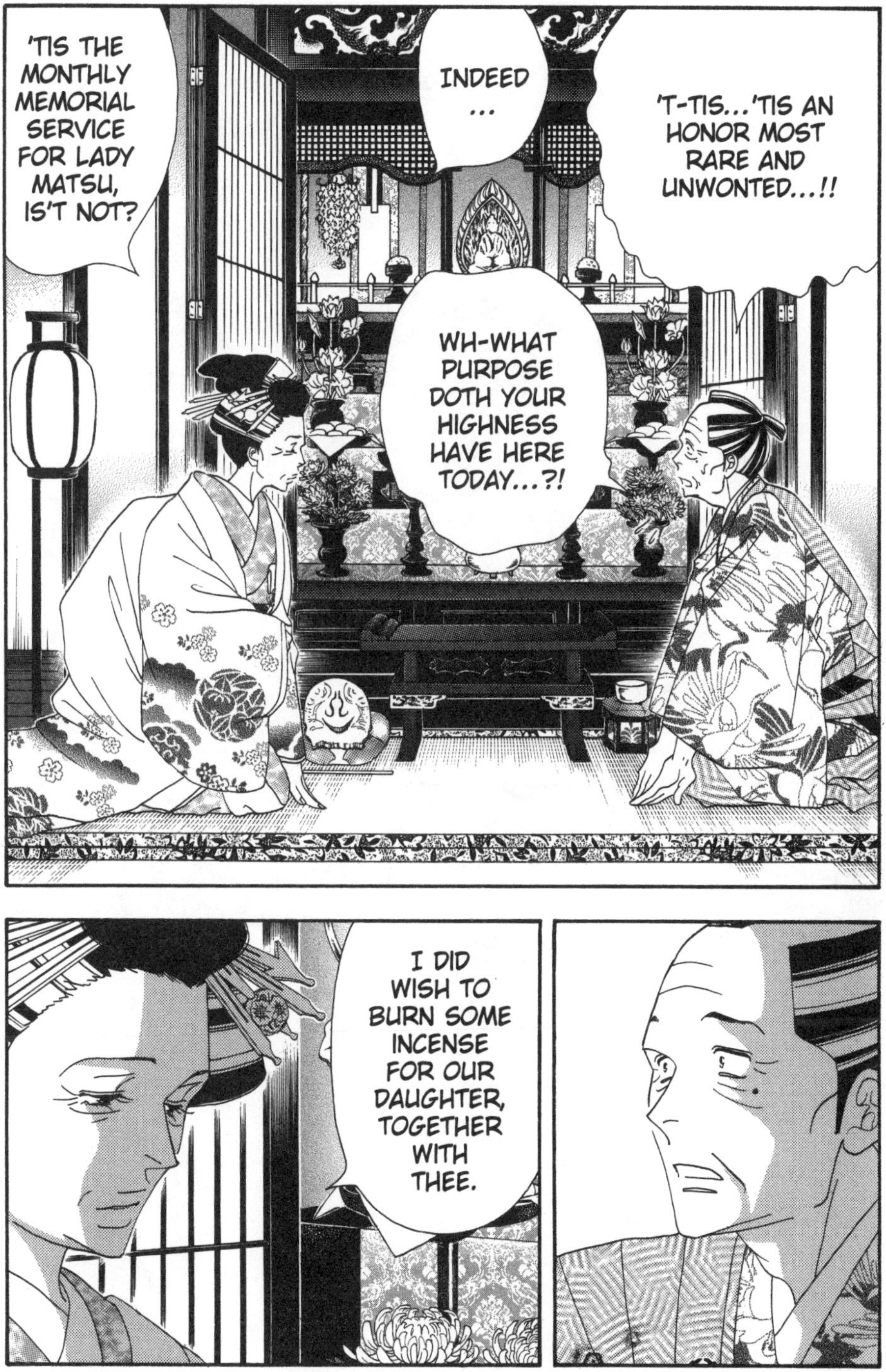
'T-TIS...'TIS AN HONOR MOST RARE AND UNWONTED...!!
WH-WHAT PURPOSE DOTH YOUR HIGHNESS HAVE HERE TODAY...?!
'TIS THE MONTHLY MEMORIAL SERVICE FOR LADY MATSU, IS'T NOT?
INDEED...
I DID WISH TO BURN SOME INCENSE FOR OUR DAUGHTER, TOGETHER WITH THEE.

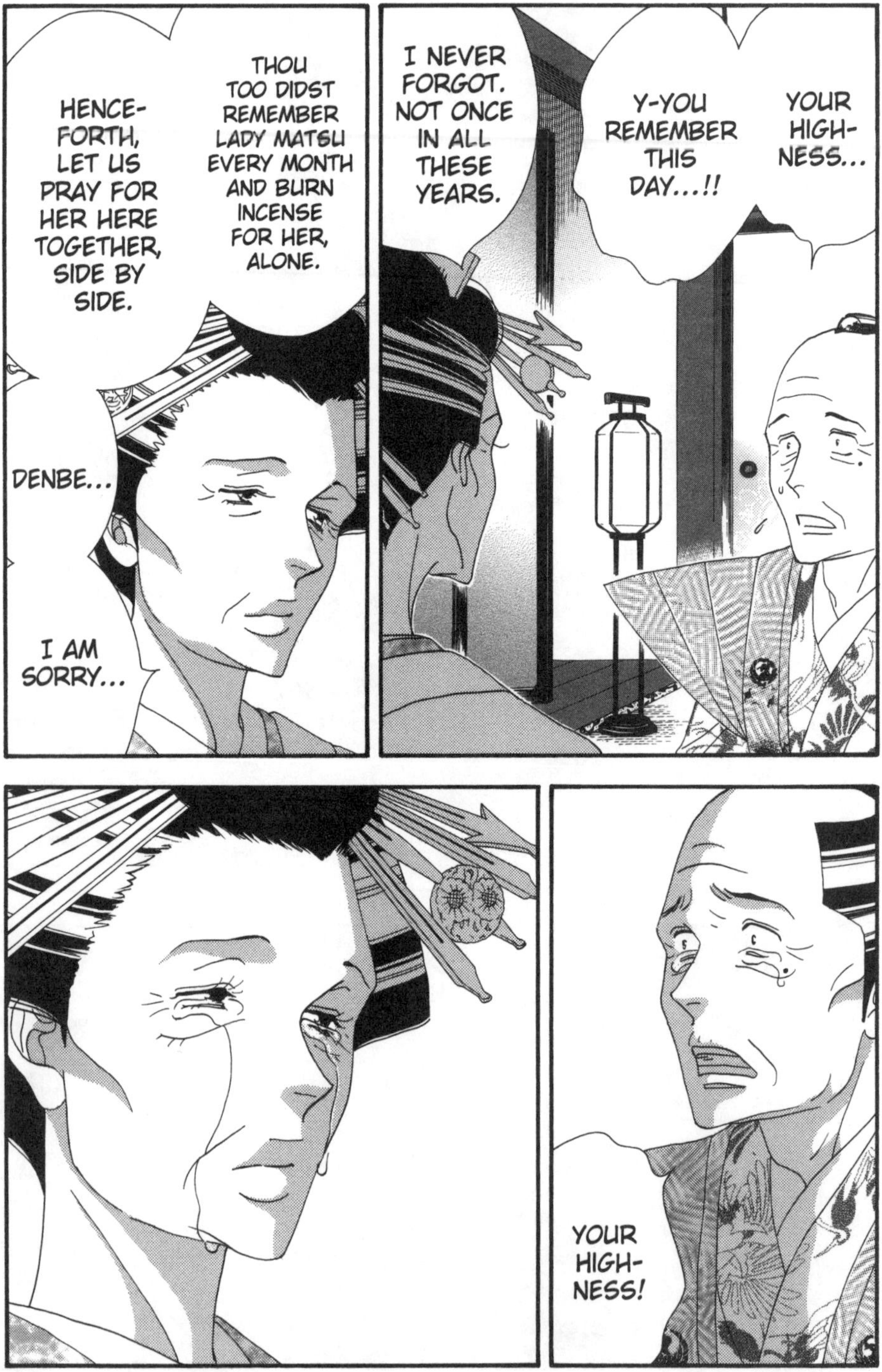
YOUR HIGHNESS...
Y-YOU REMEMBER THIS DAY...!!
I NEVER FORGOT. NOT ONCE IN ALL THESE YEARS.
THOU TOO DIDST REMEMBER LADY MATSU EVERY MONTH AND BURN INCENSE FOR HER, ALONE.
HENCEFORTH, LET US PRAY FOR HER HERE TOGETHER, SIDE BY SIDE.
DENBE...
I AM SORRY...
YOUR HIGHNESS!

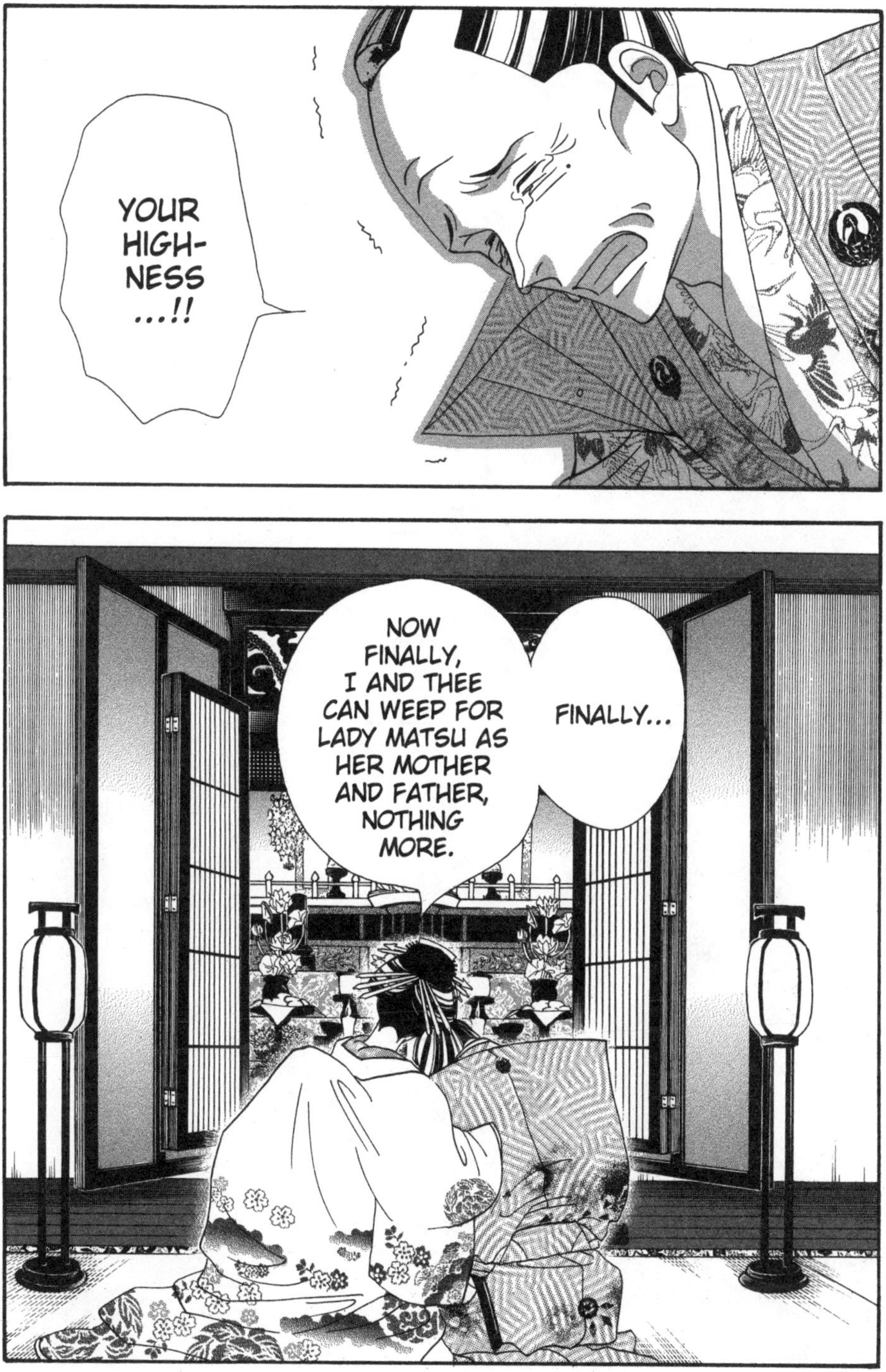
YOUR HIGH-NESS ...!!
FINALLY...
NOW FINALLY, I AND THEE CAN WEEP FOR LADY MATSU AS HER MOTHER AND FATHER, NOTHING MORE.

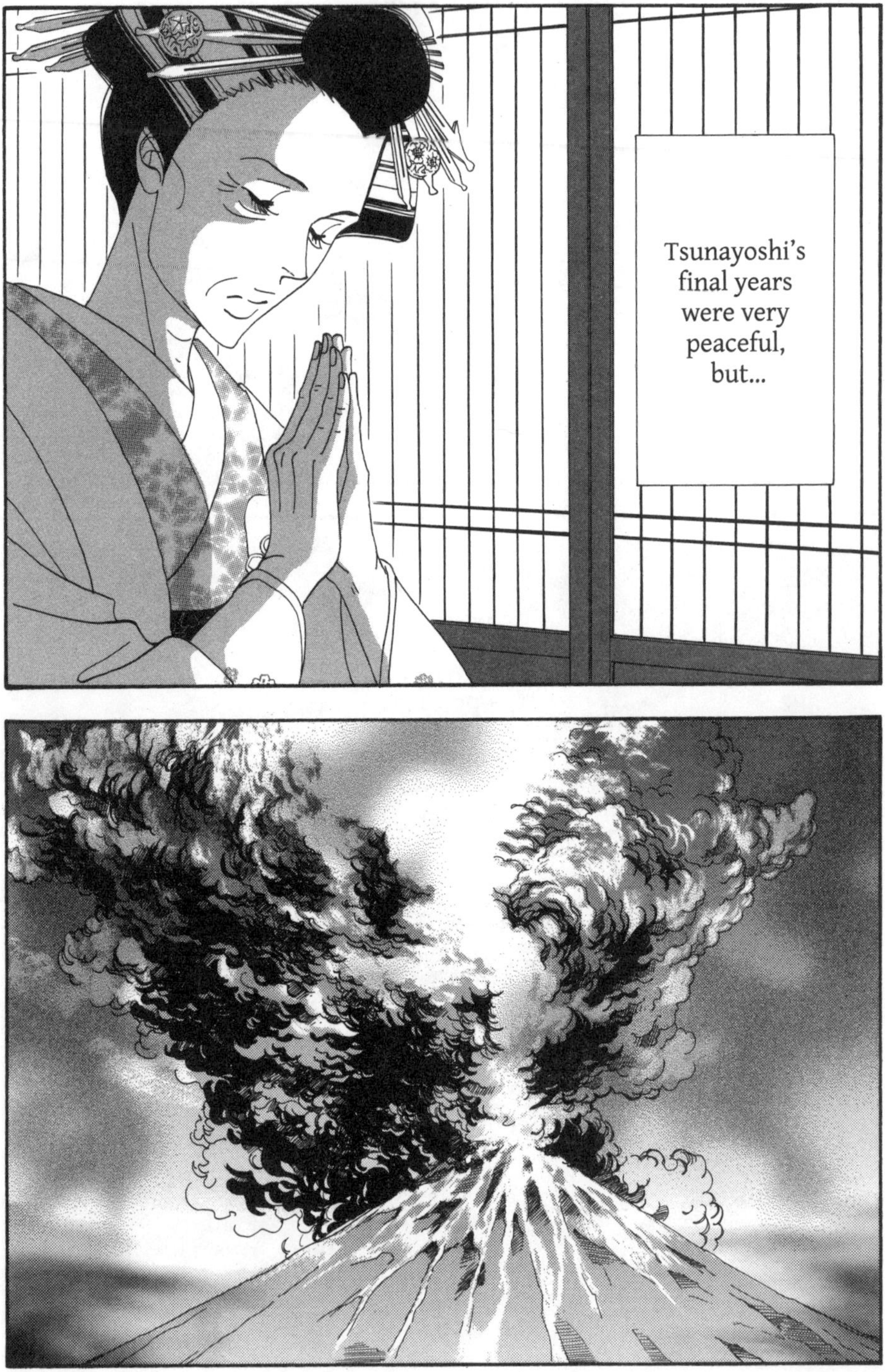
Tsunayoshi's final years were very peaceful, but...

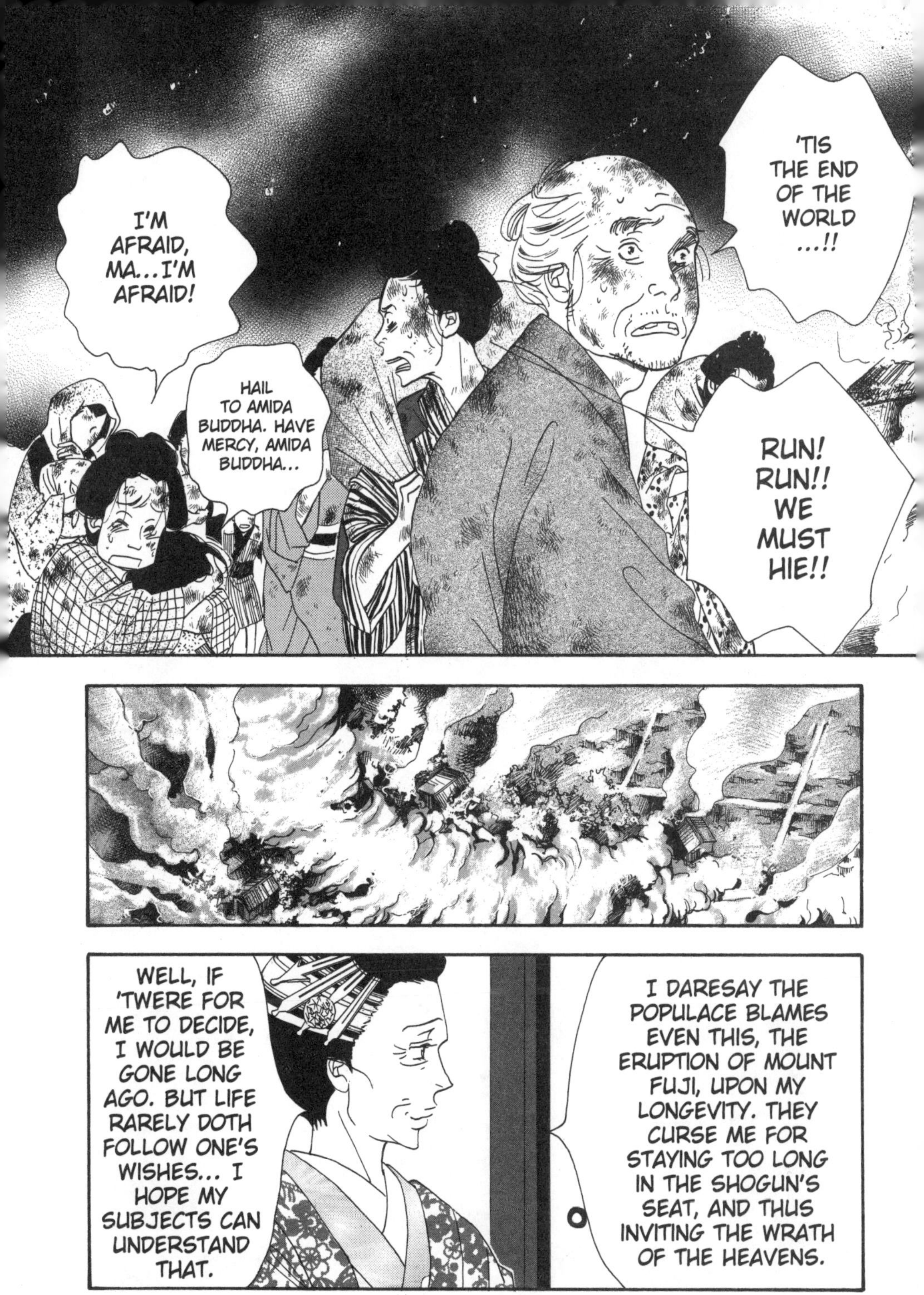
'TIS THE END OF THE WORLD...!!
RUN! RUN!! WE MUST HIE!!
HAIL TO AMIDA BUDDHA. HAVE MERCY, AMIDA BUDDHA...
I'M AFRAID, MA...I'M AFRAID!
I DARESAY THE POPULACE BLAMES EVEN THIS, THE ERUPTION OF MOUNT FUJI, UPON MY LONGEVITY. THEY CURSE ME FOR STAYING TOO LONG IN THE SHOGUN'S SEAT, AND THUS INVITING THE WRATH OF THE HEAVENS.
WELL, IF 'TWERE FOR ME TO DECIDE, I WOULD BE GONE LONG AGO. BUT LIFE RARELY DOTH FOLLOW ONE'S WISHES... I HOPE MY SUBJECTS CAN UNDERSTAND THAT.

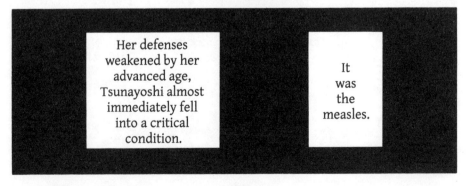

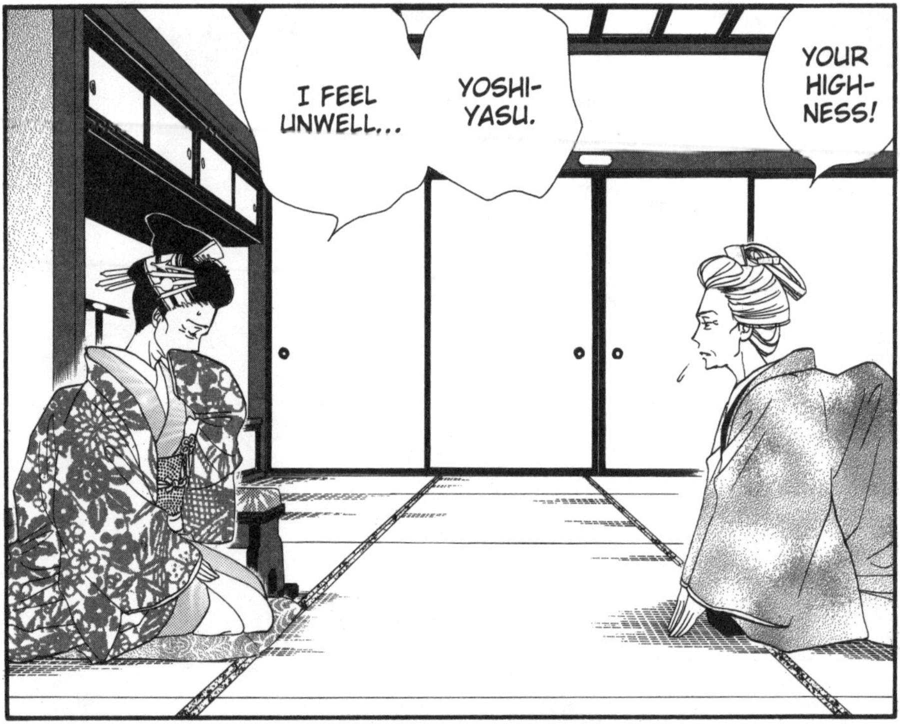
YOUR HIGHNESS!
YOSHIYASU.
I FEEL UNWELL...

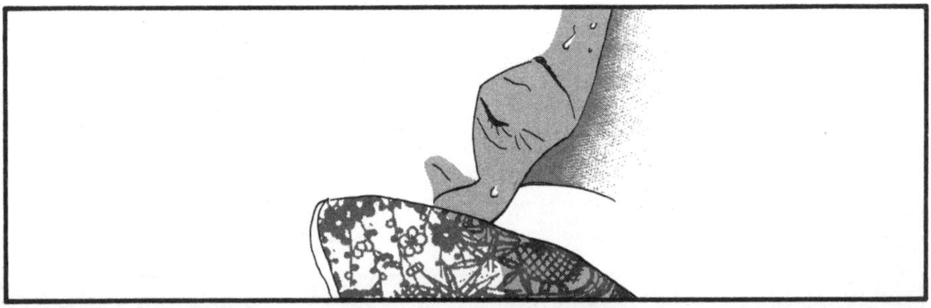

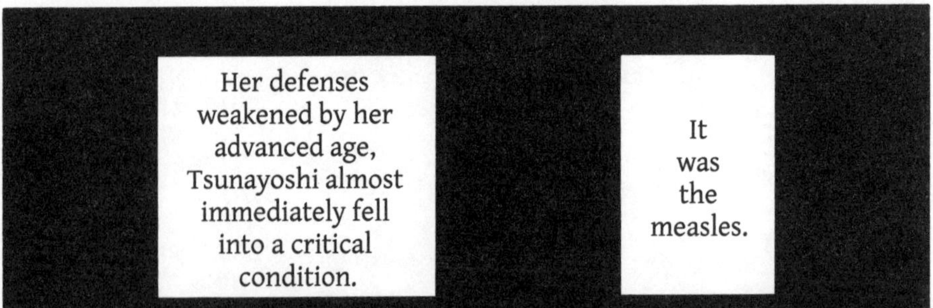
It was the measles.
Her defenses weakened by her advanced age, Tsunayoshi almost immediately fell into a critical condition.

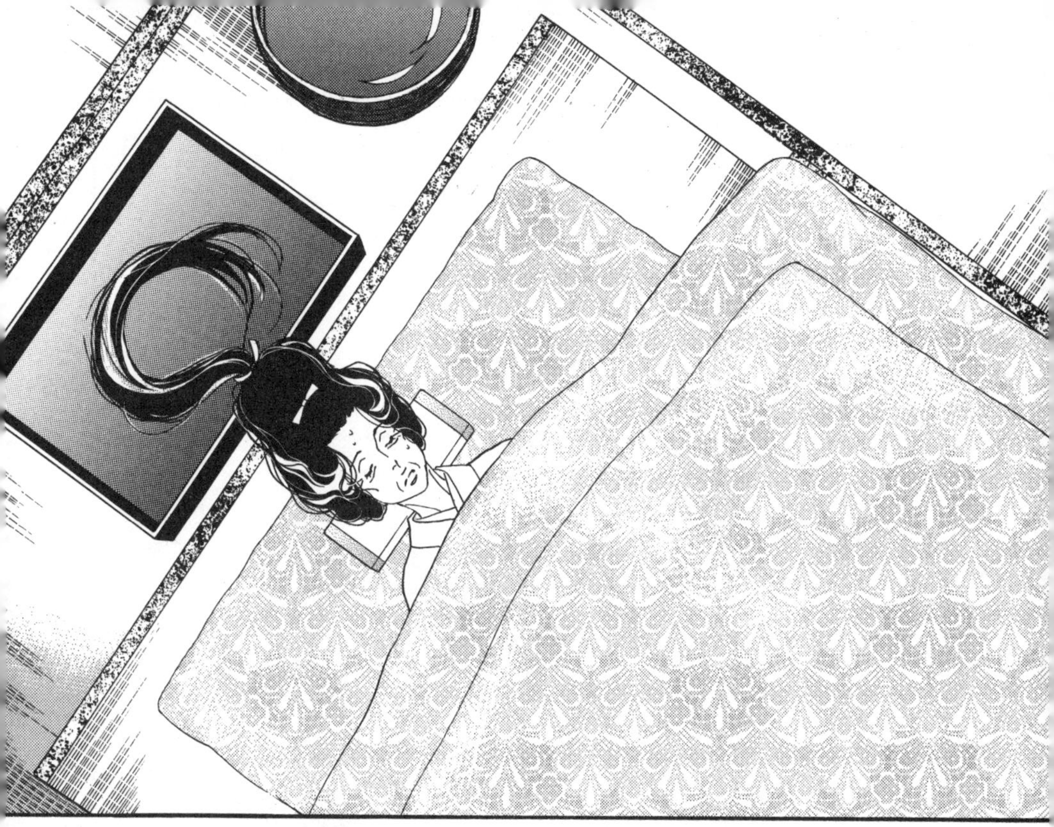

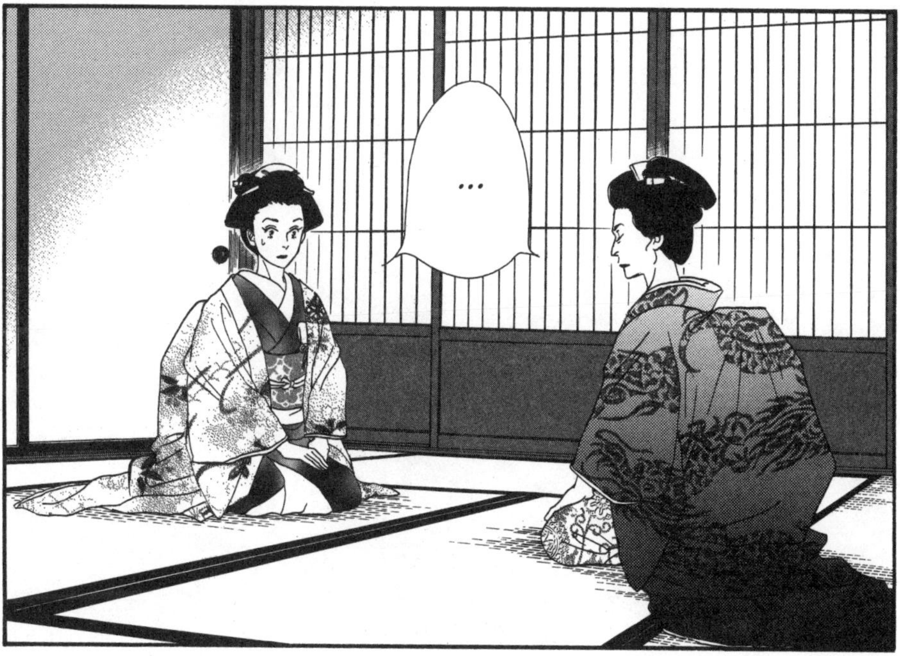
...

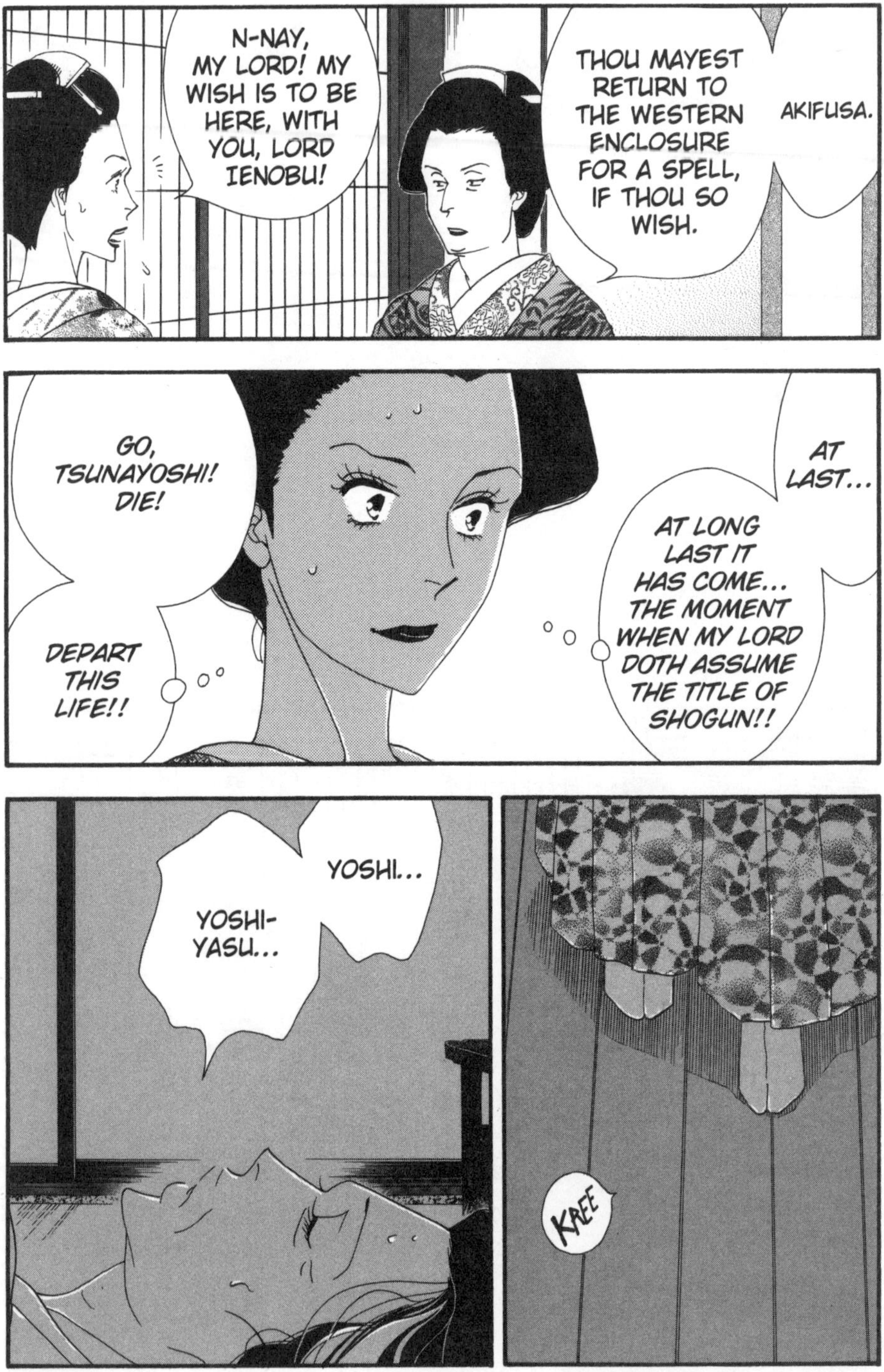
AKIFUSA.
THOU MAYEST RETURN TO THE WESTERN ENCLOSURE FOR A SPELL, IF THOU SO WISH.
N-NAY, MY LORD! MY WISH IS TO BE HERE, WITH YOU, LORD IENOBU!
AT LAST...
AT LONG LAST IT HAS COME... THE MOMENT WHEN MY LORD DOTH ASSUME THE TITLE OF SHOGUN!!
GO, TSUNAYOSHI! DIE!
DEPART THIS LIFE!!
KREE
YOSHI...
YOSHI-YASU...

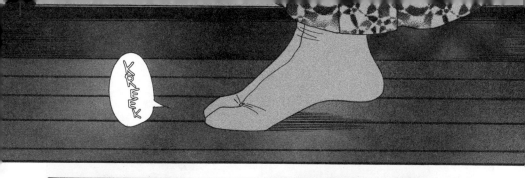

YOSHI-
YASU.
WHERE
HAST
THOU
GONE...

OH...

SWOoo

YOSHI-
YASU...

...WHO ART THOU ...?

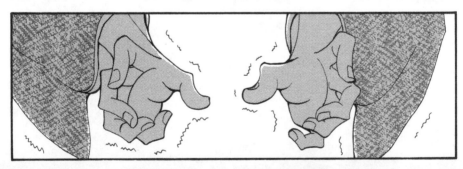

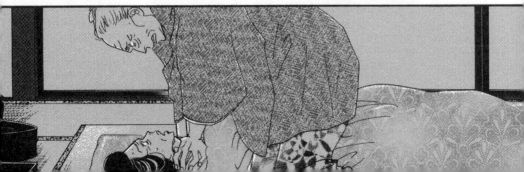

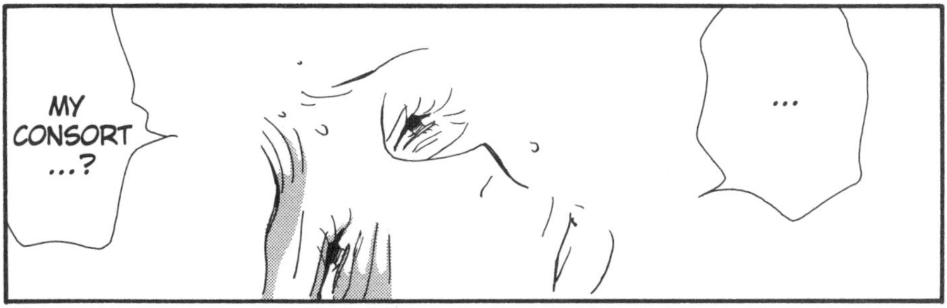
...
MY CONSORT ...?

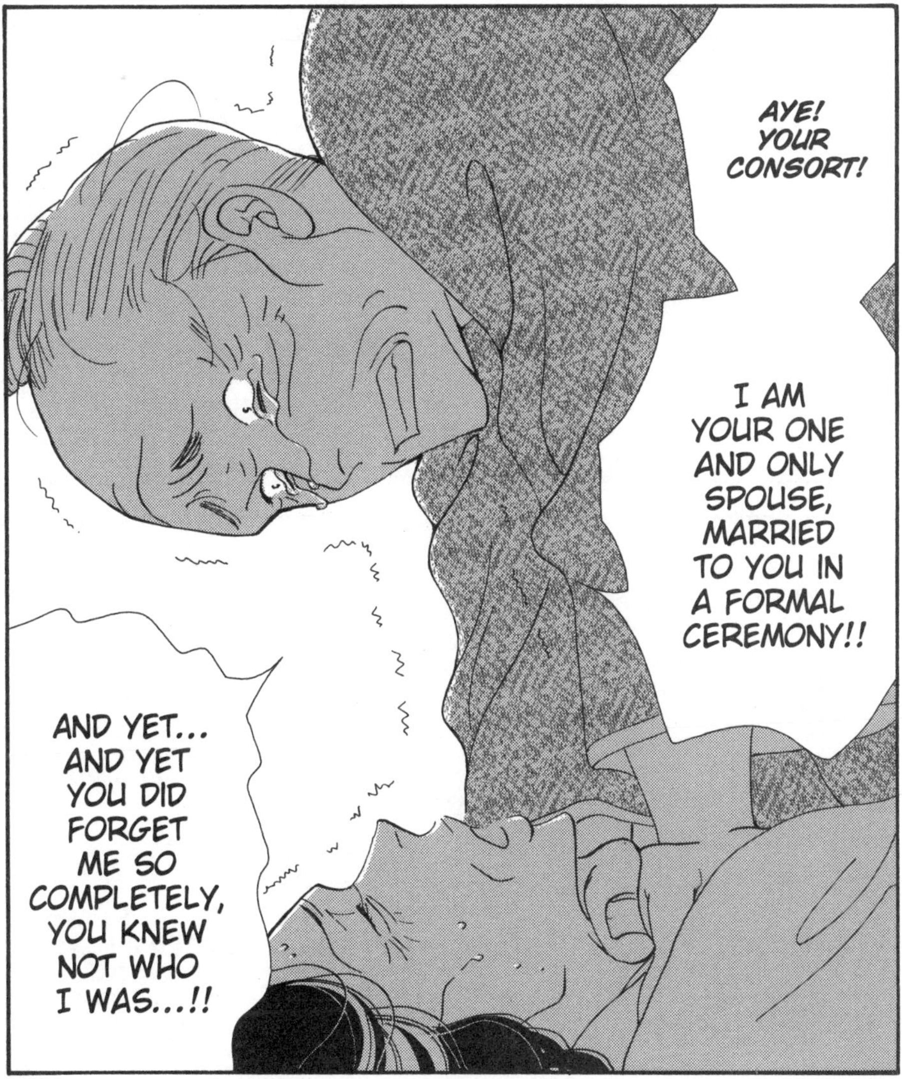
AYE! YOUR CONSORT!
I AM YOUR ONE AND ONLY SPOUSE, MARRIED TO YOU IN A FORMAL CEREMONY!!
AND YET... AND YET YOU DID FORGET ME SO COMPLETELY, YOU KNEW NOT WHO I WAS...!!

HA... HA HA...
AND WELL MAY THAT BE... 'TIS MORE THAN TEN YEARS ALREADY THAT I HAVE SUFFERED FROM GOUT, AND BECOME UNABLE TO ATTEND THE GENERAL AUDIENCE WITH YOU...
...NGH!
ARR... GH!
NO MATTER... HOW LONG... I DID AWAIT YOU, YOU NEVER CAME TO INQUIRE AFTER MY HEALTH. YOU NEVER CAME TO SEE ME...
AND SO I HAVE WAITED A LONG, LONG TIME... A LONG TIME, INDEED...
...TO BE ALONE WITH YOU... LIKE THIS... AGAIN...

THE FIRST TIME THAT I E'ER MET YOU...
YOU WERE SO LOVELY, SO VERY CHARMING, LIKE A PRETTY DOLL...
I THOUGHT, AH, HOW BLESSED I AM, TO BE WED TO SUCH A FAIR, SWEET MAIDEN...
...AND MY HEART DID RACE WITH JOY...

NO MAN IN THE IMPERIAL COURT I HAD LEFT COULD BE SO HAPPY, SO FORTUNATE AS I...

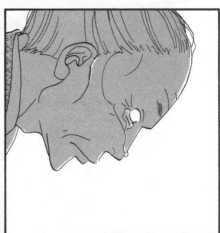

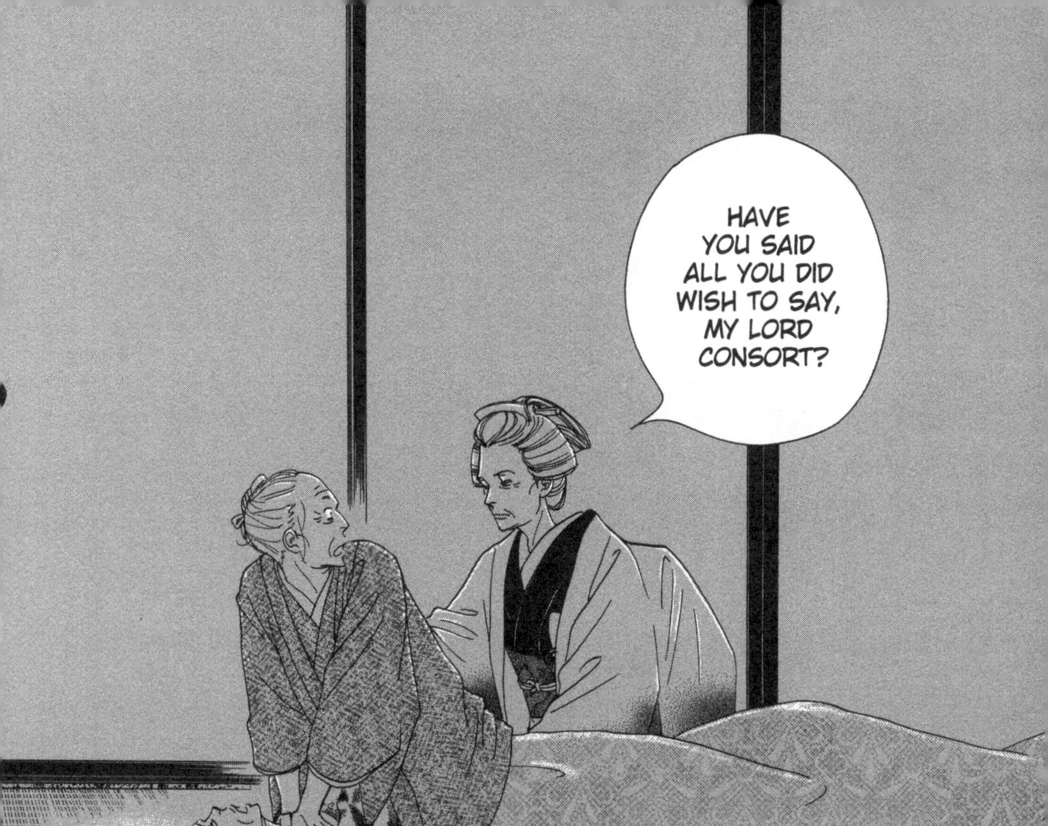
HAVE YOU SAID ALL YOU DID WISH TO SAY, MY LORD CONSORT?

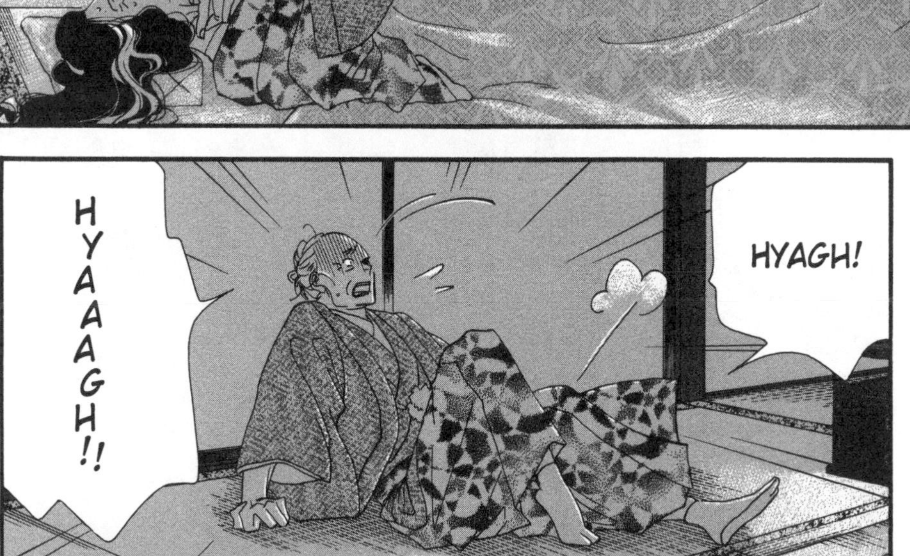
HYAGH!
HYAAAGH!!

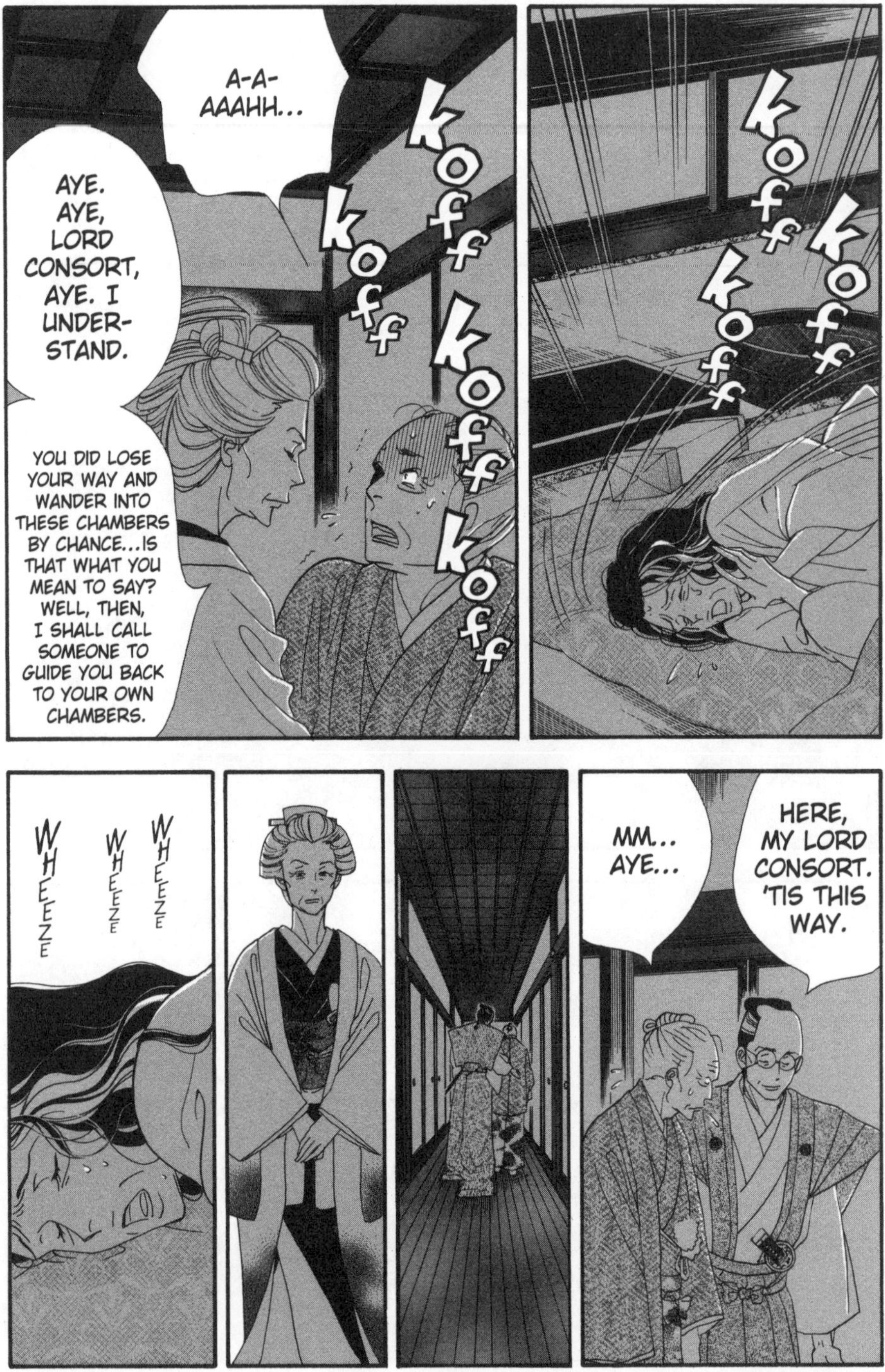

koff koff koff koff
A-A-AAAHH...
koff koff koff koff
AYE. AYE, LORD CONSORT, AYE. I UNDER-STAND.
YOU DID LOSE YOUR WAY AND WANDER INTO THESE CHAMBERS BY CHANCE...IS THAT WHAT YOU MEAN TO SAY? WELL, THEN, I SHALL CALL SOMEONE TO GUIDE YOU BACK TO YOUR OWN CHAMBERS.
HERE, MY LORD CONSORT. 'TIS THIS WAY.
MM.. AYE...
WHEEZE WHEEZE WHEEZE

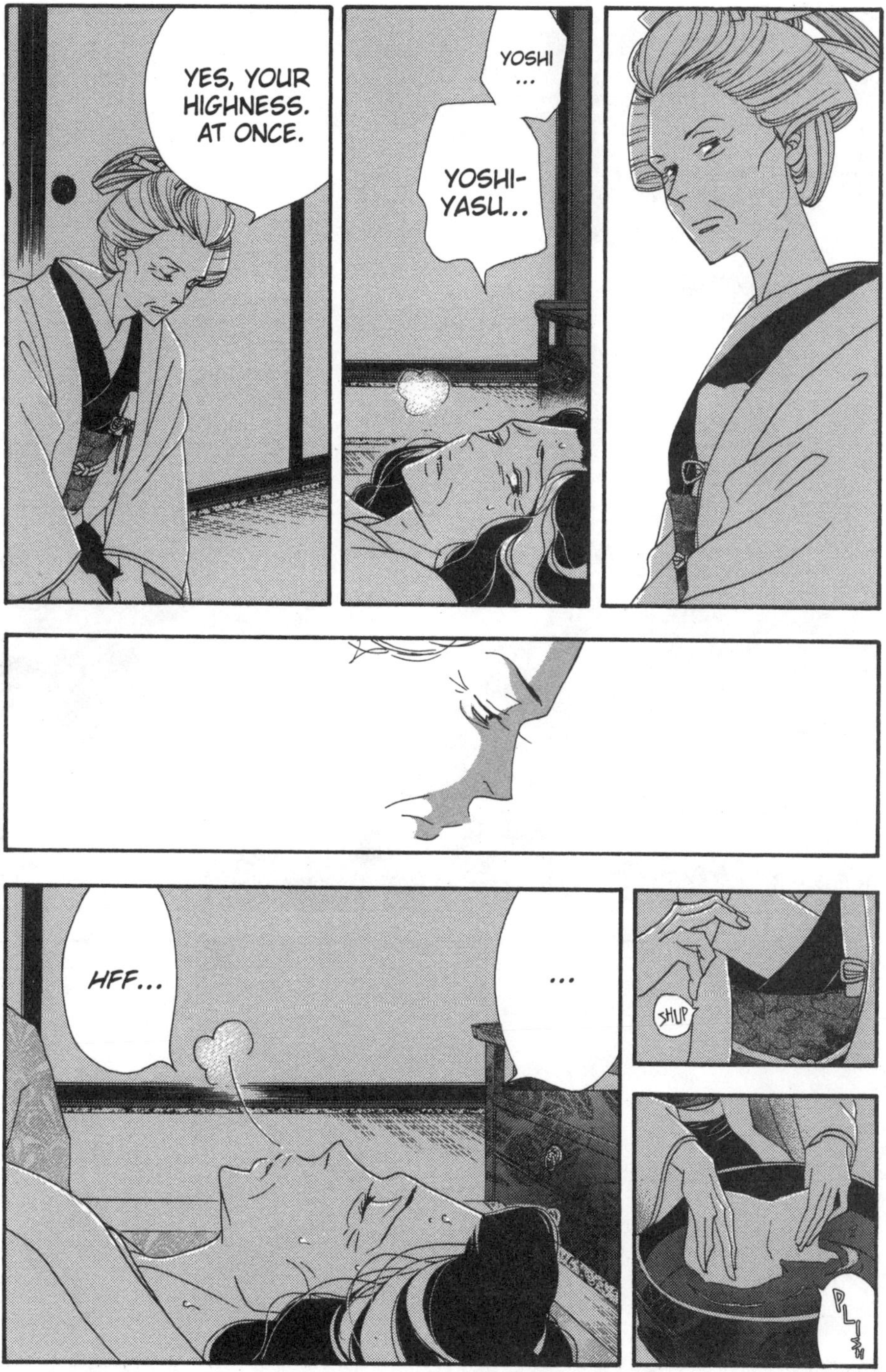
YOSHI
...
YOSHI-YASU...
YES, YOUR HIGHNESS. AT ONCE.
SHUP
PLISH
...
HFF...

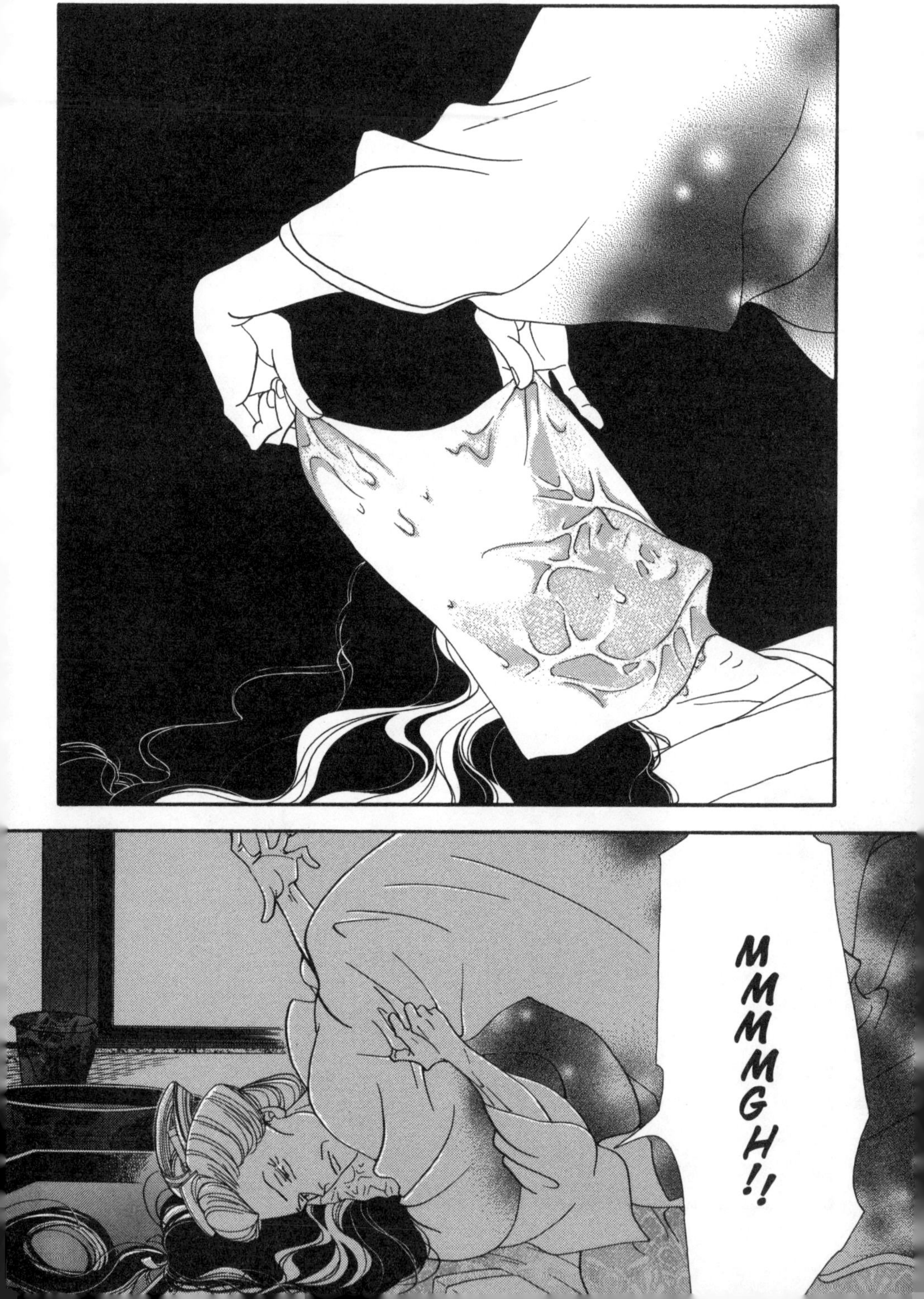
MMMMGH!!

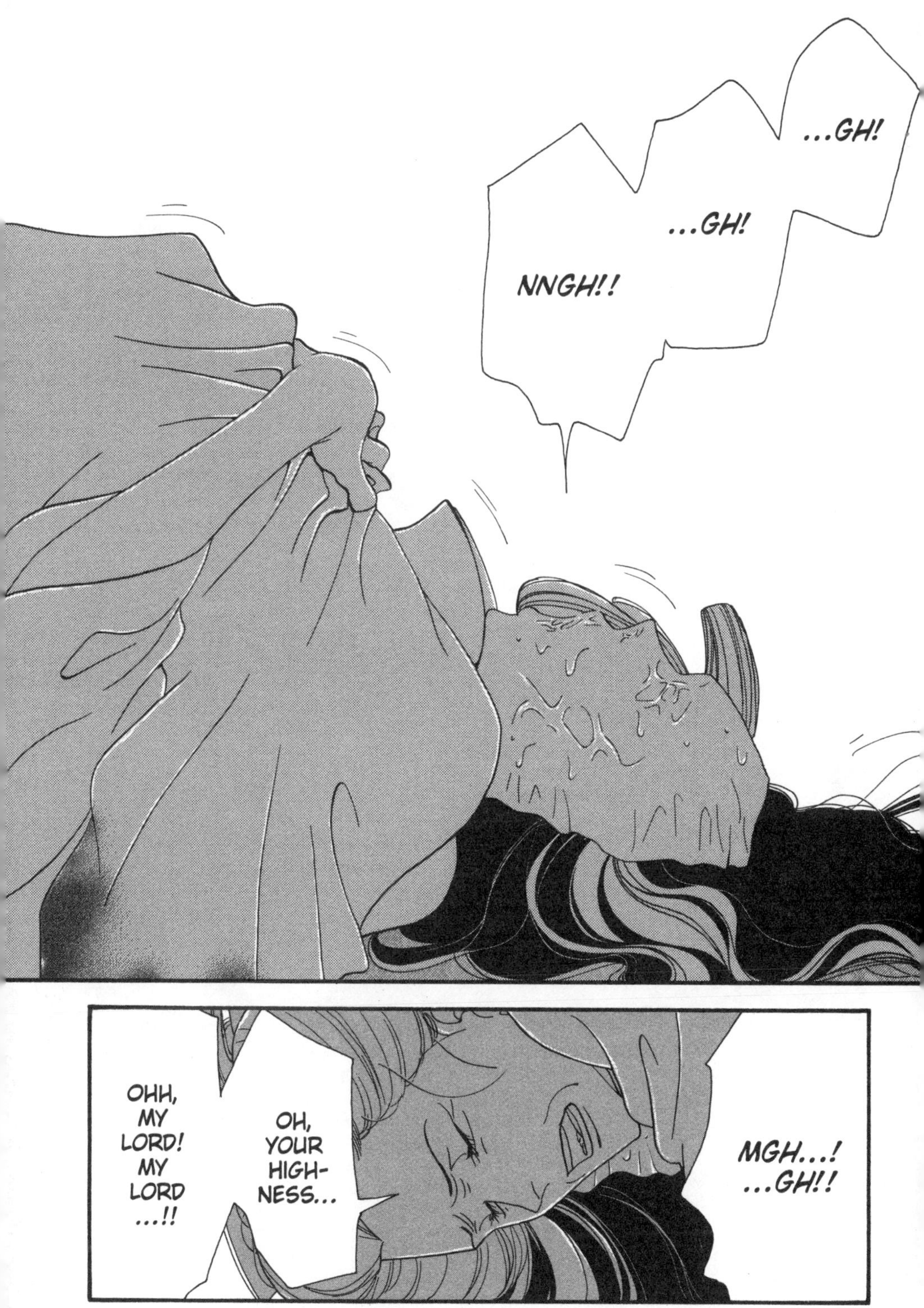
...GH!
...GH!
NNGH!!
MGH...! ...GH!!
OH, YOUR HIGH-NESS...
OHH, MY LORD! MY LORD ...!!

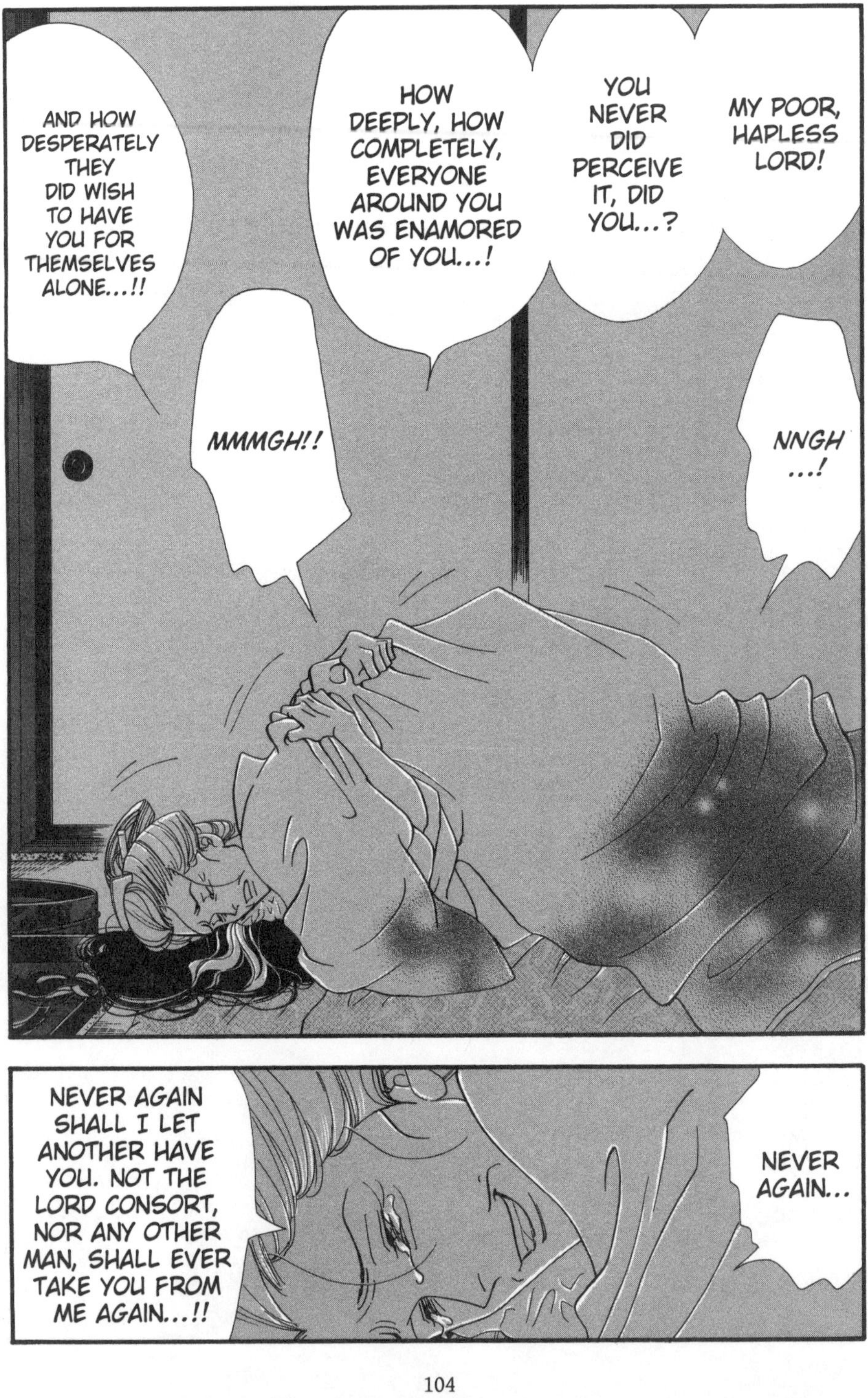
MY POOR, HAPLESS LORD!
YOU NEVER DID PERCEIVE IT, DID YOU...?
HOW DEEPLY, HOW COMPLETELY, EVERYONE AROUND YOU WAS ENAMORED OF YOU...!
AND HOW DESPERATELY THEY DID WISH TO HAVE YOU FOR THEMSELVES ALONE...!!
NNGH ...!
MMMGH!!
NEVER AGAIN...
NEVER AGAIN SHALL I LET ANOTHER HAVE YOU. NOT THE LORD CONSORT, NOR ANY OTHER MAN, SHALL EVER TAKE YOU FROM ME AGAIN...!!

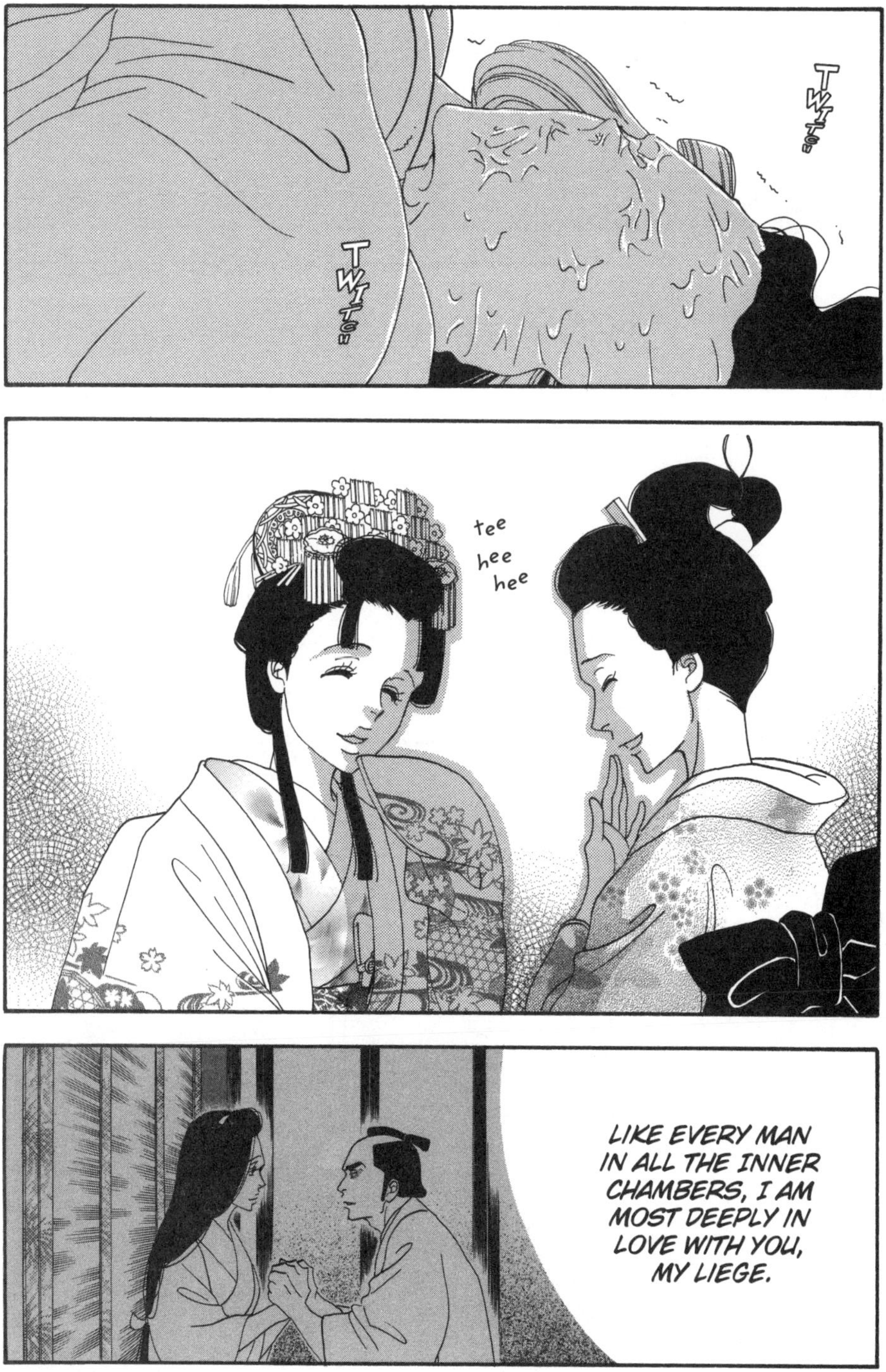
TWITCH
TWITCH
tee hee hee
LIKE EVERY MAN IN ALL THE INNER CHAMBERS, I AM MOST DEEPLY IN LOVE WITH YOU, MY LIEGE.

"EVERY MAN IN ALL THE
INNER CHAMBERS IS MOST
DEEPLY IN LOVE WITH YOU..."

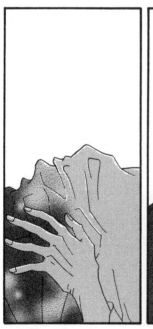

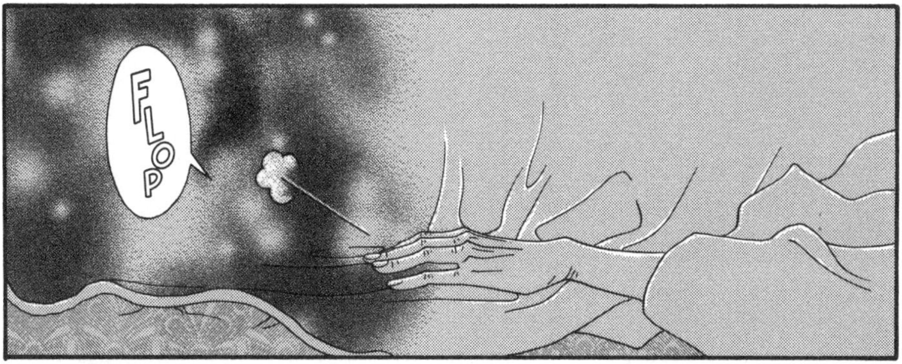
FLOP

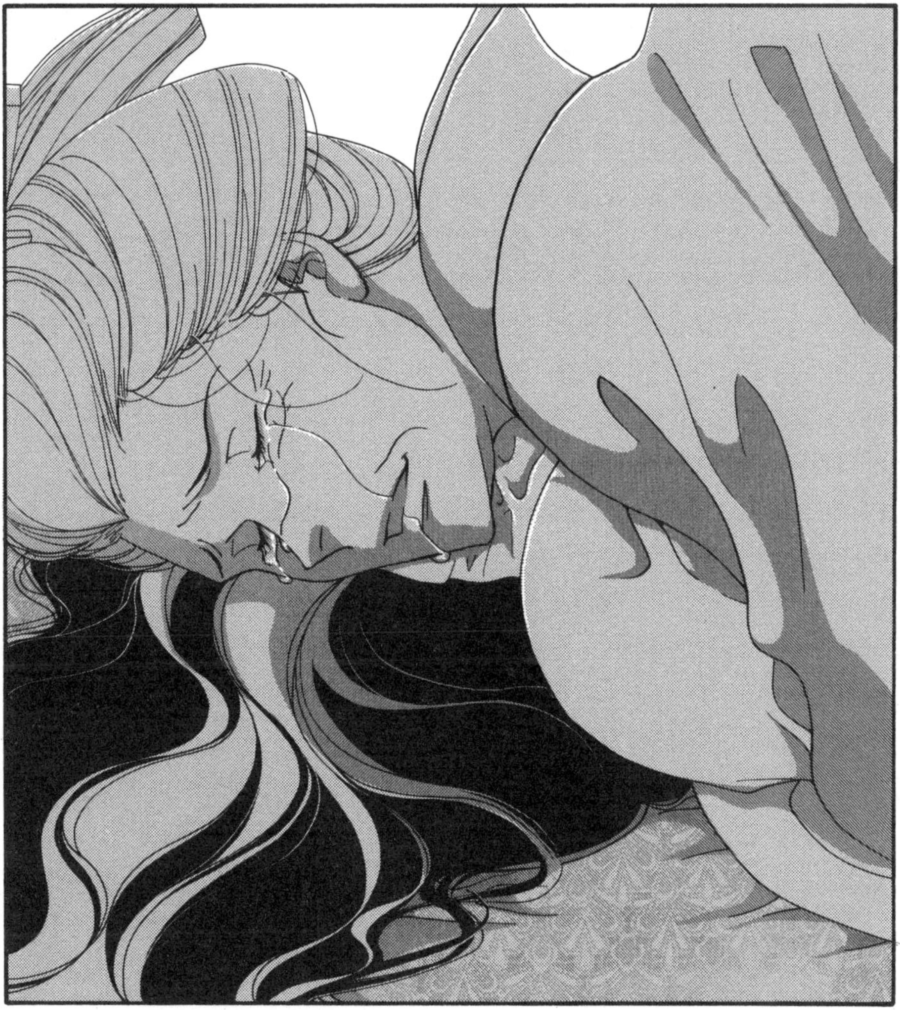

THE VIGIL IS NEEDED NO MORE.

BARON OF MINO?

HER HIGHNESS DID JUST NOW BREATHE HER LAST...

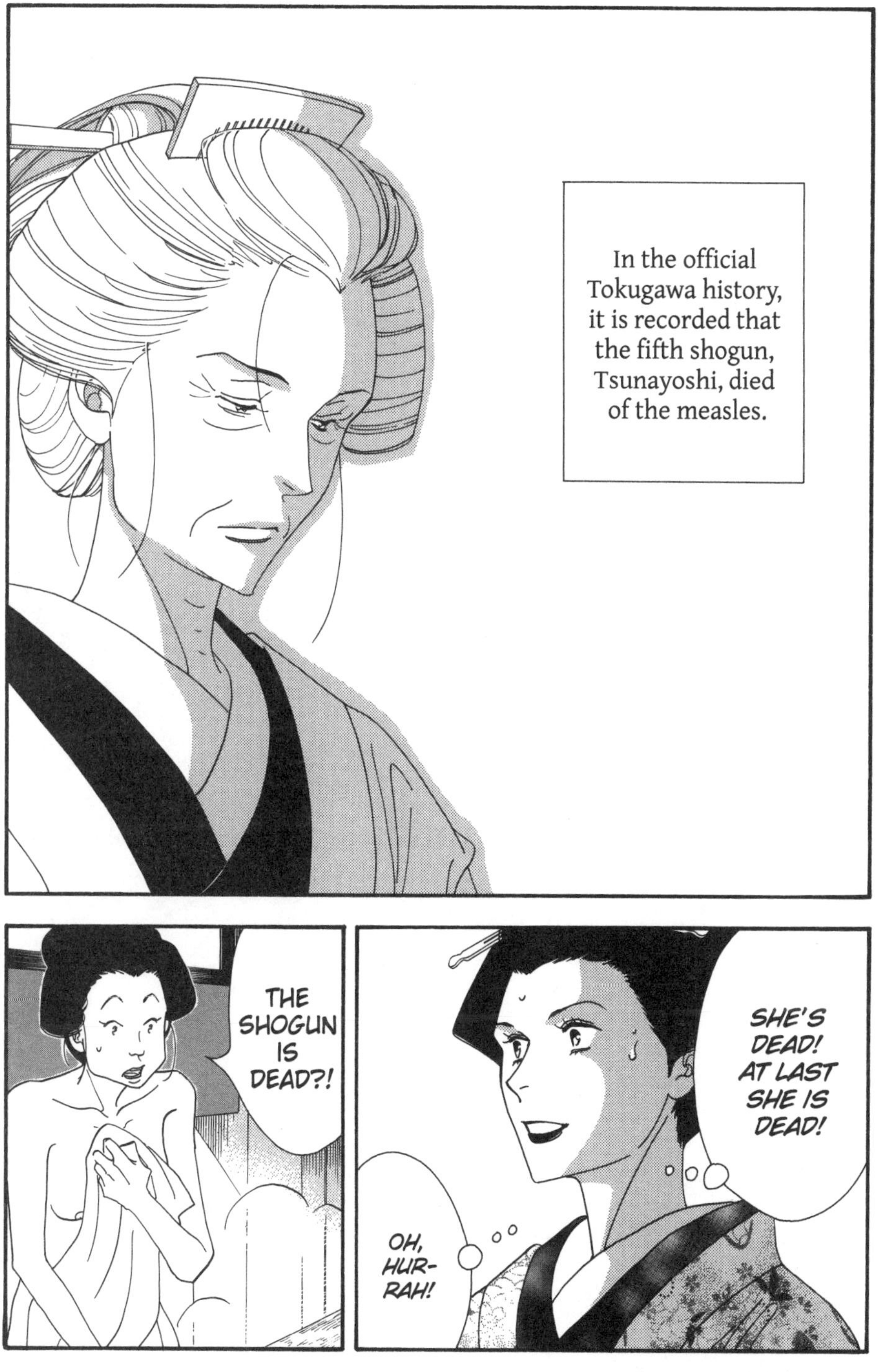
In the official Tokugawa history, it is recorded that the fifth shogun, Tsunayoshi, died of the measles.
SHE'S DEAD! AT LAST SHE IS DEAD!
OH, HUR-RAH!
THE SHOGUN IS DEAD?!

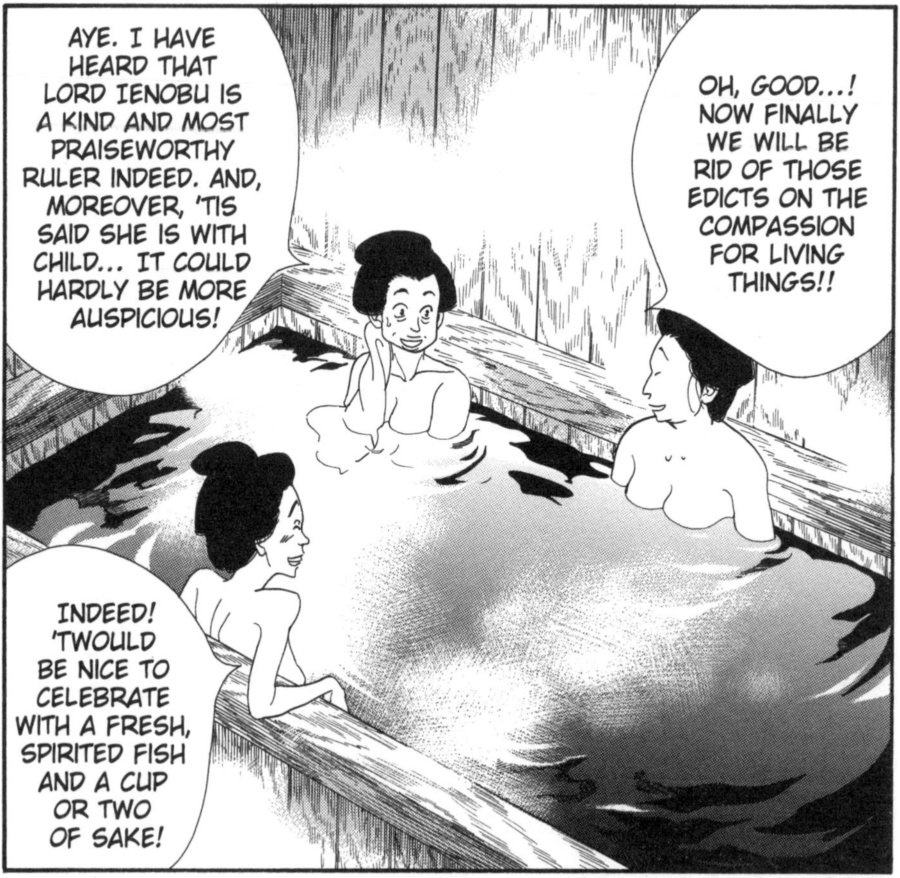
OH, GOOD...! NOW FINALLY WE WILL BE RID OF THOSE EDICTS ON THE COMPASSION FOR LIVING THINGS!!
AYE. I HAVE HEARD THAT LORD IENOBU IS A KIND AND MOST PRAISEWORTHY RULER INDEED. AND, MOREOVER, 'TIS SAID SHE IS WITH CHILD... IT COULD HARDLY BE MORE AUSPICIOUS!
INDEED! 'TWOULD BE NICE TO CELEBRATE WITH A FRESH, SPIRITED FISH AND A CUP OR TWO OF SAKE!

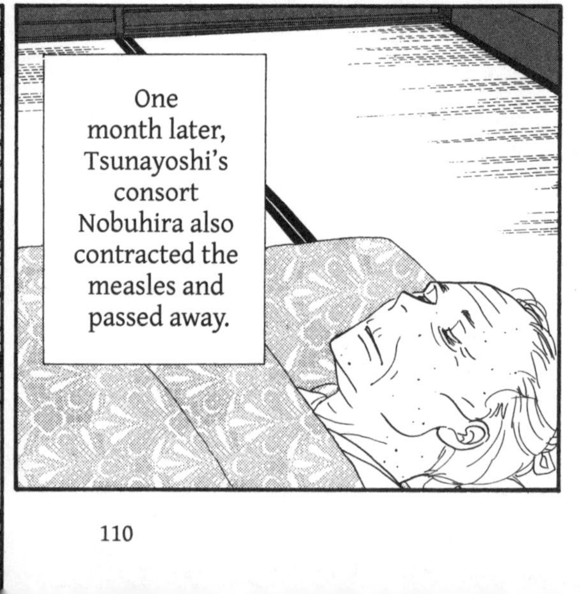
One month later, Tsunayoshi's consort Nobuhira also contracted the measles and passed away.

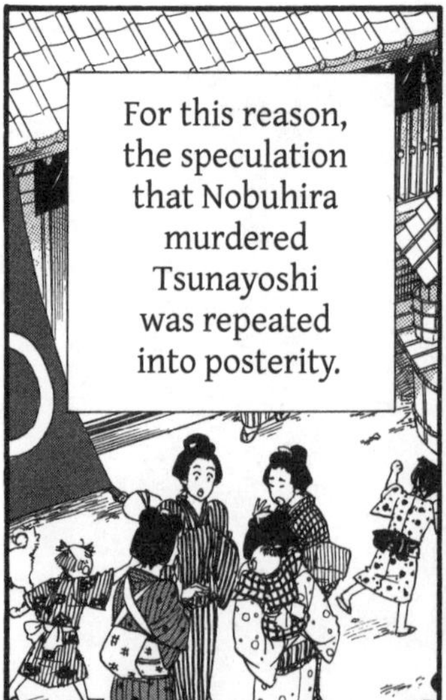
For this reason, the speculation that Nobuhira murdered Tsunayoshi was repeated into posterity.

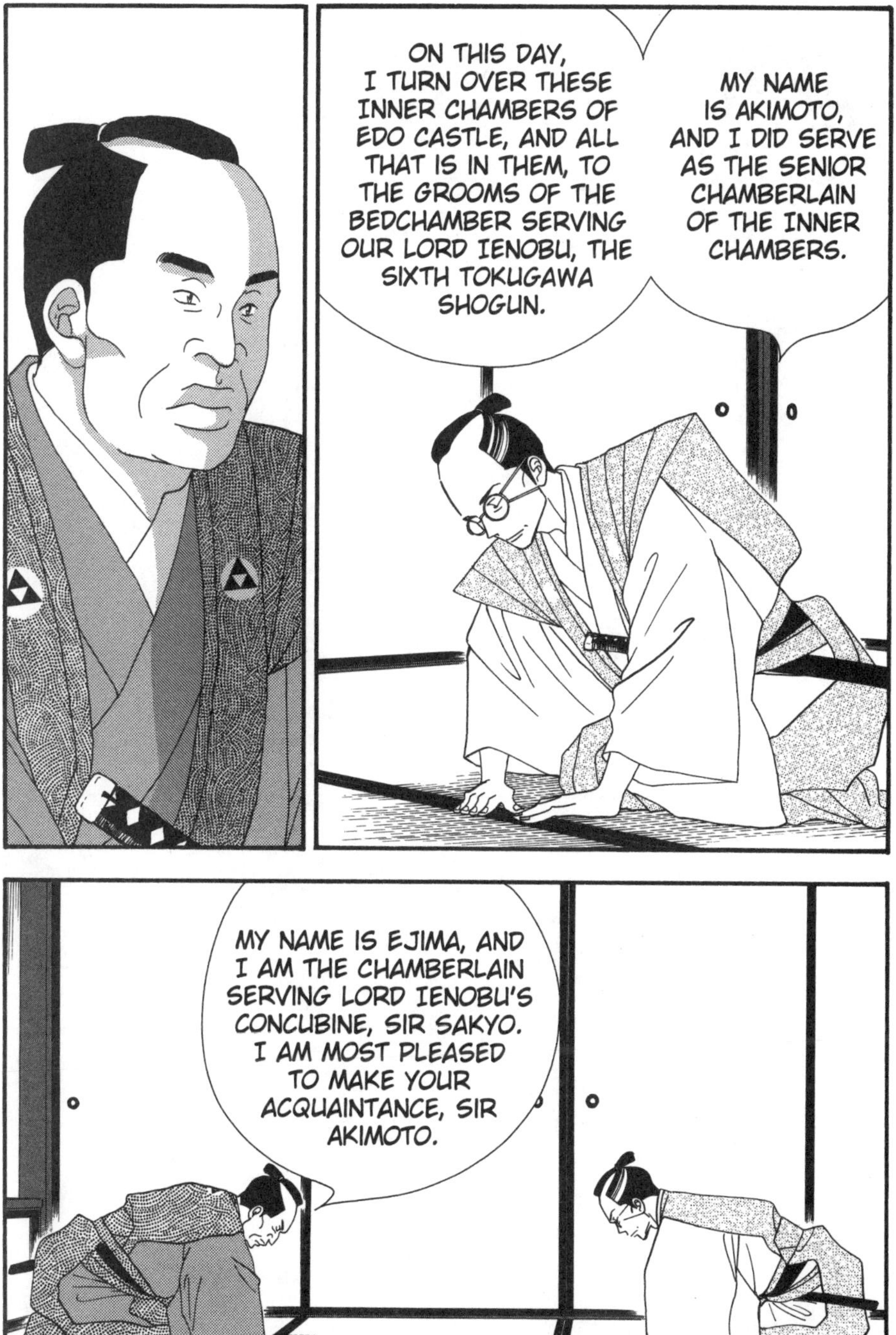
MY NAME IS AKIMOTO, AND I DID SERVE AS THE SENIOR CHAMBERLAIN OF THE INNER CHAMBERS.
ON THIS DAY, I TURN OVER THESE INNER CHAMBERS OF EDO CASTLE, AND ALL THAT IS IN THEM, TO THE GROOMS OF THE BEDCHAMBER SERVING OUR LORD IENOBU, THE SIXTH TOKUGAWA SHOGUN.
MY NAME IS EJIMA, AND I AM THE CHAMBERLAIN SERVING LORD IENOBU'S CONCUBINE, SIR SAKYO. I AM MOST PLEASED TO MAKE YOUR ACQUAINTANCE, SIR AKIMOTO.

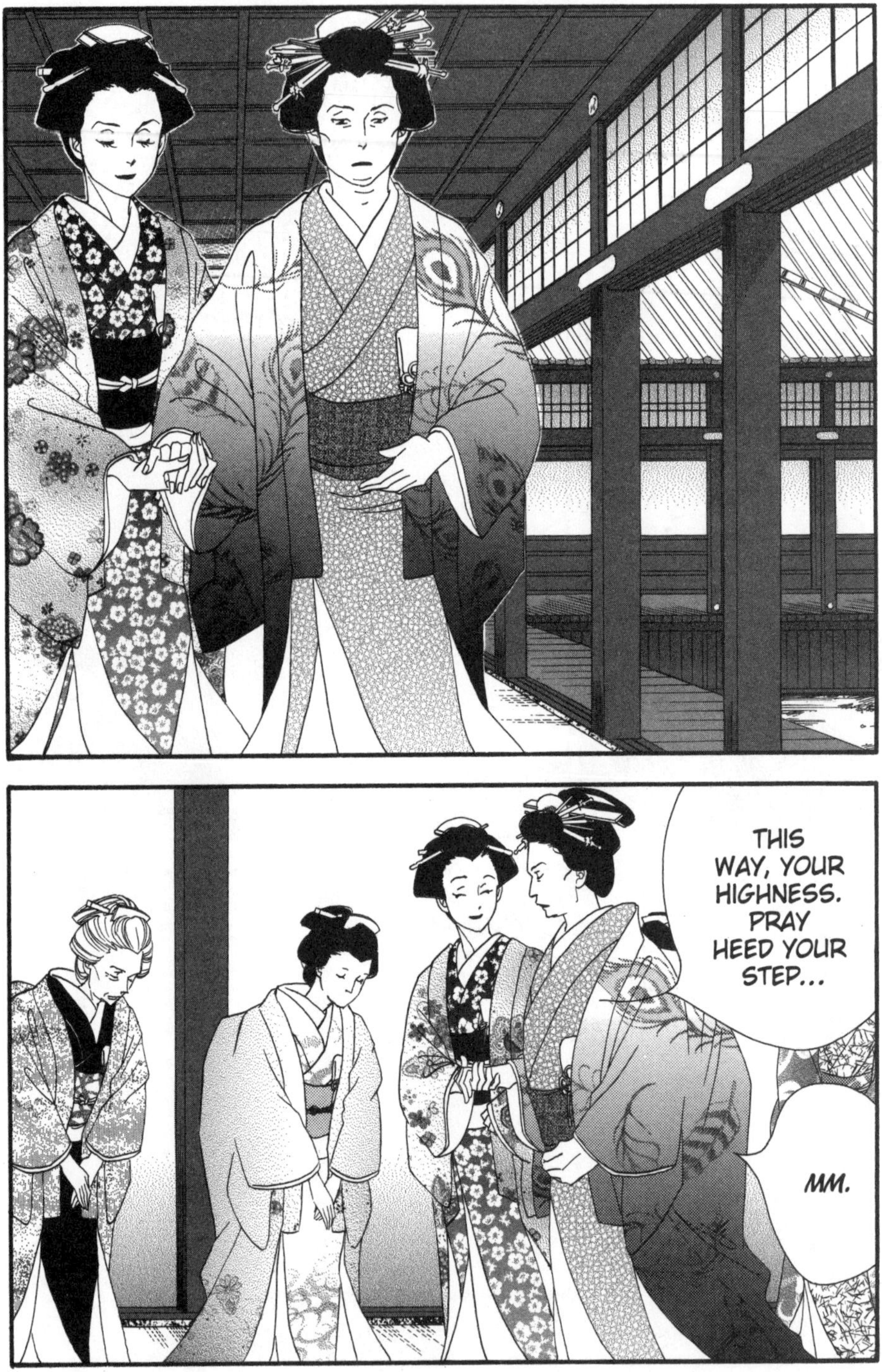
THIS WAY, YOUR HIGHNESS. PRAY HEED YOUR STEP...
MM.

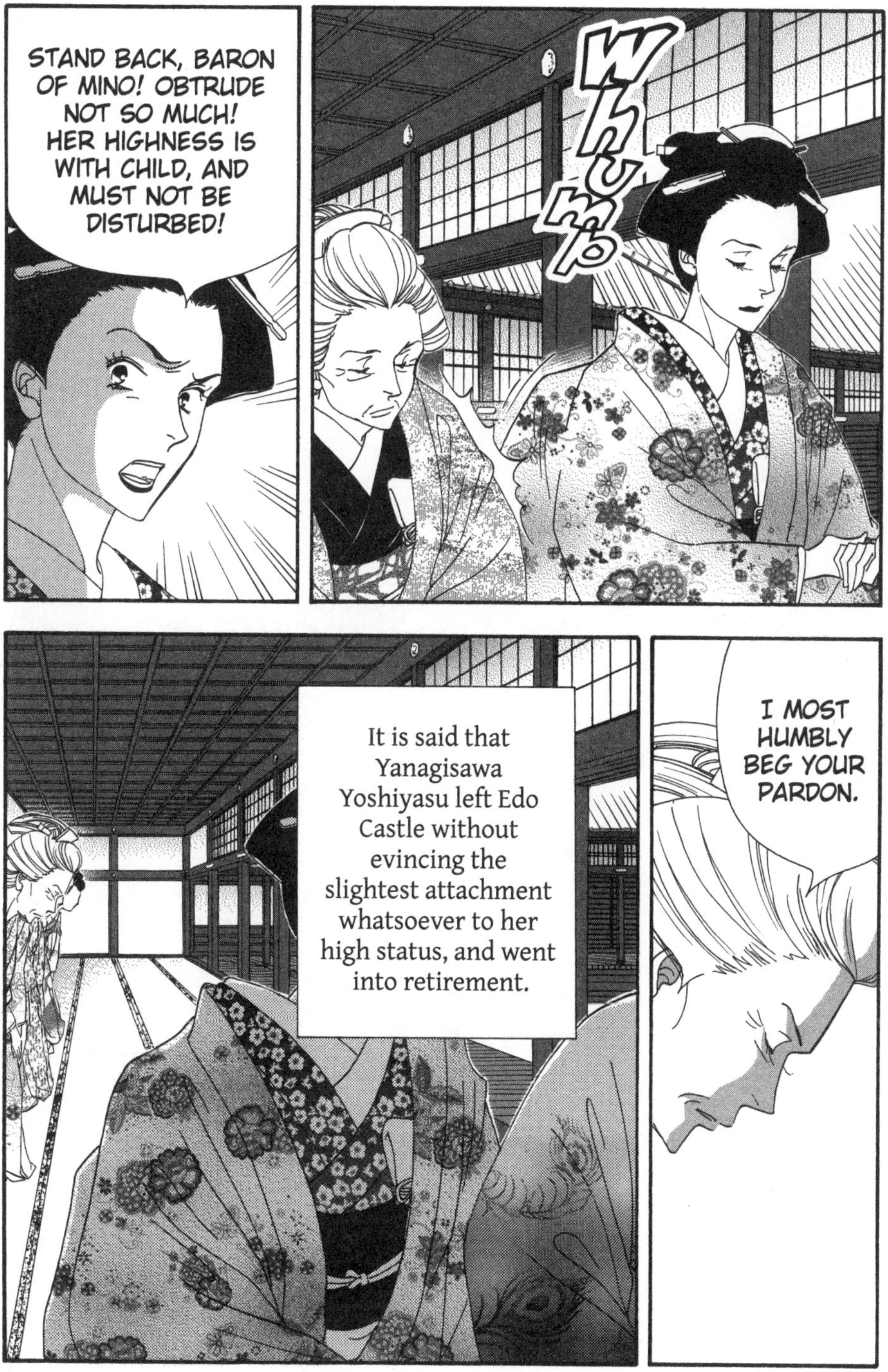
Whump
STAND BACK, BARON OF MINO! OBTRUDE NOT SO MUCH! HER HIGHNESS IS WITH CHILD, AND MUST NOT BE DISTURBED!
I MOST HUMBLY BEG YOUR PARDON.
It is said that Yanagisawa Yoshiyasu left Edo Castle without evincing the slightest attachment whatsoever to her high status, and went into retirement.

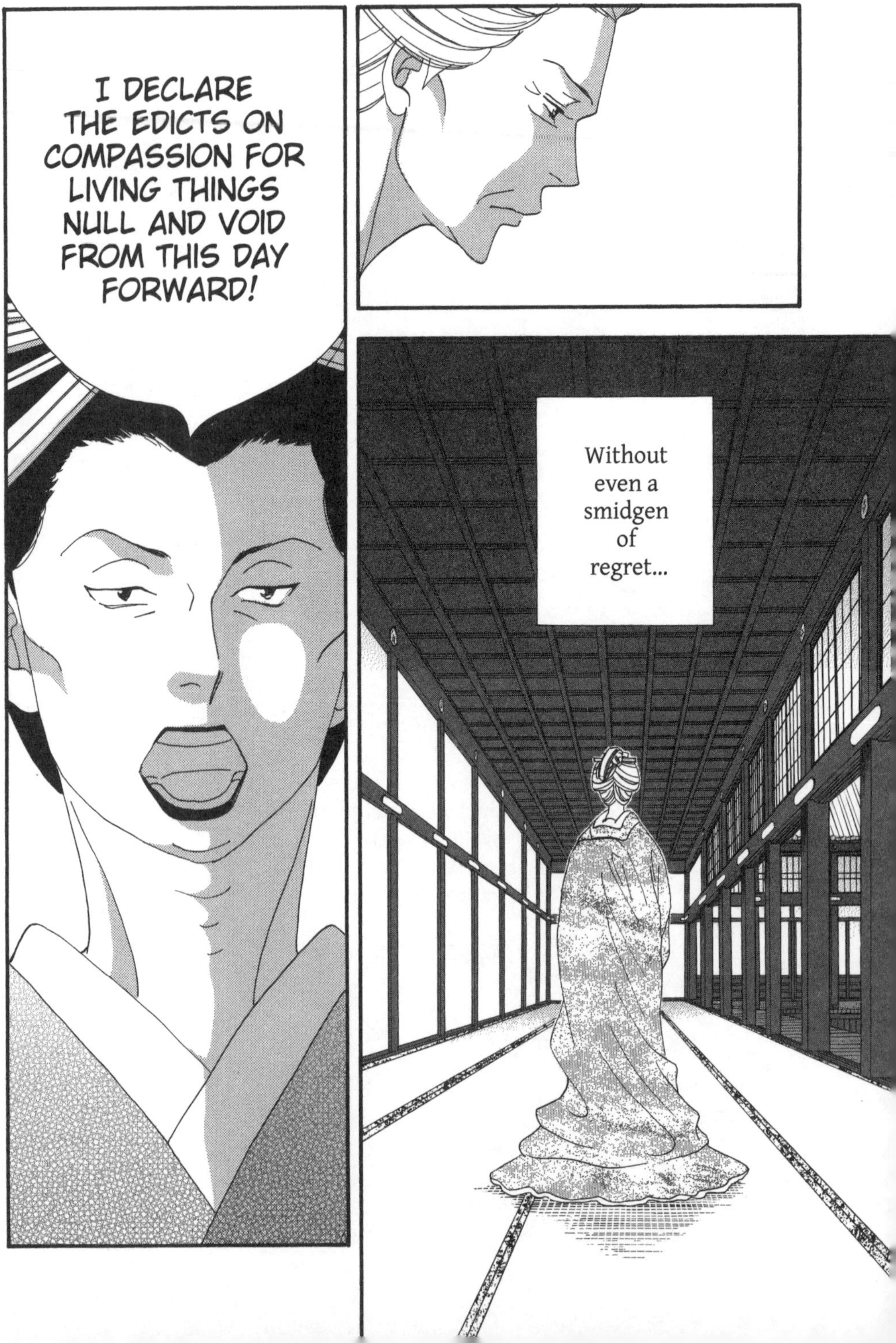
Without even a smidgen of regret...
I DECLARE THE EDICTS ON COMPASSION FOR LIVING THINGS NULL AND VOID FROM THIS DAY FORWARD!

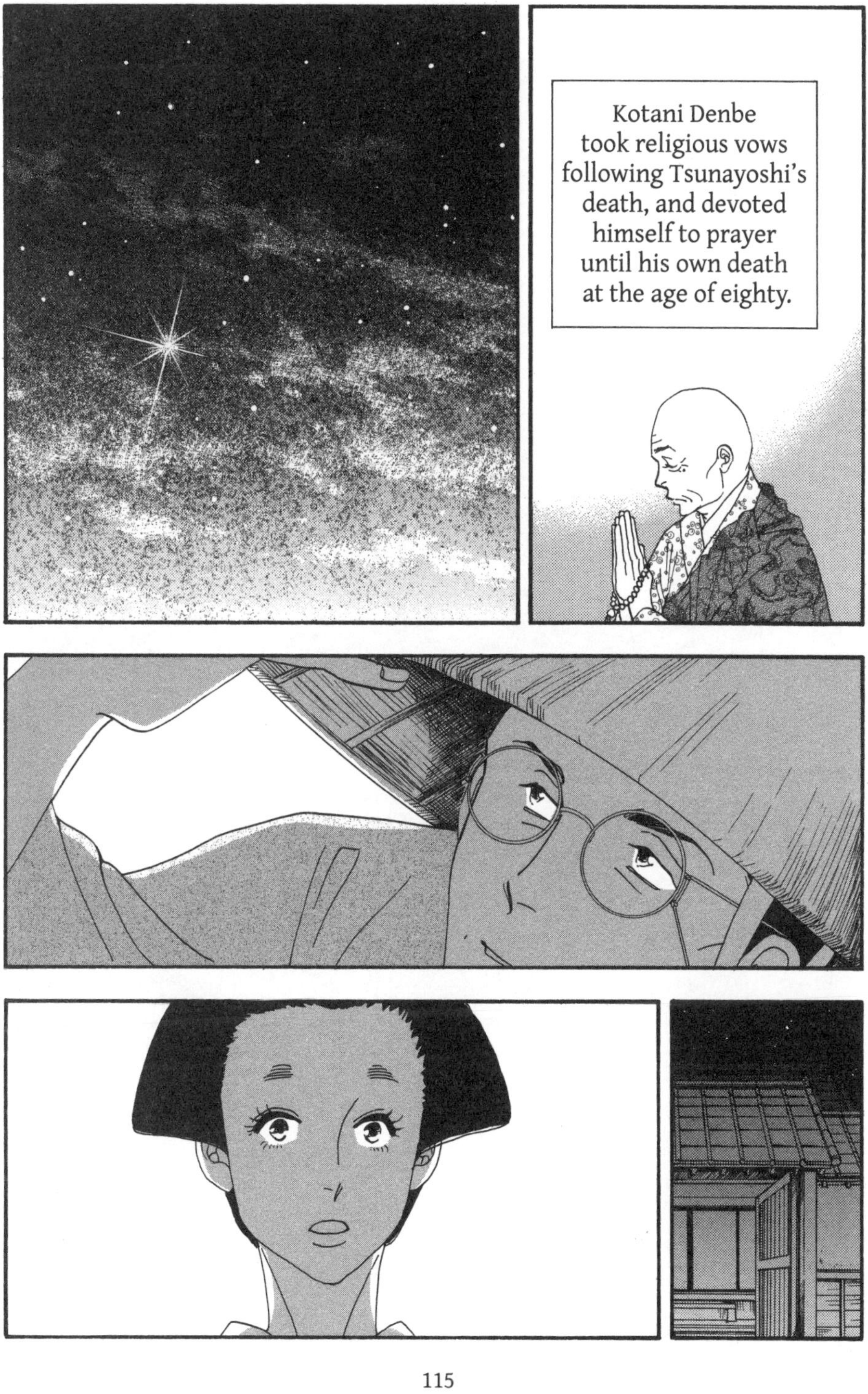
Kotani Denbe took religious vows following Tsunayoshi's death, and devoted himself to prayer until his own death at the age of eighty.

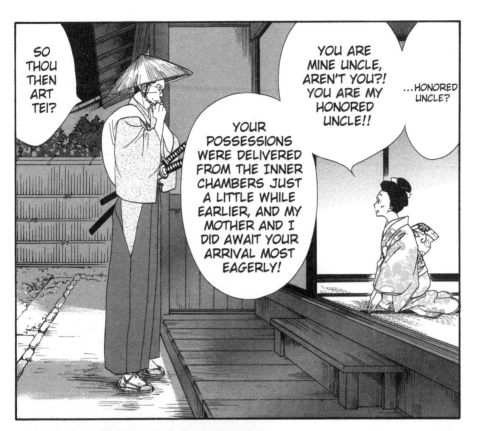

...HONORED UNCLE?
YOU ARE MINE UNCLE, AREN'T YOU?! YOU ARE MY HONORED UNCLE!!
YOUR POSSESSIONS WERE DELIVERED FROM THE INNER CHAMBERS JUST A LITTLE WHILE EARLIER, AND MY MOTHER AND I DID AWAIT YOUR ARRIVAL MOST EAGERLY!
SO THOU THEN ART TEI?
AYE, SIR! I AM YOUR NIECE, TEI!
HONORED BROTHER...

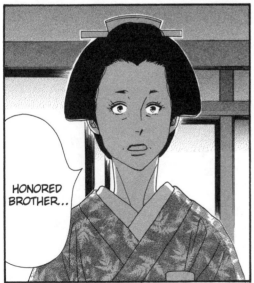

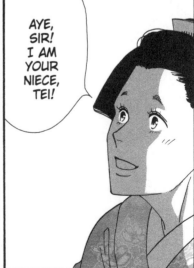

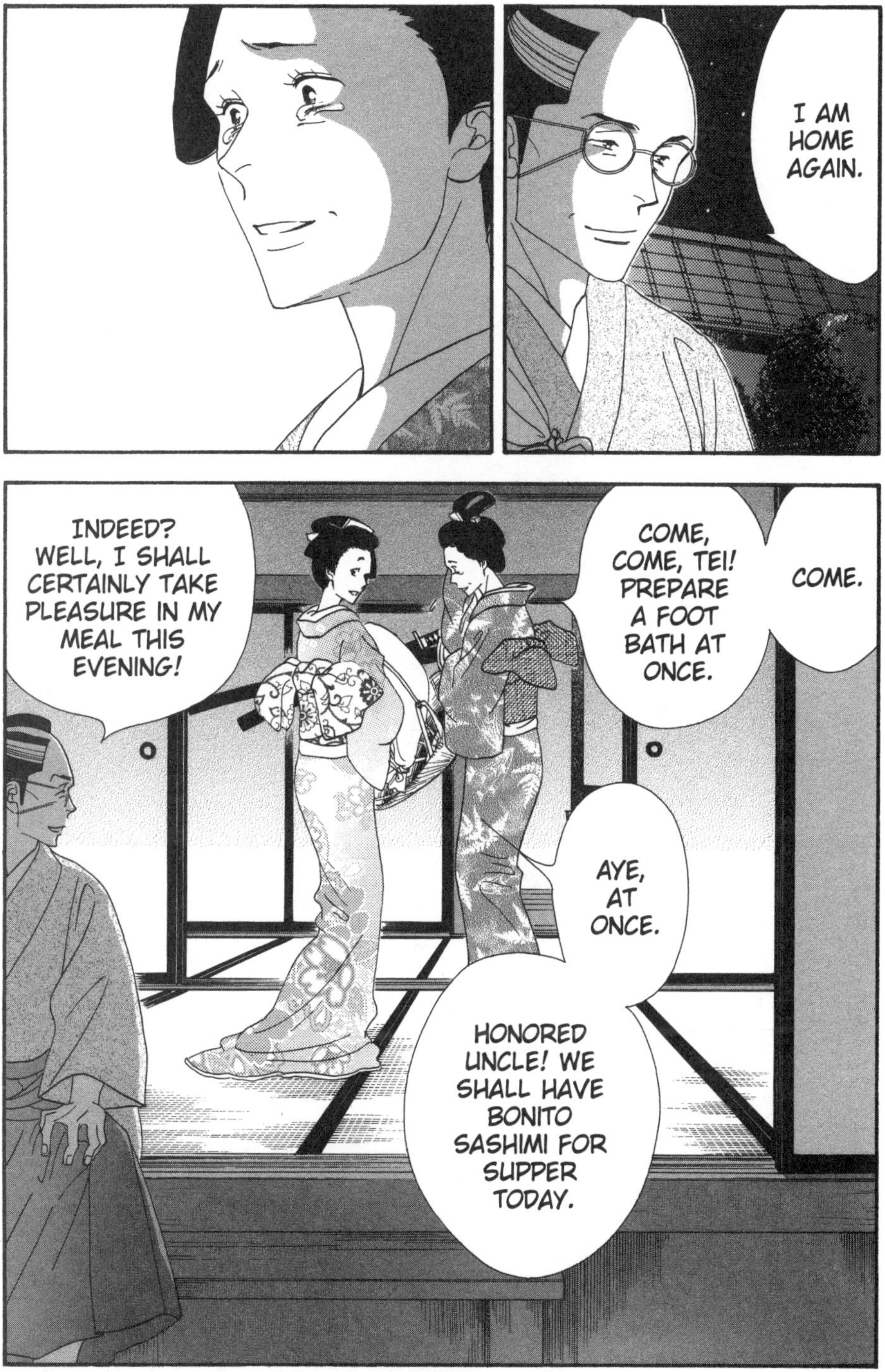
I AM HOME AGAIN.
COME.
COME, COME, TEI! PREPARE A FOOT BATH AT ONCE.
AYE, AT ONCE.
HONORED UNCLE! WE SHALL HAVE BONITO SASHIMI FOR SUPPER TODAY.
INDEED? WELL, I SHALL CERTAINLY TAKE PLEASURE IN MY MEAL THIS EVENING!

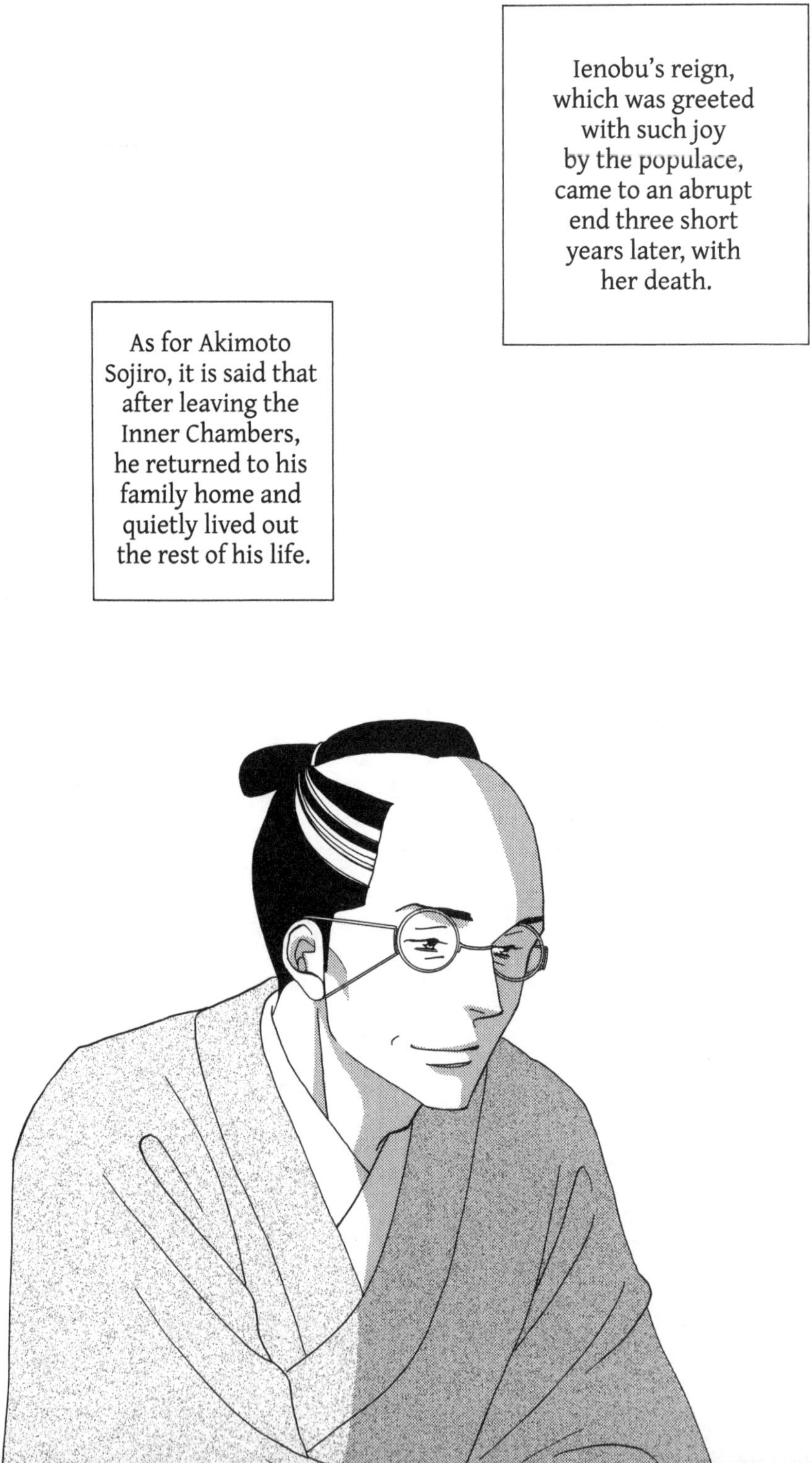
Ienobu's reign, which was greeted with such joy by the populace, came to an abrupt end three short years later, with her death.
As for Akimoto Sojiro, it is said that after leaving the Inner Chambers, he returned to his family home and quietly lived out the rest of his life.

Ōoku

THE INNER CHAMBERS

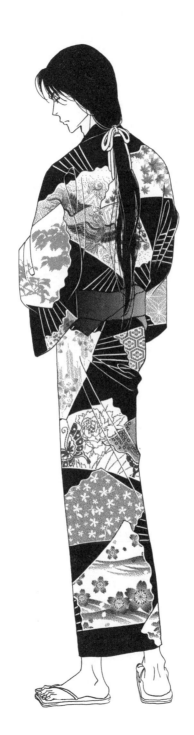

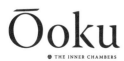

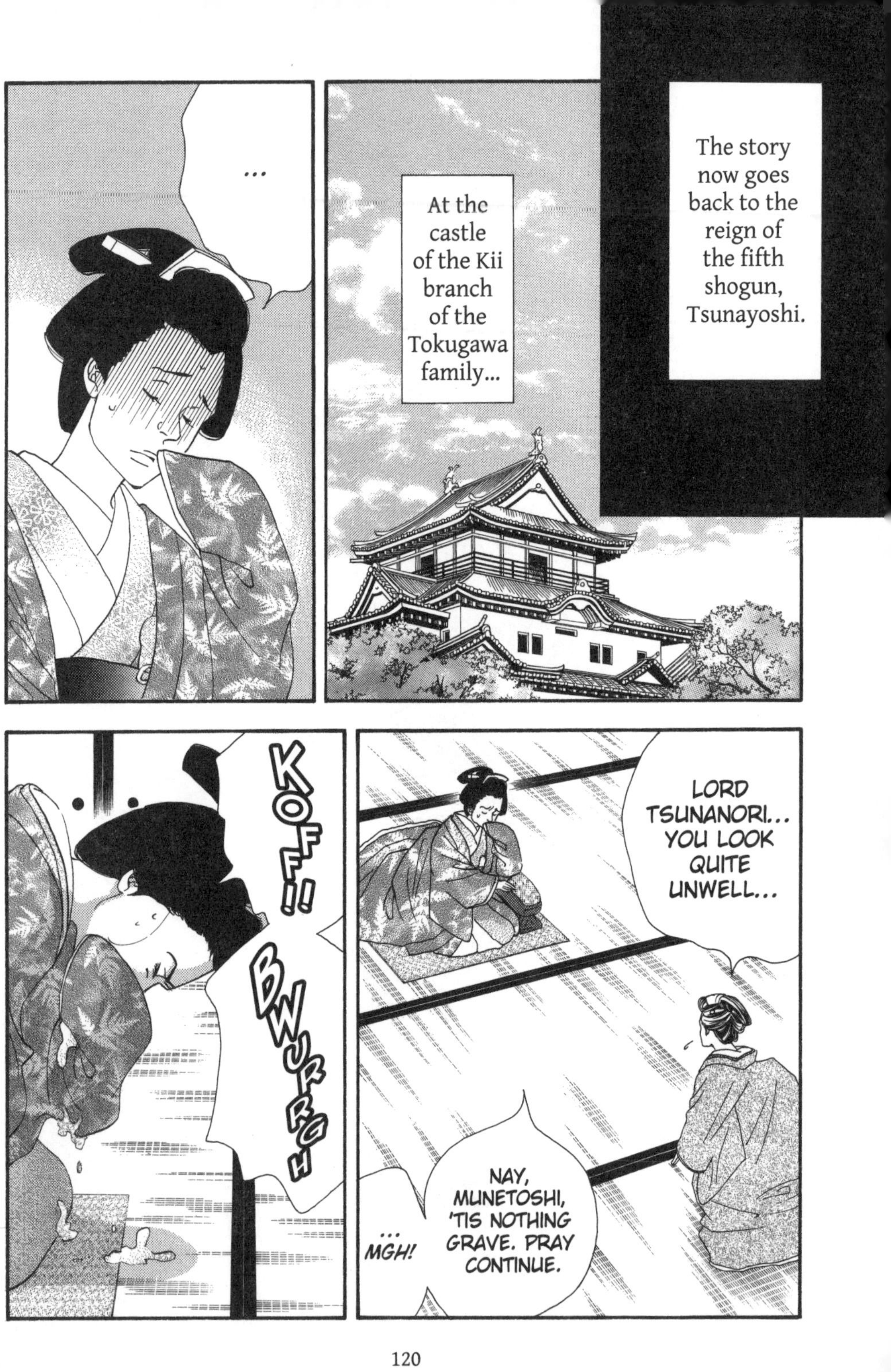
The story now goes back to the reign of the fifth shogun, Tsunayoshi.
At the castle of the Kii branch of the Tokugawa family...
...
LORD TSUNANORI... YOU LOOK QUITE UNWELL...
NAY, MUNETOSHI, 'TIS NOTHING GRAVE. PRAY CONTINUE.
... MGH!
KOFF!!
BWURRGH

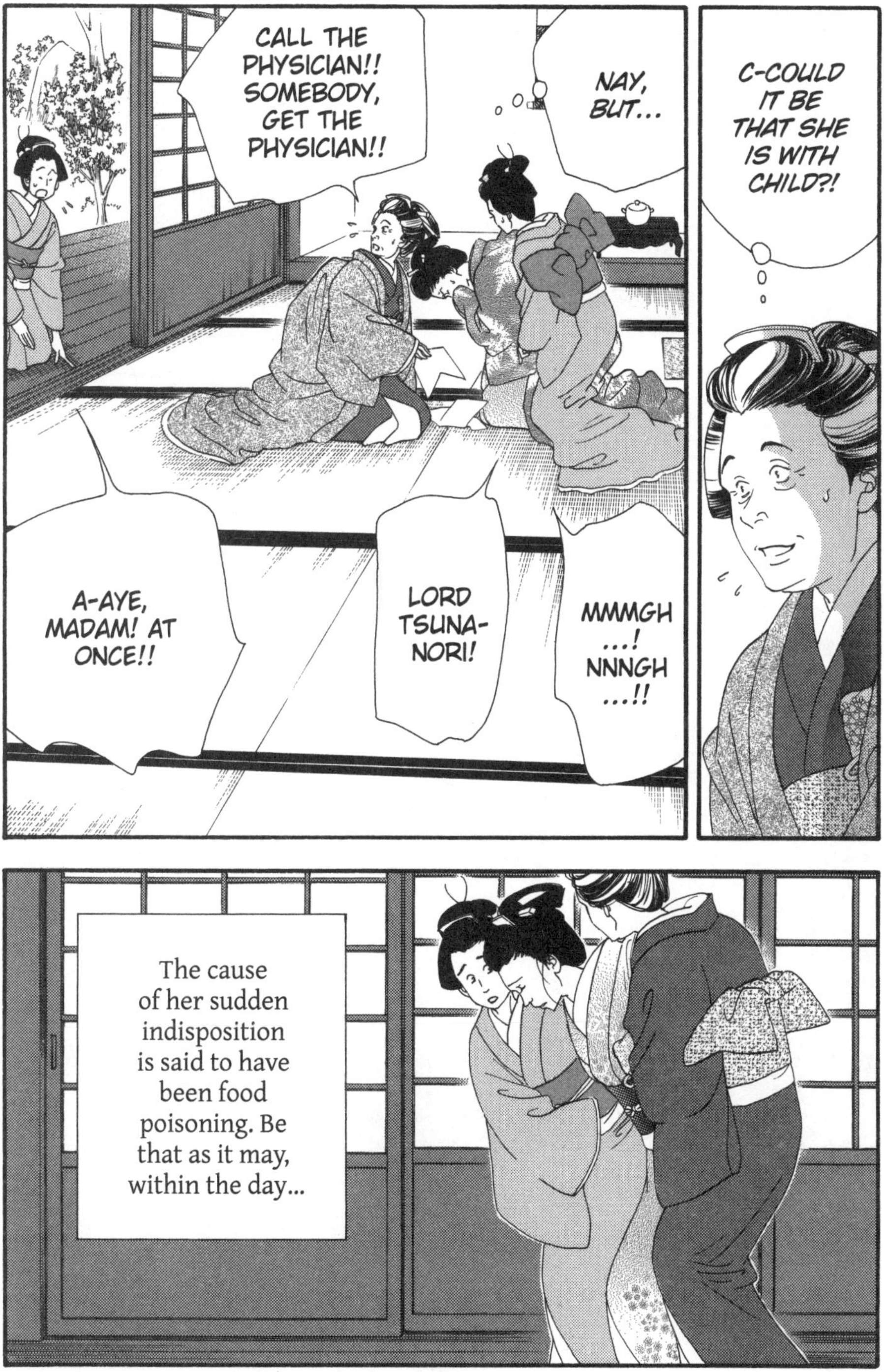
C-COULD IT BE THAT SHE IS WITH CHILD?!
NAY, BUT...
CALL THE PHYSICIAN!! SOMEBODY, GET THE PHYSICIAN!!
MMMGH ...! NNNGH ...!!
LORD TSUNA-NORI!
A-AYE, MADAM! AT ONCE!!
The cause of her sudden indisposition is said to have been food poisoning. Be that as it may, within the day...

...Tsunanori, the third lord of the Kii branch of the Tokugawa family, was dead just two years after assuming that position.

TSU-NA-NORI!!°°

TSU...
TSU...
TSU...

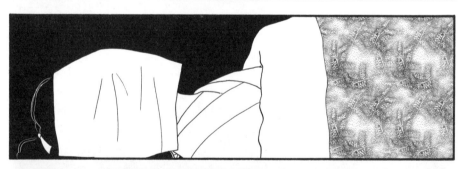

The grief of her mother, Lord Mitsusada, at the untimely loss of her intelligent, clear-sighted eldest daughter, was no doubt great.

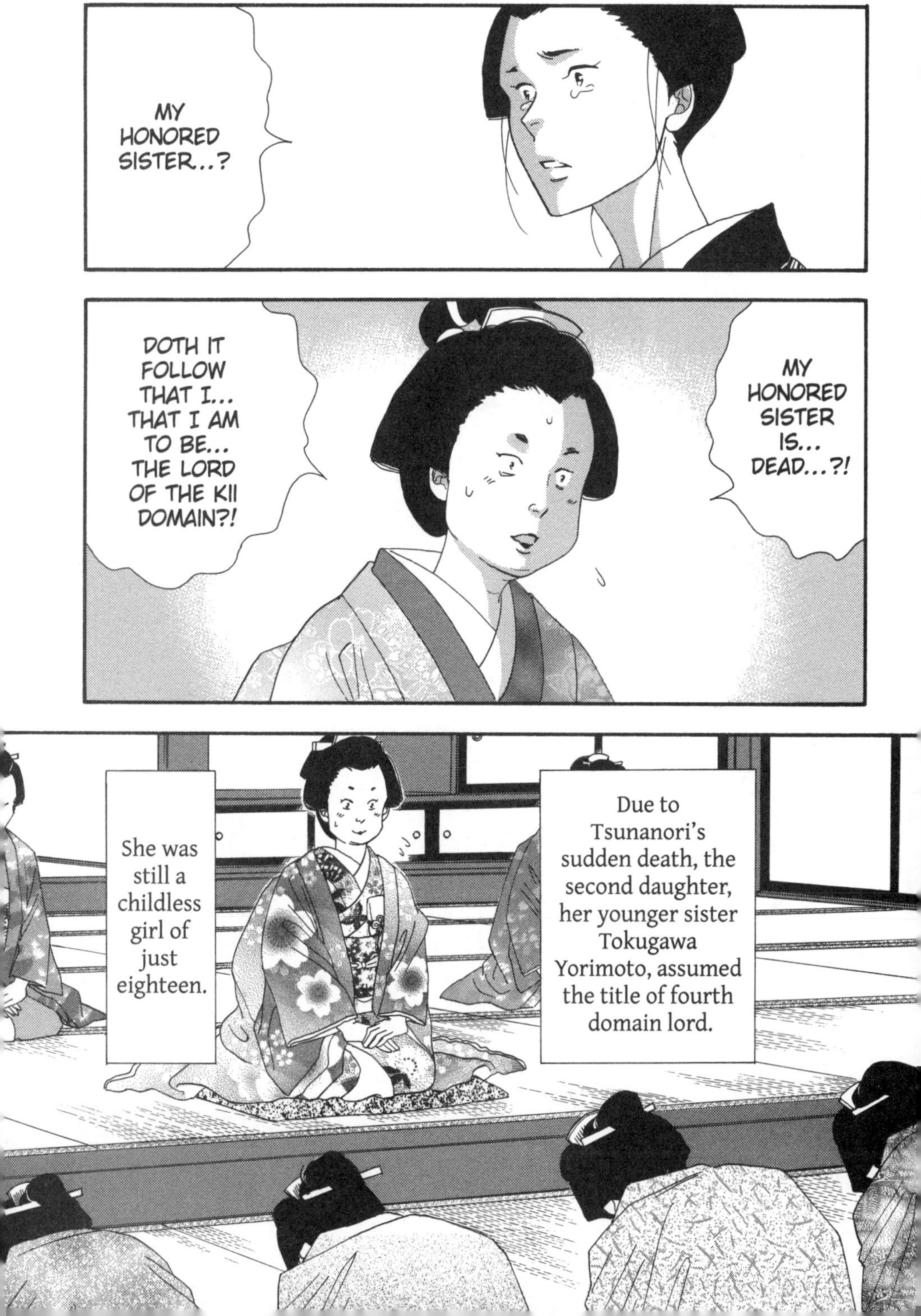
MY HONORED SISTER...?
MY HONORED SISTER IS... DEAD...?!
DOTH IT FOLLOW THAT I... THAT I AM TO BE... THE LORD OF THE KII DOMAIN?!
Due to Tsunanori's sudden death, the second daughter, her younger sister Tokugawa Yorimoto, assumed the title of fourth domain lord.
She was still a childless girl of just eighteen.

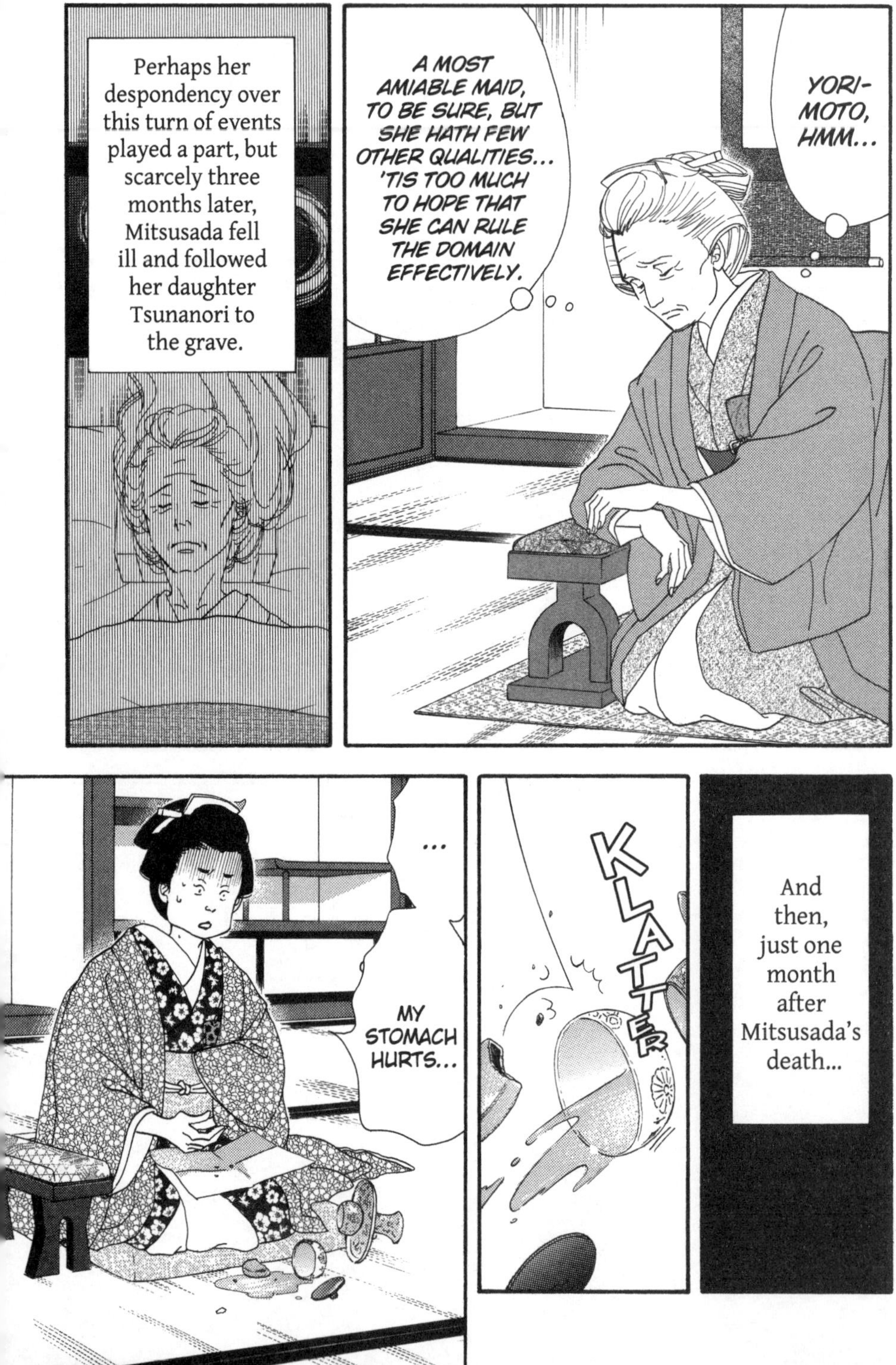

YORI-MOTO, HMM...
A MOST AMIABLE MAID, TO BE SURE, BUT SHE HATH FEW OTHER QUALITIES... 'TIS TOO MUCH TO HOPE THAT SHE CAN RULE THE DOMAIN EFFECTIVELY.
Perhaps her despondency over this turn of events played a part, but scarcely three months later, Mitsusada fell ill and followed her daughter Tsunanori to the grave.
And then, just one month after Mitsusada's death...
KLATTER
...
MY STOMACH HURTS...

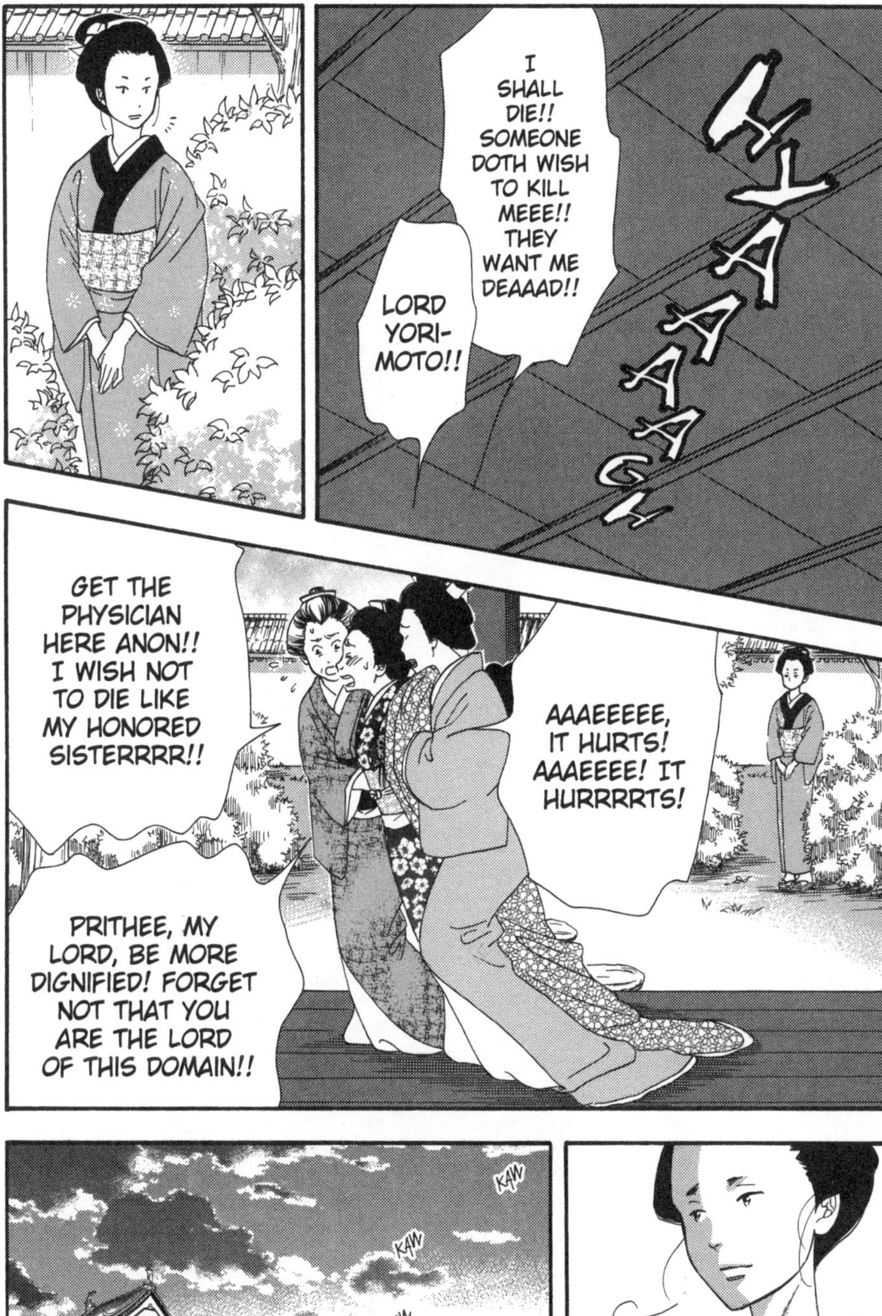
HYAAAAGH
I SHALL DIE!! SOMEONE DOTH WISH TO KILL MEEE!! THEY WANT ME DEAAAD!!
LORD YORI-MOTO!!
AAAEEEEE, IT HURTS! AAAEEEE! IT HURRRRTS!
GET THE PHYSICIAN HERE ANON!! I WISH NOT TO DIE LIKE MY HONORED SISTERRRR!!
PRITHEE, MY LORD, BE MORE DIGNIFIED! FORGET NOT THAT YOU ARE THE LORD OF THIS DOMAIN!!
KAW
KAW
KAW

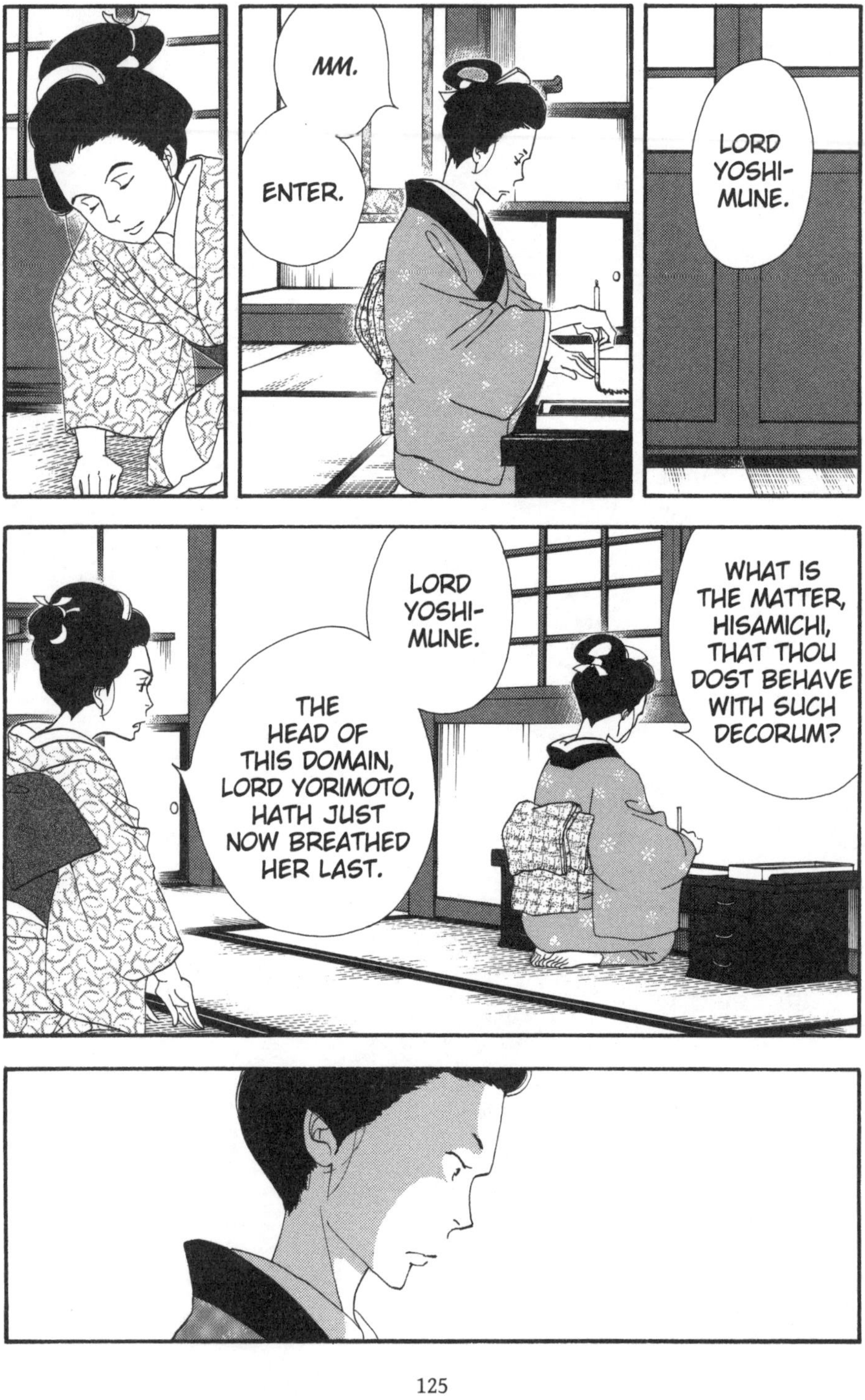
LORD YOSHI-MUNE.
MM.
ENTER.
WHAT IS THE MATTER, HISAMICHI, THAT THOU DOST BEHAVE WITH SUCH DECORUM?
LORD YOSHI-MUNE.
THE HEAD OF THIS DOMAIN, LORD YORIMOTO, HATH JUST NOW BREATHED HER LAST.

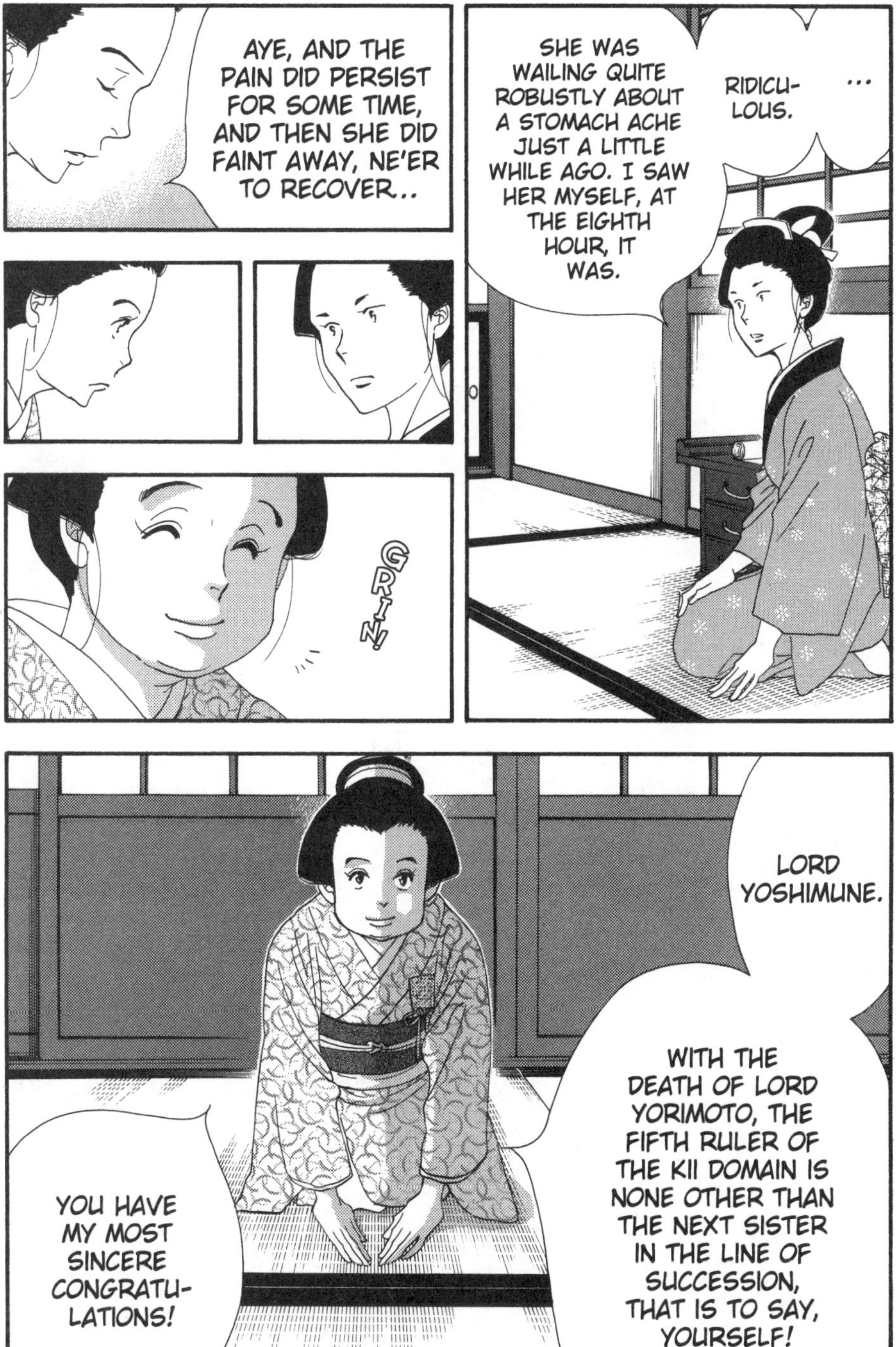
...
RIDICULOUS.
SHE WAS WAILING QUITE ROBUSTLY ABOUT A STOMACH ACHE JUST A LITTLE WHILE AGO. I SAW HER MYSELF, AT THE EIGHTH HOUR, IT WAS.
AYE, AND THE PAIN DID PERSIST FOR SOME TIME, AND THEN SHE DID FAINT AWAY, NE'ER TO RECOVER...
GRIN!
LORD YOSHIMUNE.
WITH THE DEATH OF LORD YORIMOTO, THE FIFTH RULER OF THE KII DOMAIN IS NONE OTHER THAN THE NEXT SISTER IN THE LINE OF SUCCESSION, THAT IS TO SAY, YOURSELF!
YOU HAVE MY MOST SINCERE CONGRATULATIONS!

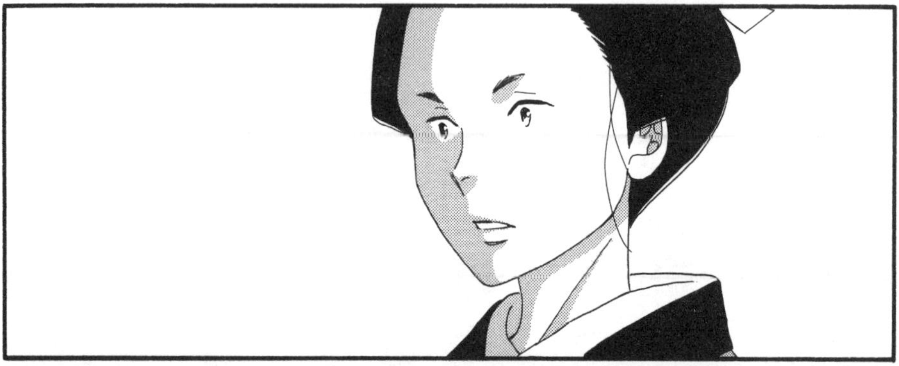

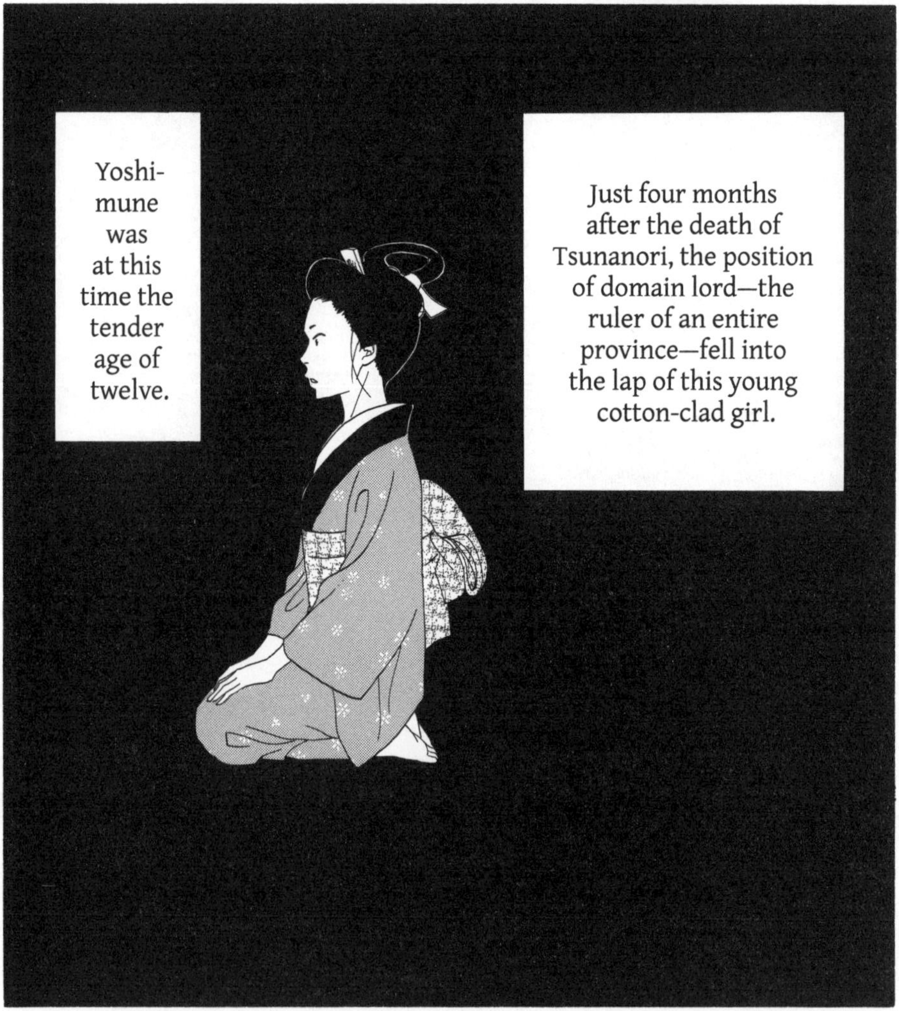
Just four months after the death of Tsunanori, the position of domain lord—the ruler of an entire province—fell into the lap of this young cotton-clad girl.
Yoshi-mune was at this time the tender age of twelve.

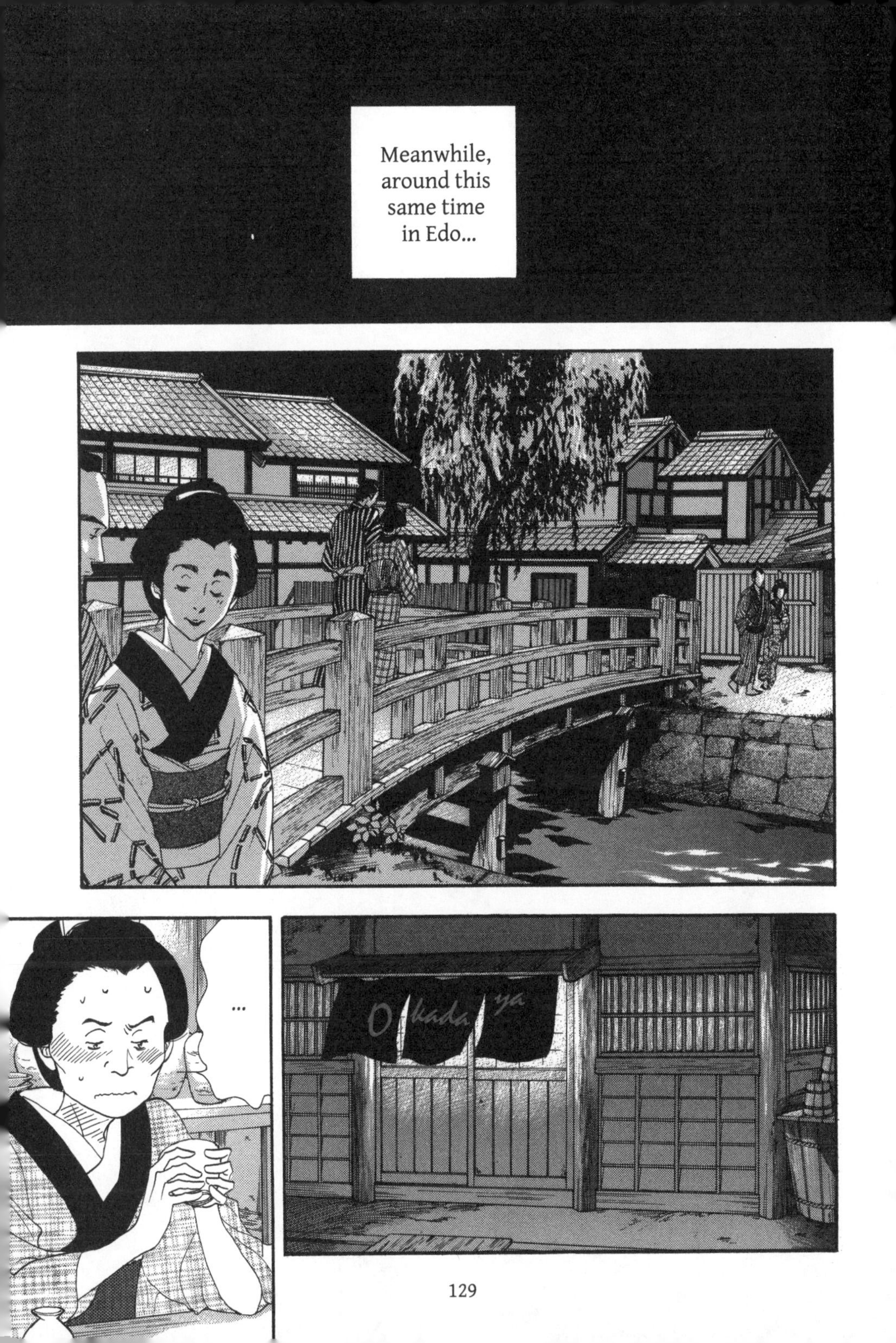
Meanwhile, around this same time in Edo...
Okadaya
...

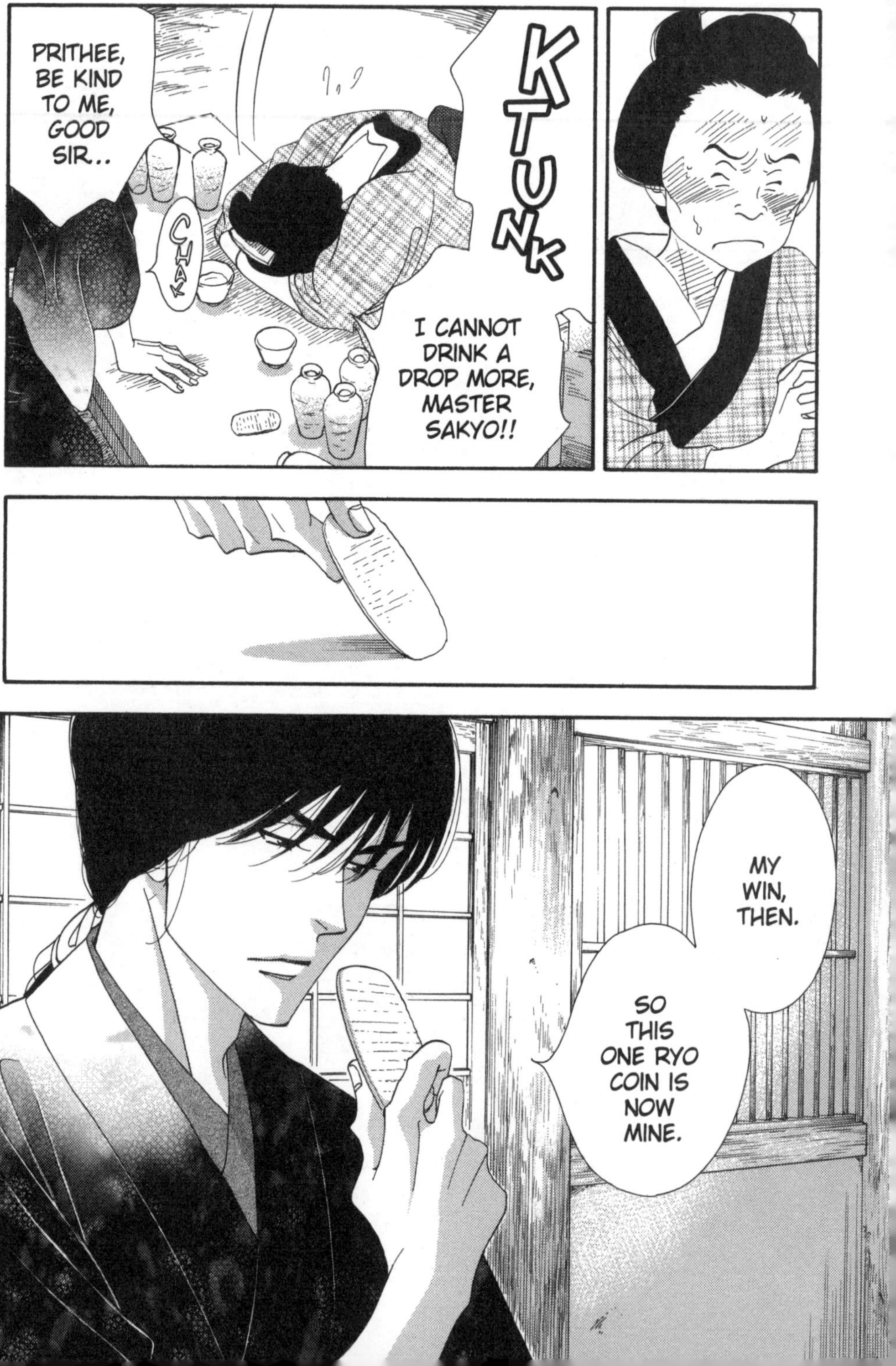
KTUNK
PRITHEE, BE KIND TO ME, GOOD SIR...
CHAK
I CANNOT DRINK A DROP MORE, MASTER SAKYO!!
MY WIN, THEN.
SO THIS ONE RYO COIN IS NOW MINE.

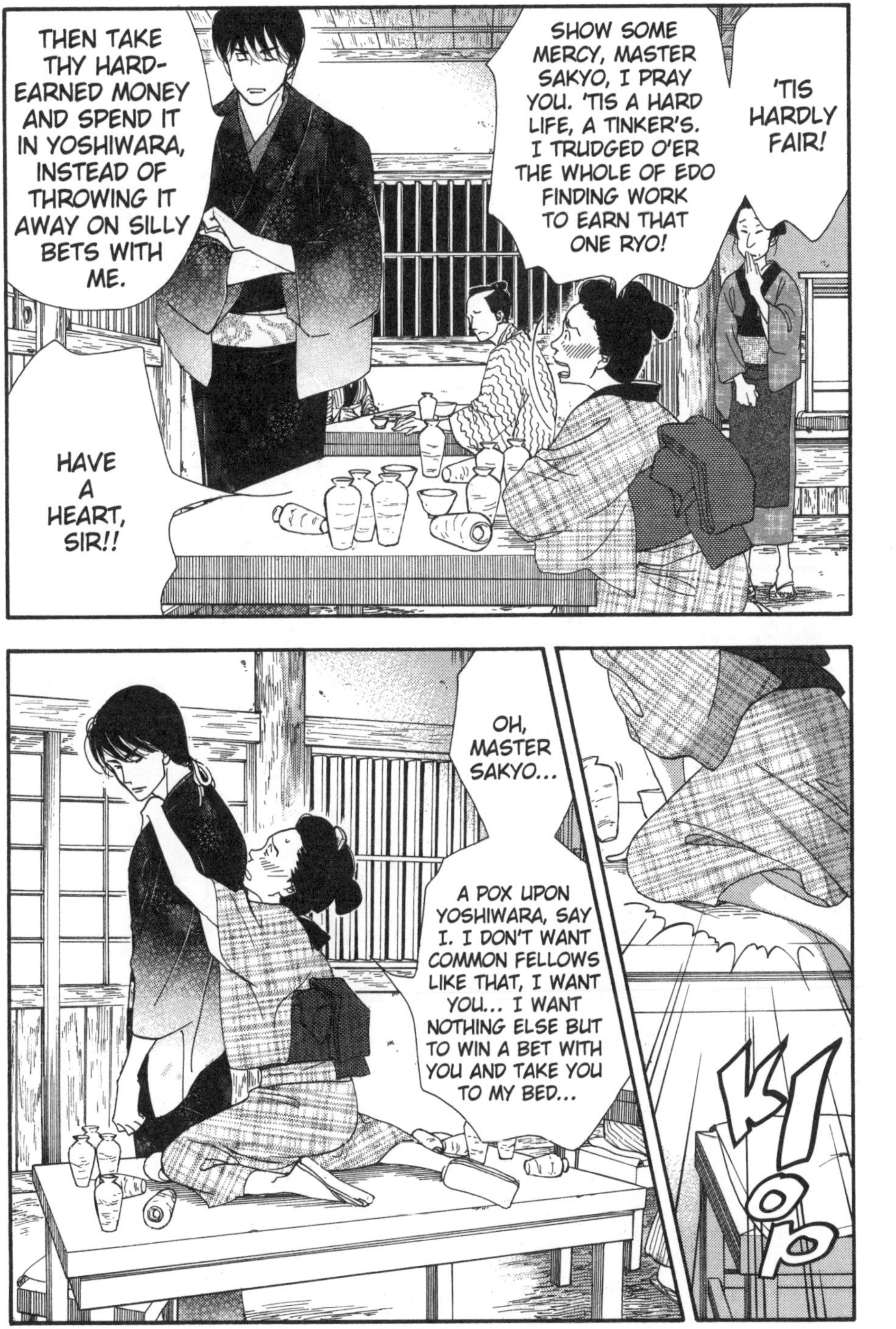
'TIS HARDLY FAIR!
SHOW SOME MERCY, MASTER SAKYO, I PRAY YOU. 'TIS A HARD LIFE, A TINKER'S. I TRUDGED O'ER THE WHOLE OF EDO FINDING WORK TO EARN THAT ONE RYO!
THEN TAKE THY HARD-EARNED MONEY AND SPEND IT IN YOSHIWARA, INSTEAD OF THROWING IT AWAY ON SILLY BETS WITH ME.
HAVE A HEART, SIR!!
KLOP
OH, MASTER SAKYO...
A POX UPON YOSHIWARA, SAY I. I DON'T WANT COMMON FELLOWS LIKE THAT, I WANT YOU... I WANT NOTHING ELSE BUT TO WIN A BET WITH YOU AND TAKE YOU TO MY BED...

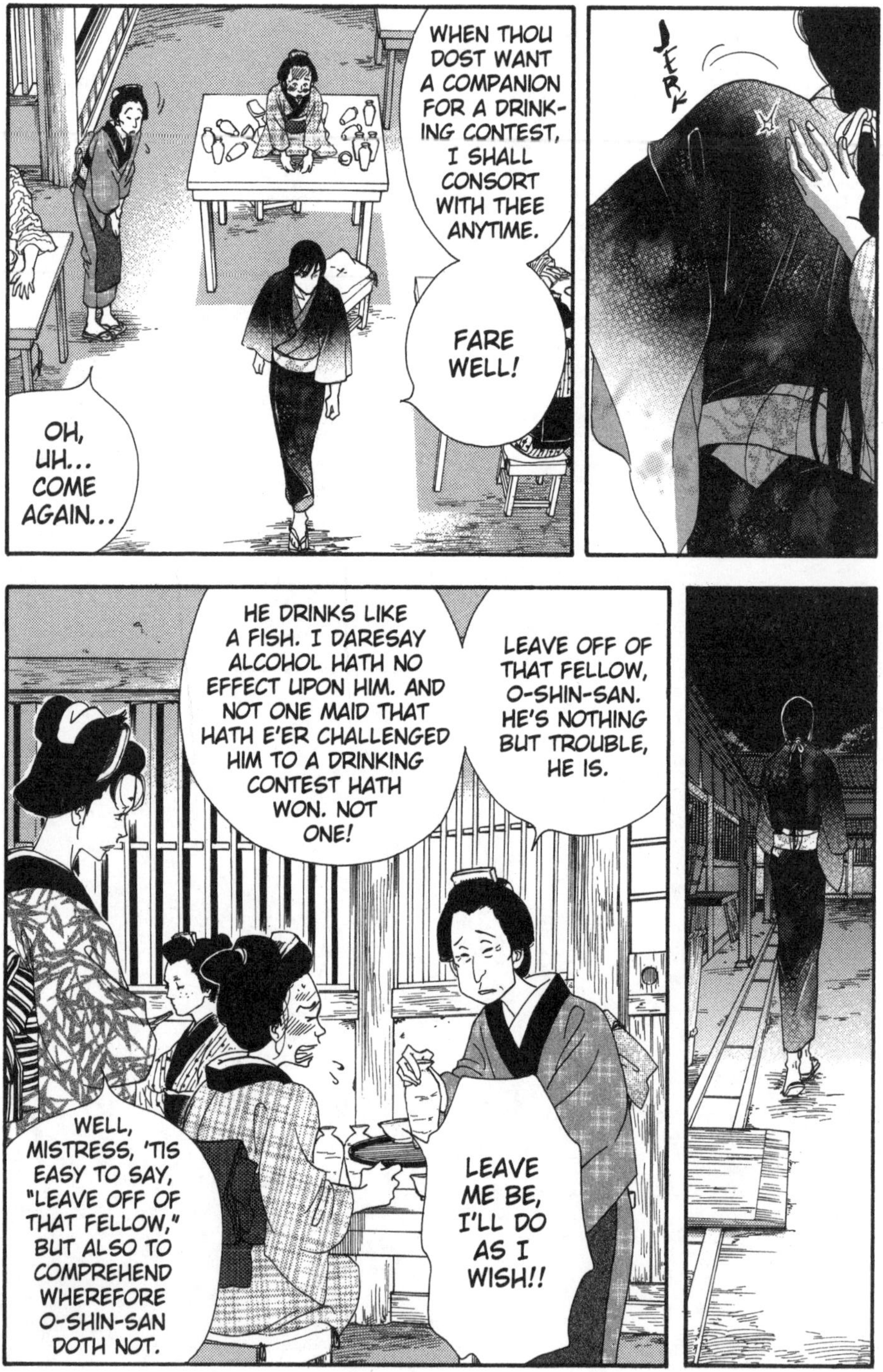
JERK
WHEN THOU DOST WANT A COMPANION FOR A DRINKING CONTEST, I SHALL CONSORT WITH THEE ANYTIME.
FARE WELL!
OH, UH... COME AGAIN...
LEAVE OFF OF THAT FELLOW, O-SHIN-SAN. HE'S NOTHING BUT TROUBLE, HE IS.
HE DRINKS LIKE A FISH. I DARESAY ALCOHOL HATH NO EFFECT UPON HIM. AND NOT ONE MAID THAT HATH E'ER CHALLENGED HIM TO A DRINKING CONTEST HATH WON. NOT ONE!
LEAVE ME BE, I'LL DO AS I WISH!!
WELL, MISTRESS, 'TIS EASY TO SAY, "LEAVE OFF OF THAT FELLOW," BUT ALSO TO COMPREHEND WHEREFORE O-SHIN-SAN DOTH NOT.

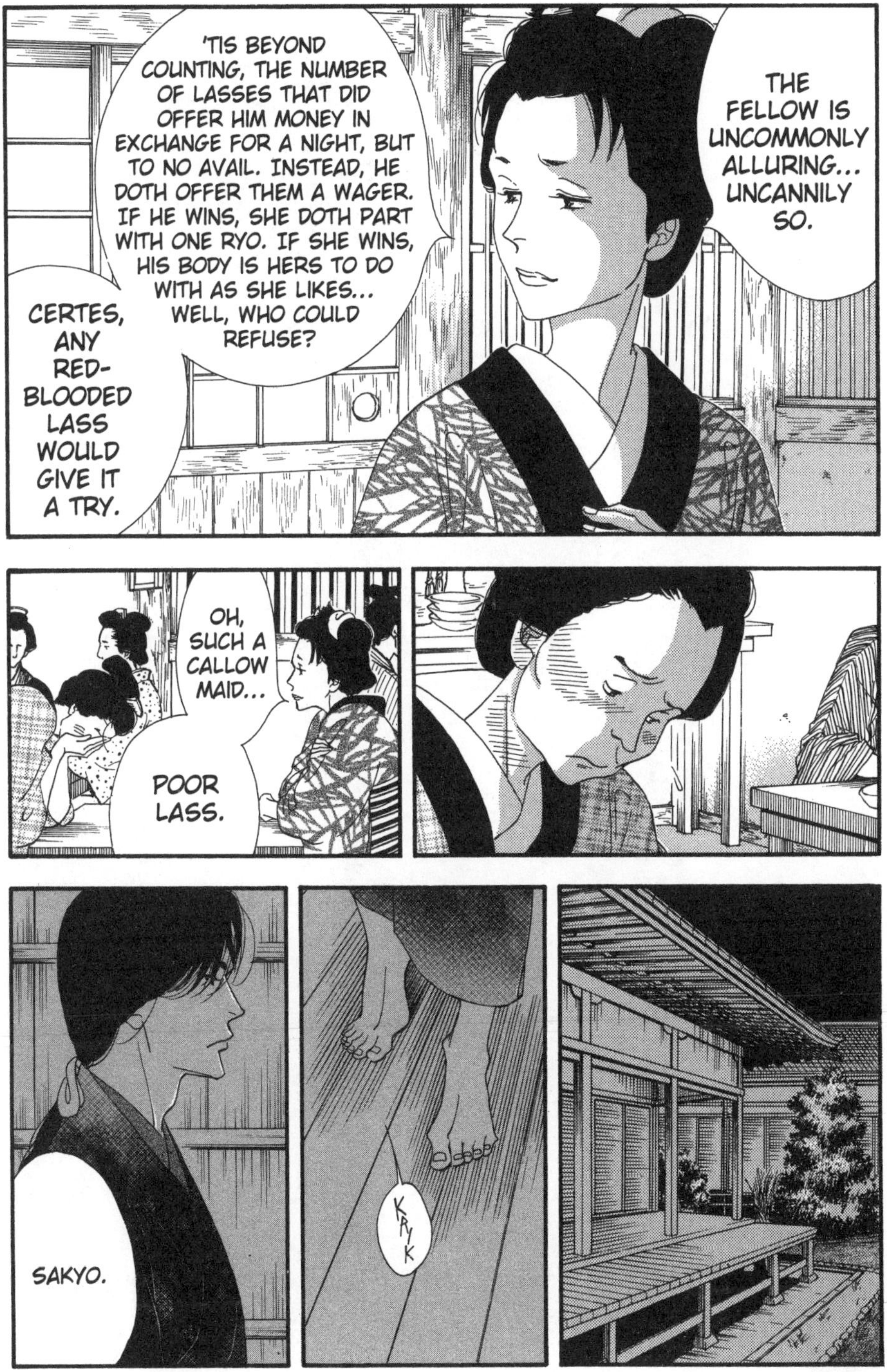
THE FELLOW IS UNCOMMONLY ALLURING... UNCANNILY SO.
'TIS BEYOND COUNTING, THE NUMBER OF LASSES THAT DID OFFER HIM MONEY IN EXCHANGE FOR A NIGHT, BUT TO NO AVAIL. INSTEAD, HE DOTH OFFER THEM A WAGER. IF HE WINS, SHE DOTH PART WITH ONE RYO. IF SHE WINS, HIS BODY IS HERS TO DO WITH AS SHE LIKES... WELL, WHO COULD REFUSE?
CERTES, ANY RED-BLOODED LASS WOULD GIVE IT A TRY.
OH, SUCH A CALLOW MAID...
POOR LASS.
KRYK
SAKYO.

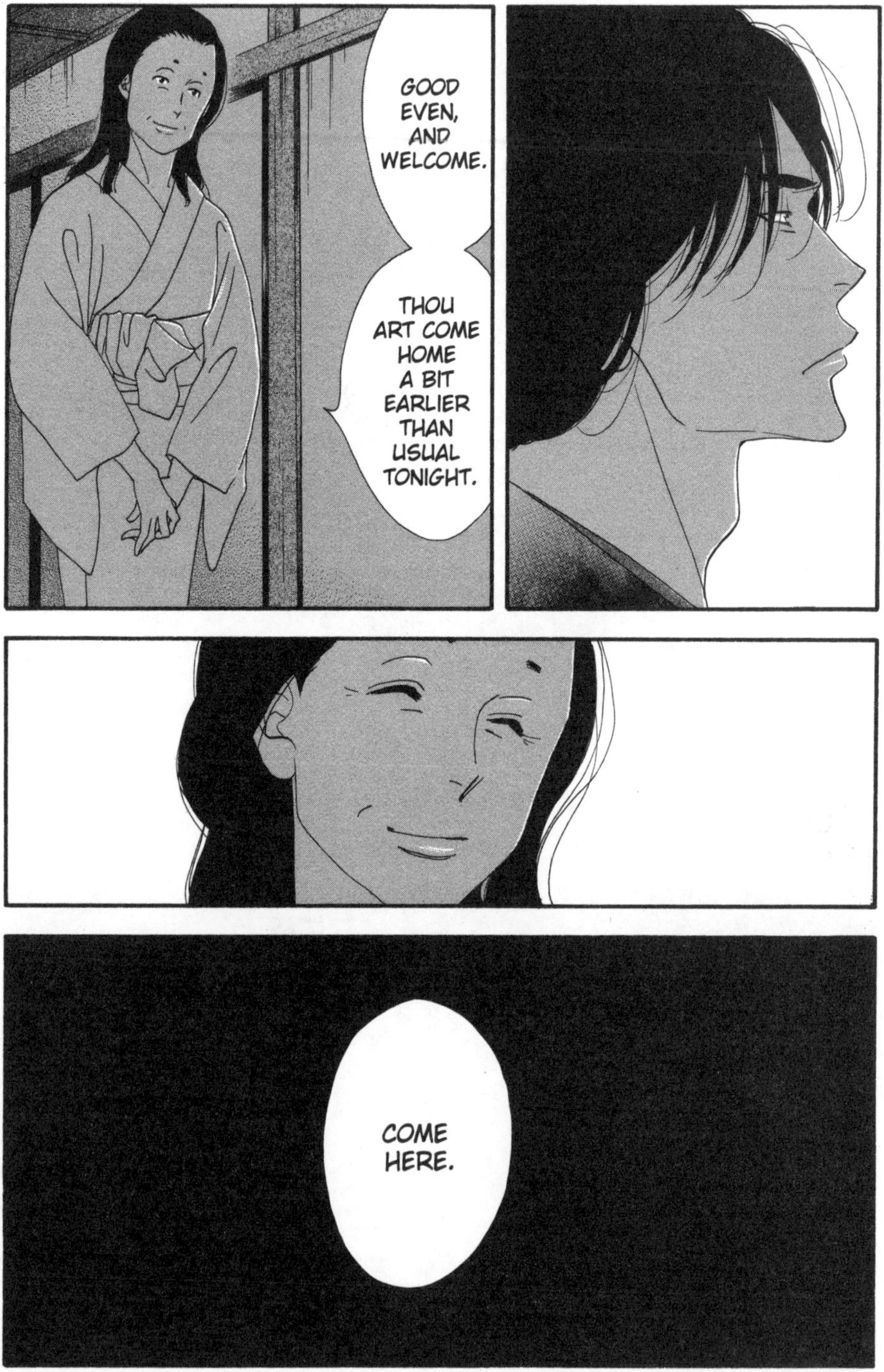
GOOD EVEN, AND WELCOME.
THOU ART COME HOME A BIT EARLIER THAN USUAL TONIGHT.
COME HERE.

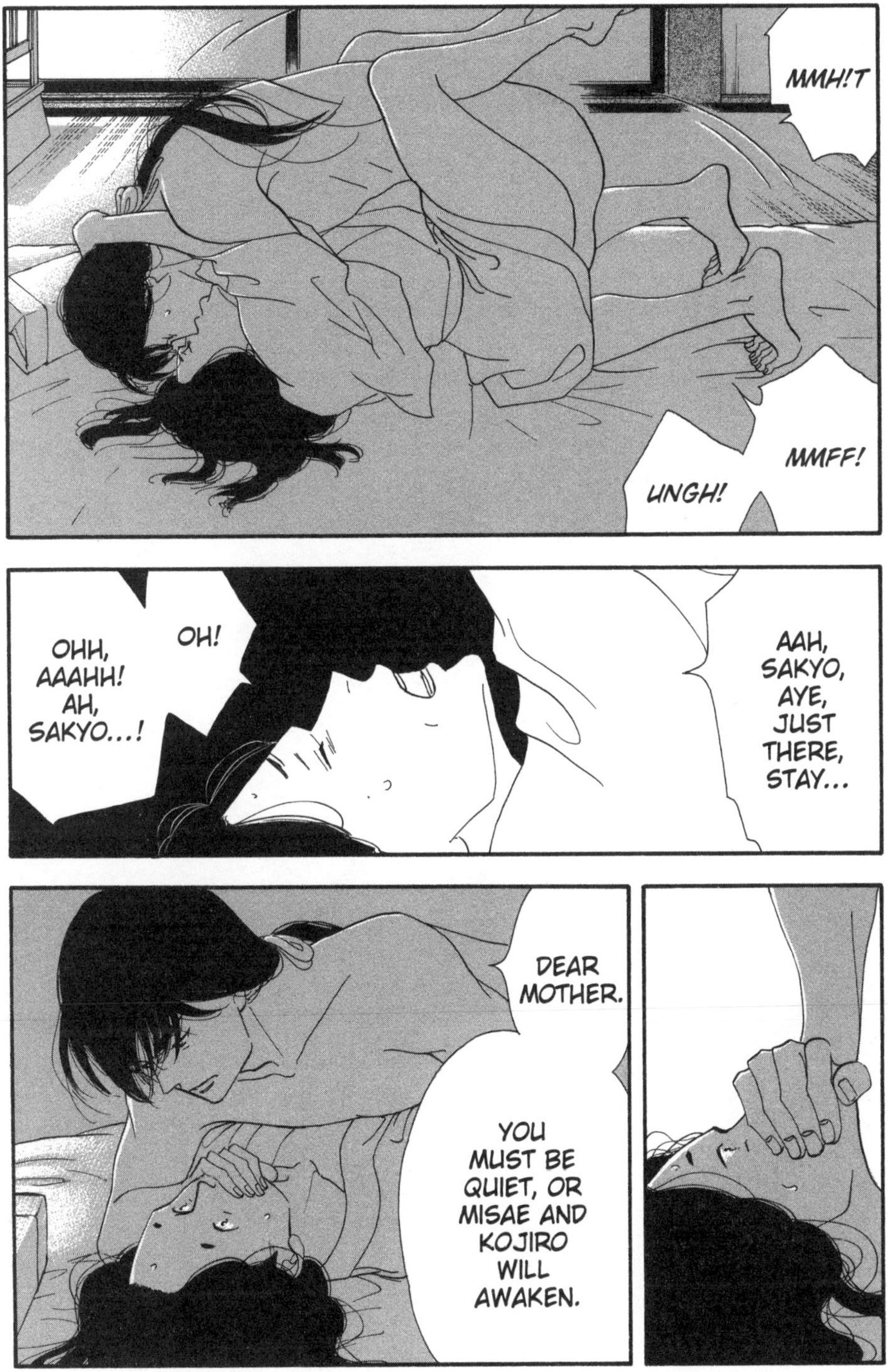
MMH!T
MMFF!
UNGH!
AAH, SAKYO, AYE, JUST THERE, STAY...
OH!
OHH, AAAHH! AH, SAKYO...!
DEAR MOTHER.
YOU MUST BE QUIET, OR MISAE AND KOJIRO WILL AWAKEN.

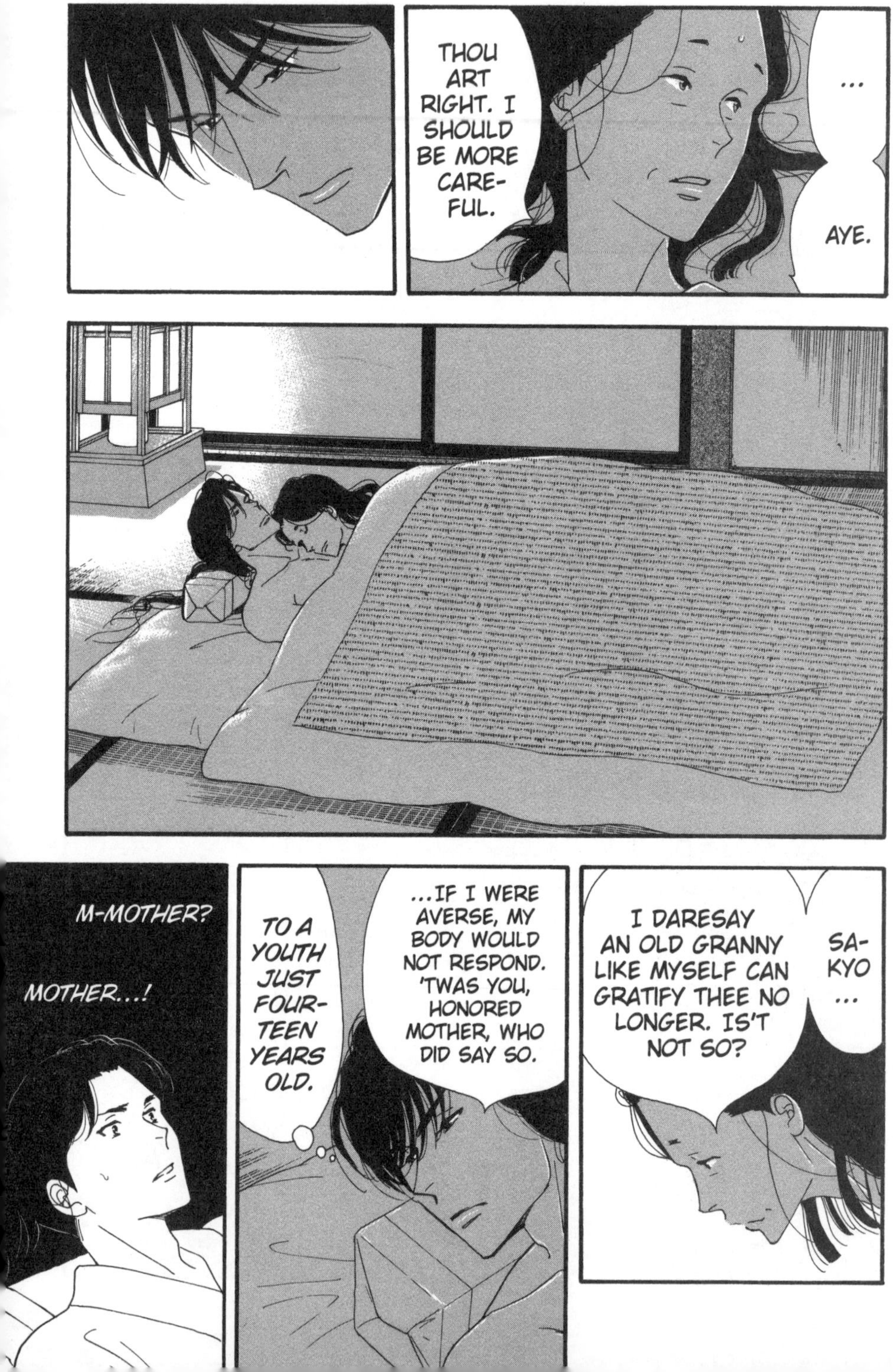
...
AYE.
THOU ART RIGHT. I SHOULD BE MORE CARE-FUL.
SA-KYO ...
I DARESAY AN OLD GRANNY LIKE MYSELF CAN GRATIFY THEE NO LONGER. IS'T NOT SO?
...IF I WERE AVERSE, MY BODY WOULD NOT RESPOND. 'TWAS YOU, HONORED MOTHER, WHO DID SAY SO.
TO A YOUTH JUST FOUR-TEEN YEARS OLD.
M-MOTHER?
MOTHER...!

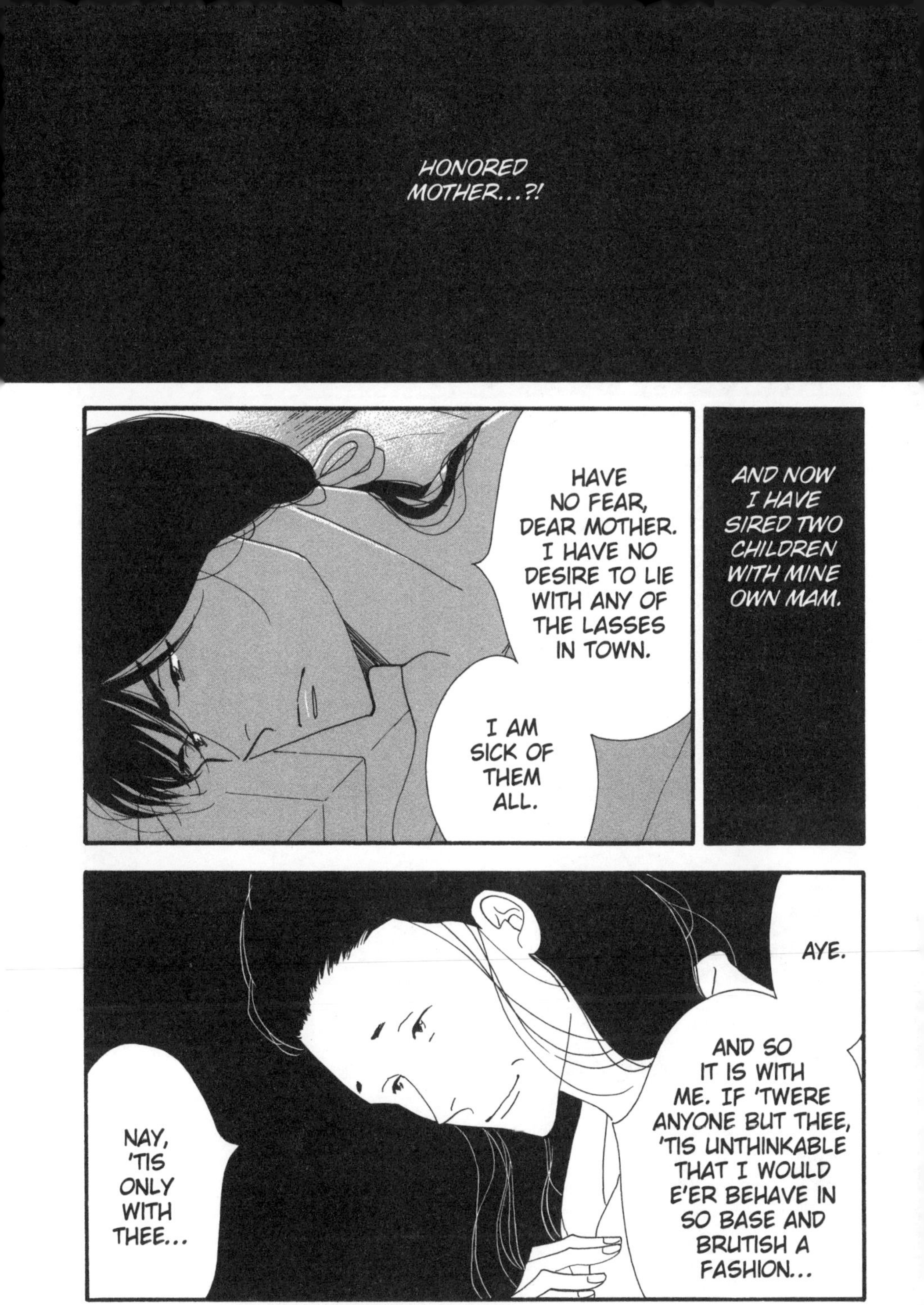
HONORED MOTHER...?!
AND NOW I HAVE SIRED TWO CHILDREN WITH MINE OWN MAM.
HAVE NO FEAR, DEAR MOTHER. I HAVE NO DESIRE TO LIE WITH ANY OF THE LASSES IN TOWN.
I AM SICK OF THEM ALL.
AYE.
AND SO IT IS WITH ME. IF 'TWERE ANYONE BUT THEE, 'TIS UNTHINKABLE THAT I WOULD E'ER BEHAVE IN SO BASE AND BRUTISH A FASHION...
NAY, 'TIS ONLY WITH THEE...

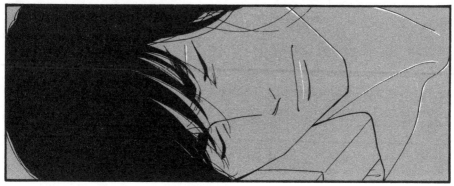

I'LL TAKE THIS ONE RYO COIN.

MY WIN.

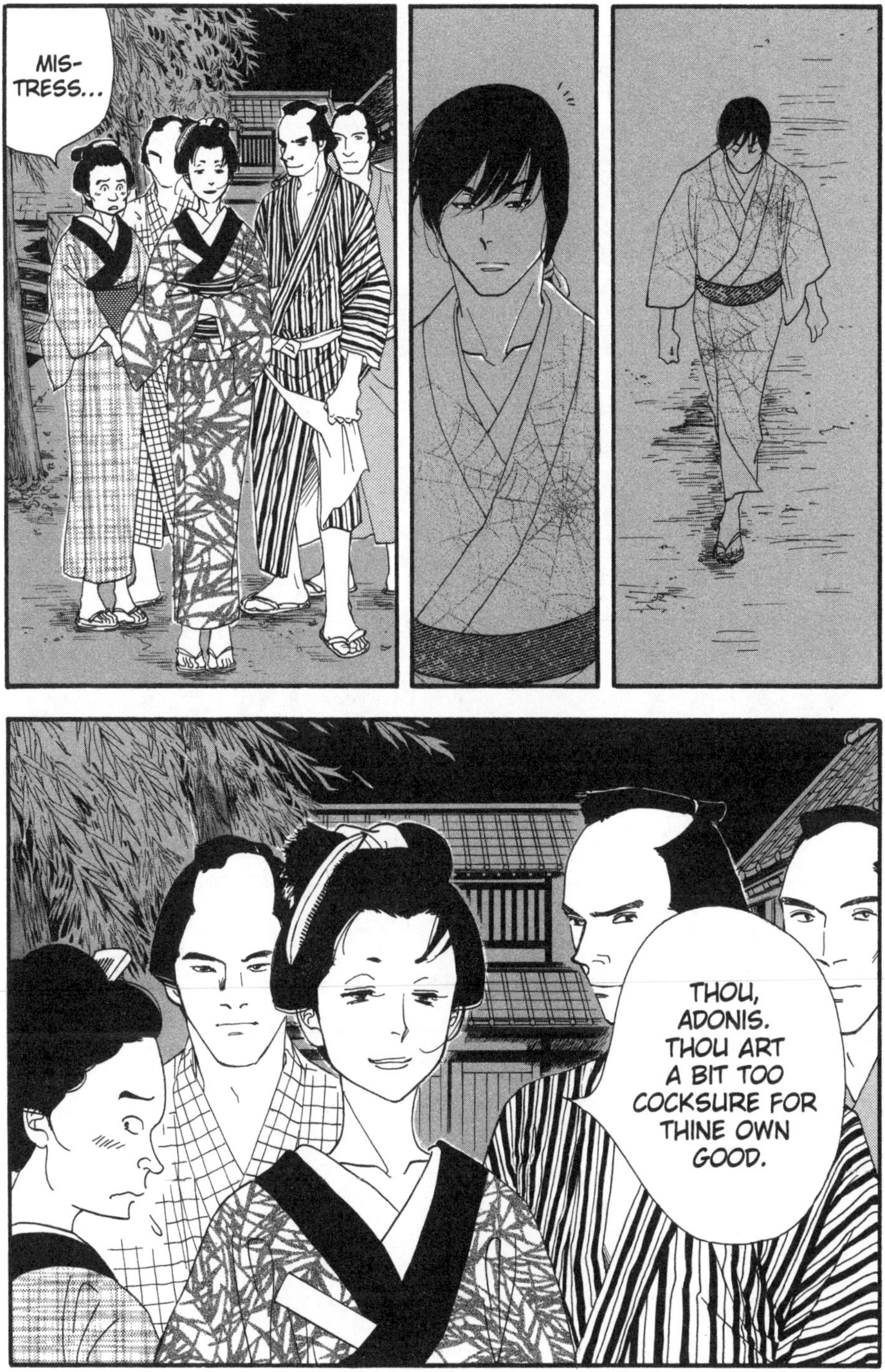
MIS-
TRESS...
THOU, ADONIS. THOU ART A BIT TOO COCKSURE FOR THINE OWN GOOD.

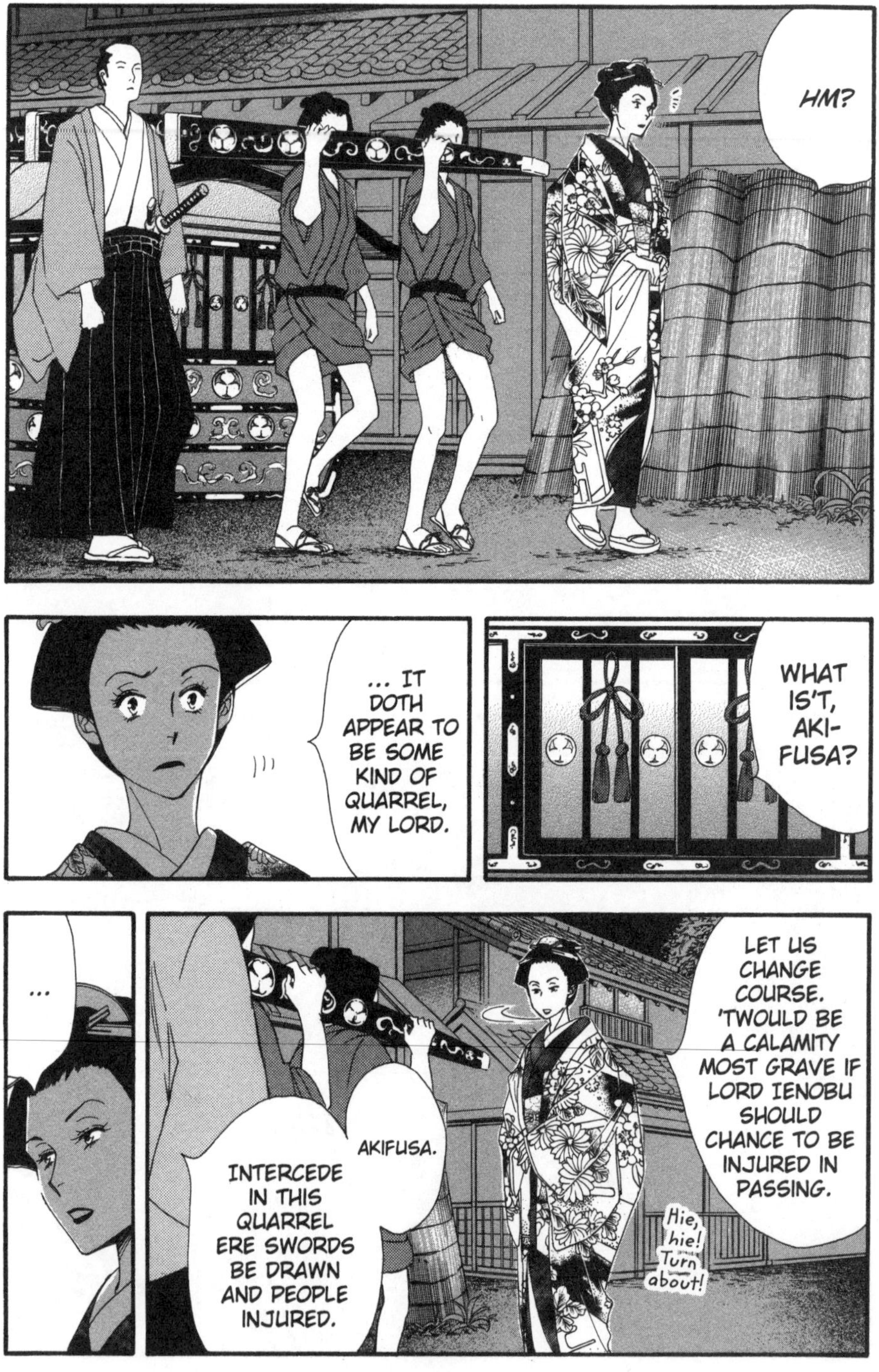
HM?
WHAT IS'T, AKI-FUSA?
... IT DOTH APPEAR TO BE SOME KIND OF QUARREL, MY LORD.
LET US CHANGE COURSE. 'TWOULD BE A CALAMITY MOST GRAVE IF LORD IENOBU SHOULD CHANCE TO BE INJURED IN PASSING.
Hie, hie! Turn about!
AKIFUSA.
INTERCEDE IN THIS QUARREL ERE SWORDS BE DRAWN AND PEOPLE INJURED.
...

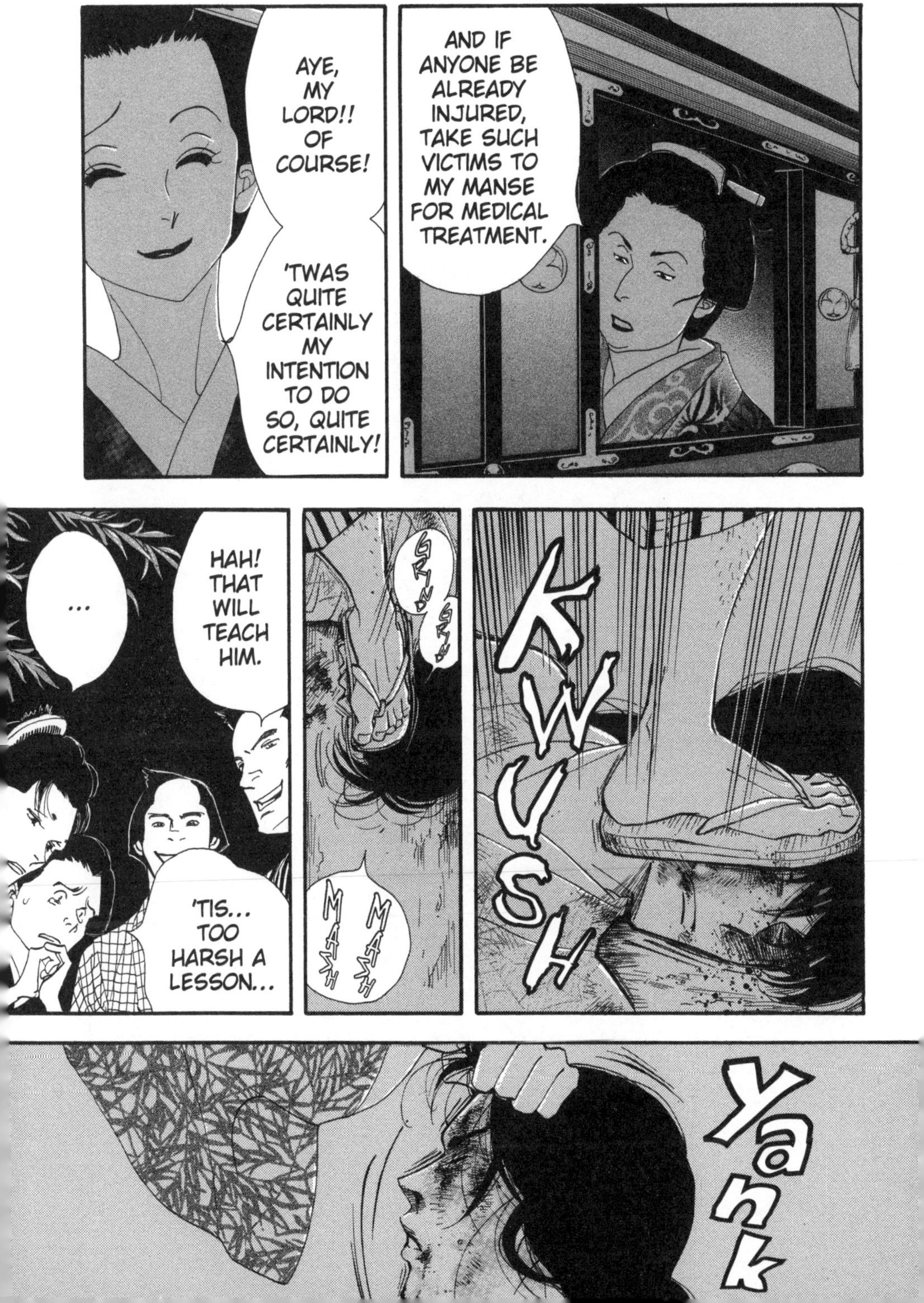
AND IF ANYONE BE ALREADY INJURED, TAKE SUCH VICTIMS TO MY MANSE FOR MEDICAL TREATMENT.
AYE, MY LORD!! OF COURSE!
'TWAS QUITE CERTAINLY MY INTENTION TO DO SO, QUITE CERTAINLY!
KWUSH
GRIND GRIND
MASH MASH
HAH! THAT WILL TEACH HIM.
...
'TIS... TOO HARSH A LESSON...
Yank

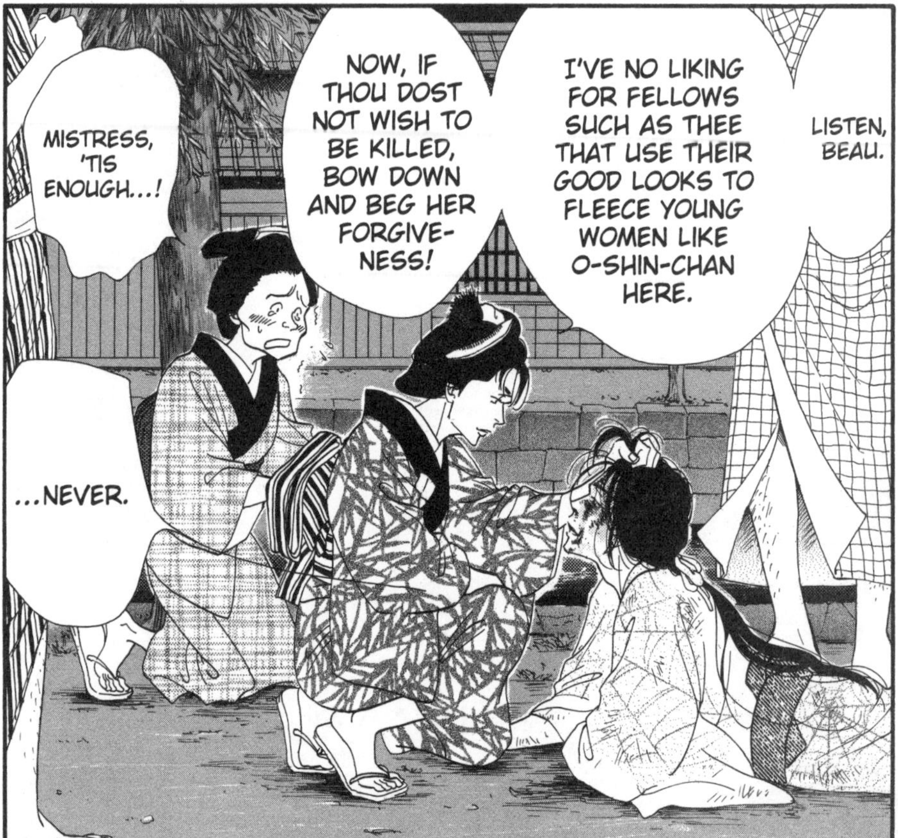
LISTEN, BEAU.
I'VE NO LIKING FOR FELLOWS SUCH AS THEE THAT USE THEIR GOOD LOOKS TO FLEECE YOUNG WOMEN LIKE O-SHIN-CHAN HERE.
NOW, IF THOU DOST NOT WISH TO BE KILLED, BOW DOWN AND BEG HER FORGIVE-NESS!
MISTRESS, 'TIS ENOUGH...!
...NEVER.

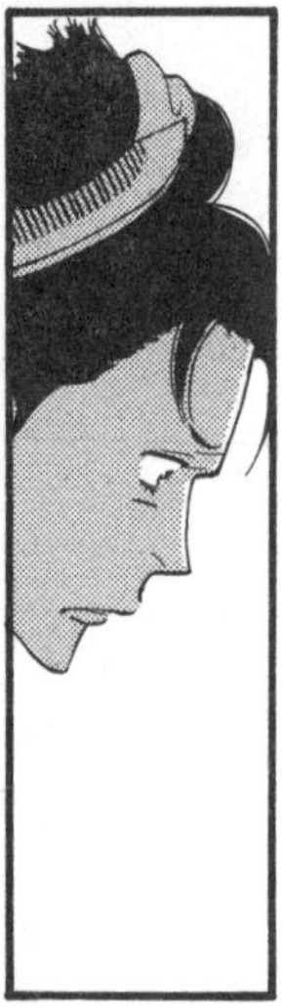

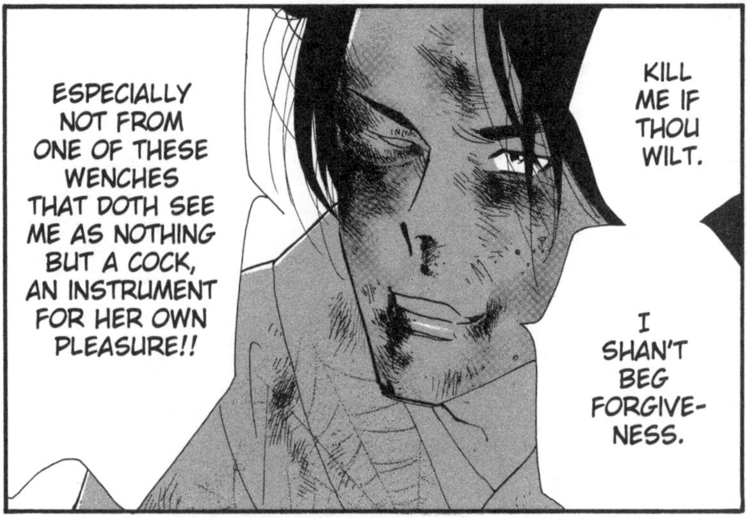
KILL ME IF THOU WILT.
I SHAN'T BEG FORGIVE-NESS.
ESPECIALLY NOT FROM ONE OF THESE WENCHES THAT DOTH SEE ME AS NOTHING BUT A COCK, AN INSTRUMENT FOR HER OWN PLEASURE!!

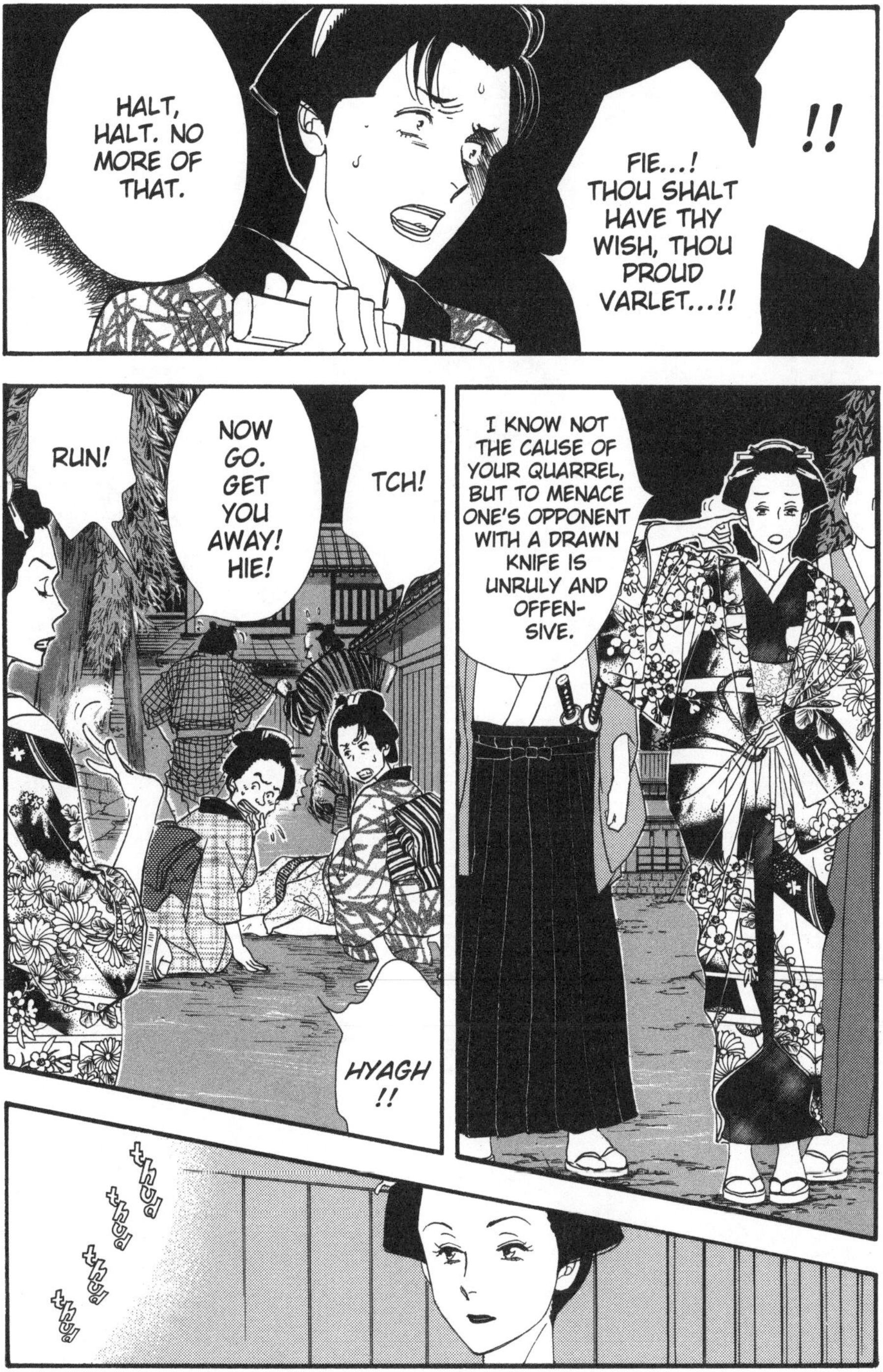
!!
FIE...! THOU SHALT HAVE THY WISH, THOU PROUD VARLET...!!
HALT, HALT. NO MORE OF THAT.
I KNOW NOT THE CAUSE OF YOUR QUARREL, BUT TO MENACE ONE'S OPPONENT WITH A DRAWN KNIFE IS UNRULY AND OFFEN-SIVE.
TCH!
NOW GO. GET YOU AWAY! HIE!
RUN!
HYAGH !!
thud thud thud thud

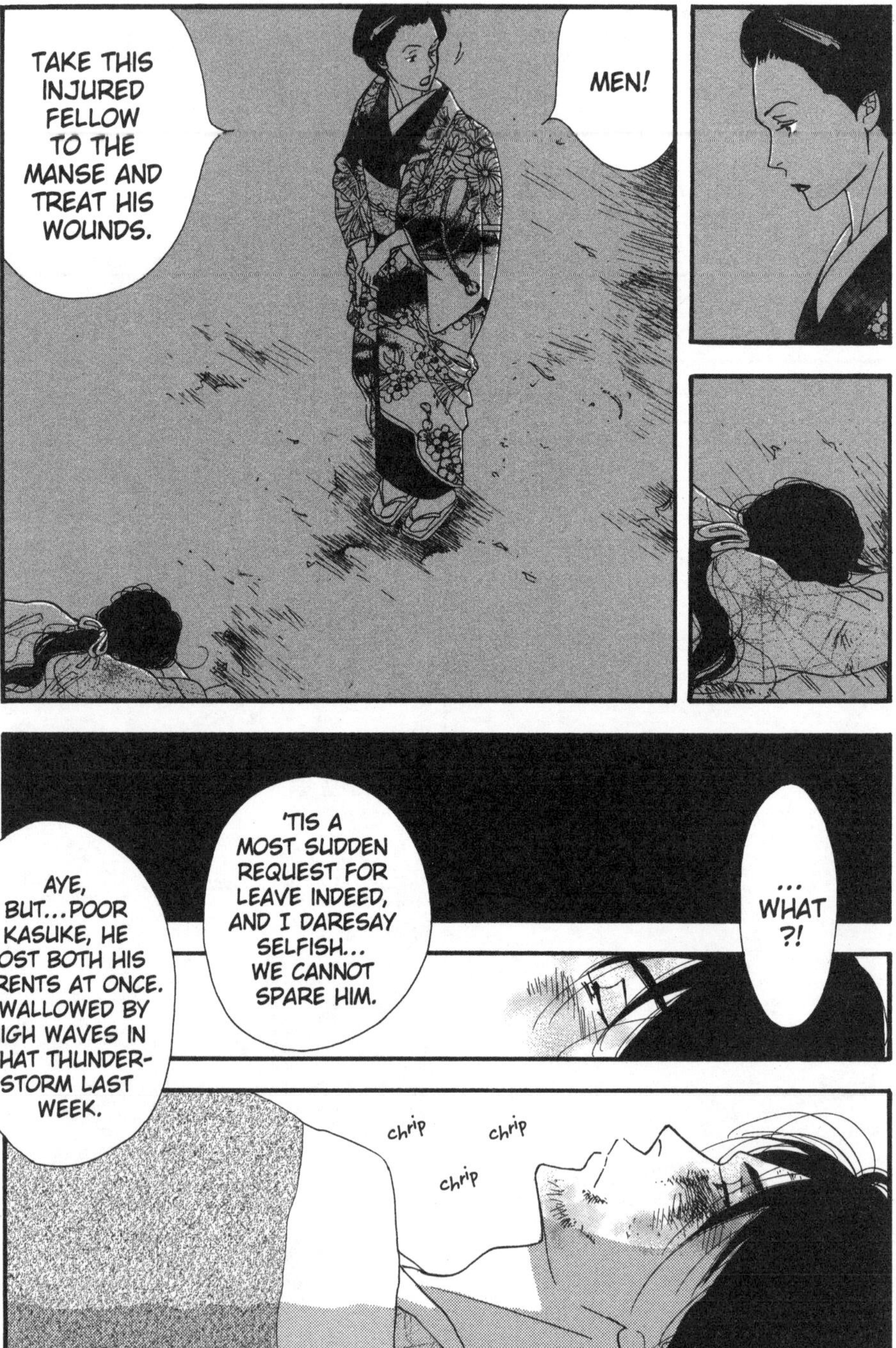
MEN!
TAKE THIS INJURED FELLOW TO THE MANSE AND TREAT HIS WOUNDS.
...WHAT?!
'TIS A MOST SUDDEN REQUEST FOR LEAVE INDEED, AND I DARESAY SELFISH... WE CANNOT SPARE HIM.
AYE, BUT...POOR KASUKE, HE LOST BOTH HIS PARENTS AT ONCE. SWALLOWED BY HIGH WAVES IN THAT THUNDER-STORM LAST WEEK.
chrip
chrip
chrip

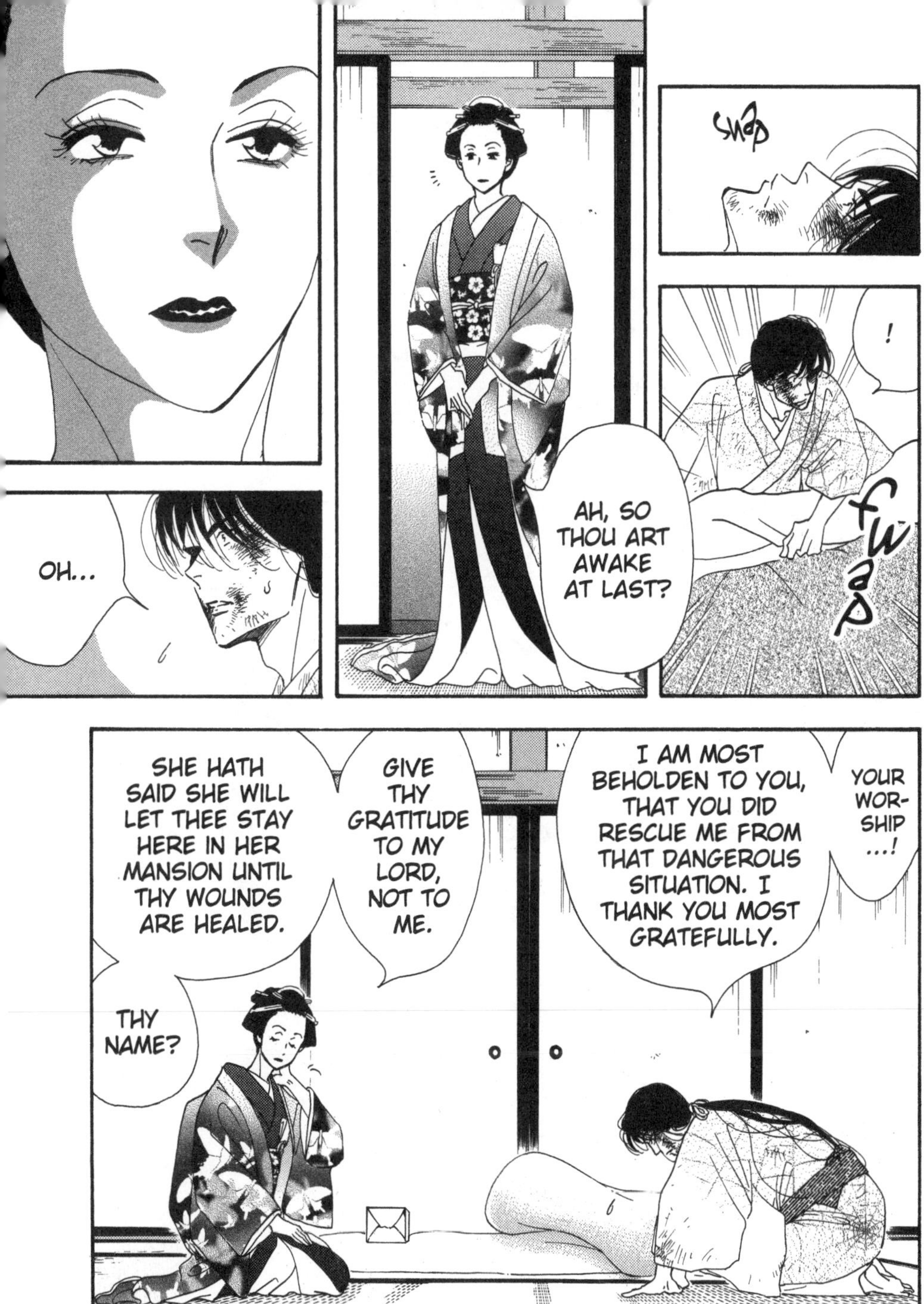
SNAP
!
FWAP
AH, SO THOU ART AWAKE AT LAST?
OH...
YOUR WORSHIP...!
I AM MOST BEHOLDEN TO YOU, THAT YOU DID RESCUE ME FROM THAT DANGEROUS SITUATION. I THANK YOU MOST GRATEFULLY.
GIVE THY GRATITUDE TO MY LORD, NOT TO ME.
SHE HATH SAID SHE WILL LET THEE STAY HERE IN HER MANSION UNTIL THY WOUNDS ARE HEALED.
THY NAME?

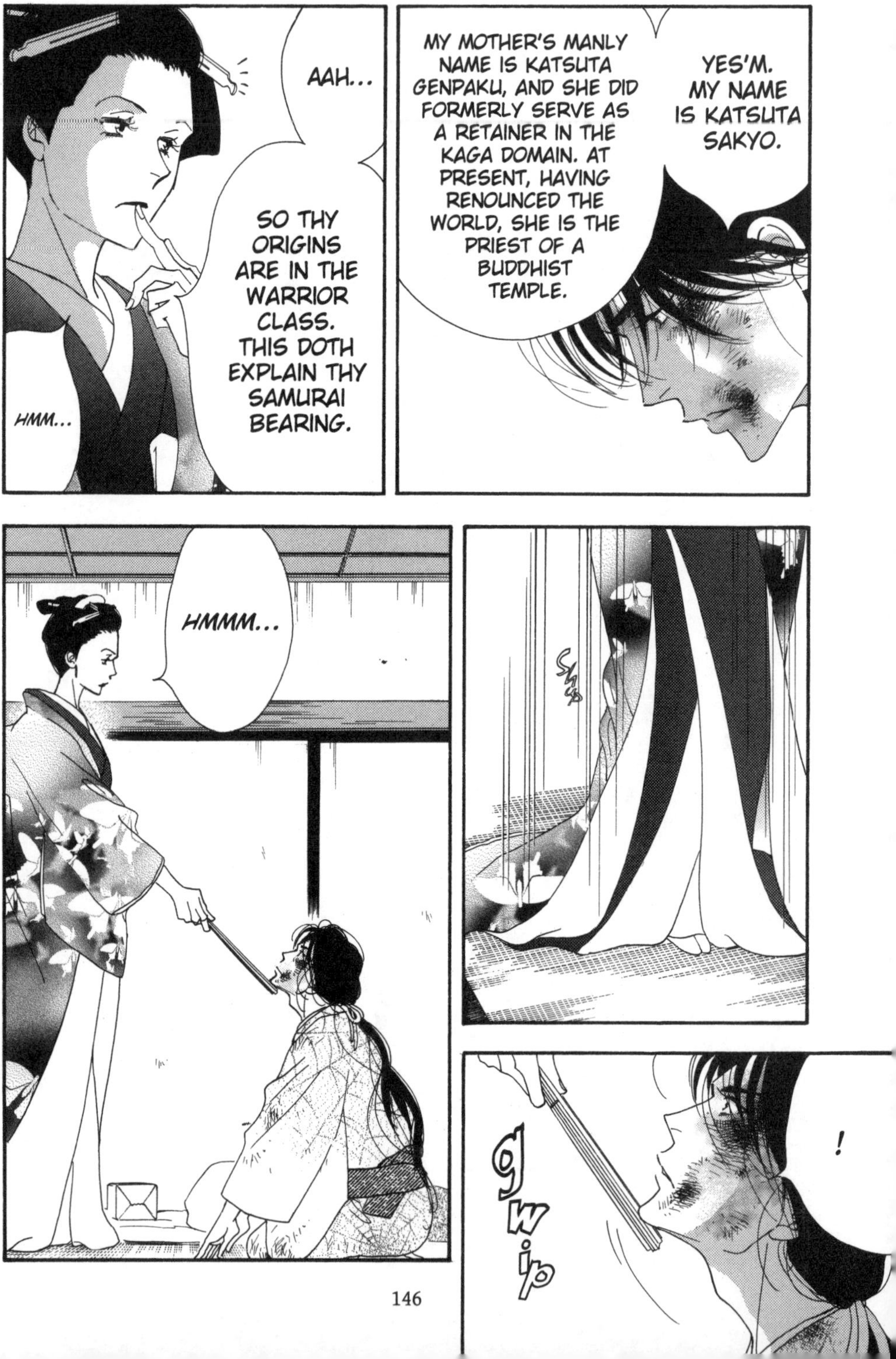
YES'M. MY NAME IS KATSUTA SAKYO.
MY MOTHER'S MANLY NAME IS KATSUTA GENPAKU, AND SHE DID FORMERLY SERVE AS A RETAINER IN THE KAGA DOMAIN. AT PRESENT, HAVING RENOUNCED THE WORLD, SHE IS THE PRIEST OF A BUDDHIST TEMPLE.
AAH...
SO THY ORIGINS ARE IN THE WARRIOR CLASS. THIS DOTH EXPLAIN THY SAMURAI BEARING.
HMM...
Shup
!
gwip
HMMM...

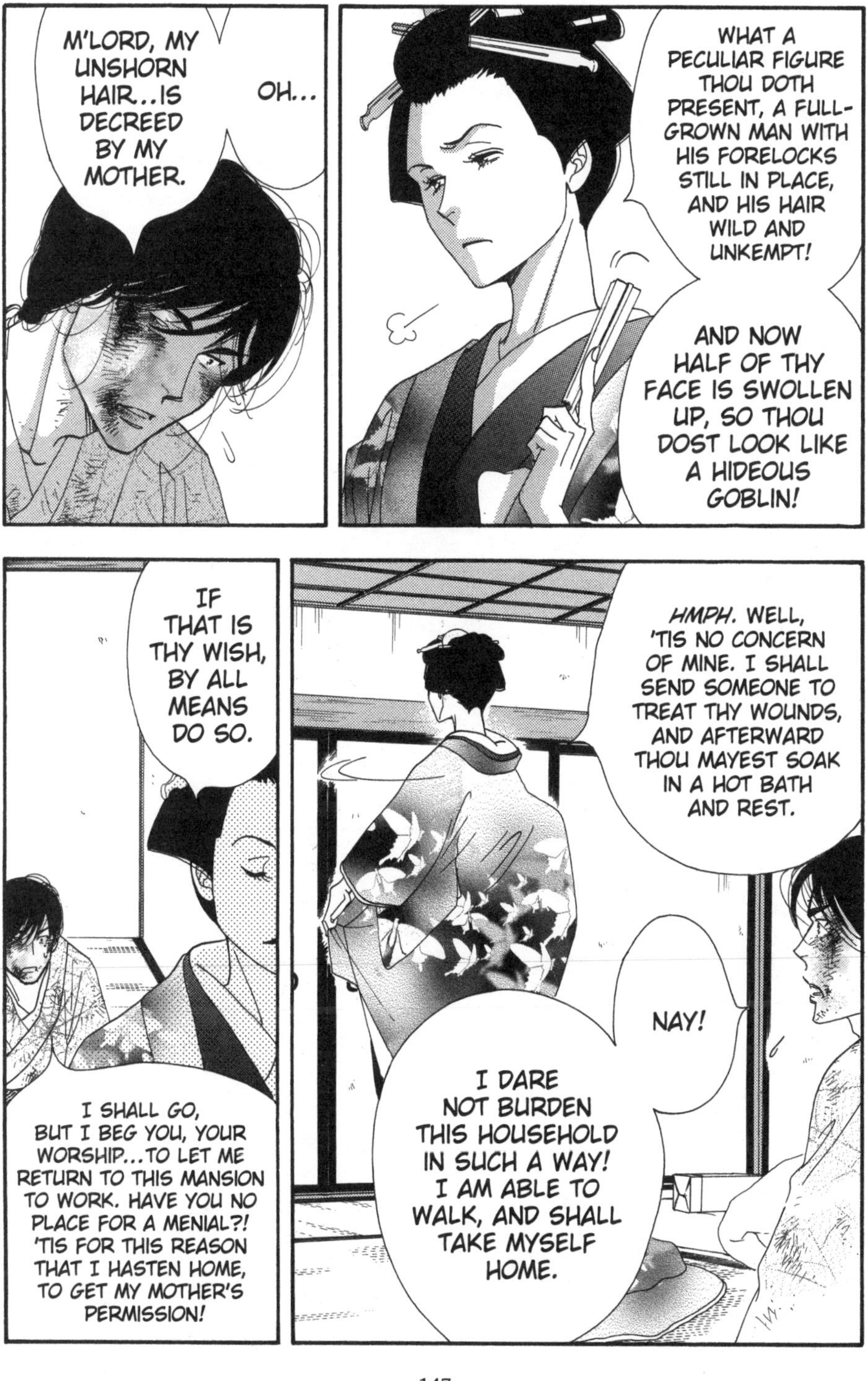
WHAT A PECULIAR FIGURE THOU DOTH PRESENT, A FULL-GROWN MAN WITH HIS FORELOCKS STILL IN PLACE, AND HIS HAIR WILD AND UNKEMPT!
AND NOW HALF OF THY FACE IS SWOLLEN UP, SO THOU DOST LOOK LIKE A HIDEOUS GOBLIN!
OH...
M'LORD, MY UNSHORN HAIR...IS DECREED BY MY MOTHER.
HMPH. WELL, 'TIS NO CONCERN OF MINE. I SHALL SEND SOMEONE TO TREAT THY WOUNDS, AND AFTERWARD THOU MAYEST SOAK IN A HOT BATH AND REST.
NAY!
I DARE NOT BURDEN THIS HOUSEHOLD IN SUCH A WAY! I AM ABLE TO WALK, AND SHALL TAKE MYSELF HOME.
IF THAT IS THY WISH, BY ALL MEANS DO SO.
I SHALL GO, BUT I BEG YOU, YOUR WORSHIP...TO LET ME RETURN TO THIS MANSION TO WORK. HAVE YOU NO PLACE FOR A MENIAL?! 'TIS FOR THIS REASON THAT I HASTEN HOME, TO GET MY MOTHER'S PERMISSION!

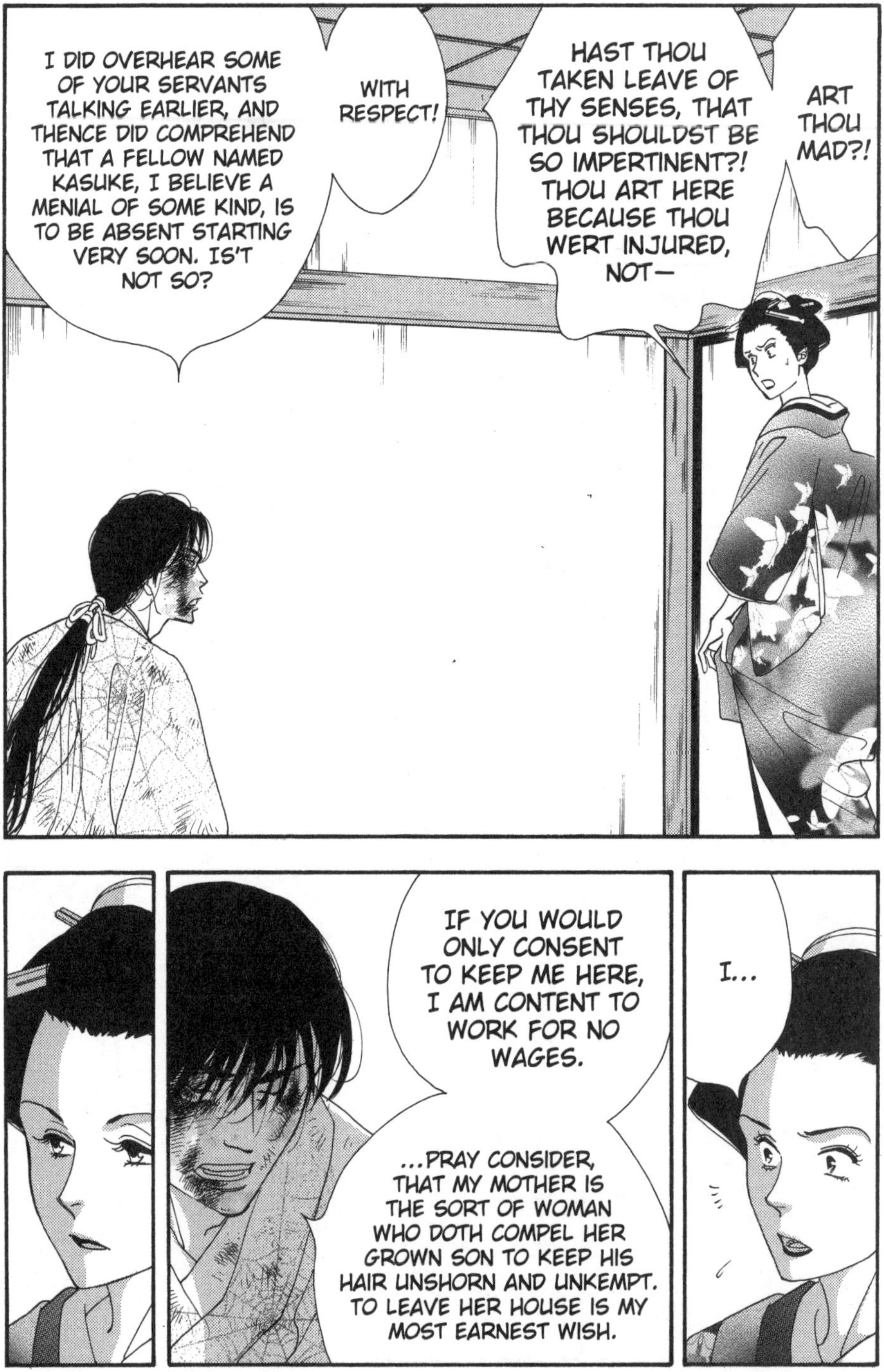
ART THOU MAD?!
HAST THOU TAKEN LEAVE OF THY SENSES, THAT THOU SHOULDST BE SO IMPERTINENT?! THOU ART HERE BECAUSE THOU WERT INJURED, NOT—
WITH RESPECT!
I DID OVERHEAR SOME OF YOUR SERVANTS TALKING EARLIER, AND THENCE DID COMPREHEND THAT A FELLOW NAMED KASUKE, I BELIEVE A MENIAL OF SOME KIND, IS TO BE ABSENT STARTING VERY SOON. IS'T NOT SO?
I...
IF YOU WOULD ONLY CONSENT TO KEEP ME HERE, I AM CONTENT TO WORK FOR NO WAGES.
...PRAY CONSIDER, THAT MY MOTHER IS THE SORT OF WOMAN WHO DOTH COMPEL HER GROWN SON TO KEEP HIS HAIR UNSHORN AND UNKEMPT. TO LEAVE HER HOUSE IS MY MOST EARNEST WISH.

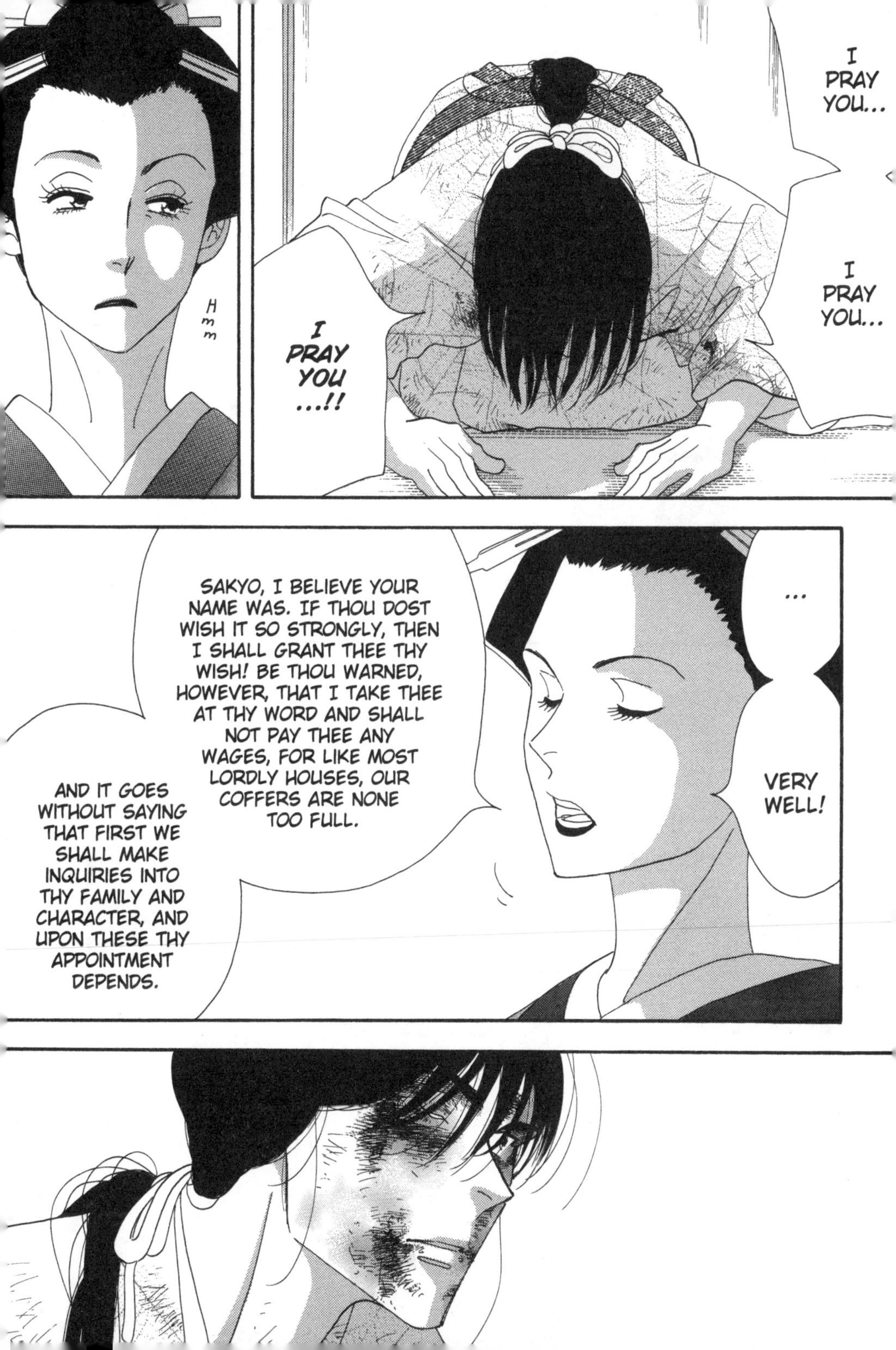
I PRAY YOU...
I PRAY YOU...
I PRAY YOU...!!
Hmm
...
VERY WELL!
SAKYO, I BELIEVE YOUR NAME WAS. IF THOU DOST WISH IT SO STRONGLY, THEN I SHALL GRANT THEE THY WISH! BE THOU WARNED, HOWEVER, THAT I TAKE THEE AT THY WORD AND SHALL NOT PAY THEE ANY WAGES, FOR LIKE MOST LORDLY HOUSES, OUR COFFERS ARE NONE TOO FULL.
AND IT GOES WITHOUT SAYING THAT FIRST WE SHALL MAKE INQUIRIES INTO THY FAMILY AND CHARACTER, AND UPON THESE THY APPOINTMENT DEPENDS.

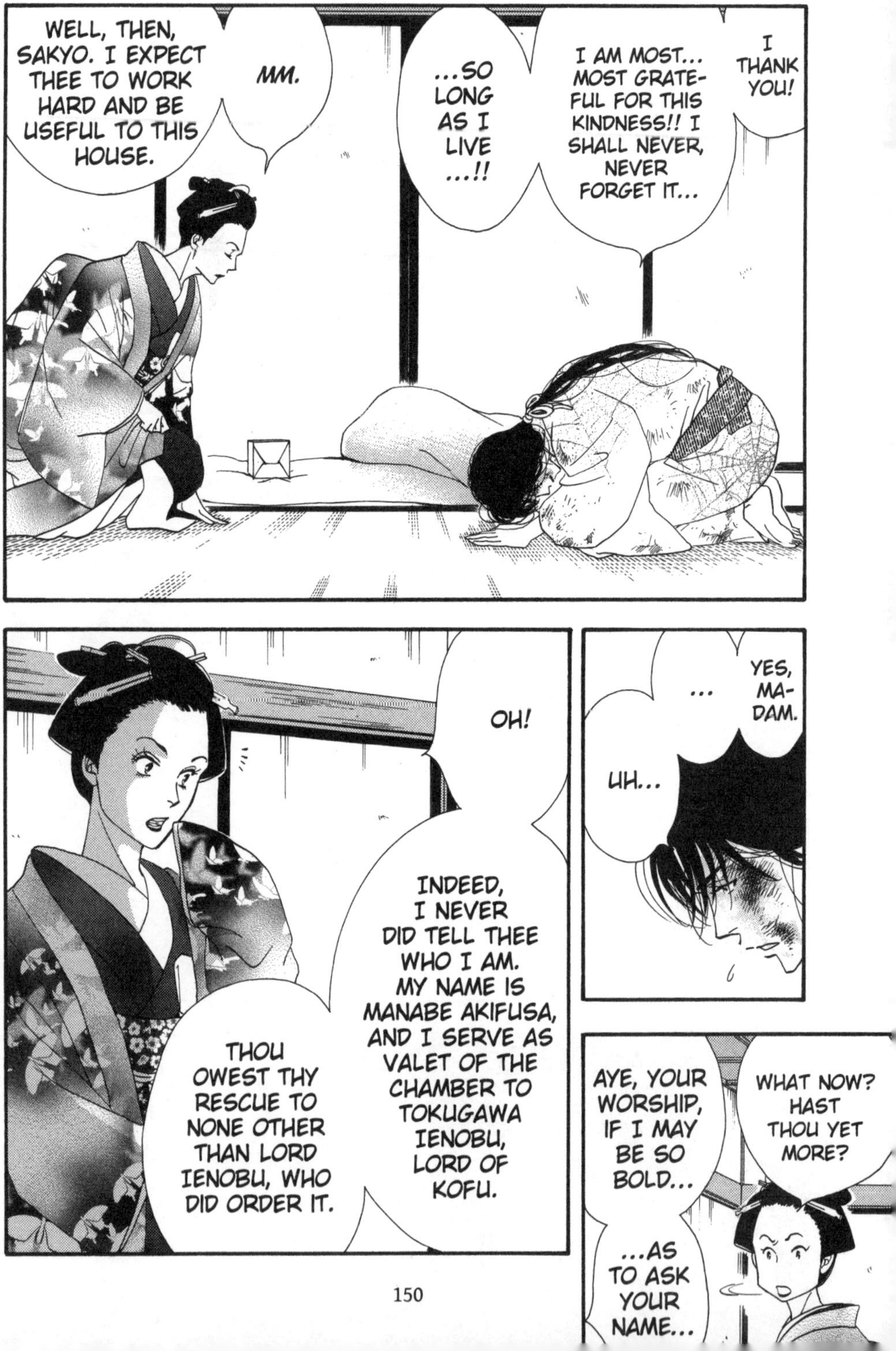
I THANK YOU!
I AM MOST... MOST GRATEFUL FOR THIS KINDNESS!! I SHALL NEVER, NEVER FORGET IT...
...SO LONG AS I LIVE...!!
MM.
WELL, THEN, SAKYO. I EXPECT THEE TO WORK HARD AND BE USEFUL TO THIS HOUSE.
YES, MADAM.
...
UH...
WHAT NOW? HAST THOU YET MORE?
AYE, YOUR WORSHIP, IF I MAY BE SO BOLD...
...AS TO ASK YOUR NAME...
OH!
INDEED, I NEVER DID TELL THEE WHO I AM. MY NAME IS MANABE AKIFUSA, AND I SERVE AS VALET OF THE CHAMBER TO TOKUGAWA IENOBU, LORD OF KOFU.
THOU OWEST THY RESCUE TO NONE OTHER THAN LORD IENOBU, WHO DID ORDER IT.

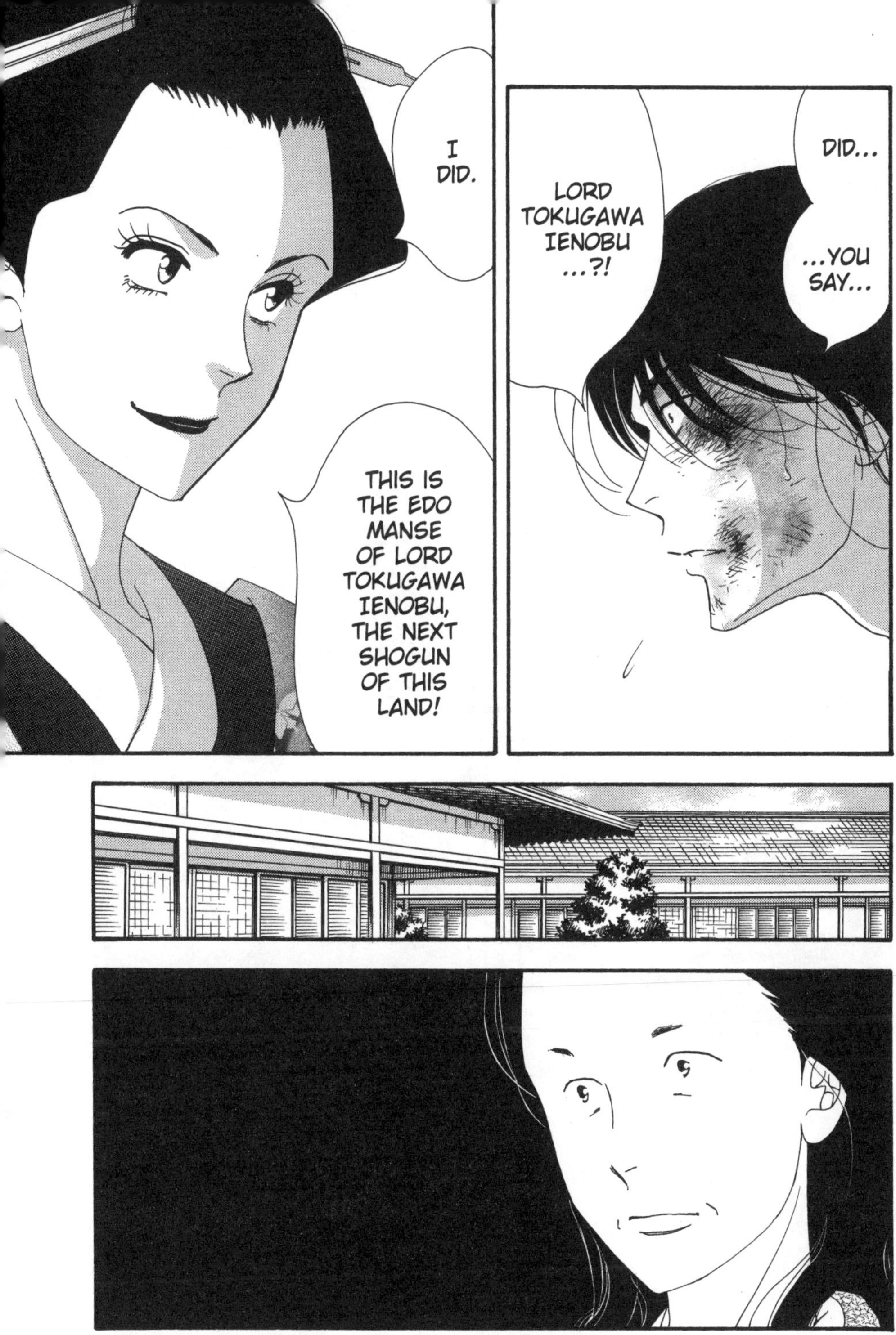
DID...
...YOU SAY...
LORD TOKUGAWA IENOBU ...?!
I DID.
THIS IS THE EDO MANSE OF LORD TOKUGAWA IENOBU, THE NEXT SHOGUN OF THIS LAND!

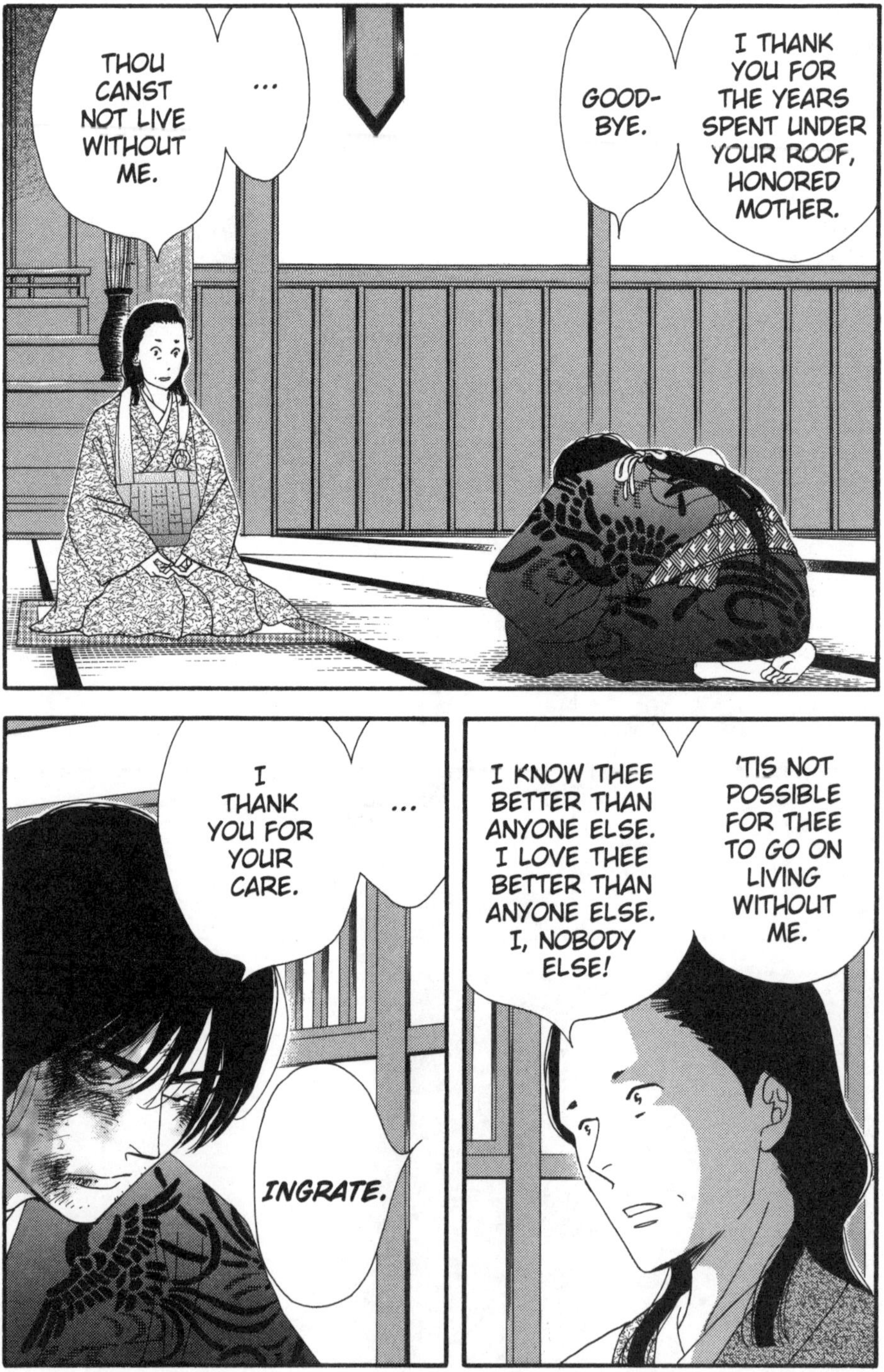
I THANK YOU FOR THE YEARS SPENT UNDER YOUR ROOF, HONORED MOTHER.
GOOD-BYE.
...
THOU CANST NOT LIVE WITHOUT ME.
'TIS NOT POSSIBLE FOR THEE TO GO ON LIVING WITHOUT ME.
I KNOW THEE BETTER THAN ANYONE ELSE. I LOVE THEE BETTER THAN ANYONE ELSE. I, NOBODY ELSE!
...
I THANK YOU FOR YOUR CARE.
INGRATE.

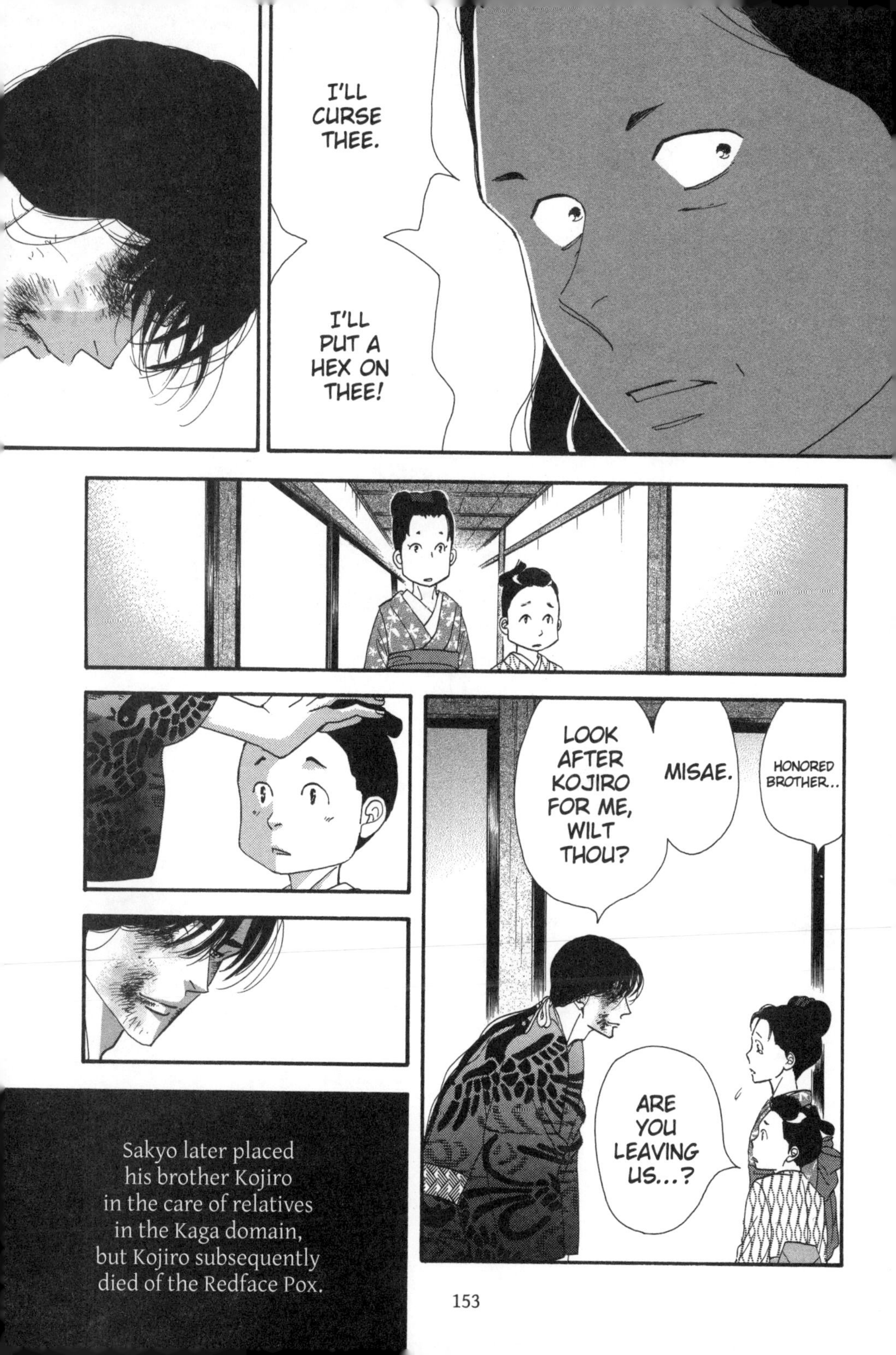
I'LL CURSE THEE.
I'LL PUT A HEX ON THEE!
HONORED BROTHER...
MISAE.
LOOK AFTER KOJIRO FOR ME, WILT THOU?
ARE YOU LEAVING US...?
Sakyo later placed his brother Kojiro in the care of relatives in the Kaga domain, but Kojiro subsequently died of the Redface Pox.

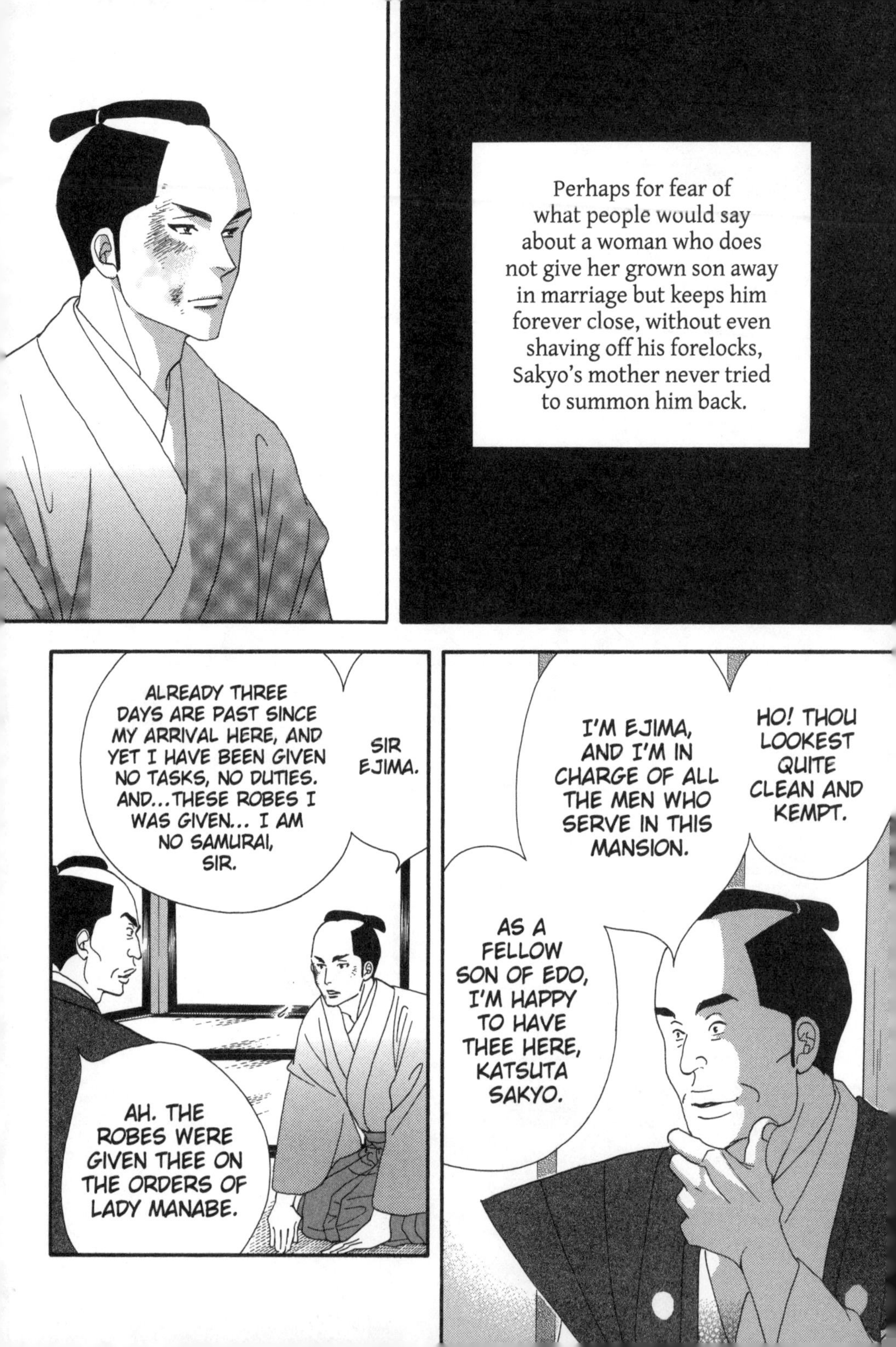
Perhaps for fear of what people would say about a woman who does not give her grown son away in marriage but keeps him forever close, without even shaving off his forelocks, Sakyo's mother never tried to summon him back.
HO! THOU LOOKEST QUITE CLEAN AND KEMPT.
I'M EJIMA, AND I'M IN CHARGE OF ALL THE MEN WHO SERVE IN THIS MANSION.
AS A FELLOW SON OF EDO, I'M HAPPY TO HAVE THEE HERE, KATSUTA SAKYO.
SIR EJIMA.
ALREADY THREE DAYS ARE PAST SINCE MY ARRIVAL HERE, AND YET I HAVE BEEN GIVEN NO TASKS, NO DUTIES. AND...THESE ROBES I WAS GIVEN... I AM NO SAMURAI, SIR.
AH. THE ROBES WERE GIVEN THEE ON THE ORDERS OF LADY MANABE.

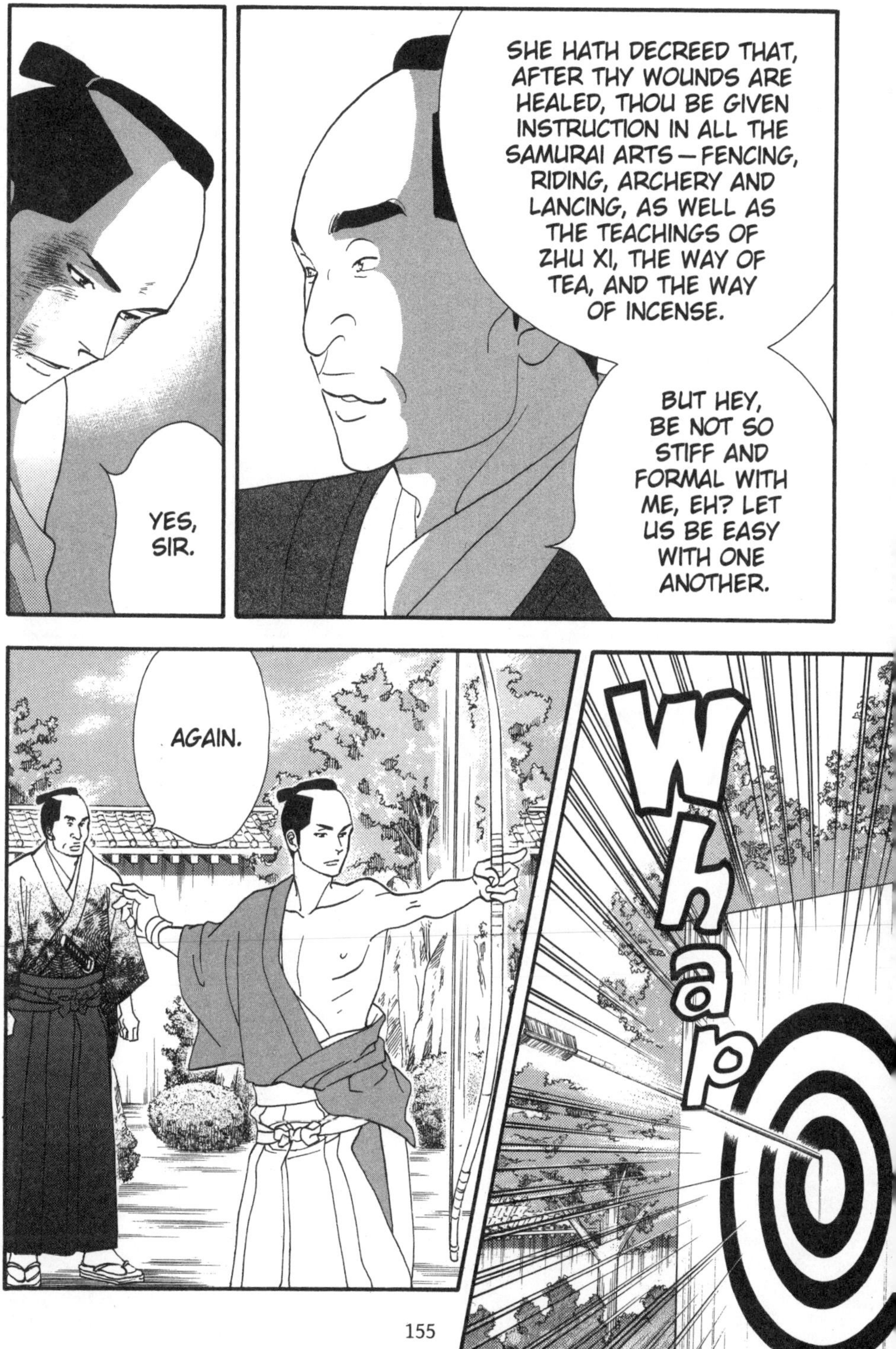
SHE HATH DECREED THAT, AFTER THY WOUNDS ARE HEALED, THOU BE GIVEN INSTRUCTION IN ALL THE SAMURAI ARTS—FENCING, RIDING, ARCHERY AND LANCING, AS WELL AS THE TEACHINGS OF ZHU XI, THE WAY OF TEA, AND THE WAY OF INCENSE.
BUT HEY, BE NOT SO STIFF AND FORMAL WITH ME, EH? LET US BE EASY WITH ONE ANOTHER.
YES, SIR.
Whap
AGAIN.

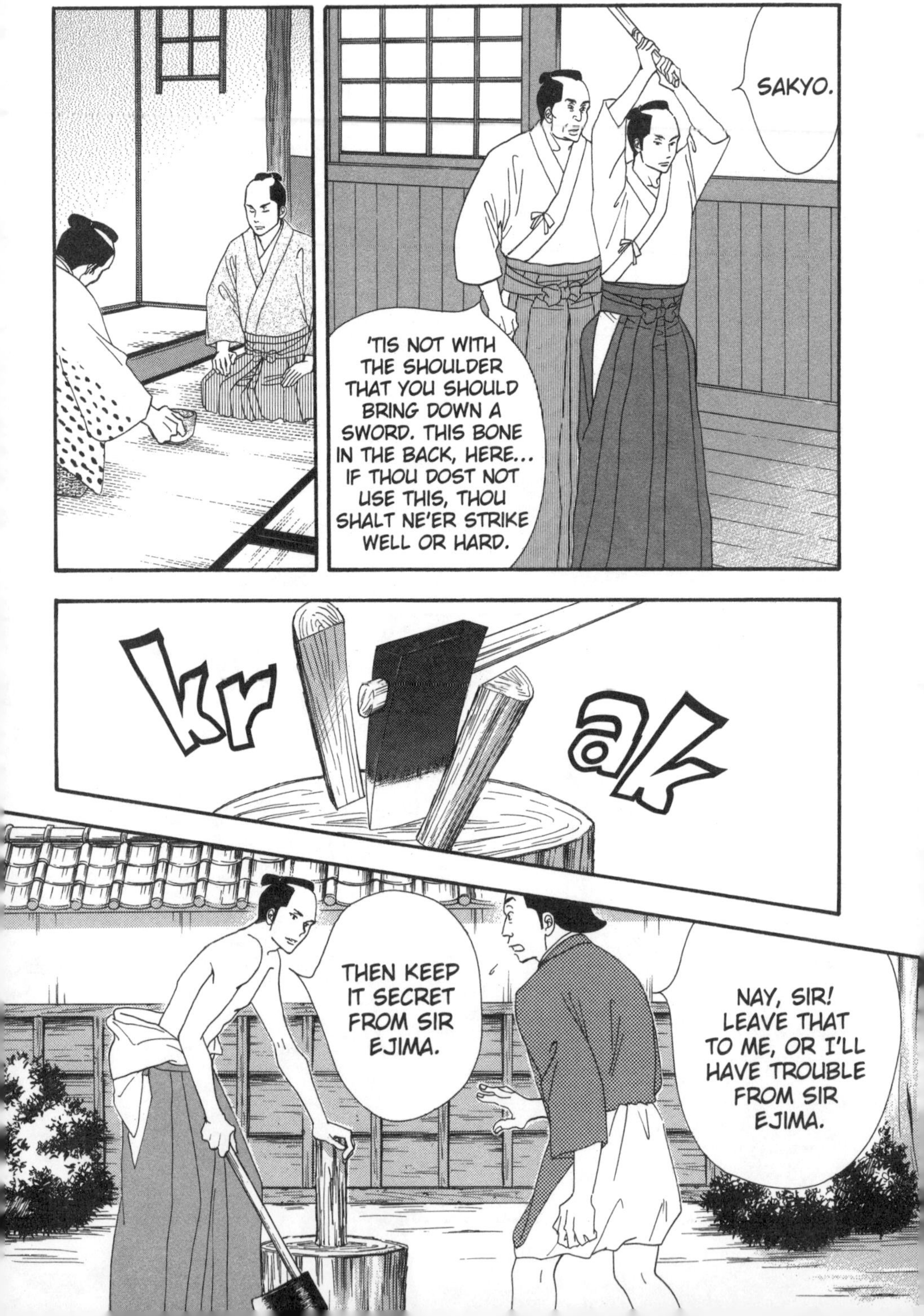
SAKYO.
'TIS NOT WITH THE SHOULDER THAT YOU SHOULD BRING DOWN A SWORD. THIS BONE IN THE BACK, HERE... IF THOU DOST NOT USE THIS, THOU SHALT NE'ER STRIKE WELL OR HARD.
kr ak
NAY, SIR! LEAVE THAT TO ME, OR I'LL HAVE TROUBLE FROM SIR EJIMA.
THEN KEEP IT SECRET FROM SIR EJIMA.

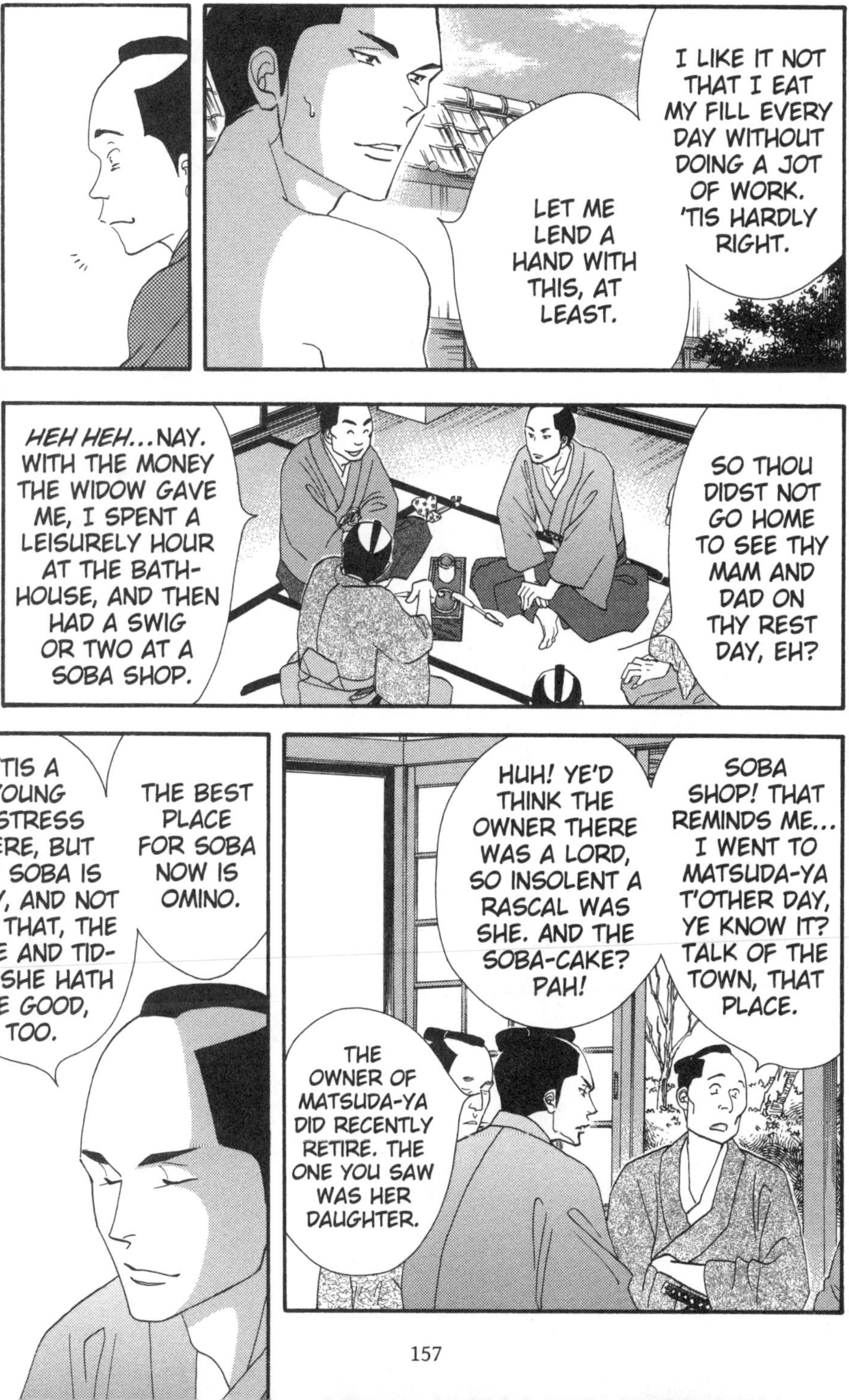
I LIKE IT NOT THAT I EAT MY FILL EVERY DAY WITHOUT DOING A JOT OF WORK. 'TIS HARDLY RIGHT.
LET ME LEND A HAND WITH THIS, AT LEAST.
SO THOU DIDST NOT GO HOME TO SEE THY MAM AND DAD ON THY REST DAY, EH?
*HEH HEH...*NAY. WITH THE MONEY THE WIDOW GAVE ME, I SPENT A LEISURELY HOUR AT THE BATH-HOUSE, AND THEN HAD A SWIG OR TWO AT A SOBA SHOP.
SOBA SHOP! THAT REMINDS ME... I WENT TO MATSUDA-YA T'OTHER DAY, YE KNOW IT? TALK OF THE TOWN, THAT PLACE.
HUH! YE'D THINK THE OWNER THERE WAS A LORD, SO INSOLENT A RASCAL WAS SHE. AND THE SOBA-CAKE? PAH!
THE OWNER OF MATSUDA-YA DID RECENTLY RETIRE. THE ONE YOU SAW WAS HER DAUGHTER.
THE BEST PLACE FOR SOBA NOW IS OMINO.
'TIS A YOUNG MISTRESS THERE, BUT HER SOBA IS TASTY, AND NOT ONLY THAT, THE SAKE AND TID-BITS SHE HATH ARE GOOD, TOO.

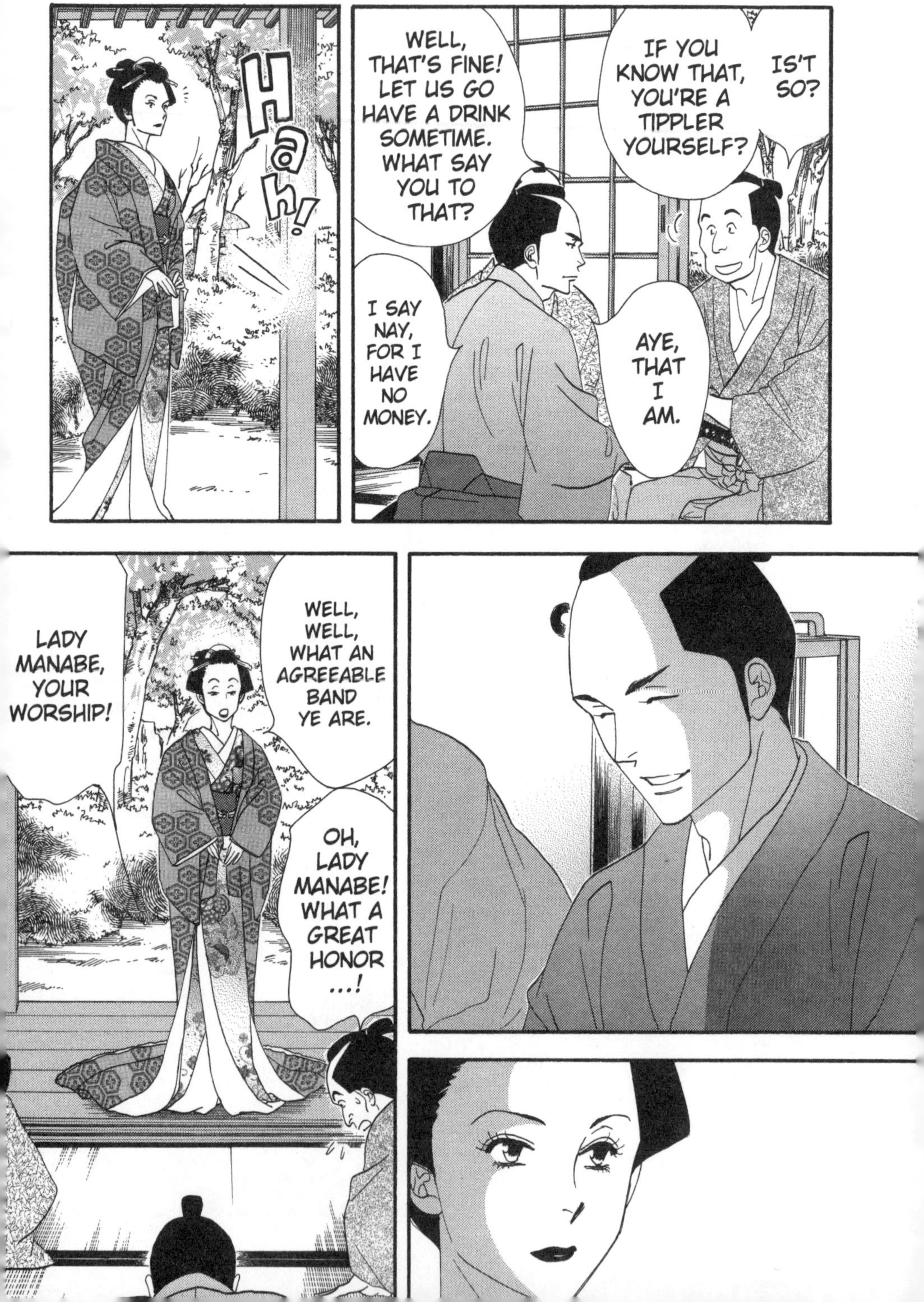
IF YOU KNOW THAT, YOU'RE A TIPPLER YOURSELF?
IS'T SO?
AYE, THAT I AM.
WELL, THAT'S FINE! LET US GO HAVE A DRINK SOMETIME. WHAT SAY YOU TO THAT?
I SAY NAY, FOR I HAVE NO MONEY.
Hah!
WELL, WELL, WHAT AN AGREEABLE BAND YE ARE.
OH, LADY MANABE! WHAT A GREAT HONOR ...!
LADY MANABE, YOUR WORSHIP!

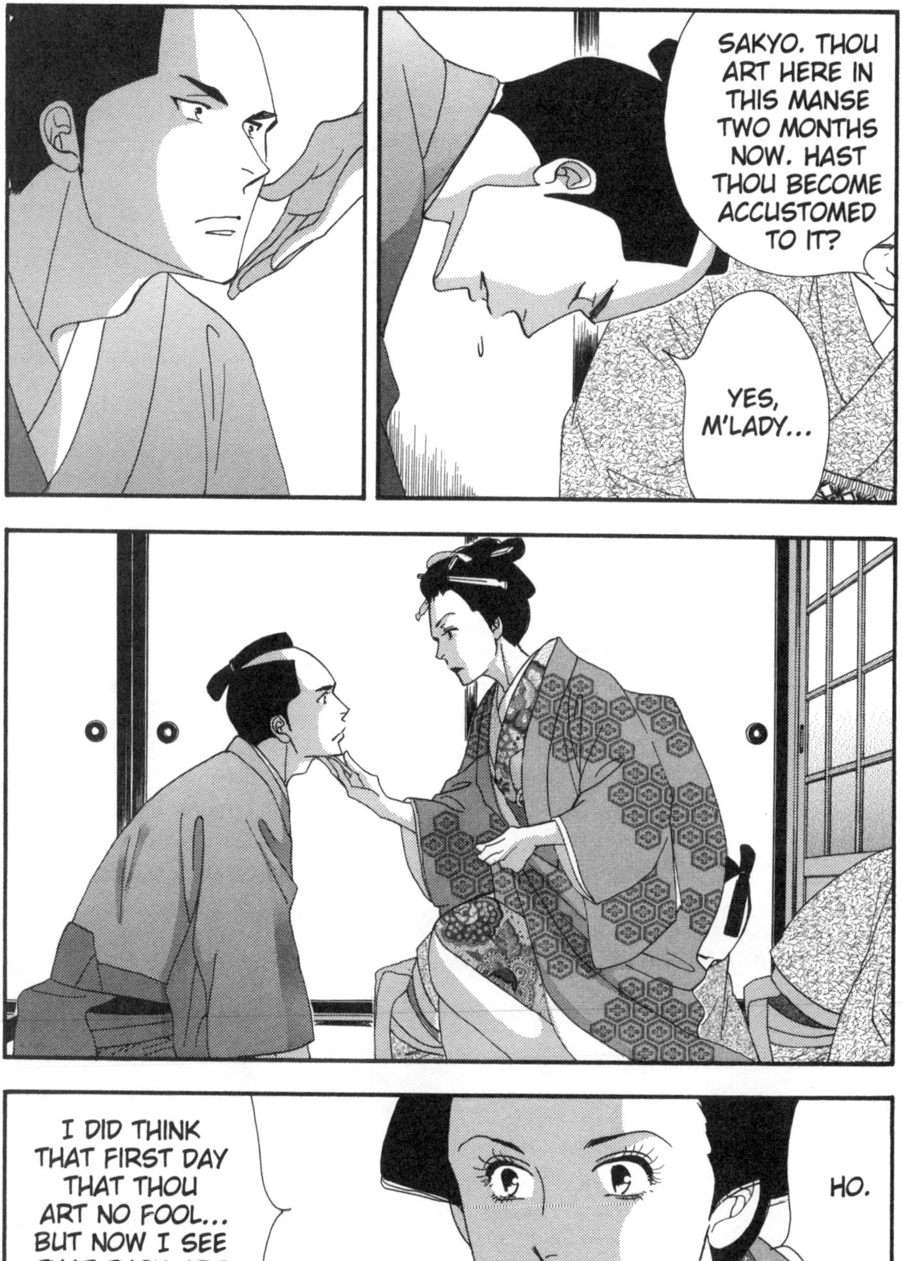
SAKYO. THOU ART HERE IN THIS MANSE TWO MONTHS NOW. HAST THOU BECOME ACCUSTOMED TO IT?
YES, M'LADY...
HO.
I DID THINK THAT FIRST DAY THAT THOU ART NO FOOL... BUT NOW I SEE THAT THOU ART FAR COMELIER THAN I DID THEN PERCEIVE.

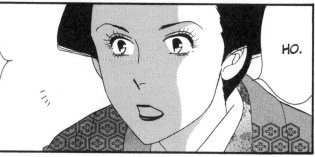

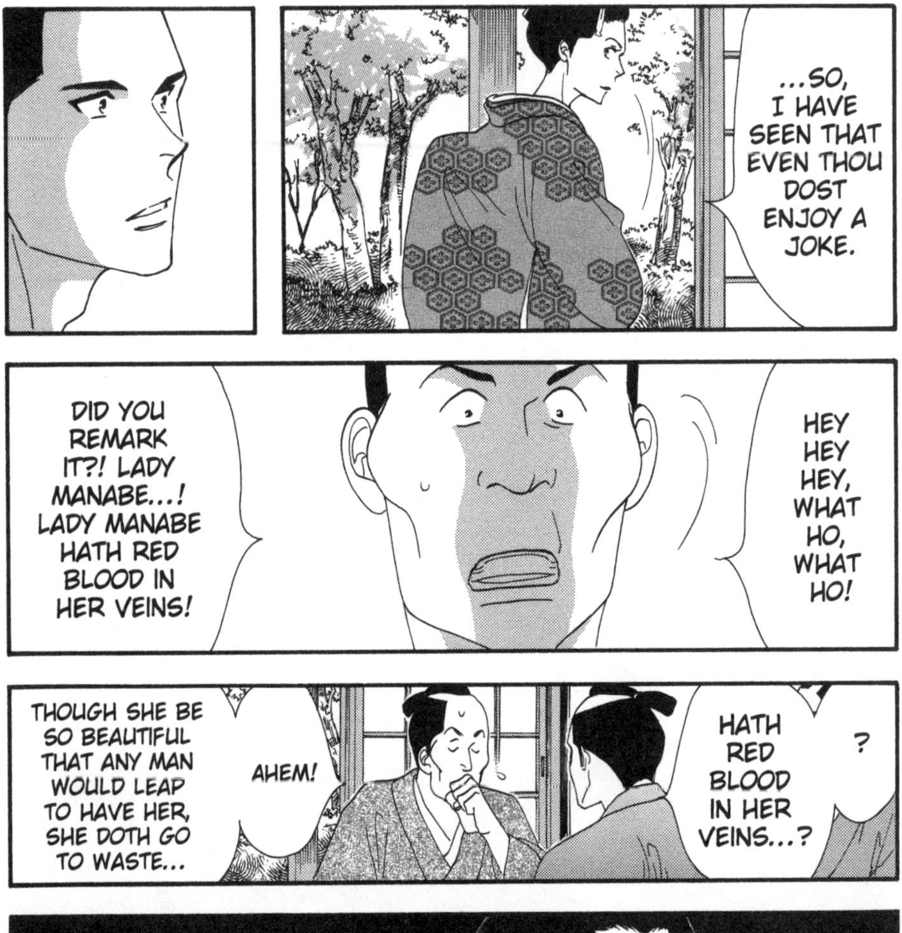
...SO, I HAVE SEEN THAT EVEN THOU DOST ENJOY A JOKE.
HEY HEY HEY, WHAT HO, WHAT HO!
DID YOU REMARK IT?! LADY MANABE...! LADY MANABE HATH RED BLOOD IN HER VEINS!
?
HATH RED BLOOD IN HER VEINS...?
AHEM!
THOUGH SHE BE SO BEAUTIFUL THAT ANY MAN WOULD LEAP TO HAVE HER, SHE DOTH GO TO WASTE...
Even Yanagisawa Yoshiyasu, Privy Councillor to the fifth shogun Tsunayoshi, had a spouse and children.
But Manabe Akifusa's defining trait was her almost abnormal fidelity to her lord, Ienobu... Although it is not known whether she and Ienobu had a sexual relationship, as was quite common at that time, it is an established fact that Manabe remained unmarried throughout her life.

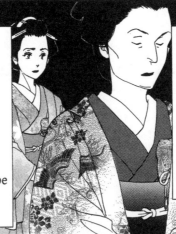

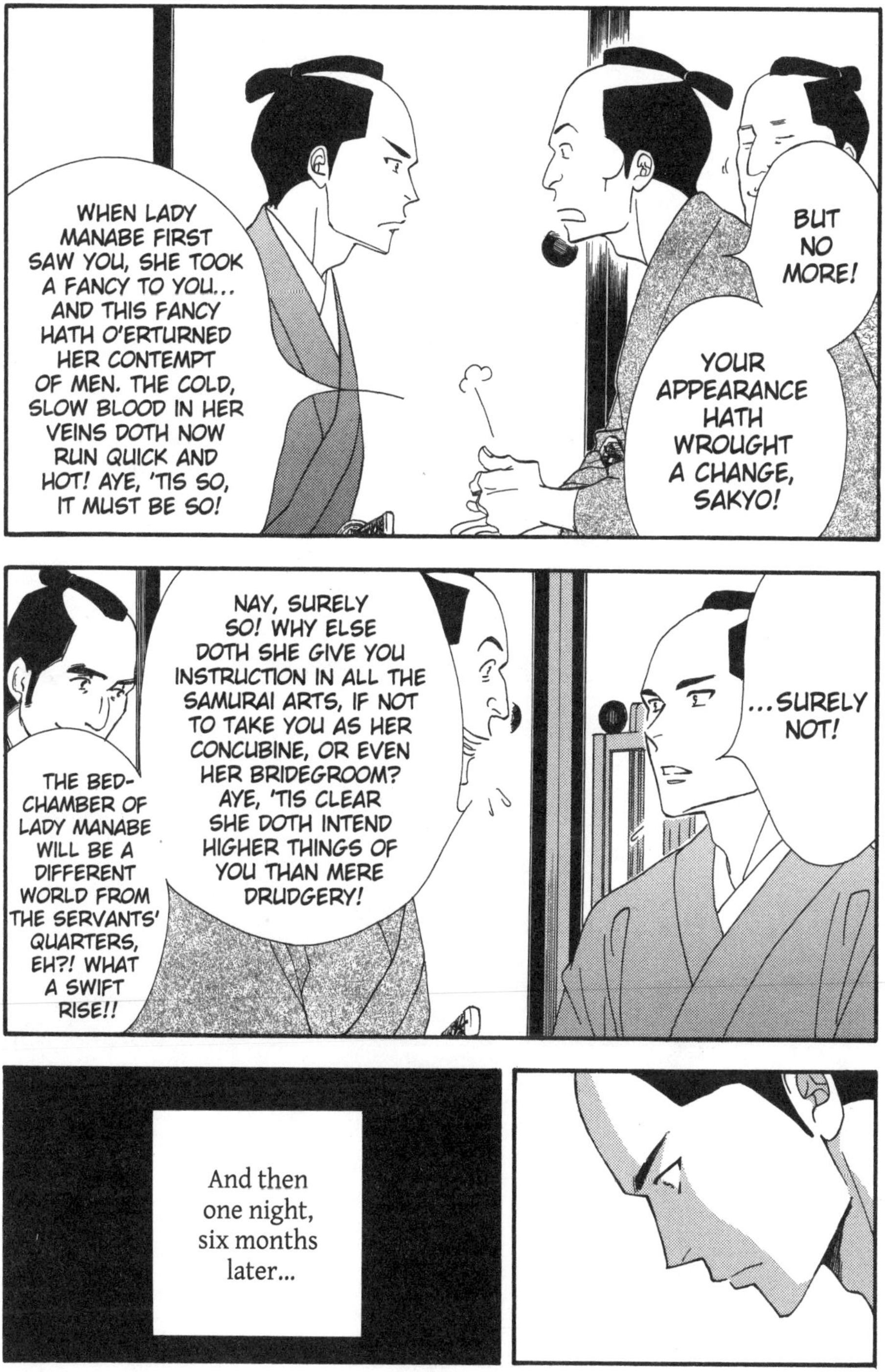
BUT NO MORE!
YOUR APPEARANCE HATH WROUGHT A CHANGE, SAKYO!
WHEN LADY MANABE FIRST SAW YOU, SHE TOOK A FANCY TO YOU... AND THIS FANCY HATH O'ERTURNED HER CONTEMPT OF MEN. THE COLD, SLOW BLOOD IN HER VEINS DOTH NOW RUN QUICK AND HOT! AYE, 'TIS SO, IT MUST BE SO!
...SURELY NOT!
NAY, SURELY SO! WHY ELSE DOTH SHE GIVE YOU INSTRUCTION IN ALL THE SAMURAI ARTS, IF NOT TO TAKE YOU AS HER CONCUBINE, OR EVEN HER BRIDEGROOM? AYE, 'TIS CLEAR SHE DOTH INTEND HIGHER THINGS OF YOU THAN MERE DRUDGERY!
THE BED-CHAMBER OF LADY MANABE WILL BE A DIFFERENT WORLD FROM THE SERVANTS' QUARTERS, EH?! WHAT A SWIFT RISE!!
And then one night, six months later...

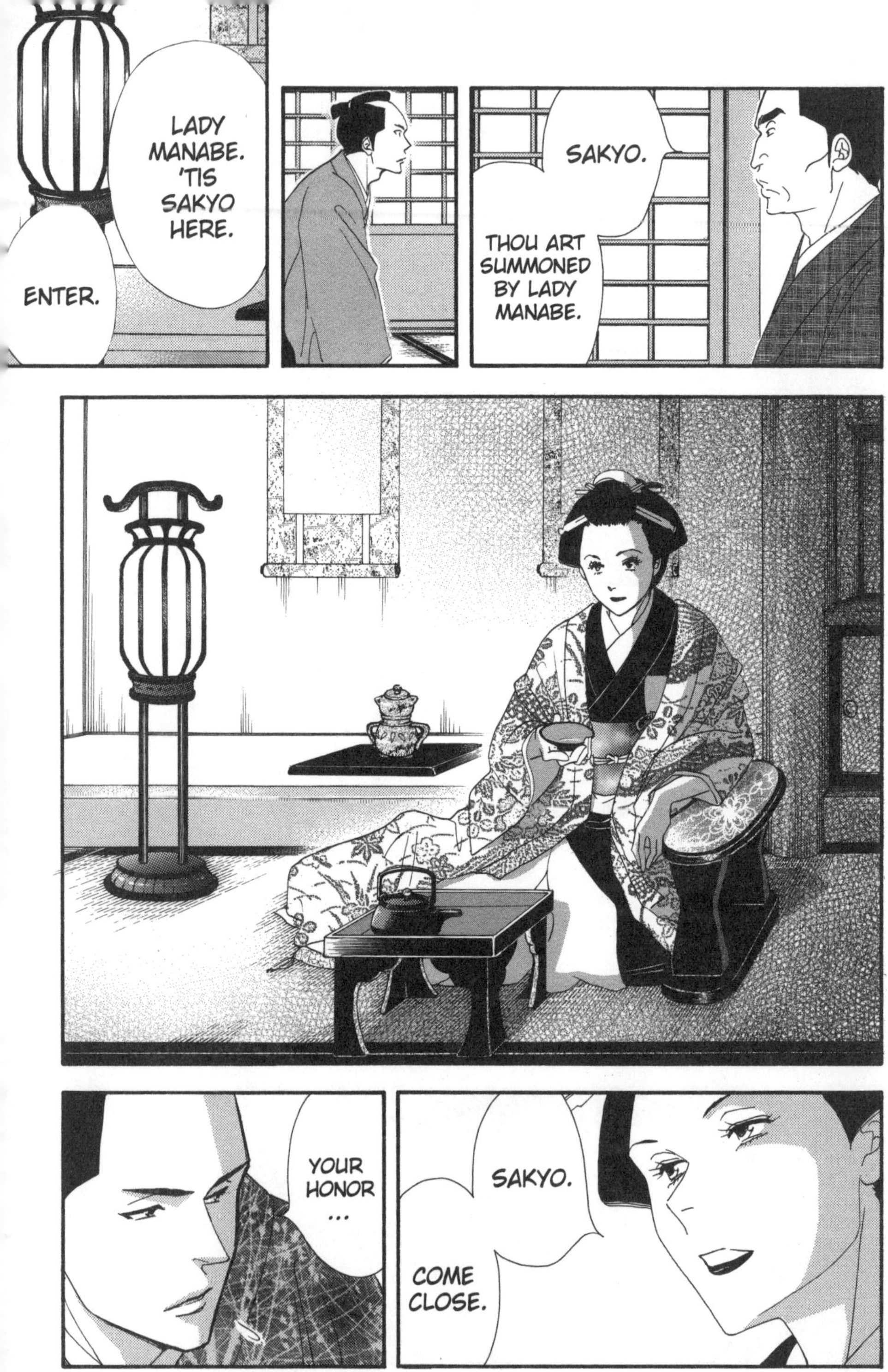
SAKYO.
THOU ART SUMMONED BY LADY MANABE.
LADY MANABE. 'TIS SAKYO HERE.
ENTER.
SAKYO.
COME CLOSE.
YOUR HONOR ...

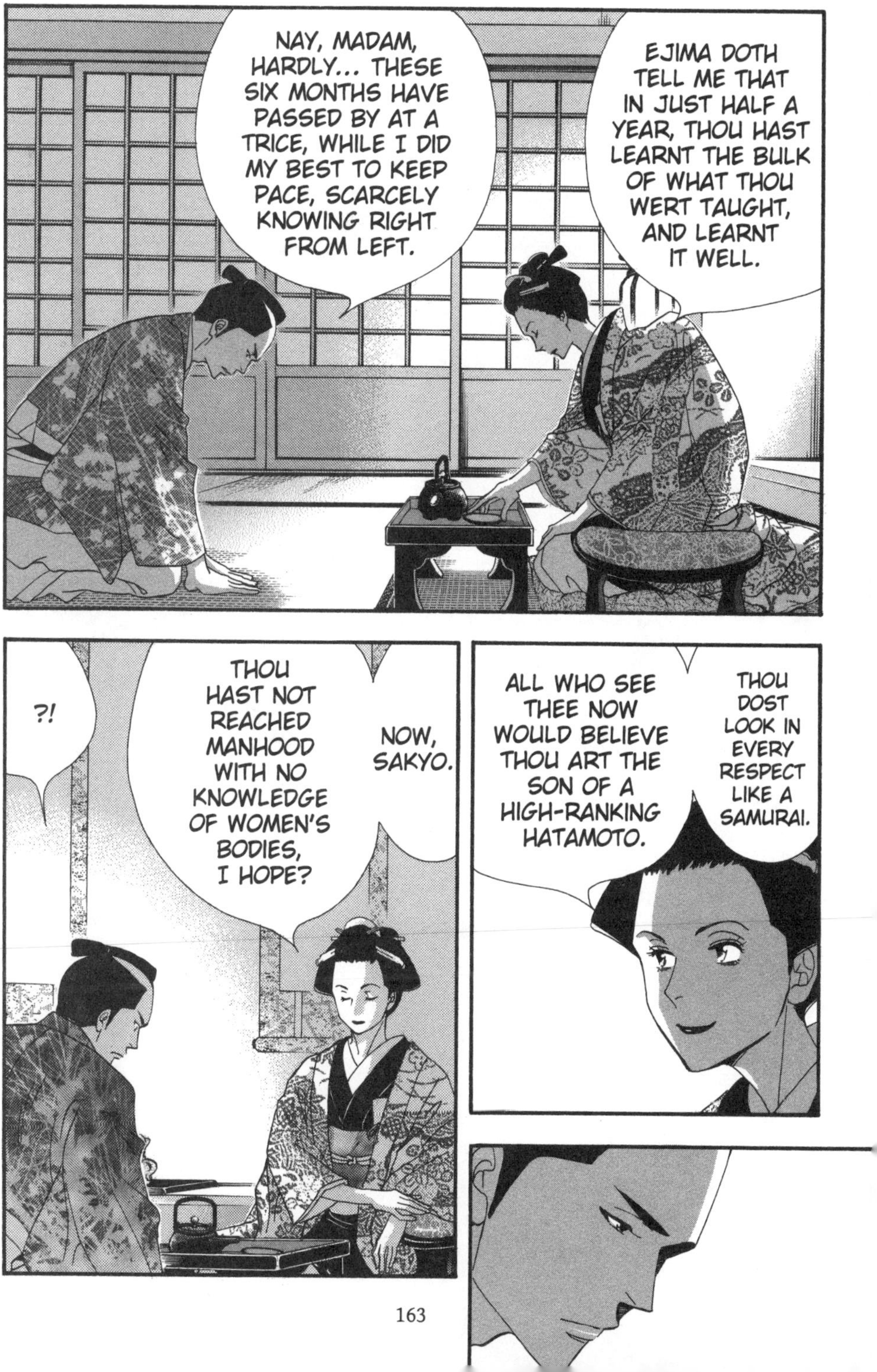
EJIMA DOTH TELL ME THAT IN JUST HALF A YEAR, THOU HAST LEARNT THE BULK OF WHAT THOU WERT TAUGHT, AND LEARNT IT WELL.
NAY, MADAM, HARDLY... THESE SIX MONTHS HAVE PASSED BY AT A TRICE, WHILE I DID MY BEST TO KEEP PACE, SCARCELY KNOWING RIGHT FROM LEFT.
THOU DOST LOOK IN EVERY RESPECT LIKE A SAMURAI.
ALL WHO SEE THEE NOW WOULD BELIEVE THOU ART THE SON OF A HIGH-RANKING HATAMOTO.
NOW, SAKYO.
THOU HAST NOT REACHED MANHOOD WITH NO KNOWLEDGE OF WOMEN'S BODIES, I HOPE?
?!

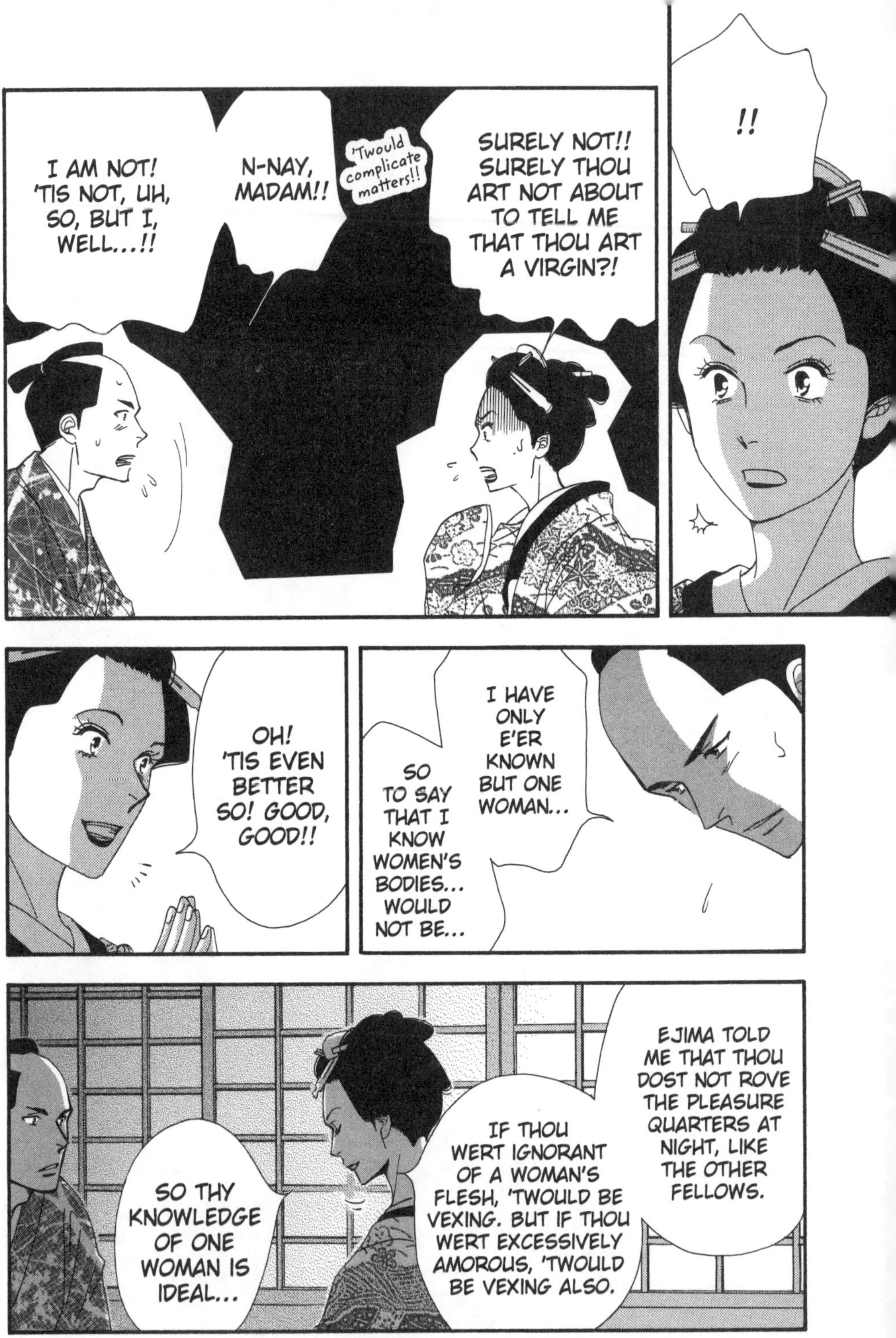
!!
SURELY NOT!! SURELY THOU ART NOT ABOUT TO TELL ME THAT THOU ART A VIRGIN?!
'Twould complicate matters!!
N-NAY, MADAM!!
I AM NOT! 'TIS NOT, UH, SO, BUT I, WELL...!!
I HAVE ONLY E'ER KNOWN BUT ONE WOMAN...
SO TO SAY THAT I KNOW WOMEN'S BODIES... WOULD NOT BE...
OH! 'TIS EVEN BETTER SO! GOOD, GOOD!!
EJIMA TOLD ME THAT THOU DOST NOT ROVE THE PLEASURE QUARTERS AT NIGHT, LIKE THE OTHER FELLOWS.
IF THOU WERT IGNORANT OF A WOMAN'S FLESH, 'TWOULD BE VEXING. BUT IF THOU WERT EXCESSIVELY AMOROUS, 'TWOULD BE VEXING ALSO.
SO THY KNOWLEDGE OF ONE WOMAN IS IDEAL...

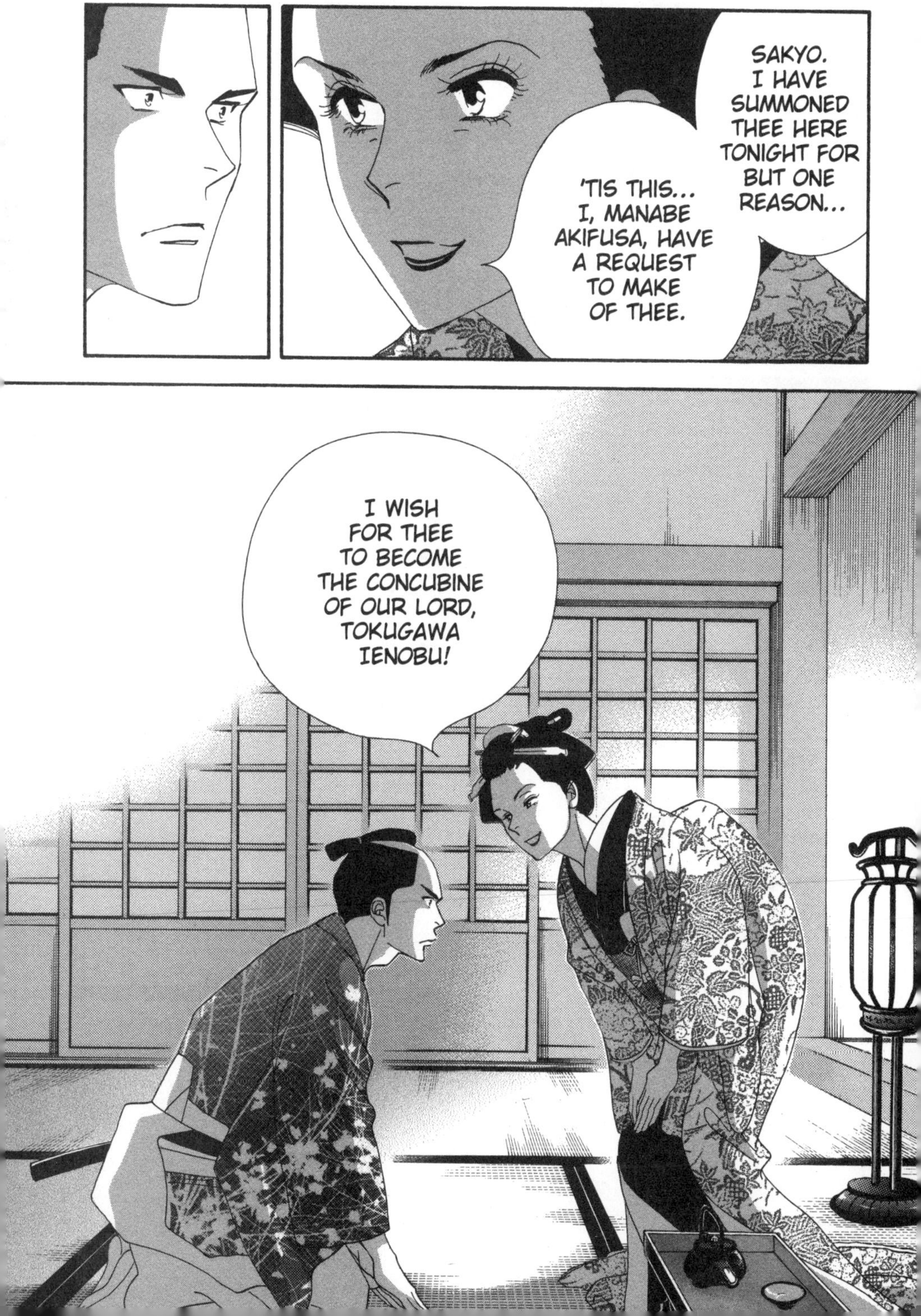
SAKYO. I HAVE SUMMONED THEE HERE TONIGHT FOR BUT ONE REASON...
'TIS THIS... I, MANABE AKIFUSA, HAVE A REQUEST TO MAKE OF THEE.
I WISH FOR THEE TO BECOME THE CONCUBINE OF OUR LORD, TOKUGAWA IENOBU!

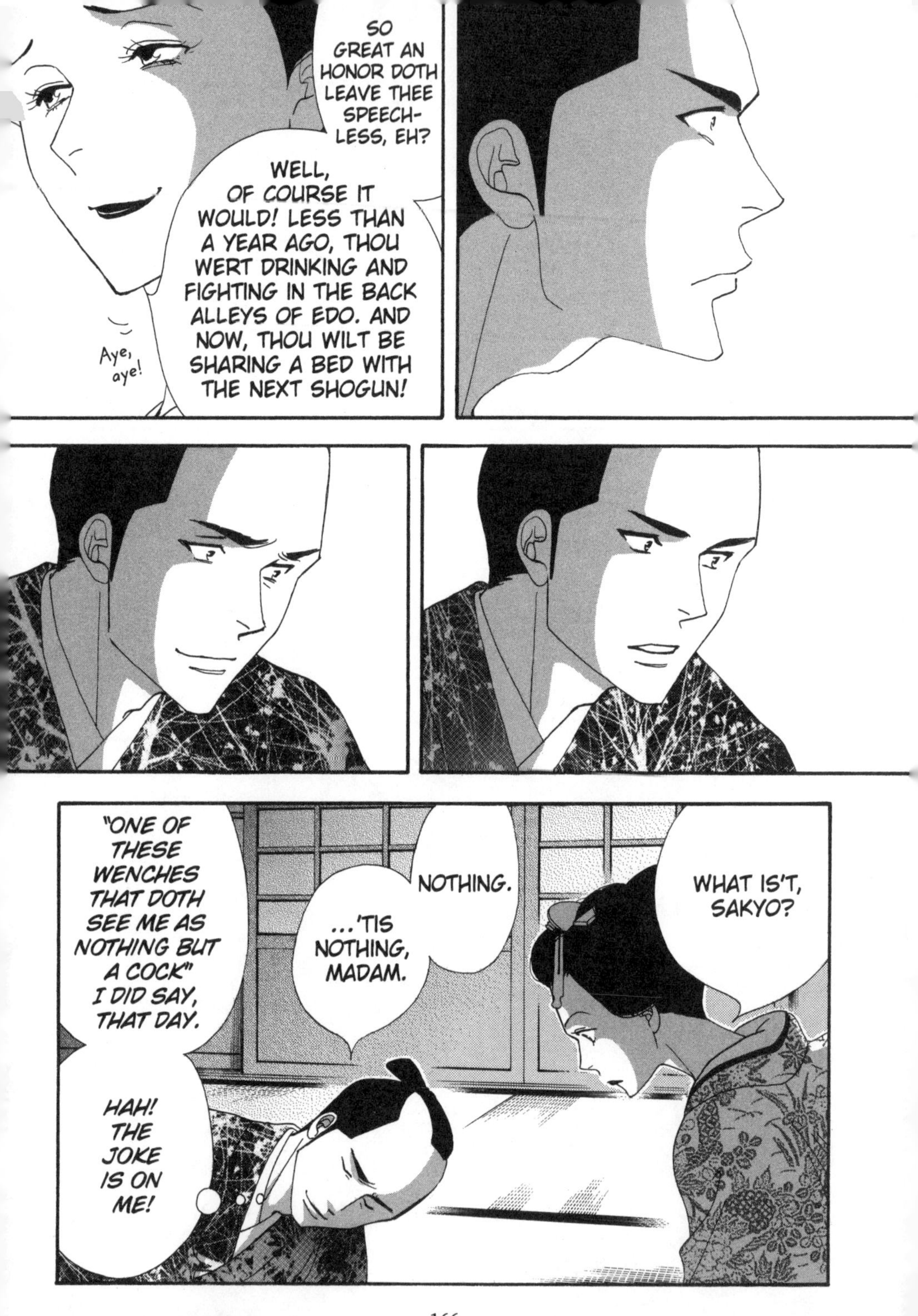
SO GREAT AN HONOR DOTH LEAVE THEE SPEECH-LESS, EH?
WELL, OF COURSE IT WOULD! LESS THAN A YEAR AGO, THOU WERT DRINKING AND FIGHTING IN THE BACK ALLEYS OF EDO. AND NOW, THOU WILT BE SHARING A BED WITH THE NEXT SHOGUN!
Aye, aye!
WHAT IS'T, SAKYO?
NOTHING.
...'TIS NOTHING, MADAM.
"ONE OF THESE WENCHES THAT DOTH SEE ME AS NOTHING BUT A COCK" I DID SAY, THAT DAY.
HAH! THE JOKE IS ON ME!

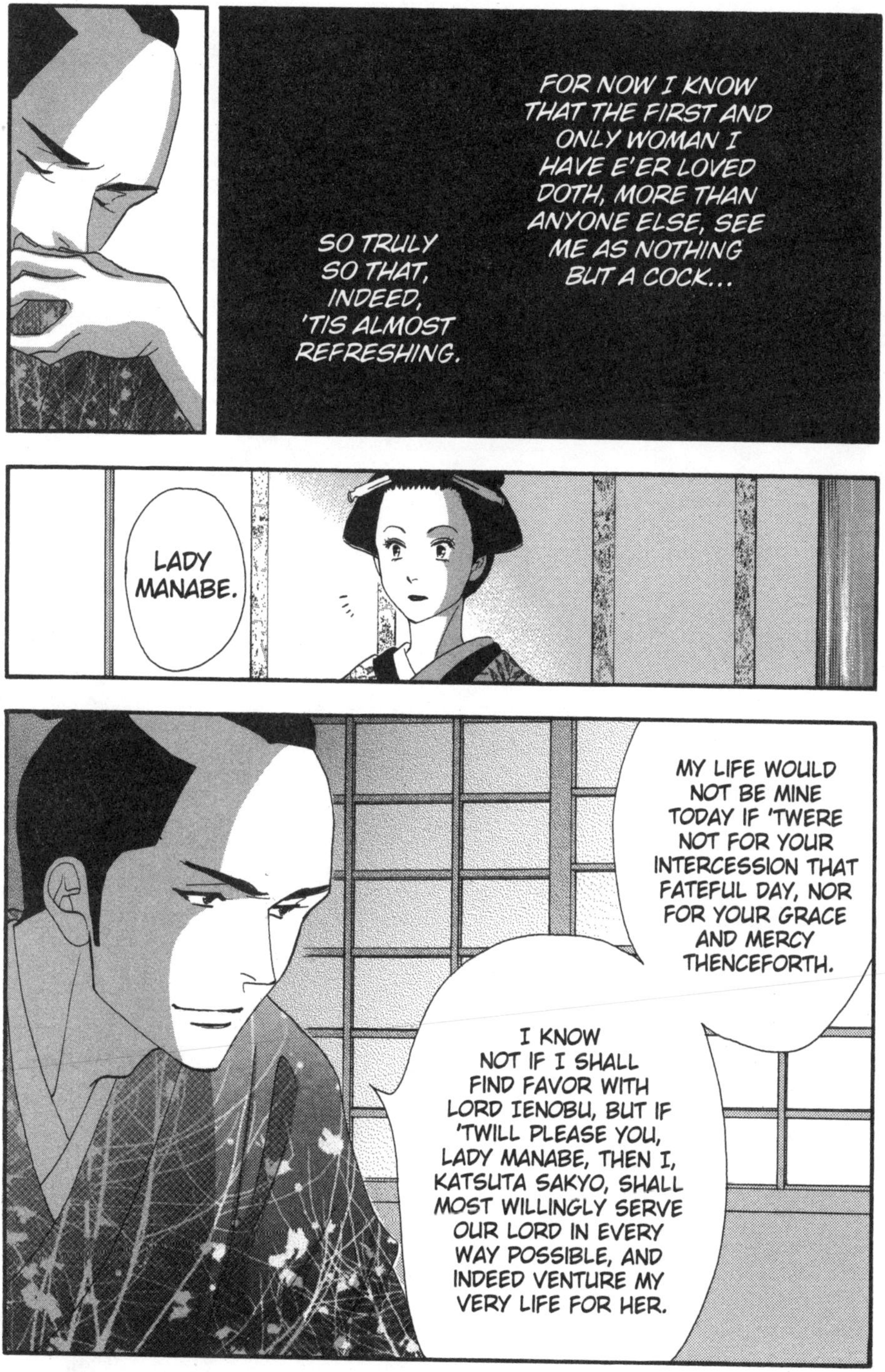
FOR NOW I KNOW THAT THE FIRST AND ONLY WOMAN I HAVE E'ER LOVED DOTH, MORE THAN ANYONE ELSE, SEE ME AS NOTHING BUT A COCK...
SO TRULY SO THAT, INDEED, 'TIS ALMOST REFRESHING.
LADY MANABE.
MY LIFE WOULD NOT BE MINE TODAY IF 'TWERE NOT FOR YOUR INTERCESSION THAT FATEFUL DAY, NOR FOR YOUR GRACE AND MERCY THENCEFORTH.
I KNOW NOT IF I SHALL FIND FAVOR WITH LORD IENOBU, BUT IF 'TWILL PLEASE YOU, LADY MANABE, THEN I, KATSUTA SAKYO, SHALL MOST WILLINGLY SERVE OUR LORD IN EVERY WAY POSSIBLE, AND INDEED VENTURE MY VERY LIFE FOR HER.

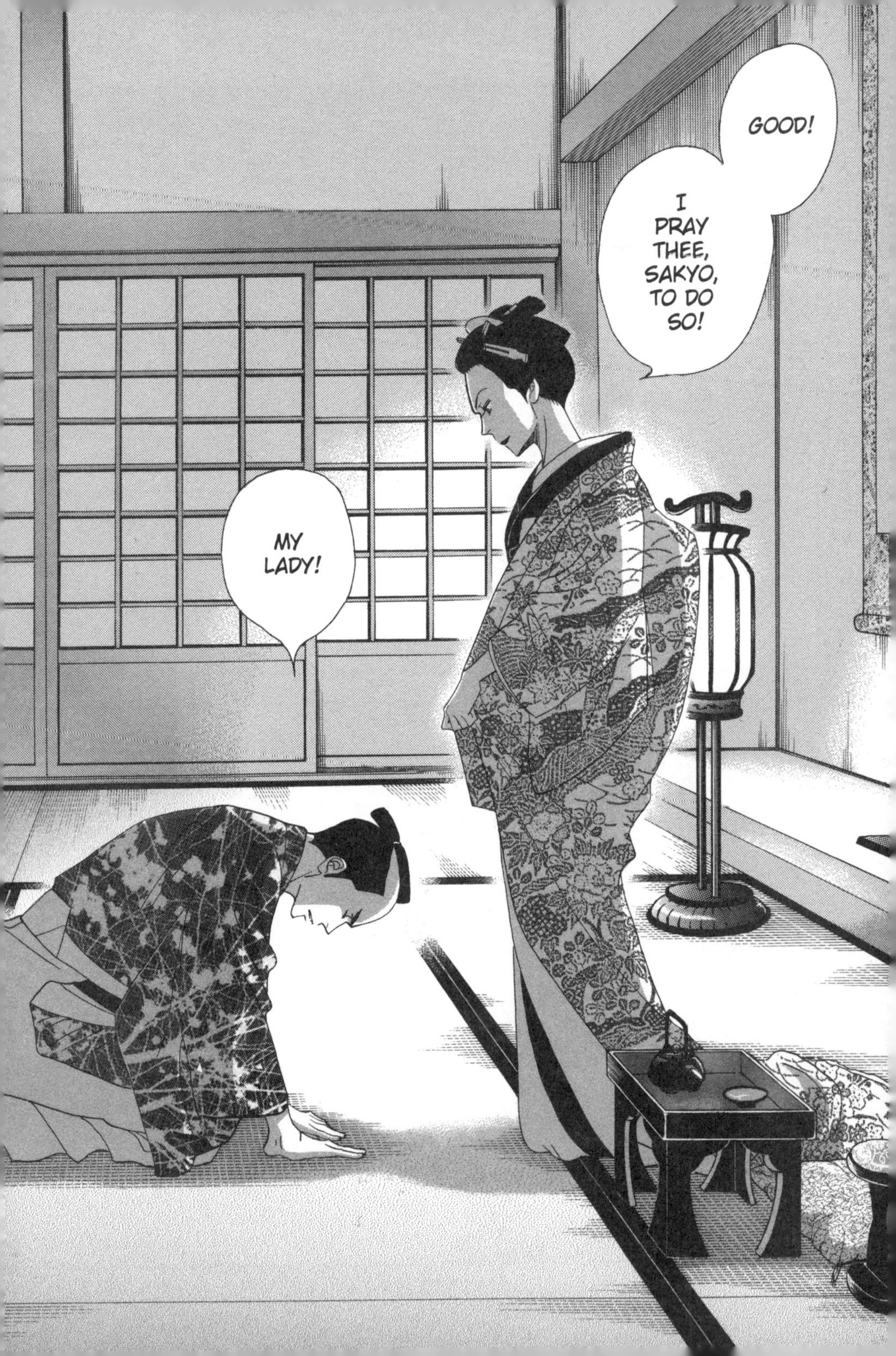
GOOD!
I PRAY THEE, SAKYO, TO DO SO!
MY LADY!

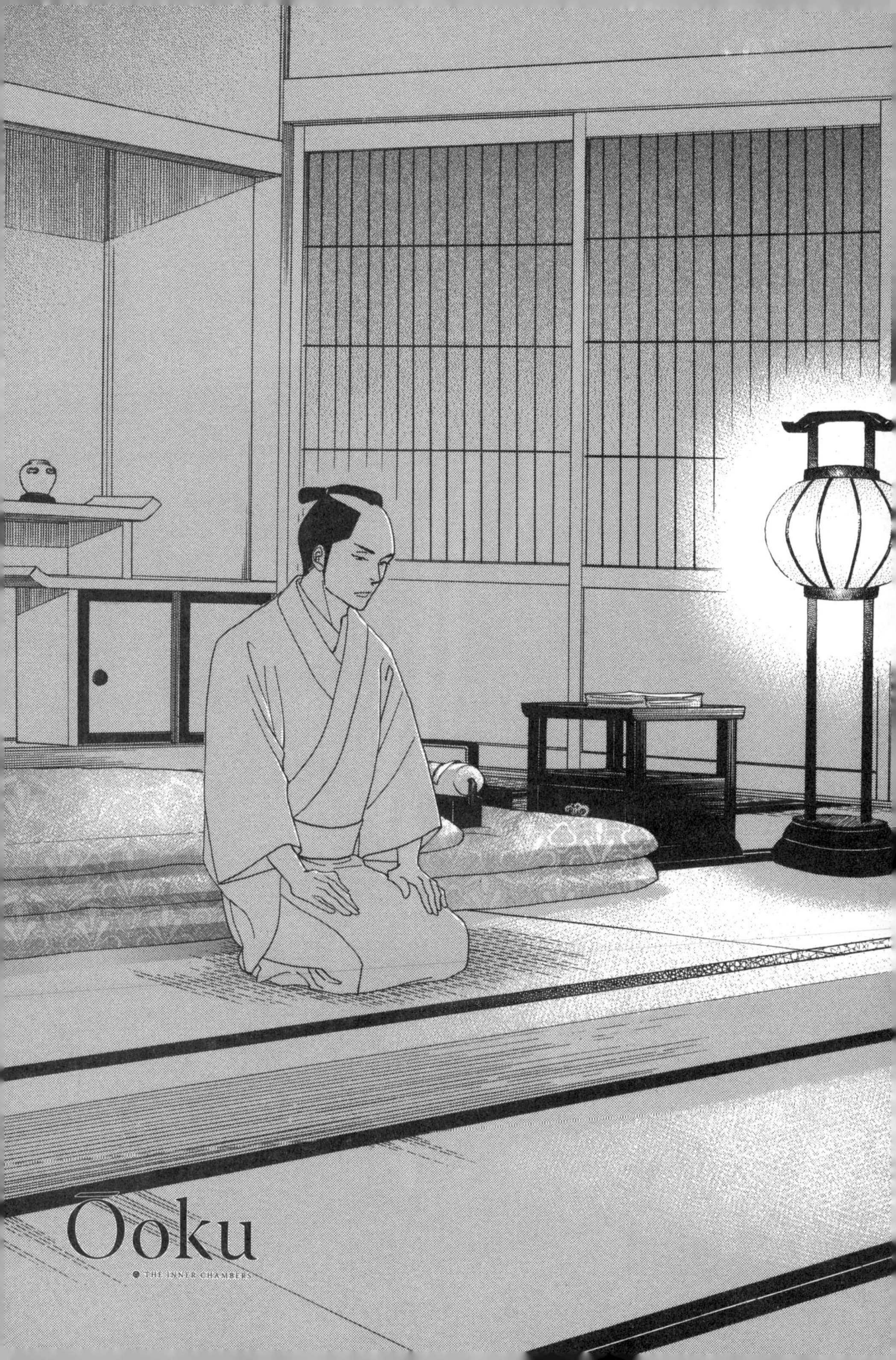
Ōoku
THE INNER CHAMBERS

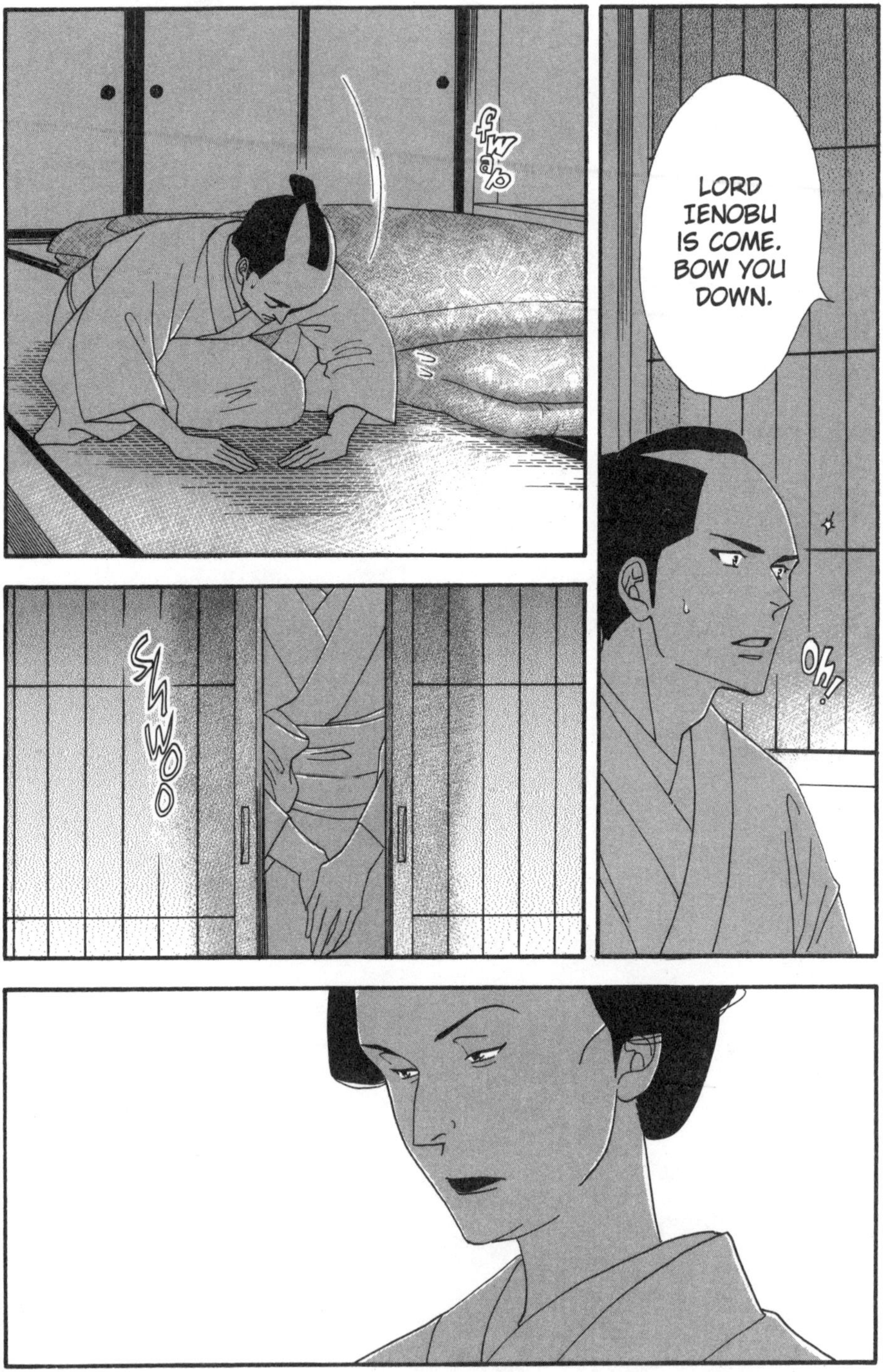
LORD IENOBU IS COME. BOW YOU DOWN.
Oh!
fwap
SHWOO

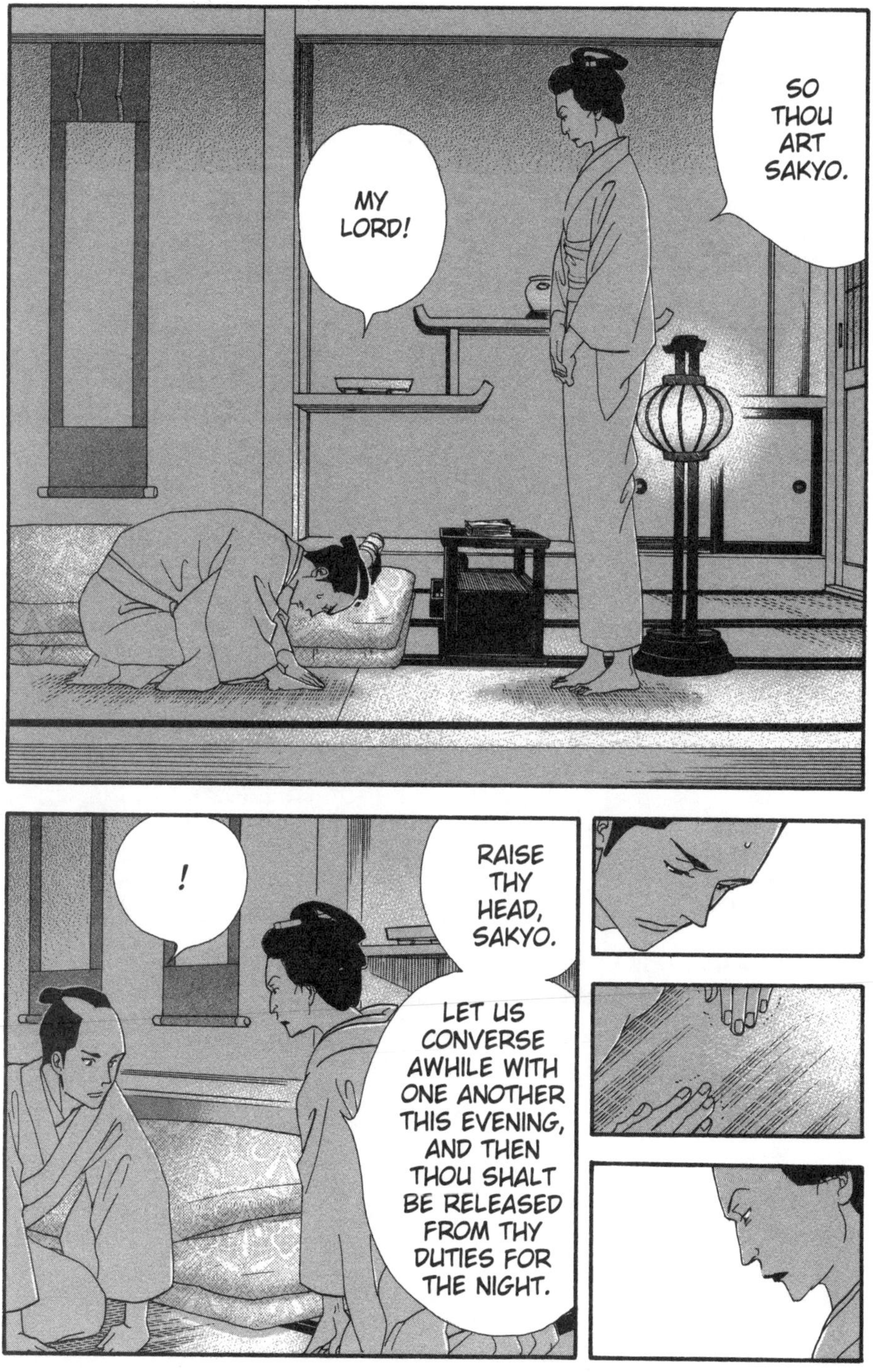
SO THOU ART SAKYO.
MY LORD!
RAISE THY HEAD, SAKYO.
!
LET US CONVERSE AWHILE WITH ONE ANOTHER THIS EVENING, AND THEN THOU SHALT BE RELEASED FROM THY DUTIES FOR THE NIGHT.

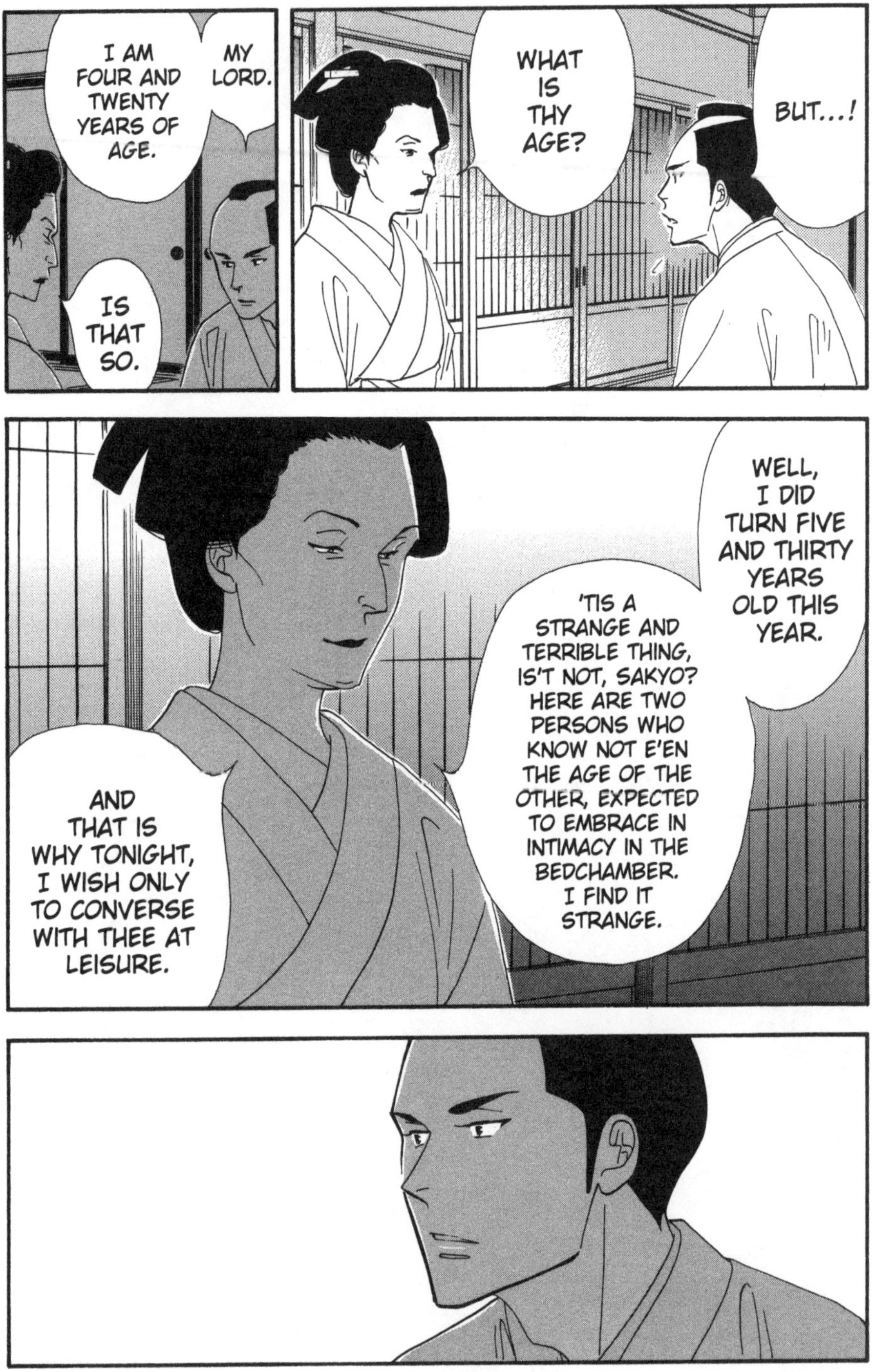
BUT...!
WHAT IS THY AGE?
MY LORD.
I AM FOUR AND TWENTY YEARS OF AGE.
IS THAT SO.
WELL, I DID TURN FIVE AND THIRTY YEARS OLD THIS YEAR.
'TIS A STRANGE AND TERRIBLE THING, IS'T NOT, SAKYO? HERE ARE TWO PERSONS WHO KNOW NOT E'EN THE AGE OF THE OTHER, EXPECTED TO EMBRACE IN INTIMACY IN THE BEDCHAMBER. I FIND IT STRANGE.
AND THAT IS WHY TONIGHT, I WISH ONLY TO CONVERSE WITH THEE AT LEISURE.

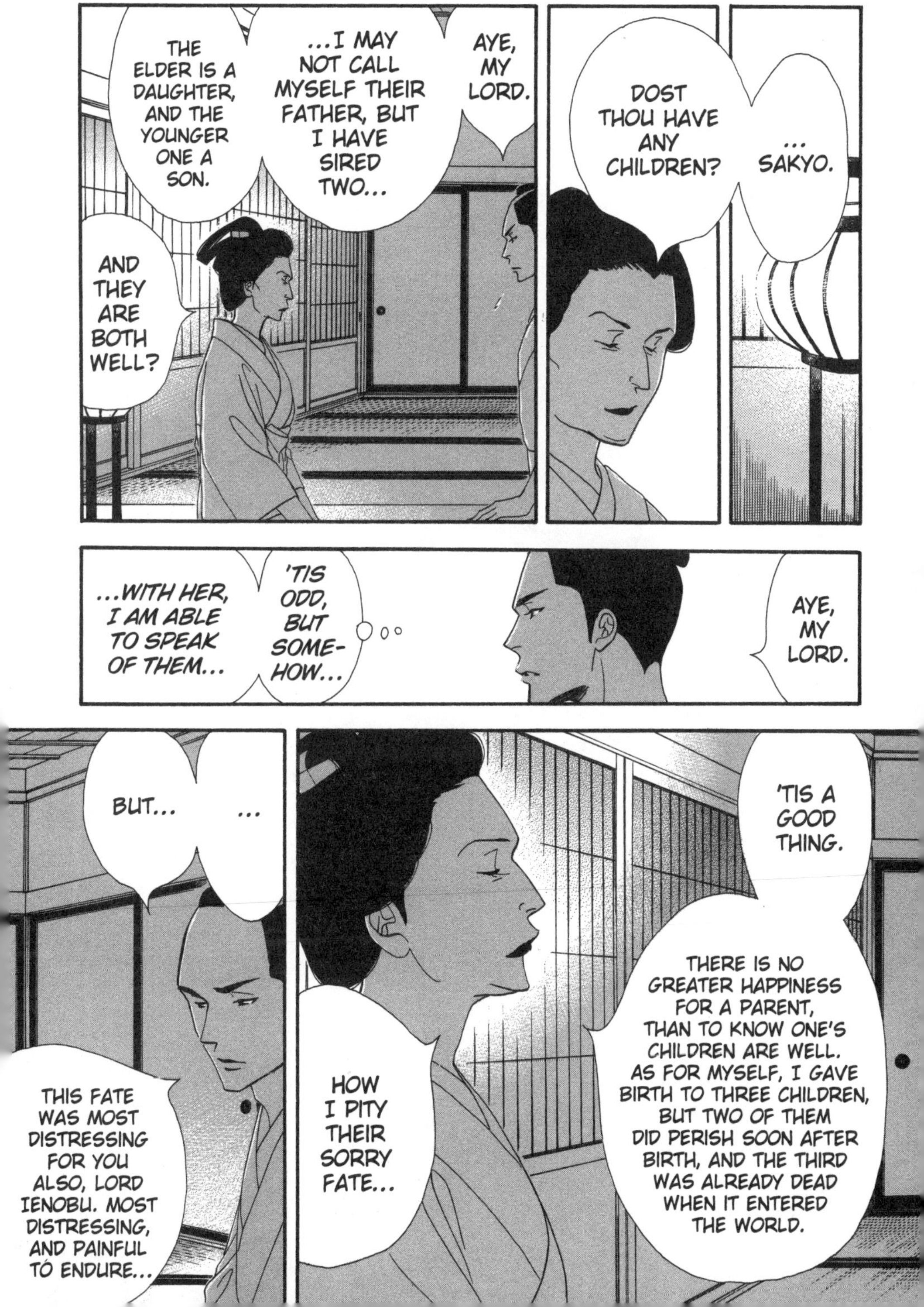
... SAKYO.
DOST THOU HAVE ANY CHILDREN?
AYE, MY LORD.
...I MAY NOT CALL MYSELF THEIR FATHER, BUT I HAVE SIRED TWO...
THE ELDER IS A DAUGHTER, AND THE YOUNGER ONE A SON.
AND THEY ARE BOTH WELL?
AYE, MY LORD.
'TIS ODD, BUT SOME-HOW...
...WITH HER, I AM ABLE TO SPEAK OF THEM...
'TIS A GOOD THING.
THERE IS NO GREATER HAPPINESS FOR A PARENT, THAN TO KNOW ONE'S CHILDREN ARE WELL. AS FOR MYSELF, I GAVE BIRTH TO THREE CHILDREN, BUT TWO OF THEM DID PERISH SOON AFTER BIRTH, AND THE THIRD WAS ALREADY DEAD WHEN IT ENTERED THE WORLD.
HOW I PITY THEIR SORRY FATE...
...
BUT...
THIS FATE WAS MOST DISTRESSING FOR YOU ALSO, LORD IENOBU. MOST DISTRESSING, AND PAINFUL TO ENDURE...

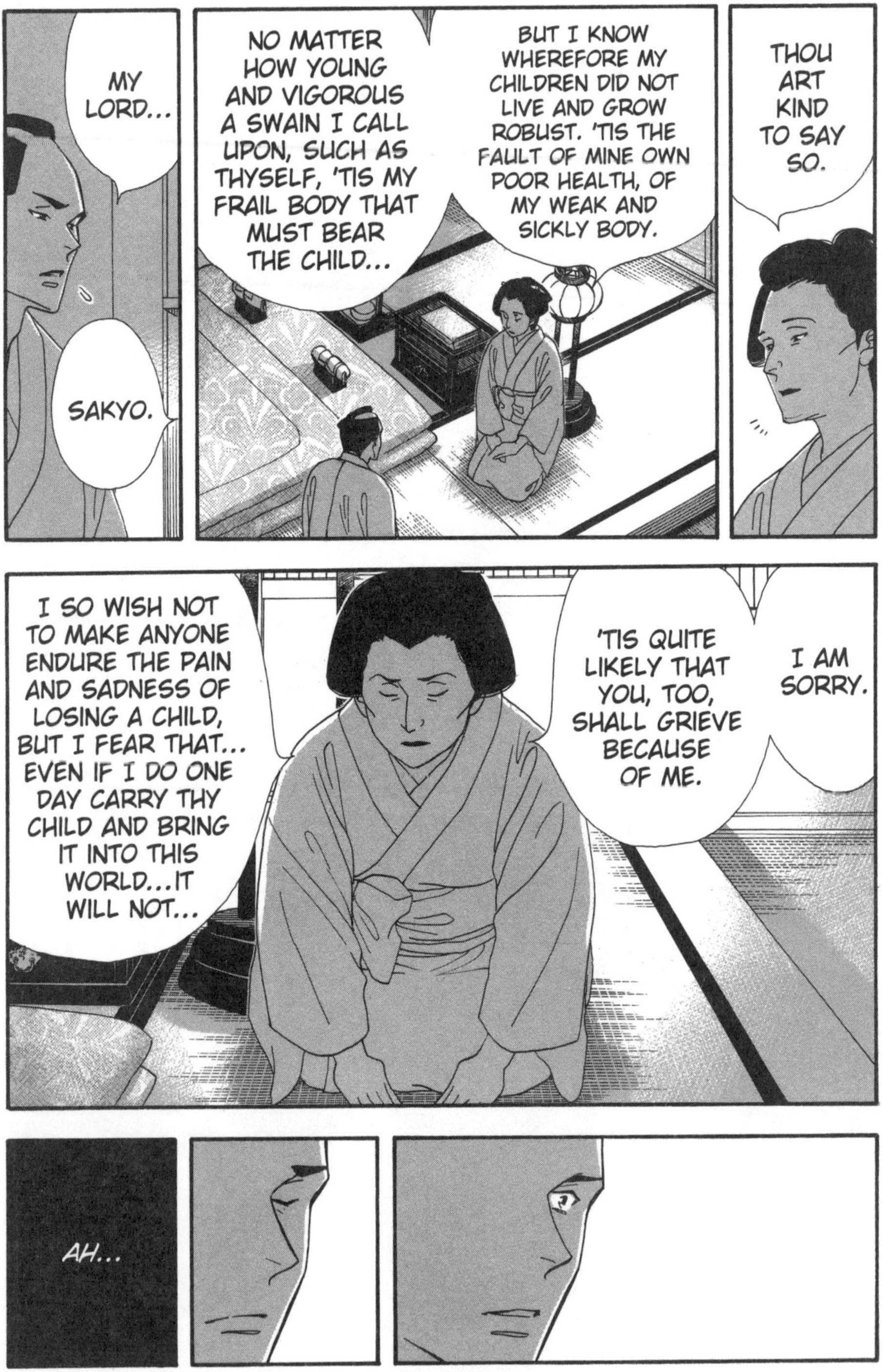
THOU ART KIND TO SAY SO.
BUT I KNOW WHEREFORE MY CHILDREN DID NOT LIVE AND GROW ROBUST. 'TIS THE FAULT OF MINE OWN POOR HEALTH, OF MY WEAK AND SICKLY BODY.
NO MATTER HOW YOUNG AND VIGOROUS A SWAIN I CALL UPON, SUCH AS THYSELF, 'TIS MY FRAIL BODY THAT MUST BEAR THE CHILD...
MY LORD...
SAKYO.
I AM SORRY.
'TIS QUITE LIKELY THAT YOU, TOO, SHALL GRIEVE BECAUSE OF ME.
I SO WISH NOT TO MAKE ANYONE ENDURE THE PAIN AND SADNESS OF LOSING A CHILD, BUT I FEAR THAT... EVEN IF I DO ONE DAY CARRY THY CHILD AND BRING IT INTO THIS WORLD...IT WILL NOT...
AH...

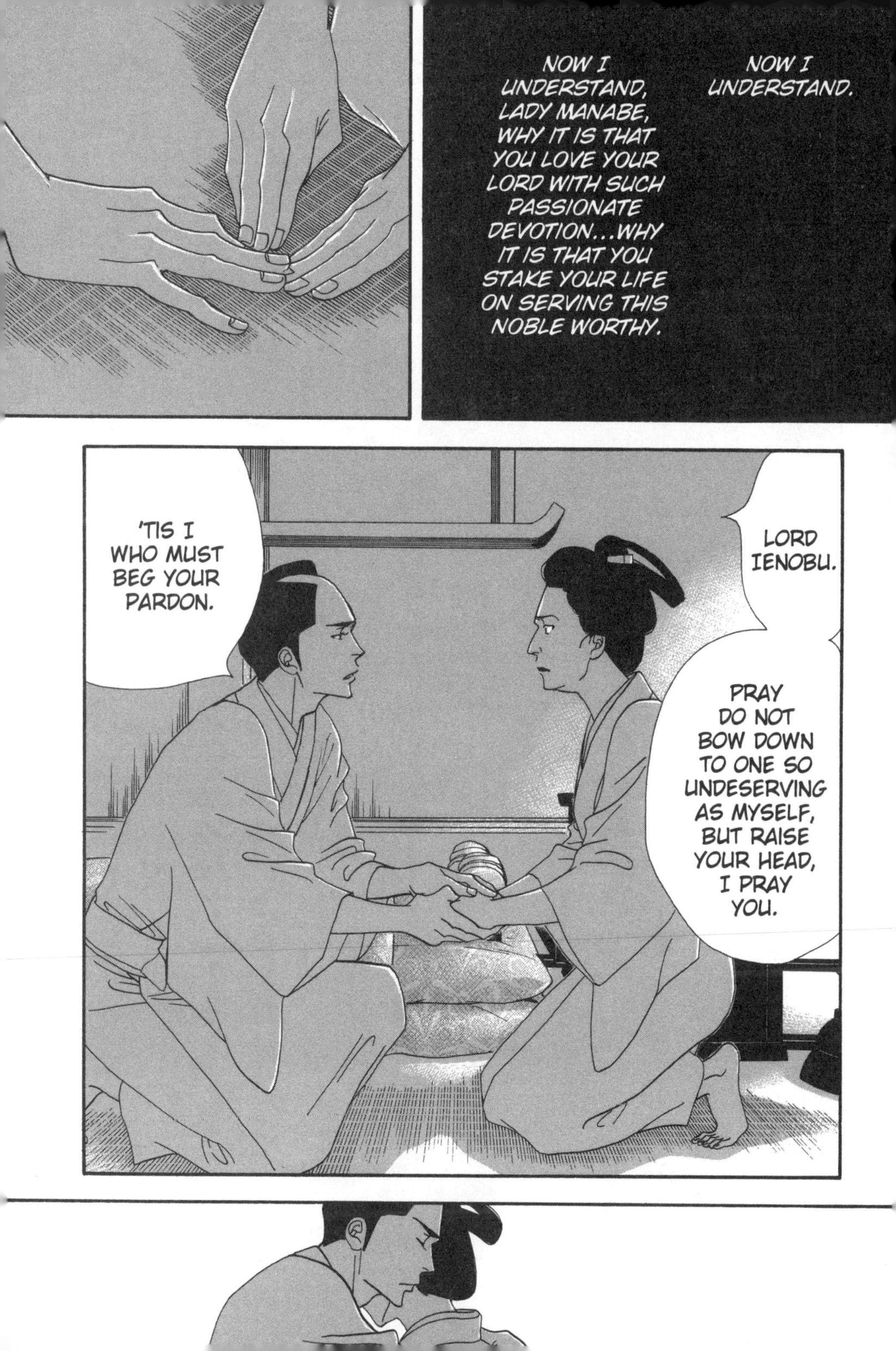
NOW I UNDERSTAND.
NOW I UNDERSTAND, LADY MANABE, WHY IT IS THAT YOU LOVE YOUR LORD WITH SUCH PASSIONATE DEVOTION...WHY IT IS THAT YOU STAKE YOUR LIFE ON SERVING THIS NOBLE WORTHY.
LORD IENOBU.
PRAY DO NOT BOW DOWN TO ONE SO UNDESERVING AS MYSELF, BUT RAISE YOUR HEAD, I PRAY YOU.
'TIS I WHO MUST BEG YOUR PARDON.

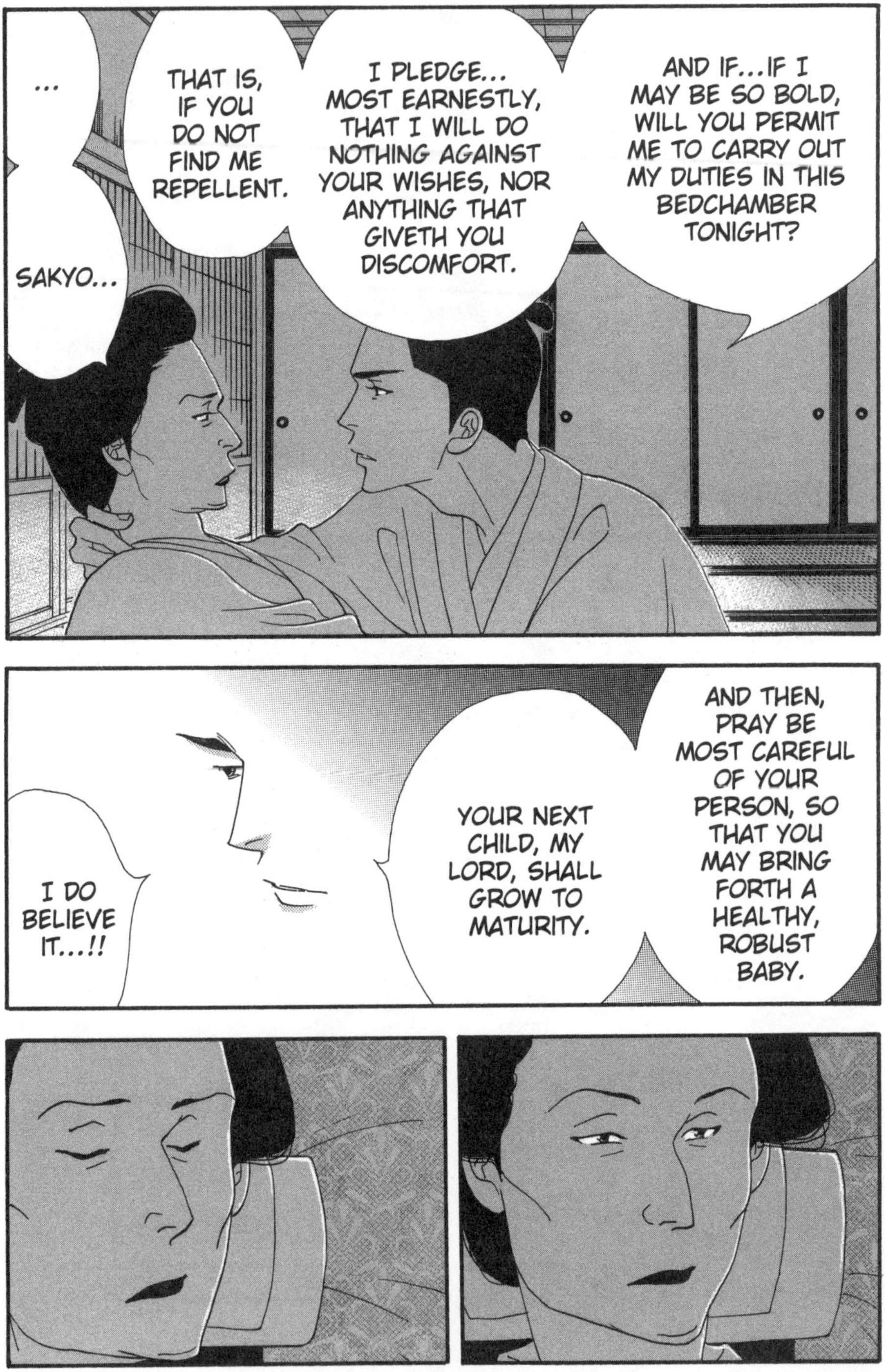
AND IF…IF I MAY BE SO BOLD, WILL YOU PERMIT ME TO CARRY OUT MY DUTIES IN THIS BEDCHAMBER TONIGHT?
I PLEDGE… MOST EARNESTLY, THAT I WILL DO NOTHING AGAINST YOUR WISHES, NOR ANYTHING THAT GIVETH YOU DISCOMFORT.
THAT IS, IF YOU DO NOT FIND ME REPELLENT.
…
SAKYO…
AND THEN, PRAY BE MOST CAREFUL OF YOUR PERSON, SO THAT YOU MAY BRING FORTH A HEALTHY, ROBUST BABY.
YOUR NEXT CHILD, MY LORD, SHALL GROW TO MATURITY.
I DO BELIEVE IT…!!

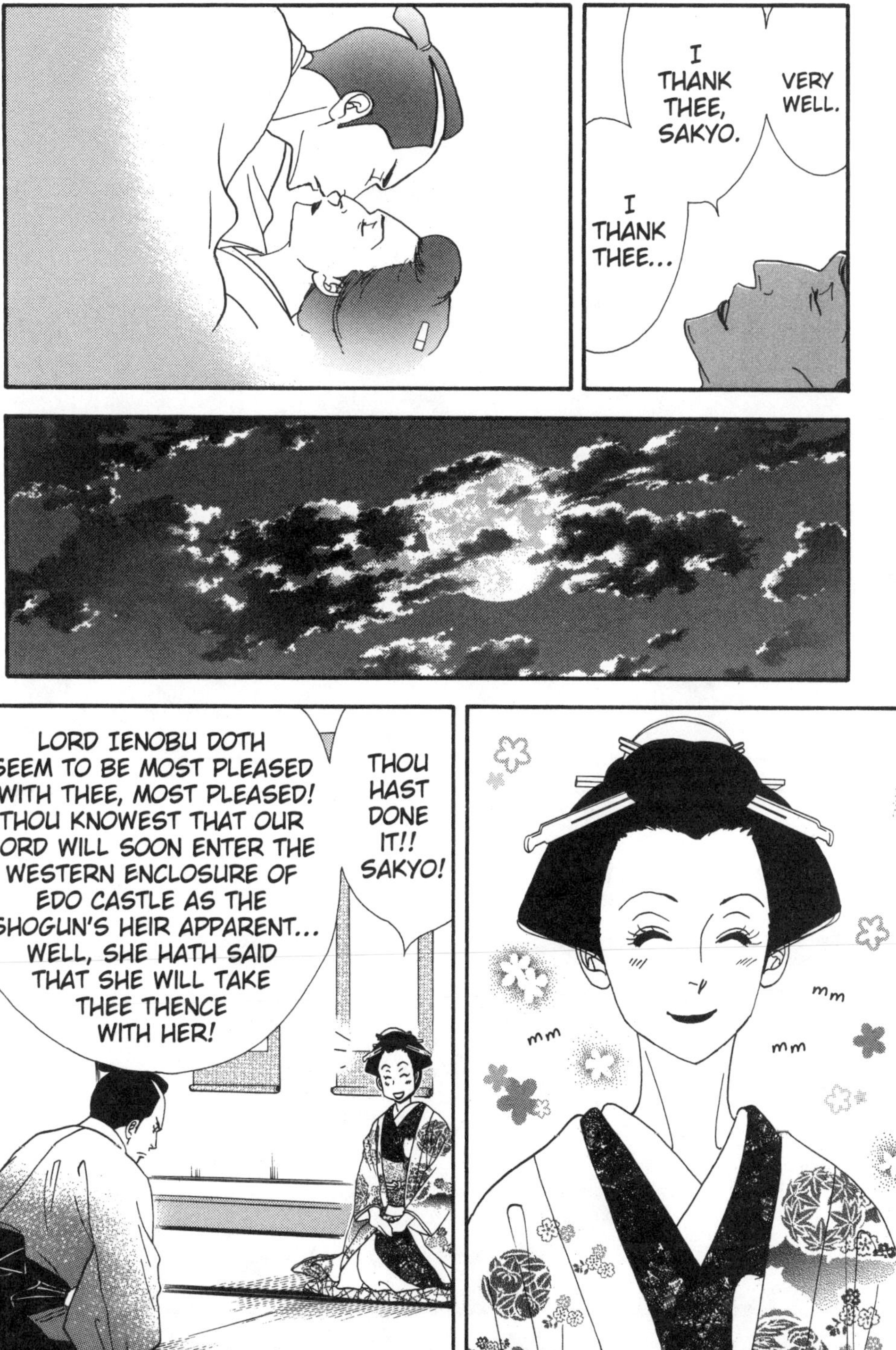
VERY WELL.
I THANK THEE, SAKYO.
I THANK THEE...
mm
mm
mm
THOU HAST DONE IT!! SAKYO!
LORD IENOBU DOTH SEEM TO BE MOST PLEASED WITH THEE, MOST PLEASED! THOU KNOWEST THAT OUR LORD WILL SOON ENTER THE WESTERN ENCLOSURE OF EDO CASTLE AS THE SHOGUN'S HEIR APPARENT... WELL, SHE HATH SAID THAT SHE WILL TAKE THEE THENCE WITH HER!

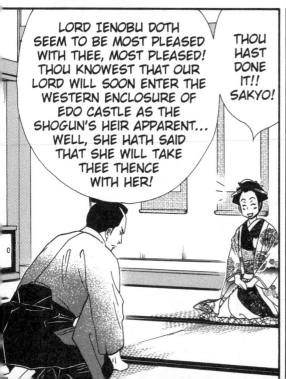

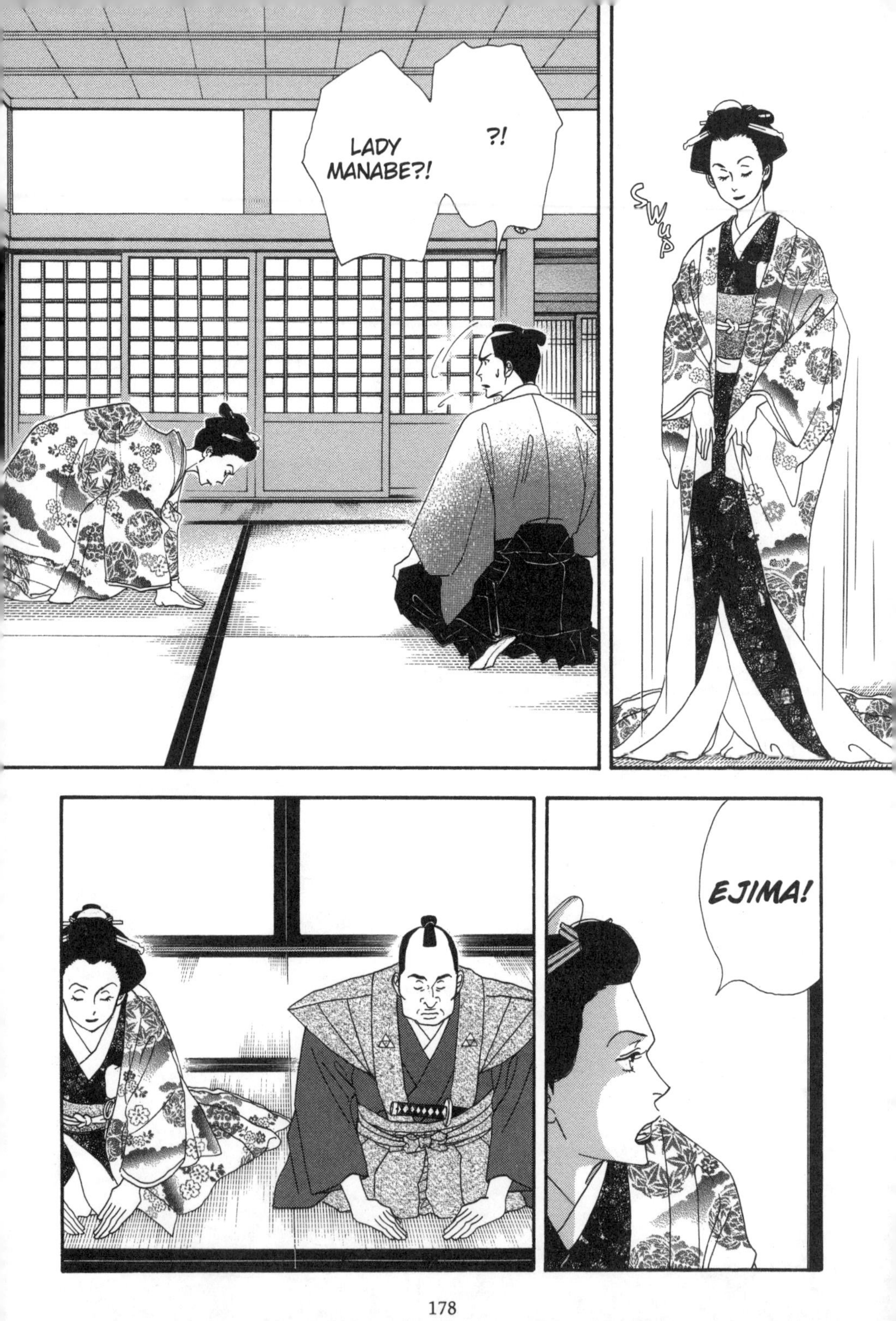
SWUP
?!
LADY MANABE?!
EJIMA!

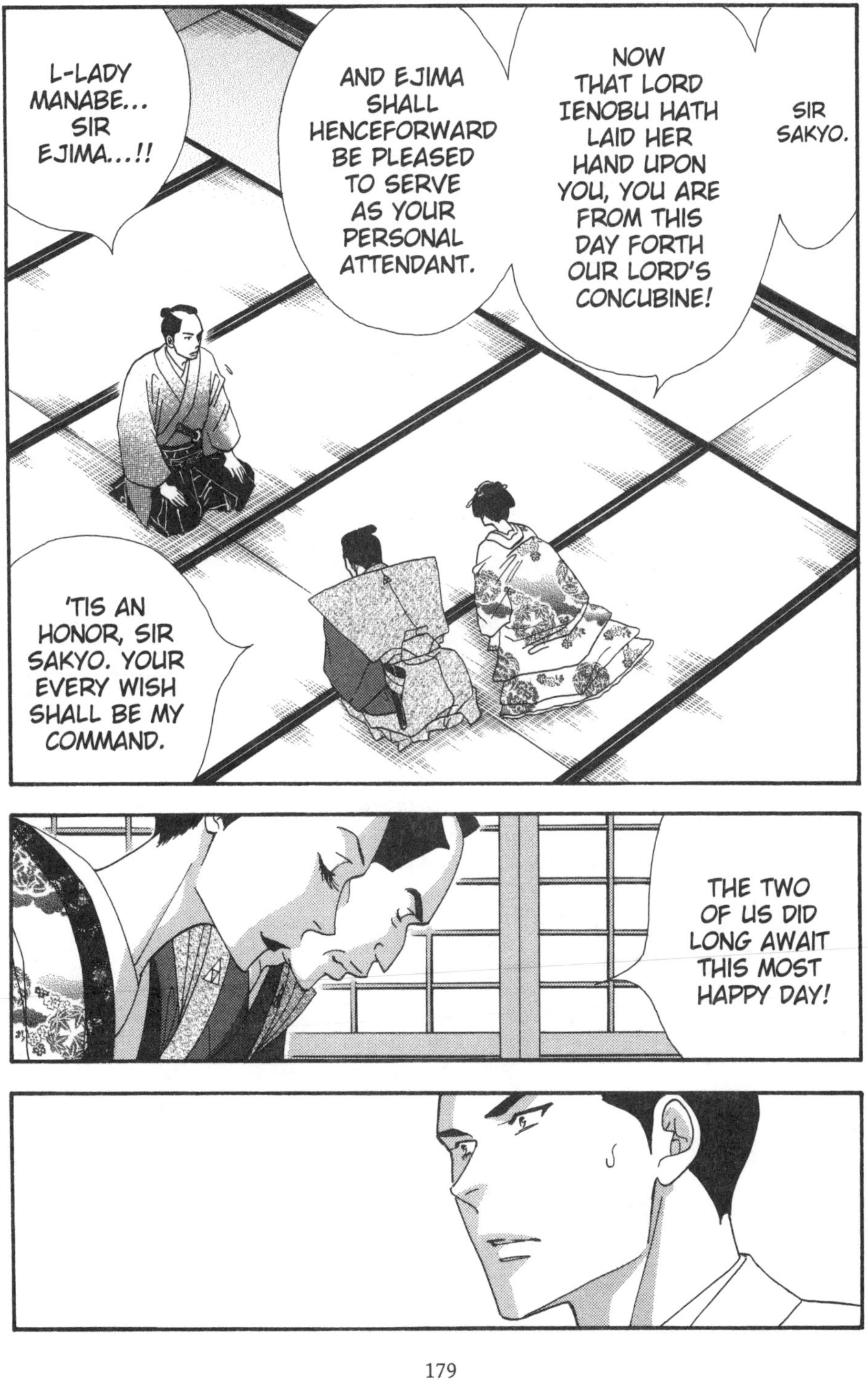
SIR SAKYO.
NOW THAT LORD IENOBU HATH LAID HER HAND UPON YOU, YOU ARE FROM THIS DAY FORTH OUR LORD'S CONCUBINE!
AND EJIMA SHALL HENCEFORWARD BE PLEASED TO SERVE AS YOUR PERSONAL ATTENDANT.
L-LADY MANABE... SIR EJIMA...!!
'TIS AN HONOR, SIR SAKYO. YOUR EVERY WISH SHALL BE MY COMMAND.
THE TWO OF US DID LONG AWAIT THIS MOST HAPPY DAY!

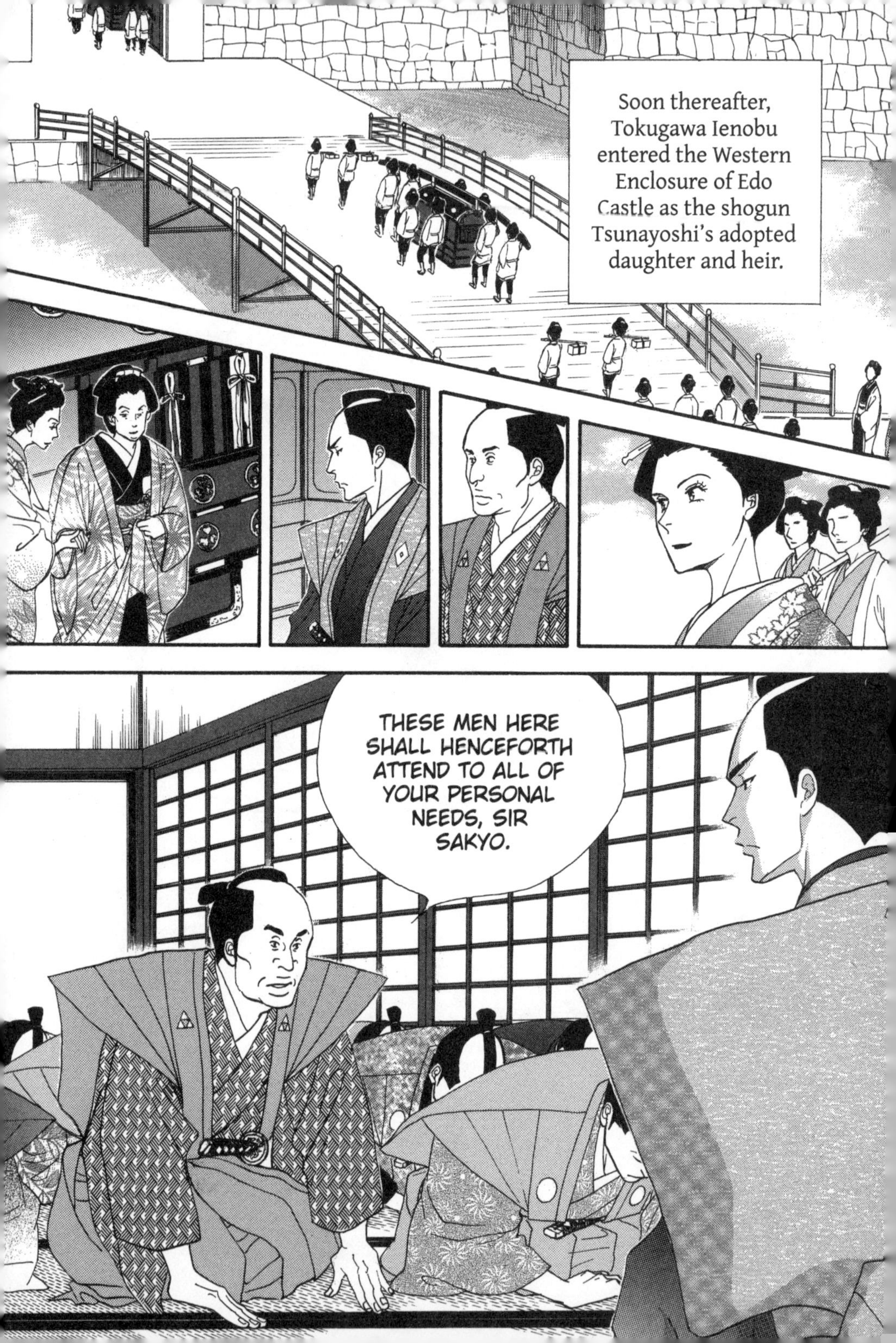
Soon thereafter, Tokugawa Ienobu entered the Western Enclosure of Edo Castle as the shogun Tsunayoshi's adopted daughter and heir.
THESE MEN HERE SHALL HENCEFORTH ATTEND TO ALL OF YOUR PERSONAL NEEDS, SIR SAKYO.

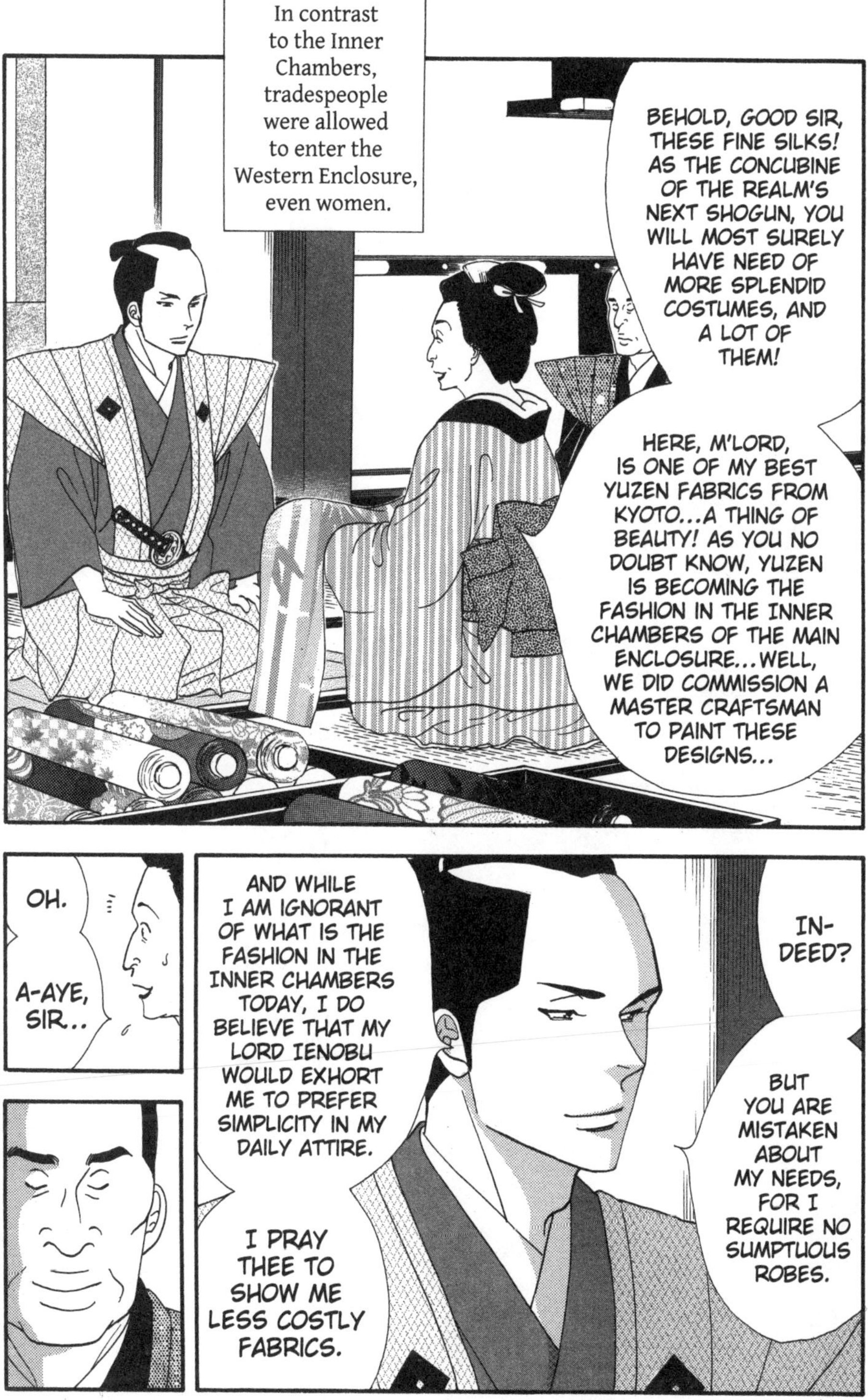
In contrast to the Inner Chambers, tradespeople were allowed to enter the Western Enclosure, even women.
BEHOLD, GOOD SIR, THESE FINE SILKS! AS THE CONCUBINE OF THE REALM'S NEXT SHOGUN, YOU WILL MOST SURELY HAVE NEED OF MORE SPLENDID COSTUMES, AND A LOT OF THEM!
HERE, M'LORD, IS ONE OF MY BEST YUZEN FABRICS FROM KYOTO...A THING OF BEAUTY! AS YOU NO DOUBT KNOW, YUZEN IS BECOMING THE FASHION IN THE INNER CHAMBERS OF THE MAIN ENCLOSURE...WELL, WE DID COMMISSION A MASTER CRAFTSMAN TO PAINT THESE DESIGNS...
IN-DEED?
BUT YOU ARE MISTAKEN ABOUT MY NEEDS, FOR I REQUIRE NO SUMPTUOUS ROBES.
AND WHILE I AM IGNORANT OF WHAT IS THE FASHION IN THE INNER CHAMBERS TODAY, I DO BELIEVE THAT MY LORD IENOBU WOULD EXHORT ME TO PREFER SIMPLICITY IN MY DAILY ATTIRE.
I PRAY THEE TO SHOW ME LESS COSTLY FABRICS.
OH.
A-AYE, SIR...

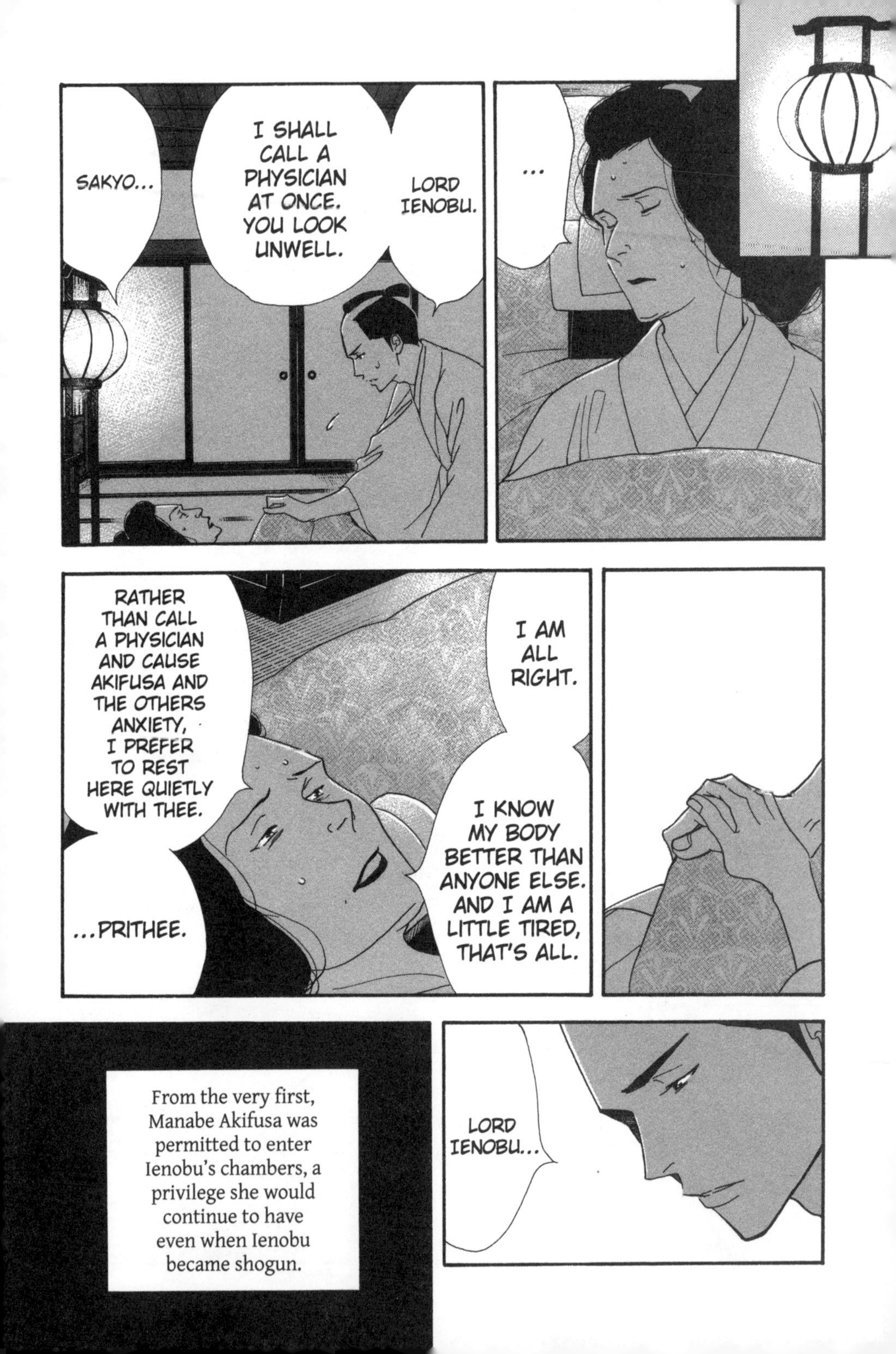
...
LORD IENOBU.
I SHALL CALL A PHYSICIAN AT ONCE. YOU LOOK UNWELL.
SAKYO...
I AM ALL RIGHT.
I KNOW MY BODY BETTER THAN ANYONE ELSE. AND I AM A LITTLE TIRED, THAT'S ALL.
RATHER THAN CALL A PHYSICIAN AND CAUSE AKIFUSA AND THE OTHERS ANXIETY, I PREFER TO REST HERE QUIETLY WITH THEE.
...PRITHEE.
LORD IENOBU...
From the very first, Manabe Akifusa was permitted to enter Ienobu's chambers, a privilege she would continue to have even when Ienobu became shogun.

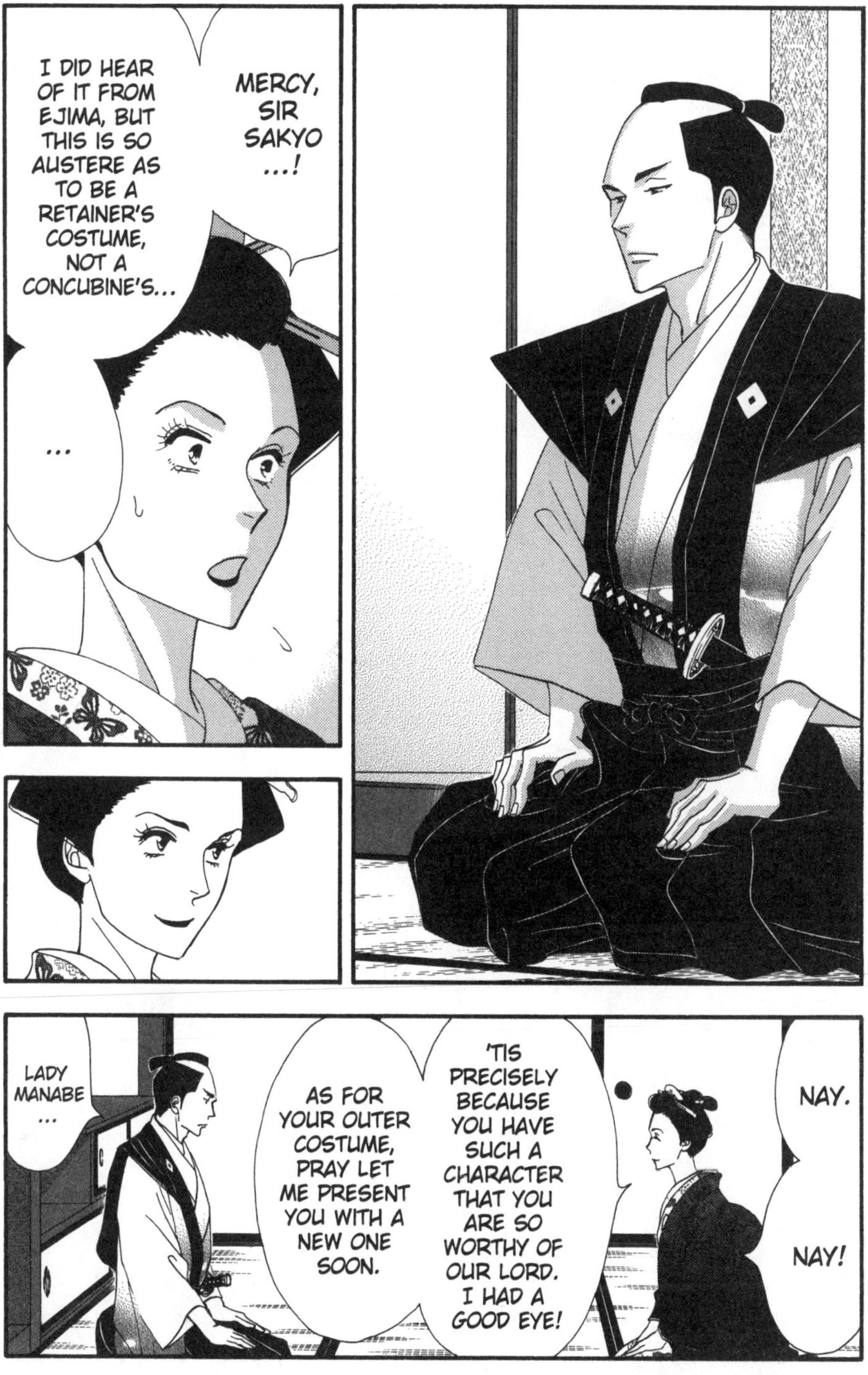
MERCY, SIR SAKYO ...!
I DID HEAR OF IT FROM EJIMA, BUT THIS IS SO AUSTERE AS TO BE A RETAINER'S COSTUME, NOT A CONCUBINE'S...
...
NAY.
NAY!
'TIS PRECISELY BECAUSE YOU HAVE SUCH A CHARACTER THAT YOU ARE SO WORTHY OF OUR LORD. I HAD A GOOD EYE!
AS FOR YOUR OUTER COSTUME, PRAY LET ME PRESENT YOU WITH A NEW ONE SOON.
LADY MANABE ...

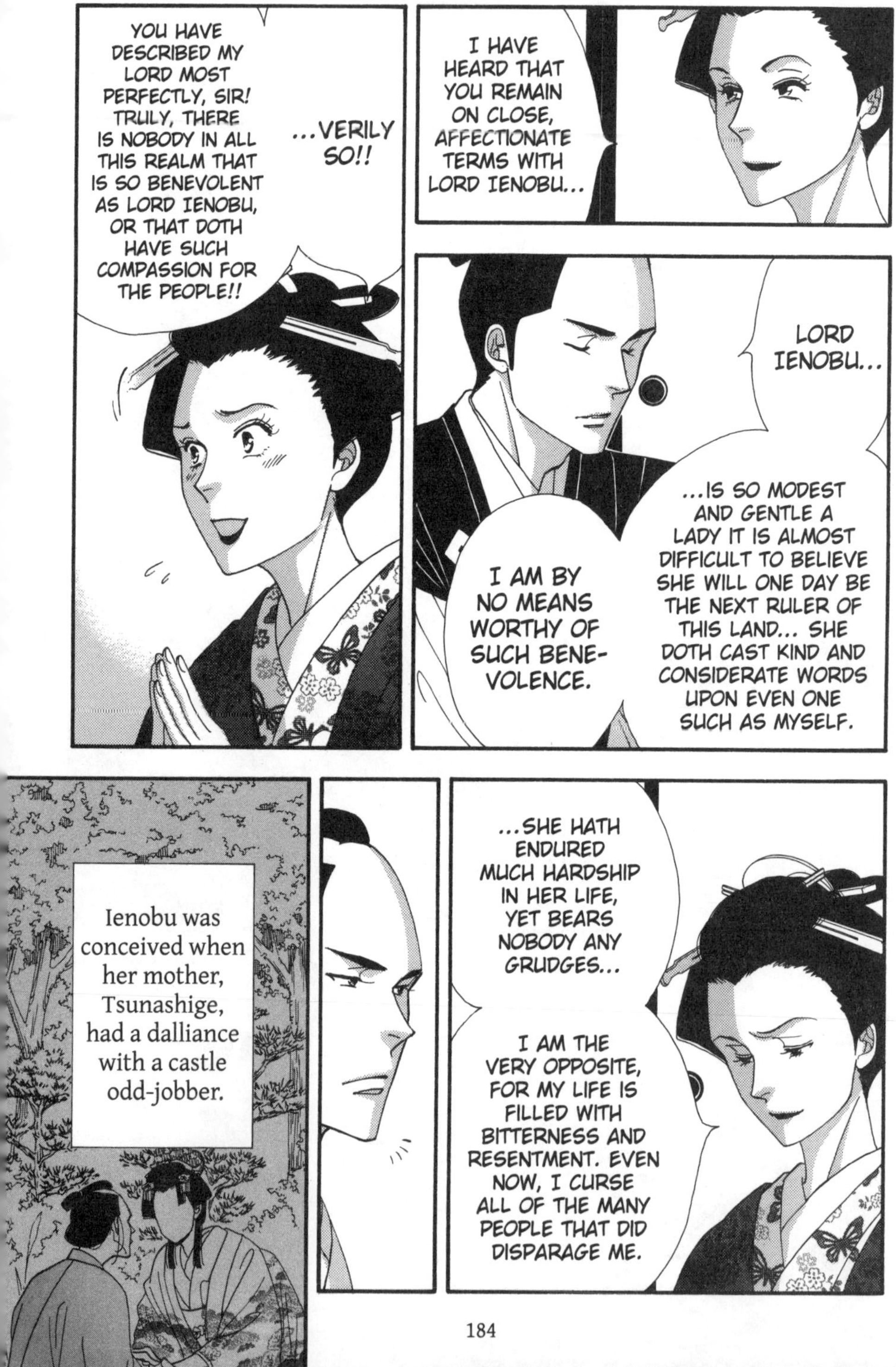
I HAVE HEARD THAT YOU REMAIN ON CLOSE, AFFECTIONATE TERMS WITH LORD IENOBU...
LORD IENOBU...
...IS SO MODEST AND GENTLE A LADY IT IS ALMOST DIFFICULT TO BELIEVE SHE WILL ONE DAY BE THE NEXT RULER OF THIS LAND... SHE DOTH CAST KIND AND CONSIDERATE WORDS UPON EVEN ONE SUCH AS MYSELF.
I AM BY NO MEANS WORTHY OF SUCH BENE-VOLENCE.
YOU HAVE DESCRIBED MY LORD MOST PERFECTLY, SIR! TRULY, THERE IS NOBODY IN ALL THIS REALM THAT IS SO BENEVOLENT AS LORD IENOBU, OR THAT DOTH HAVE SUCH COMPASSION FOR THE PEOPLE!!
...VERILY SO!!
...SHE HATH ENDURED MUCH HARDSHIP IN HER LIFE, YET BEARS NOBODY ANY GRUDGES...
I AM THE VERY OPPOSITE, FOR MY LIFE IS FILLED WITH BITTERNESS AND RESENTMENT. EVEN NOW, I CURSE ALL OF THE MANY PEOPLE THAT DID DISPARAGE ME.
Ienobu was conceived when her mother, Tsunashige, had a dalliance with a castle odd-jobber.

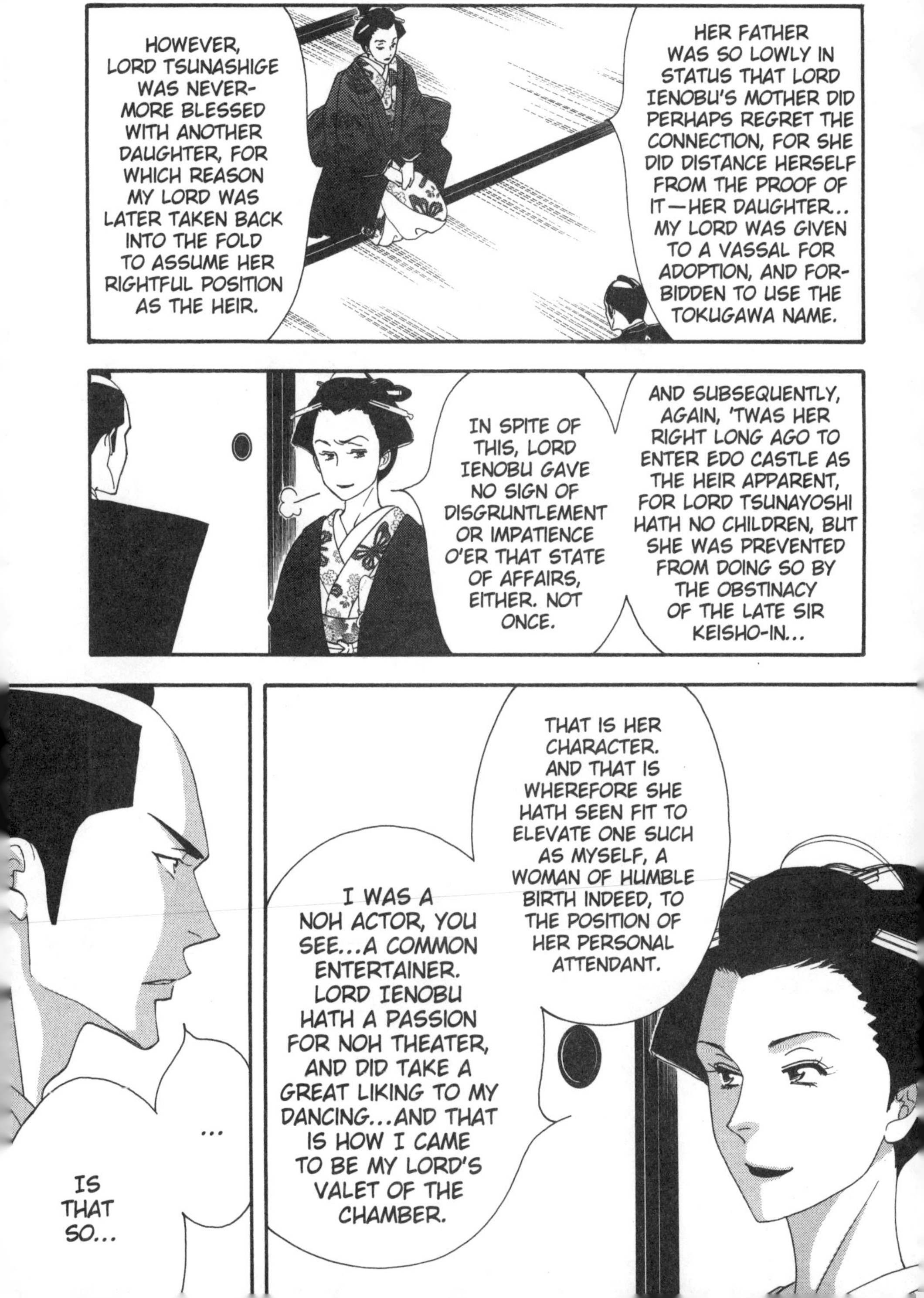
HER FATHER WAS SO LOWLY IN STATUS THAT LORD IENOBU'S MOTHER DID PERHAPS REGRET THE CONNECTION, FOR SHE DID DISTANCE HERSELF FROM THE PROOF OF IT—HER DAUGHTER... MY LORD WAS GIVEN TO A VASSAL FOR ADOPTION, AND FOR-BIDDEN TO USE THE TOKUGAWA NAME.
HOWEVER, LORD TSUNASHIGE WAS NEVER-MORE BLESSED WITH ANOTHER DAUGHTER, FOR WHICH REASON MY LORD WAS LATER TAKEN BACK INTO THE FOLD TO ASSUME HER RIGHTFUL POSITION AS THE HEIR.
AND SUBSEQUENTLY, AGAIN, 'TWAS HER RIGHT LONG AGO TO ENTER EDO CASTLE AS THE HEIR APPARENT, FOR LORD TSUNAYOSHI HATH NO CHILDREN, BUT SHE WAS PREVENTED FROM DOING SO BY THE OBSTINACY OF THE LATE SIR KEISHO-IN...
IN SPITE OF THIS, LORD IENOBU GAVE NO SIGN OF DISGRUNTLEMENT OR IMPATIENCE O'ER THAT STATE OF AFFAIRS, EITHER. NOT ONCE.
THAT IS HER CHARACTER. AND THAT IS WHEREFORE SHE HATH SEEN FIT TO ELEVATE ONE SUCH AS MYSELF, A WOMAN OF HUMBLE BIRTH INDEED, TO THE POSITION OF HER PERSONAL ATTENDANT.
I WAS A NOH ACTOR, YOU SEE...A COMMON ENTERTAINER. LORD IENOBU HATH A PASSION FOR NOH THEATER, AND DID TAKE A GREAT LIKING TO MY DANCING...AND THAT IS HOW I CAME TO BE MY LORD'S VALET OF THE CHAMBER.
...
IS THAT SO...

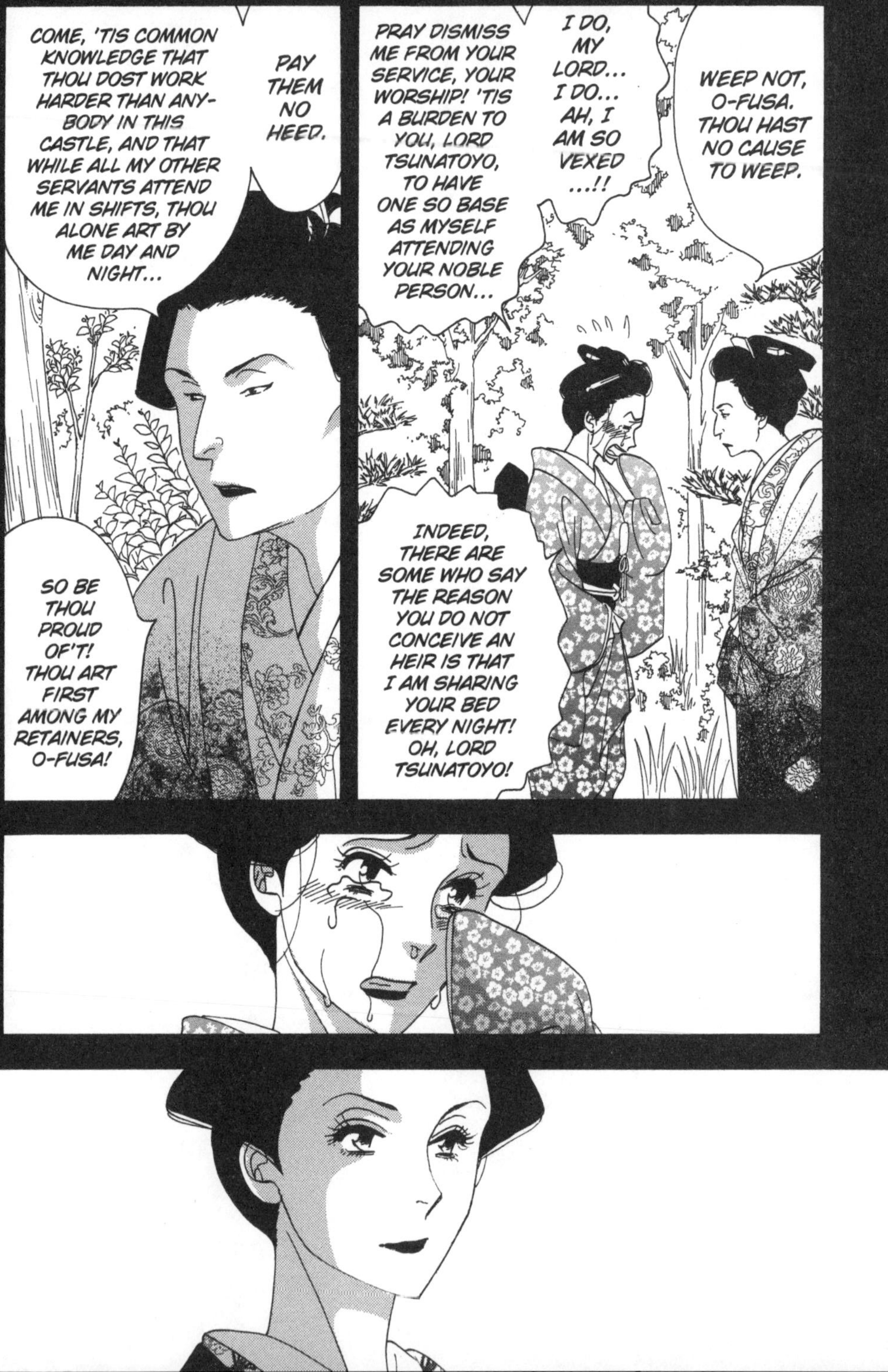
WEEP NOT, O-FUSA. THOU HAST NO CAUSE TO WEEP.
I DO, MY LORD... I DO... AH, I AM SO VEXED ...!!
PRAY DISMISS ME FROM YOUR SERVICE, YOUR WORSHIP! 'TIS A BURDEN TO YOU, LORD TSUNATOYO, TO HAVE ONE SO BASE AS MYSELF ATTENDING YOUR NOBLE PERSON...
INDEED, THERE ARE SOME WHO SAY THE REASON YOU DO NOT CONCEIVE AN HEIR IS THAT I AM SHARING YOUR BED EVERY NIGHT! OH, LORD TSUNATOYO!
PAY THEM NO HEED.
COME, 'TIS COMMON KNOWLEDGE THAT THOU DOST WORK HARDER THAN ANY-BODY IN THIS CASTLE, AND THAT WHILE ALL MY OTHER SERVANTS ATTEND ME IN SHIFTS, THOU ALONE ART BY ME DAY AND NIGHT...
SO BE THOU PROUD OF'T! THOU ART FIRST AMONG MY RETAINERS, O-FUSA!

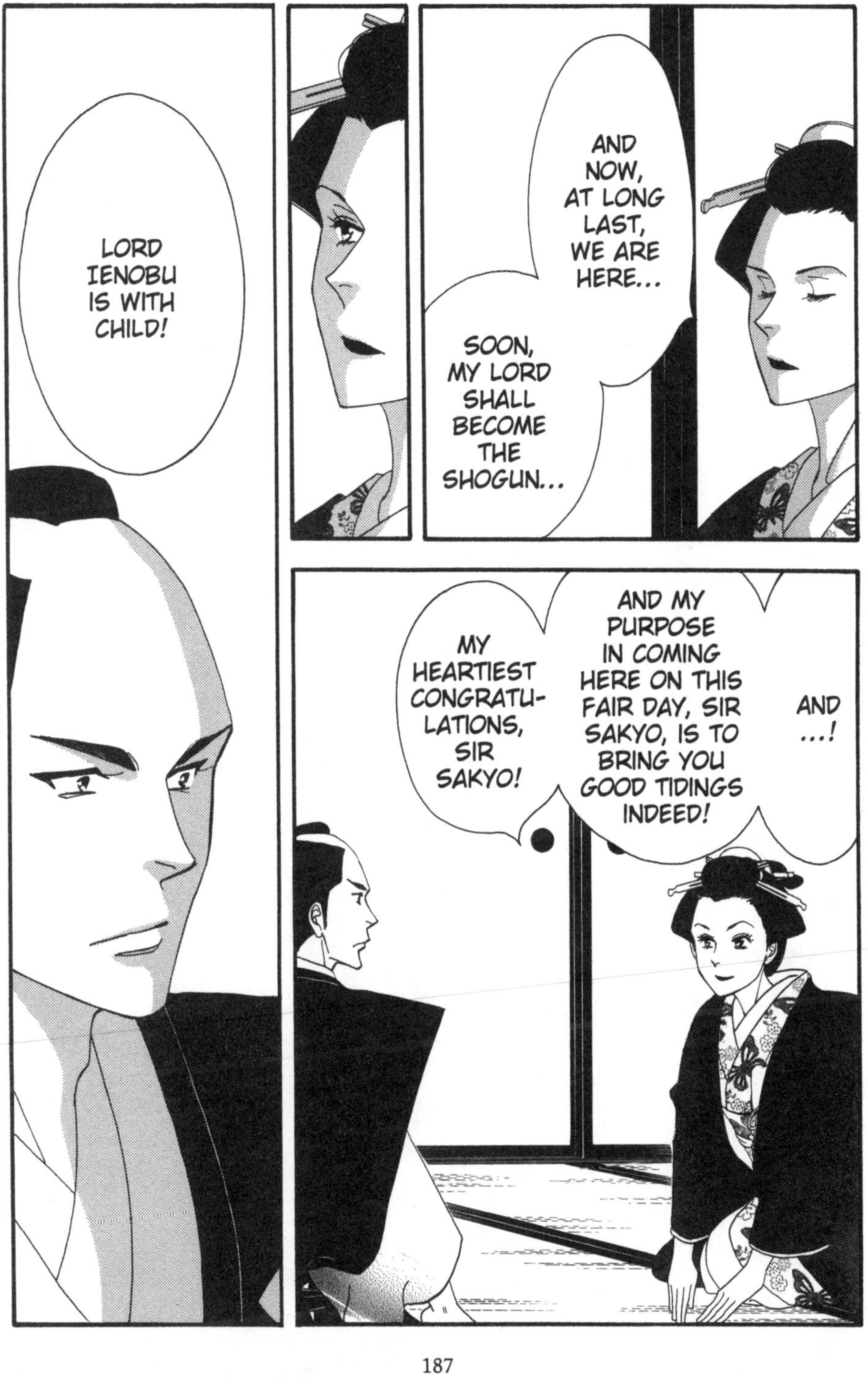
AND NOW, AT LONG LAST, WE ARE HERE...
SOON, MY LORD SHALL BECOME THE SHOGUN...
AND ...!
AND MY PURPOSE IN COMING HERE ON THIS FAIR DAY, SIR SAKYO, IS TO BRING YOU GOOD TIDINGS INDEED!
MY HEARTIEST CONGRATU-LATIONS, SIR SAKYO!
LORD IENOBU IS WITH CHILD!

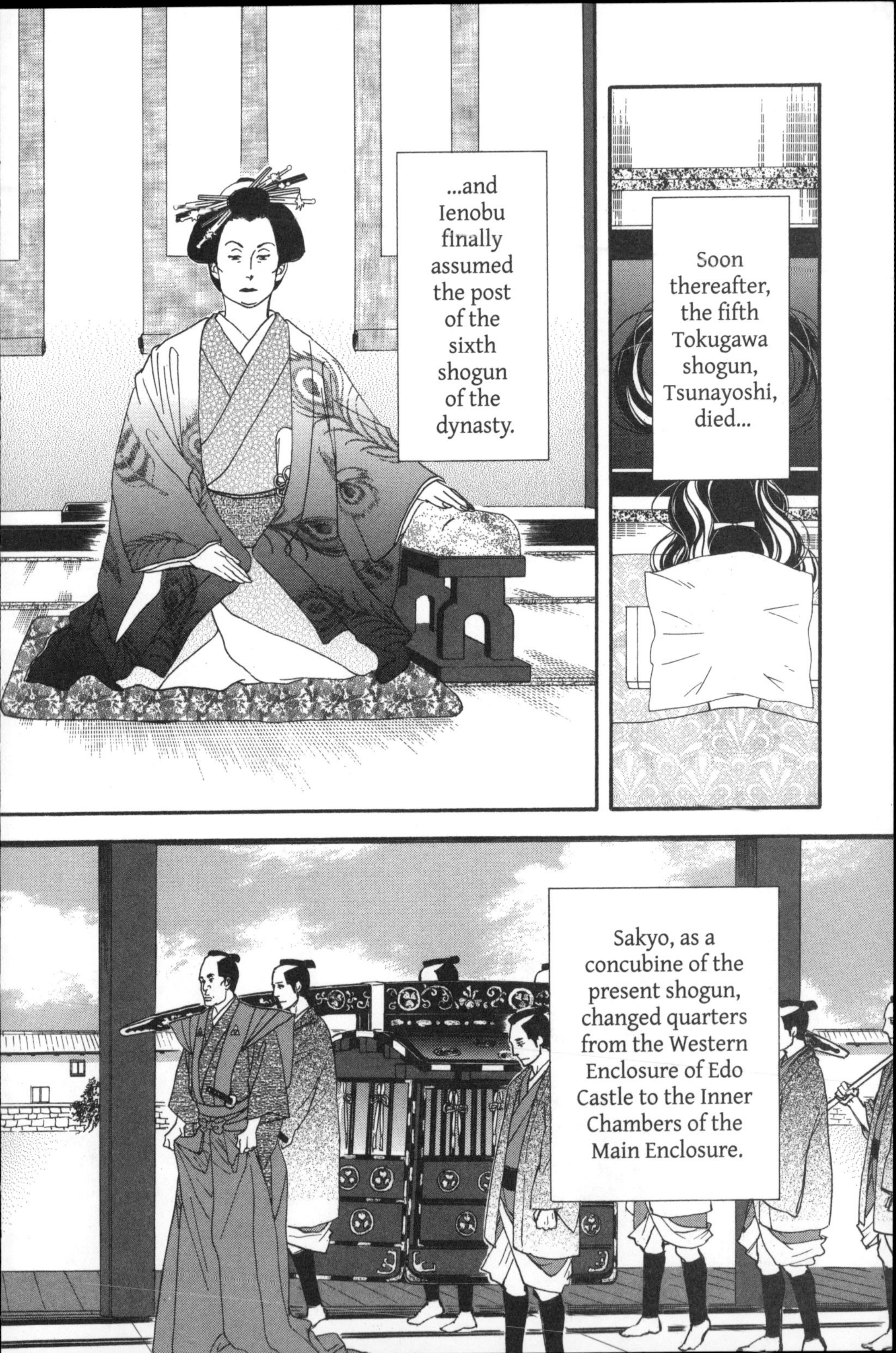
Soon thereafter, the fifth Tokugawa shogun, Tsunayoshi, died...
...and Ienobu finally assumed the post of the sixth shogun of the dynasty.
Sakyo, as a concubine of the present shogun, changed quarters from the Western Enclosure of Edo Castle to the Inner Chambers of the Main Enclosure.

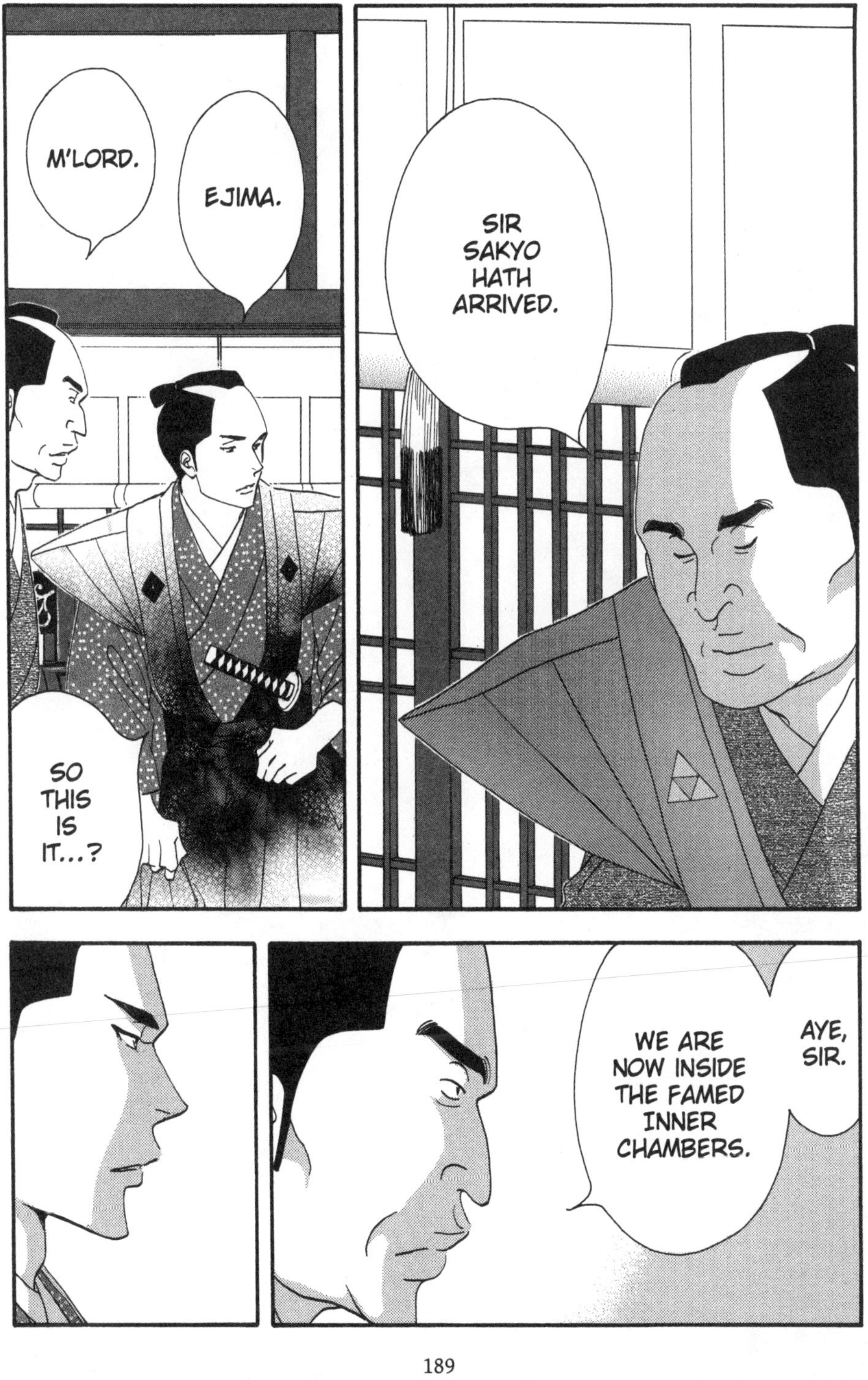
SIR SAKYO HATH ARRIVED.
EJIMA.
M'LORD.
SO THIS IS IT...?
AYE, SIR.
WE ARE NOW INSIDE THE FAMED INNER CHAMBERS.

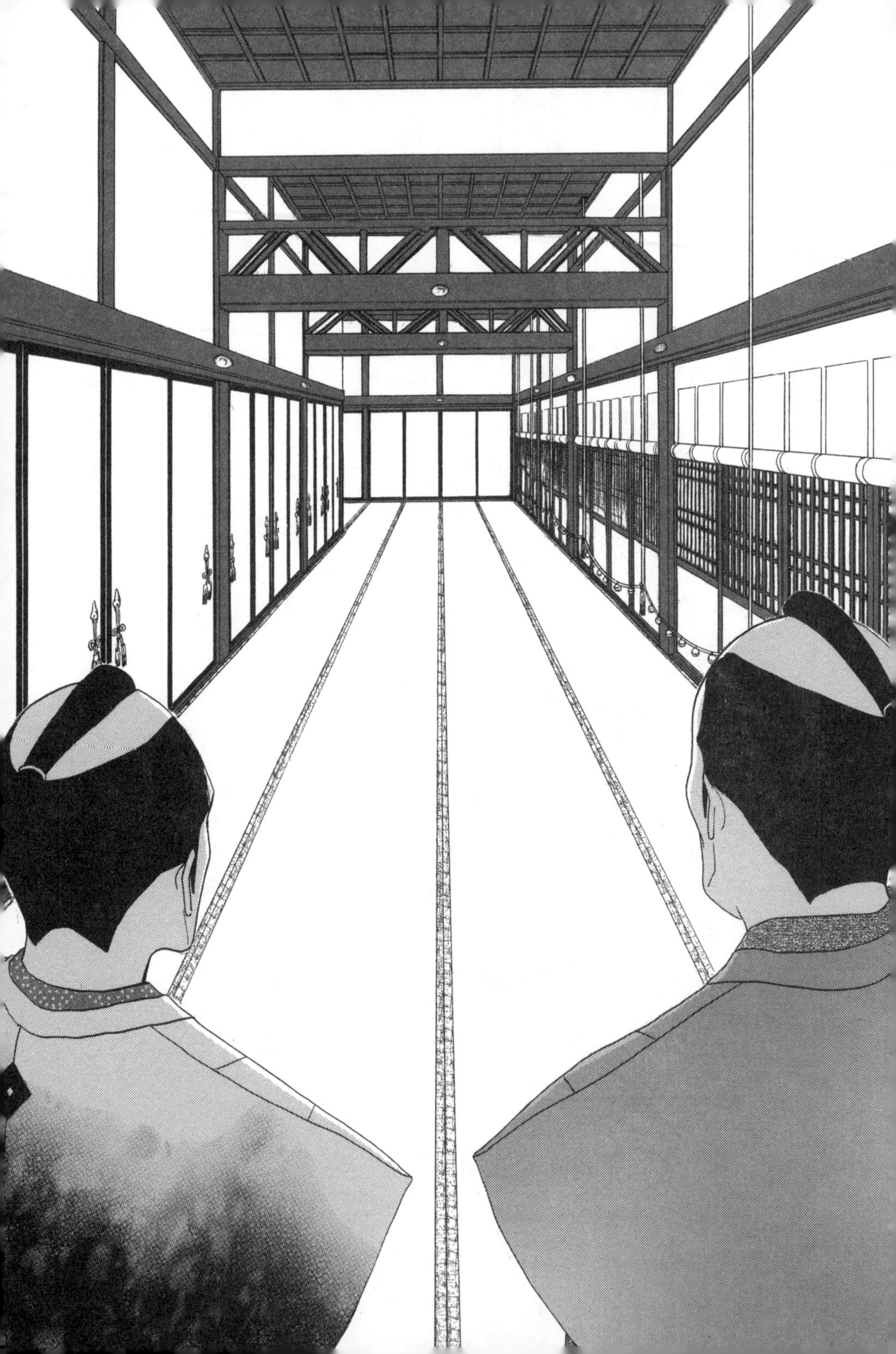

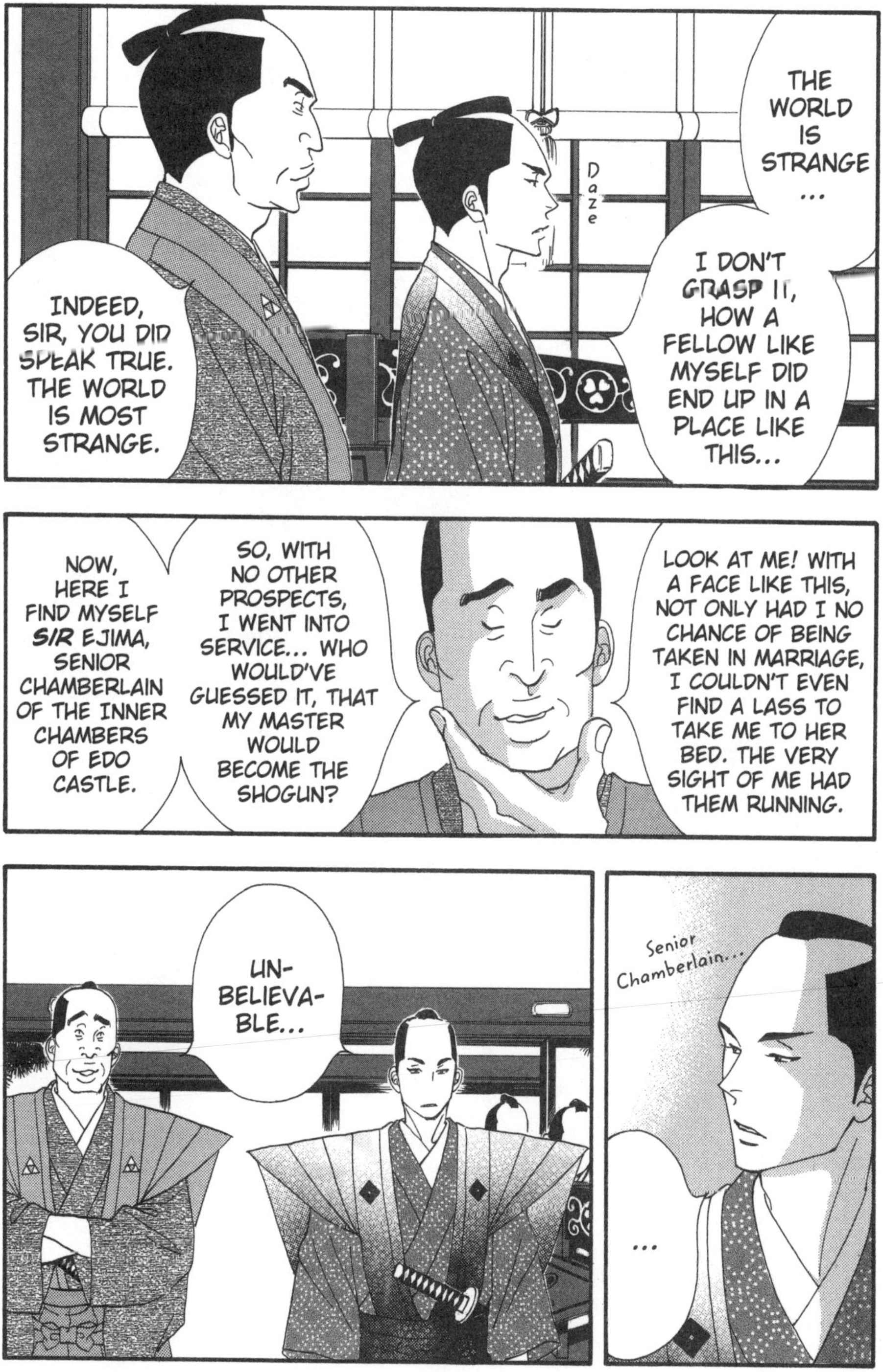
THE WORLD IS STRANGE...
I DON'T GRASP IT, HOW A FELLOW LIKE MYSELF DID END UP IN A PLACE LIKE THIS...
Daze
INDEED, SIR, YOU DID SPEAK TRUE. THE WORLD IS MOST STRANGE.
LOOK AT ME! WITH A FACE LIKE THIS, NOT ONLY HAD I NO CHANCE OF BEING TAKEN IN MARRIAGE, I COULDN'T EVEN FIND A LASS TO TAKE ME TO HER BED. THE VERY SIGHT OF ME HAD THEM RUNNING.
SO, WITH NO OTHER PROSPECTS, I WENT INTO SERVICE... WHO WOULD'VE GUESSED IT, THAT MY MASTER WOULD BECOME THE SHOGUN?
NOW, HERE I FIND MYSELF *SIR* EJIMA, SENIOR CHAMBERLAIN OF THE INNER CHAMBERS OF EDO CASTLE.
Senior Chamberlain...
...
UN-BELIEVA-BLE...

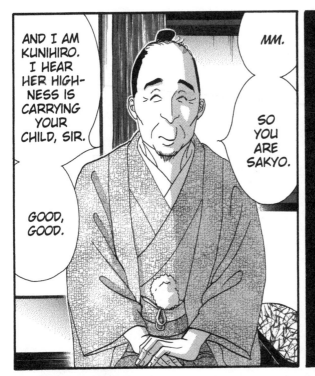

It was only after entering the Inner Chambers that Sakyo visited Ienobu's official consort, Sir Kunihiro, for the first time.
MM.
SO YOU ARE SAKYO.
AND I AM KUNIHIRO. I HEAR HER HIGHNESS IS CARRYING YOUR CHILD, SIR.
GOOD, GOOD.
DEAR SIR!
I AM MOST GRATIFIED TO MAKE YOUR ACQUAINTANCE, LORD CONSORT, AND TO BEHOLD HOW HALE YOU ARE.
AH HA HA! NO NEED FOR SUCH STIFFNESS OF MANNER, GOOD FELLOW.

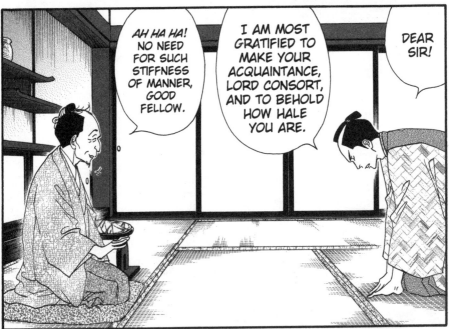

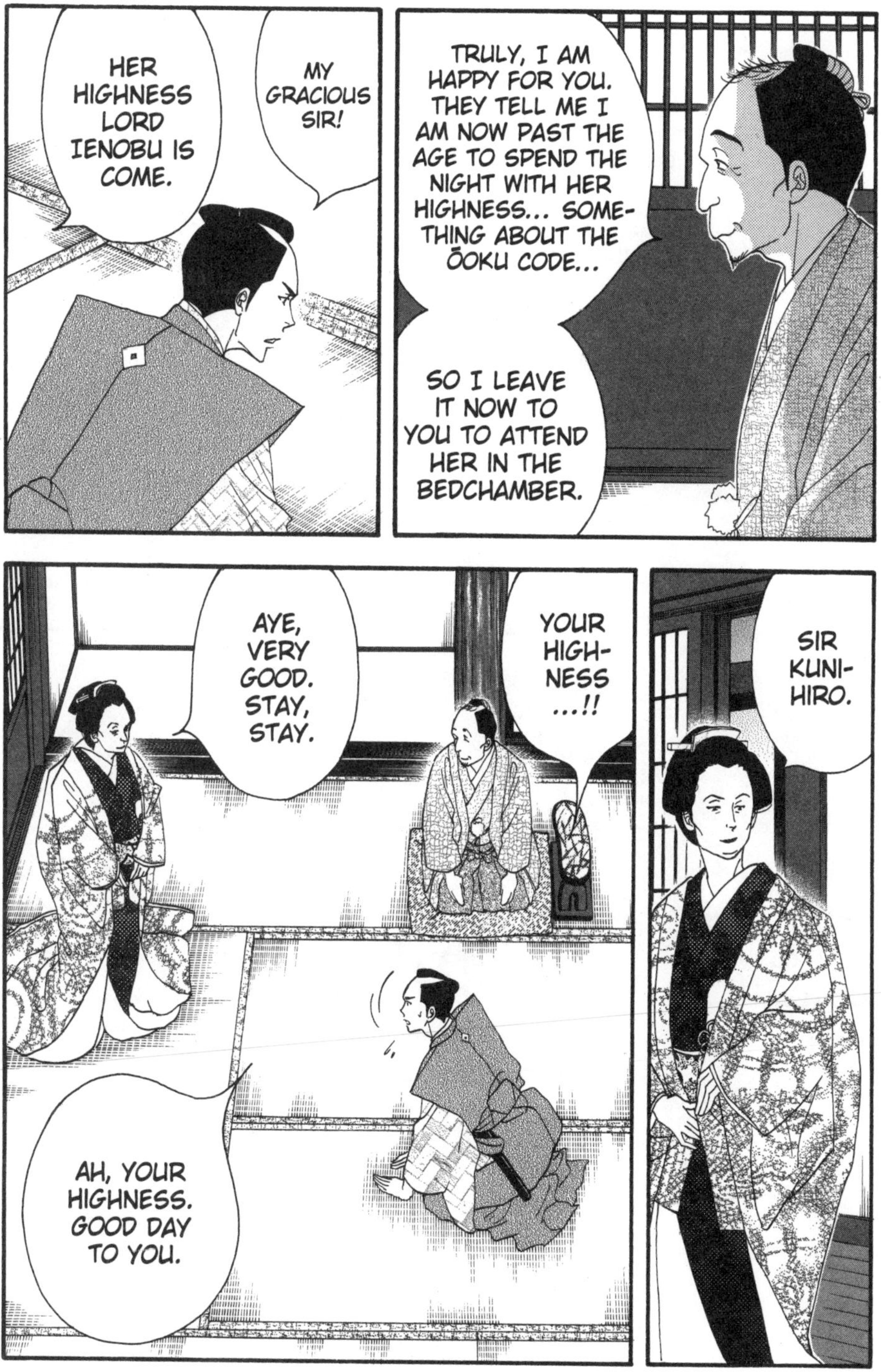
TRULY, I AM HAPPY FOR YOU. THEY TELL ME I AM NOW PAST THE AGE TO SPEND THE NIGHT WITH HER HIGHNESS... SOMETHING ABOUT THE ŌOKU CODE...
SO I LEAVE IT NOW TO YOU TO ATTEND HER IN THE BEDCHAMBER.
MY GRACIOUS SIR!
HER HIGHNESS LORD IENOBU IS COME.
SIR KUNIHIRO.
YOUR HIGHNESS...!!
AYE, VERY GOOD. STAY, STAY.
AH, YOUR HIGHNESS. GOOD DAY TO YOU.

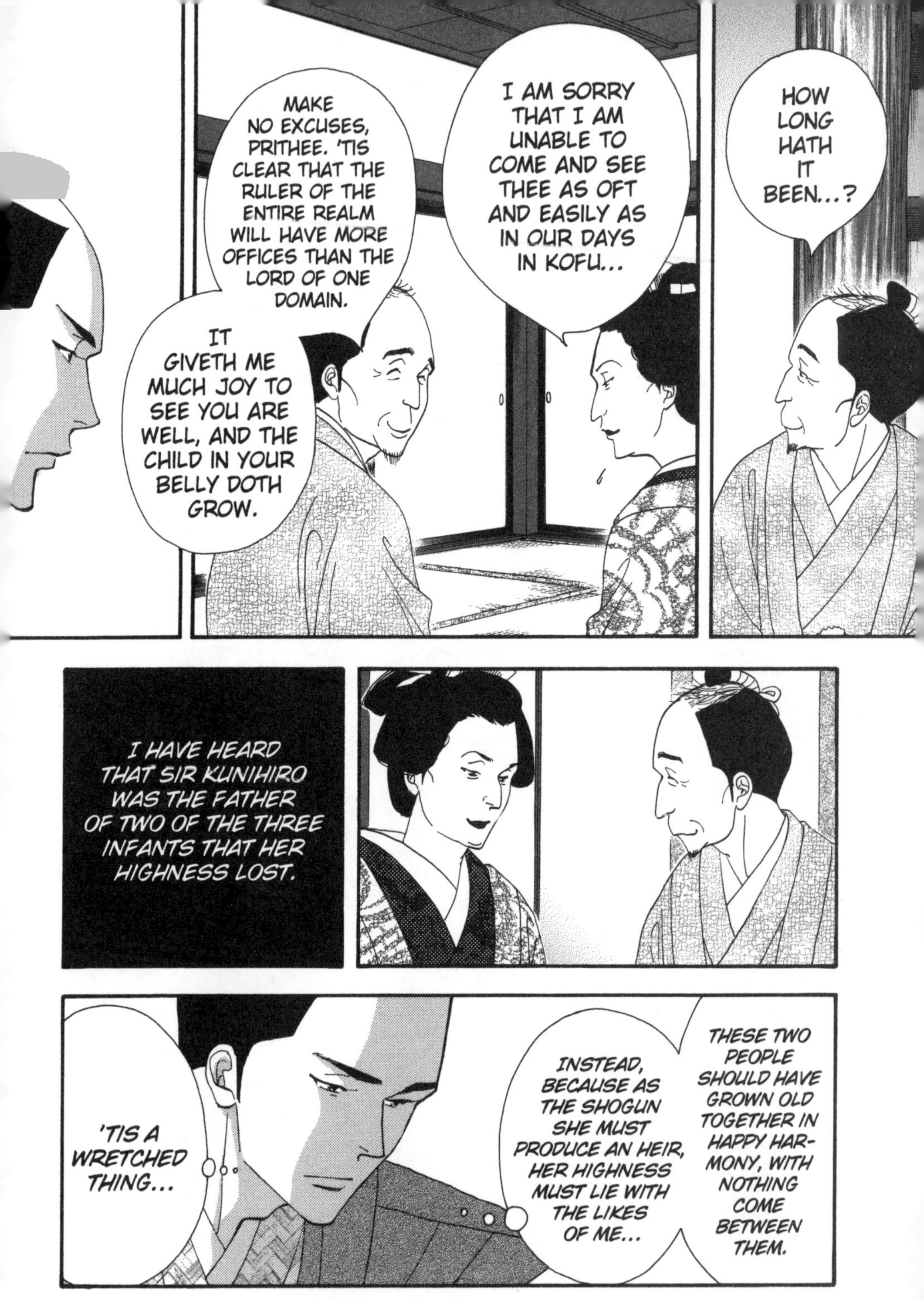
HOW LONG HATH IT BEEN...?
I AM SORRY THAT I AM UNABLE TO COME AND SEE THEE AS OFT AND EASILY AS IN OUR DAYS IN KOFU...
MAKE NO EXCUSES, PRITHEE. 'TIS CLEAR THAT THE RULER OF THE ENTIRE REALM WILL HAVE MORE OFFICES THAN THE LORD OF ONE DOMAIN.
IT GIVETH ME MUCH JOY TO SEE YOU ARE WELL, AND THE CHILD IN YOUR BELLY DOTH GROW.
I HAVE HEARD THAT SIR KUNIHIRO WAS THE FATHER OF TWO OF THE THREE INFANTS THAT HER HIGHNESS LOST.
THESE TWO PEOPLE SHOULD HAVE GROWN OLD TOGETHER IN HAPPY HAR-MONY, WITH NOTHING COME BETWEEN THEM.
INSTEAD, BECAUSE AS THE SHOGUN SHE MUST PRODUCE AN HEIR, HER HIGHNESS MUST LIE WITH THE LIKES OF ME...
'TIS A WRETCHED THING...

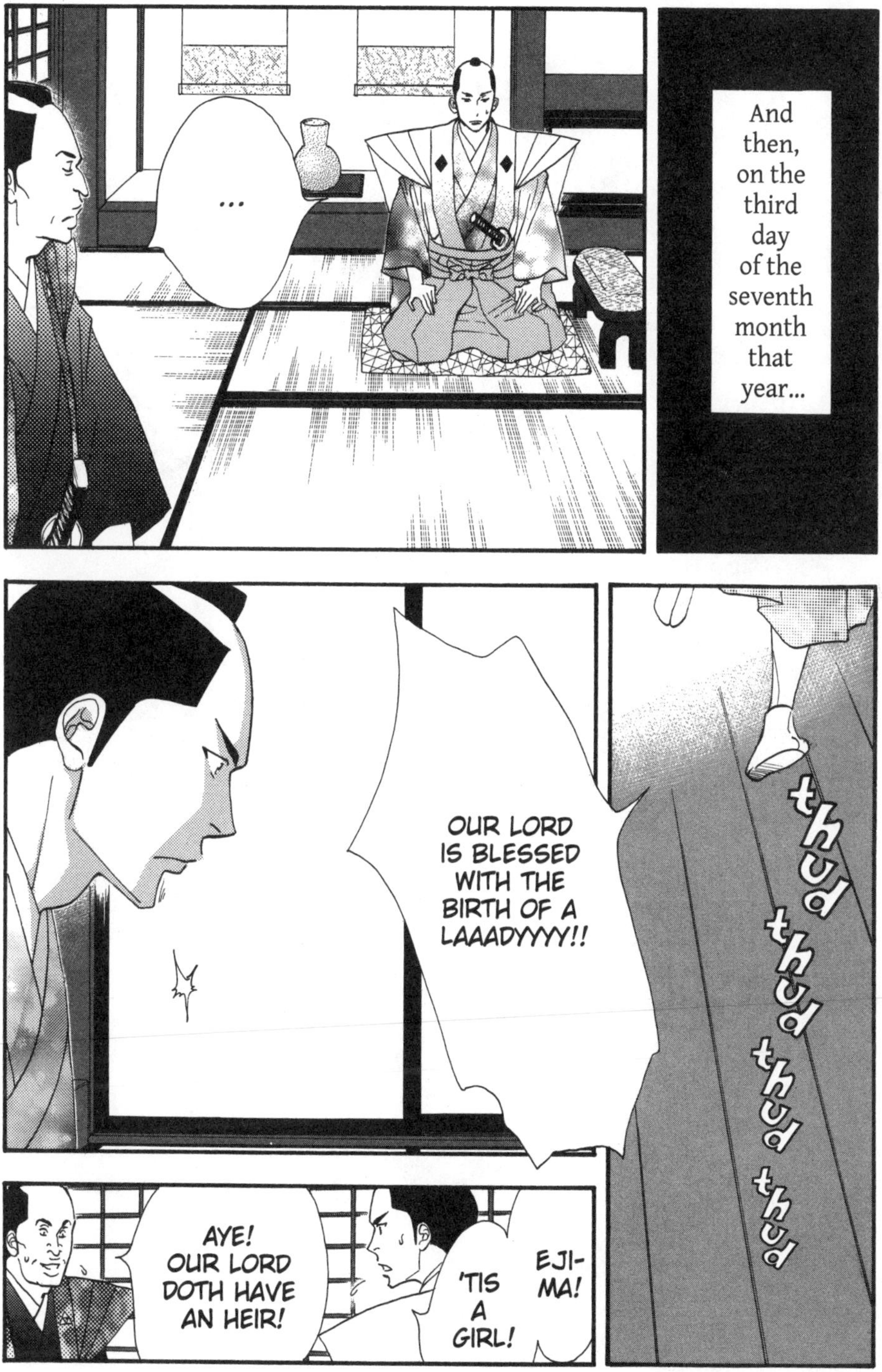
And then, on the third day of the seventh month that year...
...
thud thud thud thud
OUR LORD IS BLESSED WITH THE BIRTH OF A LAAADYYYY!!
EJI-MA!
'TIS A GIRL!
AYE! OUR LORD DOTH HAVE AN HEIR!

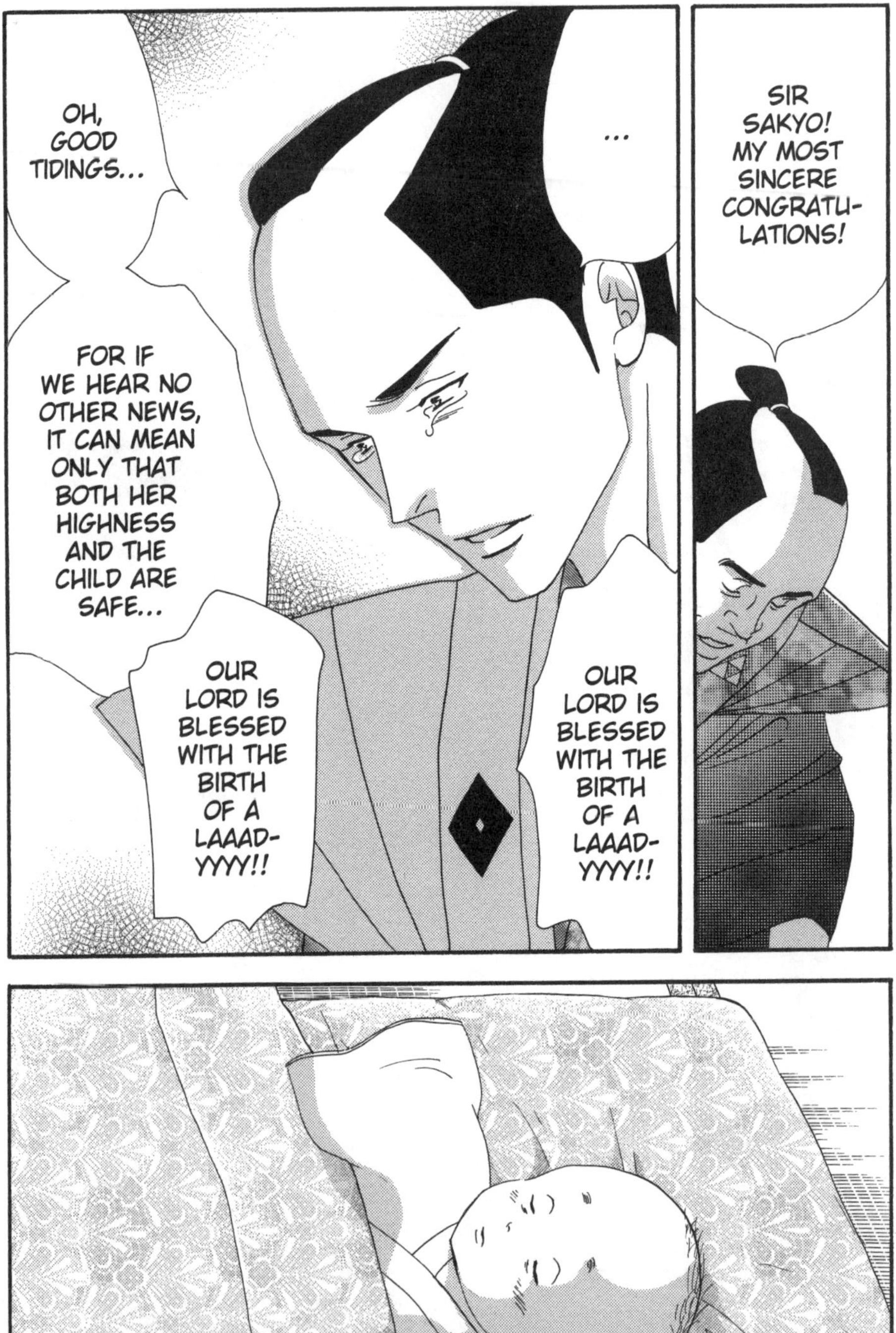
SIR SAKYO! MY MOST SINCERE CONGRATULATIONS!
...
OH, GOOD TIDINGS...
FOR IF WE HEAR NO OTHER NEWS, IT CAN MEAN ONLY THAT BOTH HER HIGHNESS AND THE CHILD ARE SAFE...
OUR LORD IS BLESSED WITH THE BIRTH OF A LAAAD-YYYY!!
OUR LORD IS BLESSED WITH THE BIRTH OF A LAAAD-YYYY!!

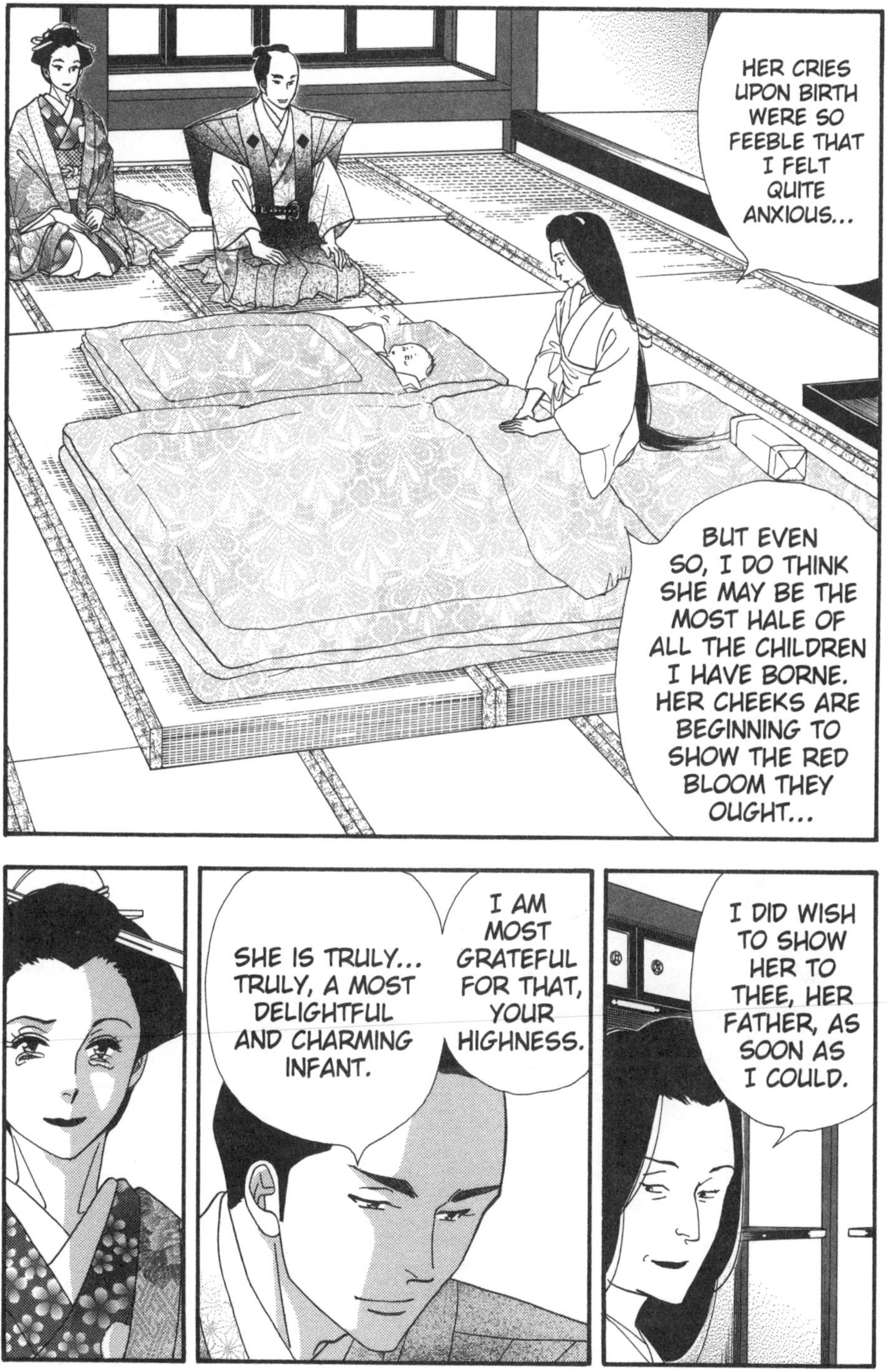
HER CRIES UPON BIRTH WERE SO FEEBLE THAT I FELT QUITE ANXIOUS...
BUT EVEN SO, I DO THINK SHE MAY BE THE MOST HALE OF ALL THE CHILDREN I HAVE BORNE. HER CHEEKS ARE BEGINNING TO SHOW THE RED BLOOM THEY OUGHT...
I DID WISH TO SHOW HER TO THEE, HER FATHER, AS SOON AS I COULD.
I AM MOST GRATEFUL FOR THAT, YOUR HIGHNESS.
SHE IS TRULY... TRULY, A MOST DELIGHTFUL AND CHARMING INFANT.

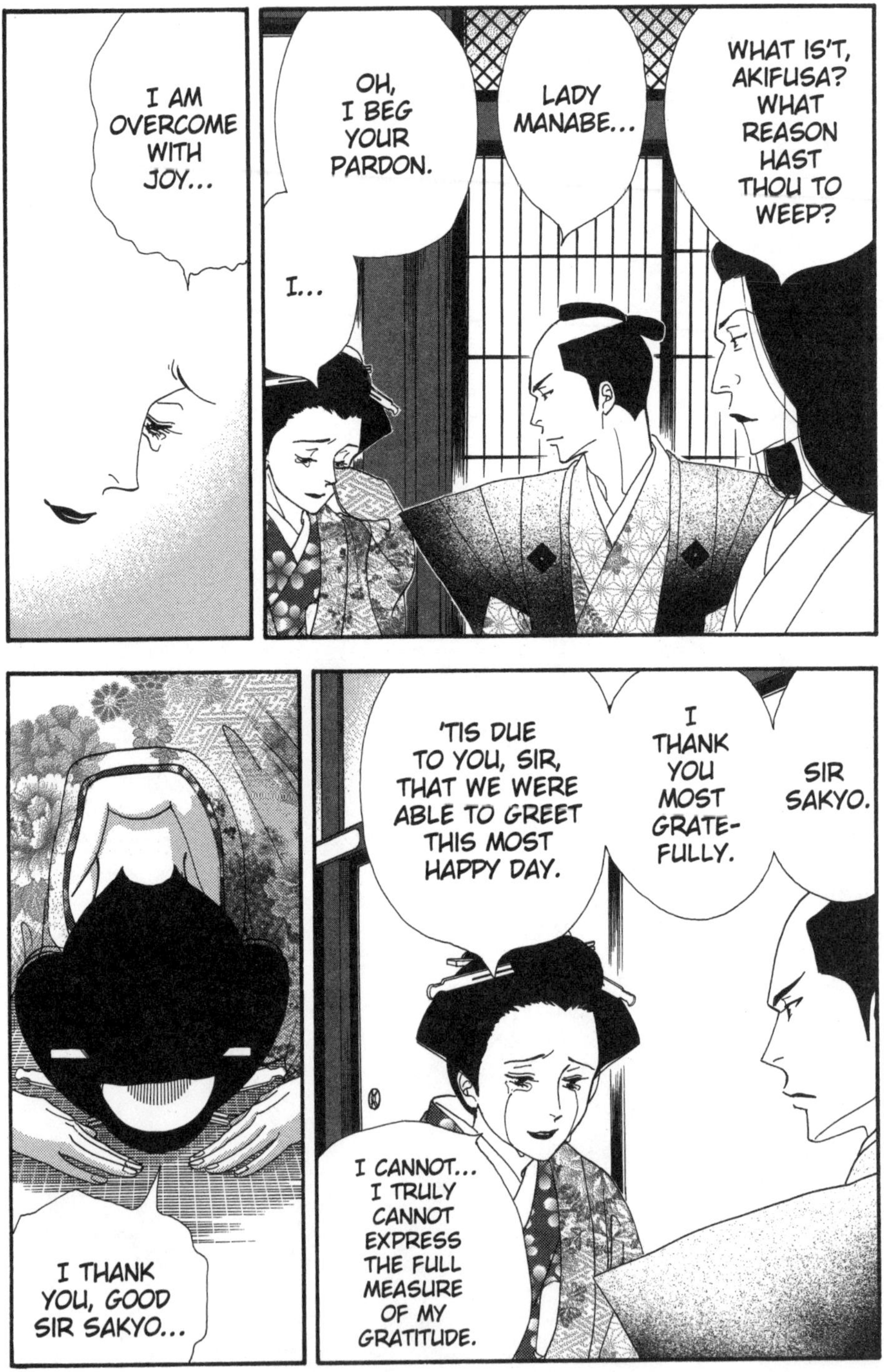
WHAT IS'T, AKIFUSA? WHAT REASON HAST THOU TO WEEP?
LADY MANABE...
OH, I BEG YOUR PARDON.
I...
I AM OVERCOME WITH JOY...
SIR SAKYO.
I THANK YOU MOST GRATE-FULLY.
'TIS DUE TO YOU, SIR, THAT WE WERE ABLE TO GREET THIS MOST HAPPY DAY.
I CANNOT... I TRULY CANNOT EXPRESS THE FULL MEASURE OF MY GRATITUDE.
I THANK YOU, GOOD SIR SAKYO...

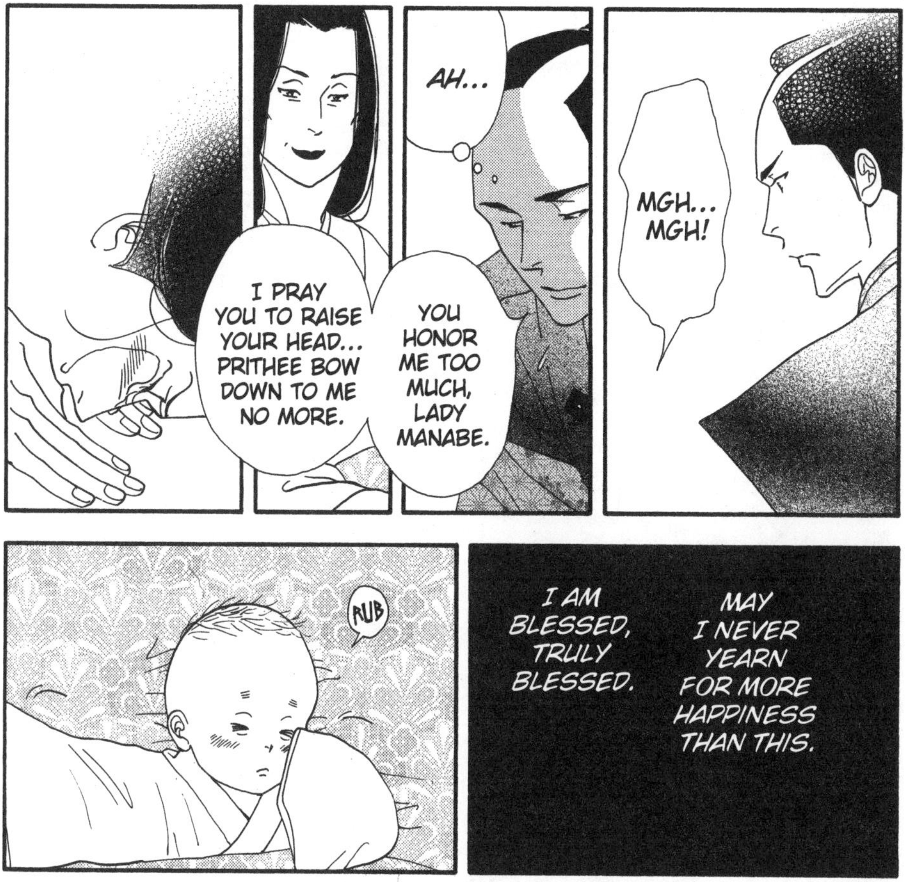
MGH... MGH!
AH...
YOU HONOR ME TOO MUCH, LADY MANABE.
I PRAY YOU TO RAISE YOUR HEAD... PRITHEE BOW DOWN TO ME NO MORE.
I AM BLESSED, TRULY BLESSED.
MAY I NEVER YEARN FOR MORE HAPPINESS THAN THIS.
RUB

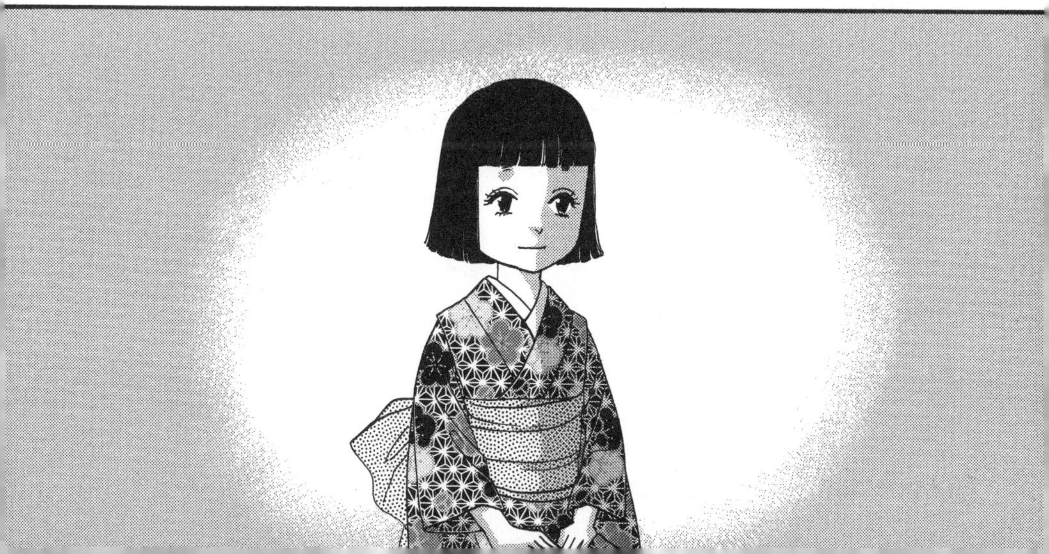

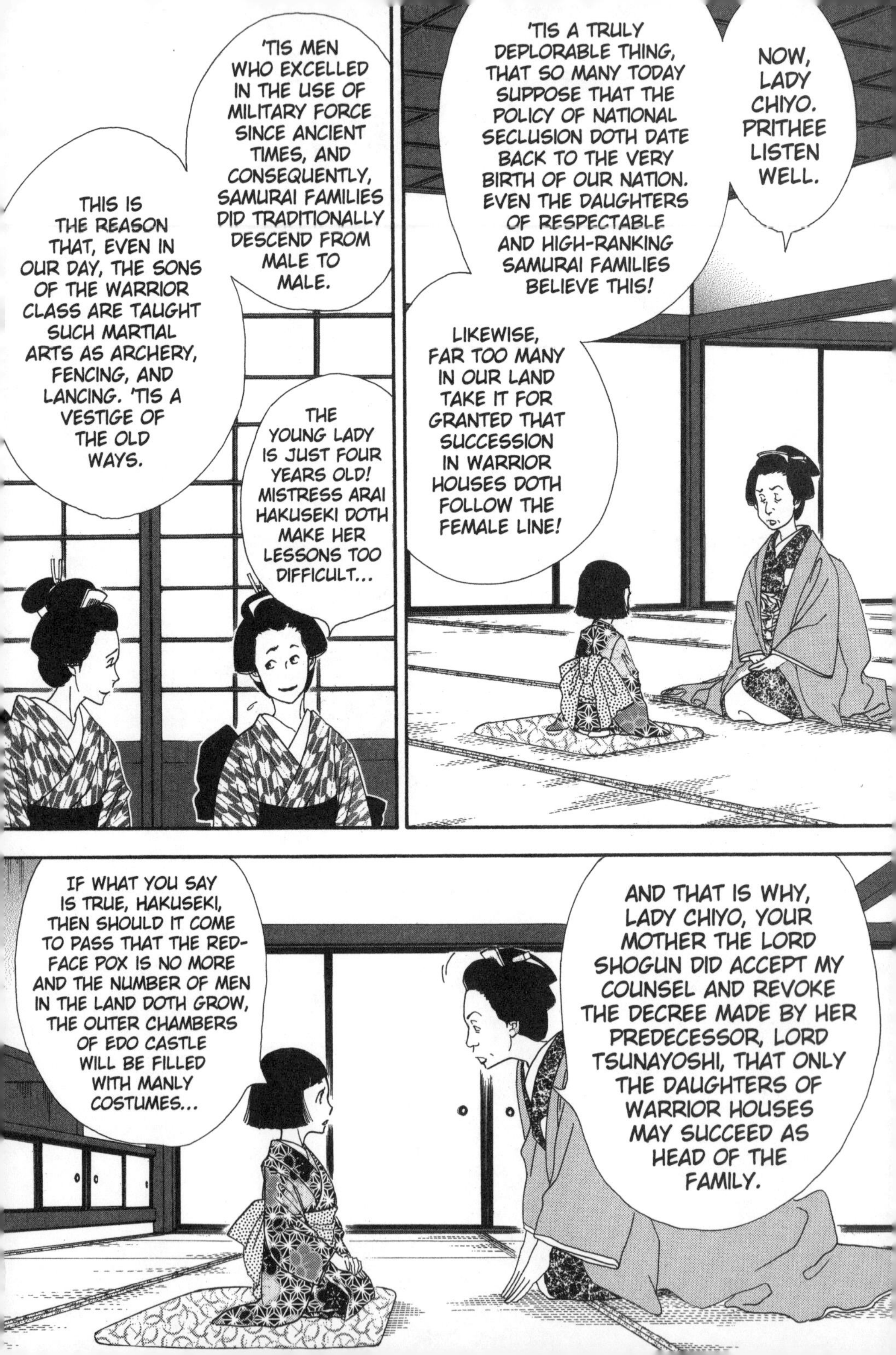
NOW, LADY CHIYO. PRITHEE LISTEN WELL.
'TIS A TRULY DEPLORABLE THING, THAT SO MANY TODAY SUPPOSE THAT THE POLICY OF NATIONAL SECLUSION DOTH DATE BACK TO THE VERY BIRTH OF OUR NATION. EVEN THE DAUGHTERS OF RESPECTABLE AND HIGH-RANKING SAMURAI FAMILIES BELIEVE THIS!
LIKEWISE, FAR TOO MANY IN OUR LAND TAKE IT FOR GRANTED THAT SUCCESSION IN WARRIOR HOUSES DOTH FOLLOW THE FEMALE LINE!
'TIS MEN WHO EXCELLED IN THE USE OF MILITARY FORCE SINCE ANCIENT TIMES, AND CONSEQUENTLY, SAMURAI FAMILIES DID TRADITIONALLY DESCEND FROM MALE TO MALE.
THIS IS THE REASON THAT, EVEN IN OUR DAY, THE SONS OF THE WARRIOR CLASS ARE TAUGHT SUCH MARTIAL ARTS AS ARCHERY, FENCING, AND LANCING. 'TIS A VESTIGE OF THE OLD WAYS.
THE YOUNG LADY IS JUST FOUR YEARS OLD! MISTRESS ARAI HAKUSEKI DOTH MAKE HER LESSONS TOO DIFFICULT...
AND THAT IS WHY, LADY CHIYO, YOUR MOTHER THE LORD SHOGUN DID ACCEPT MY COUNSEL AND REVOKE THE DECREE MADE BY HER PREDECESSOR, LORD TSUNAYOSHI, THAT ONLY THE DAUGHTERS OF WARRIOR HOUSES MAY SUCCEED AS HEAD OF THE FAMILY.
IF WHAT YOU SAY IS TRUE, HAKUSEKI, THEN SHOULD IT COME TO PASS THAT THE RED-FACE POX IS NO MORE AND THE NUMBER OF MEN IN THE LAND DOTH GROW, THE OUTER CHAMBERS OF EDO CASTLE WILL BE FILLED WITH MANLY COSTUMES...

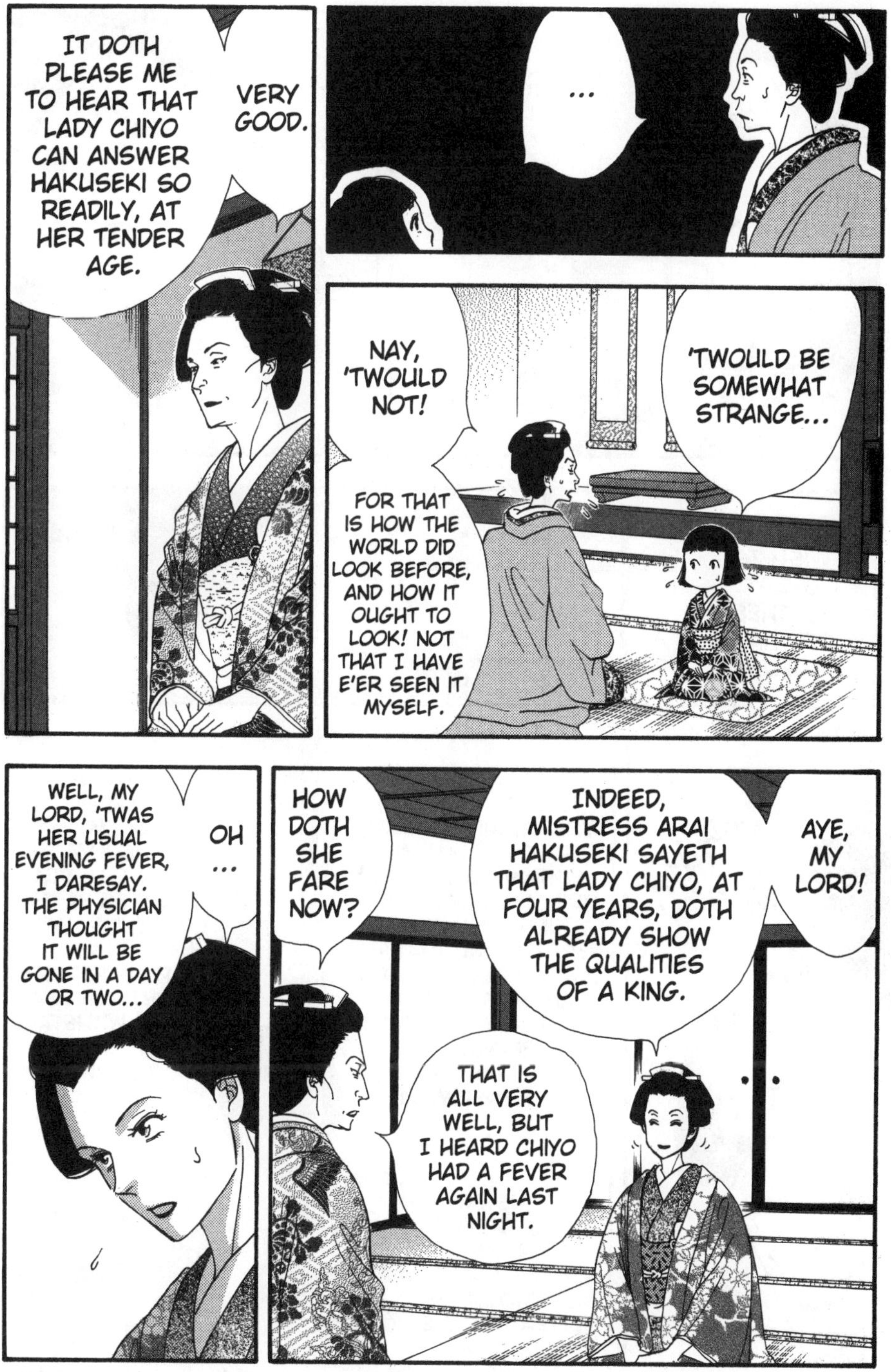
...
'TWOULD BE SOMEWHAT STRANGE...
NAY, 'TWOULD NOT!
FOR THAT IS HOW THE WORLD DID LOOK BEFORE, AND HOW IT OUGHT TO LOOK! NOT THAT I HAVE E'ER SEEN IT MYSELF.
VERY GOOD.
IT DOTH PLEASE ME TO HEAR THAT LADY CHIYO CAN ANSWER HAKUSEKI SO READILY, AT HER TENDER AGE.
AYE, MY LORD!
INDEED, MISTRESS ARAI HAKUSEKI SAYETH THAT LADY CHIYO, AT FOUR YEARS, DOTH ALREADY SHOW THE QUALITIES OF A KING.
THAT IS ALL VERY WELL, BUT I HEARD CHIYO HAD A FEVER AGAIN LAST NIGHT.
HOW DOTH SHE FARE NOW?
OH ...
WELL, MY LORD, 'TWAS HER USUAL EVENING FEVER, I DARESAY. THE PHYSICIAN THOUGHT IT WILL BE GONE IN A DAY OR TWO...

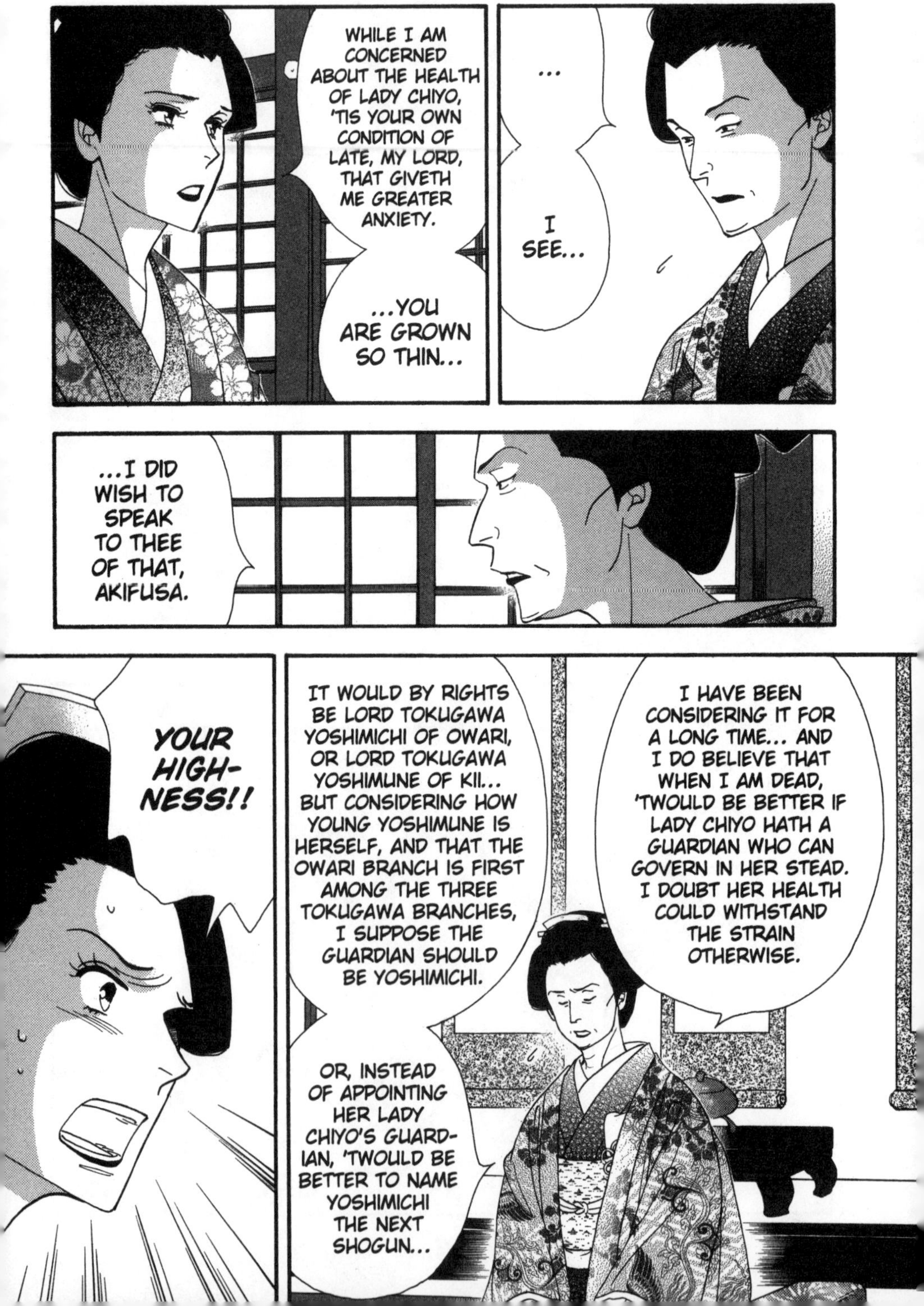
...
I SEE...
WHILE I AM CONCERNED ABOUT THE HEALTH OF LADY CHIYO, 'TIS YOUR OWN CONDITION OF LATE, MY LORD, THAT GIVETH ME GREATER ANXIETY.
...YOU ARE GROWN SO THIN...
...I DID WISH TO SPEAK TO THEE OF THAT, AKIFUSA.
I HAVE BEEN CONSIDERING IT FOR A LONG TIME... AND I DO BELIEVE THAT WHEN I AM DEAD, 'TWOULD BE BETTER IF LADY CHIYO HATH A GUARDIAN WHO CAN GOVERN IN HER STEAD. I DOUBT HER HEALTH COULD WITHSTAND THE STRAIN OTHERWISE.
IT WOULD BY RIGHTS BE LORD TOKUGAWA YOSHIMICHI OF OWARI, OR LORD TOKUGAWA YOSHIMUNE OF KII... BUT CONSIDERING HOW YOUNG YOSHIMUNE IS HERSELF, AND THAT THE OWARI BRANCH IS FIRST AMONG THE THREE TOKUGAWA BRANCHES, I SUPPOSE THE GUARDIAN SHOULD BE YOSHIMICHI.
OR, INSTEAD OF APPOINTING HER LADY CHIYO'S GUARDIAN, 'TWOULD BE BETTER TO NAME YOSHIMICHI THE NEXT SHOGUN...
YOUR HIGHNESS!!

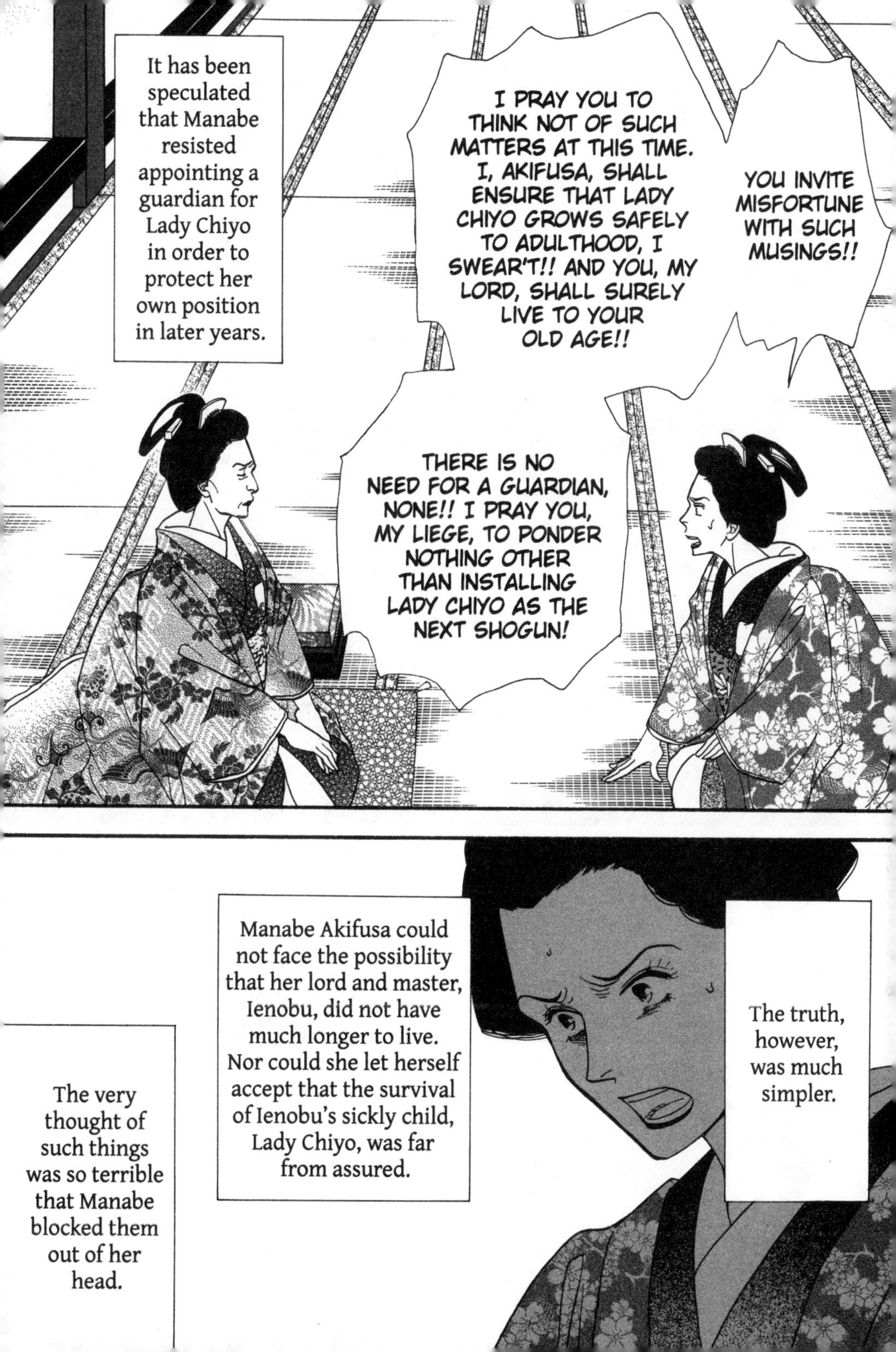
YOU INVITE MISFORTUNE WITH SUCH MUSINGS!!
I PRAY YOU TO THINK NOT OF SUCH MATTERS AT THIS TIME. I, AKIFUSA, SHALL ENSURE THAT LADY CHIYO GROWS SAFELY TO ADULTHOOD, I SWEAR'T!! AND YOU, MY LORD, SHALL SURELY LIVE TO YOUR OLD AGE!!
It has been speculated that Manabe resisted appointing a guardian for Lady Chiyo in order to protect her own position in later years.
THERE IS NO NEED FOR A GUARDIAN, NONE!! I PRAY YOU, MY LIEGE, TO PONDER NOTHING OTHER THAN INSTALLING LADY CHIYO AS THE NEXT SHOGUN!
The truth, however, was much simpler.
Manabe Akifusa could not face the possibility that her lord and master, Ienobu, did not have much longer to live. Nor could she let herself accept that the survival of Ienobu's sickly child, Lady Chiyo, was far from assured.
The very thought of such things was so terrible that Manabe blocked them out of her head.

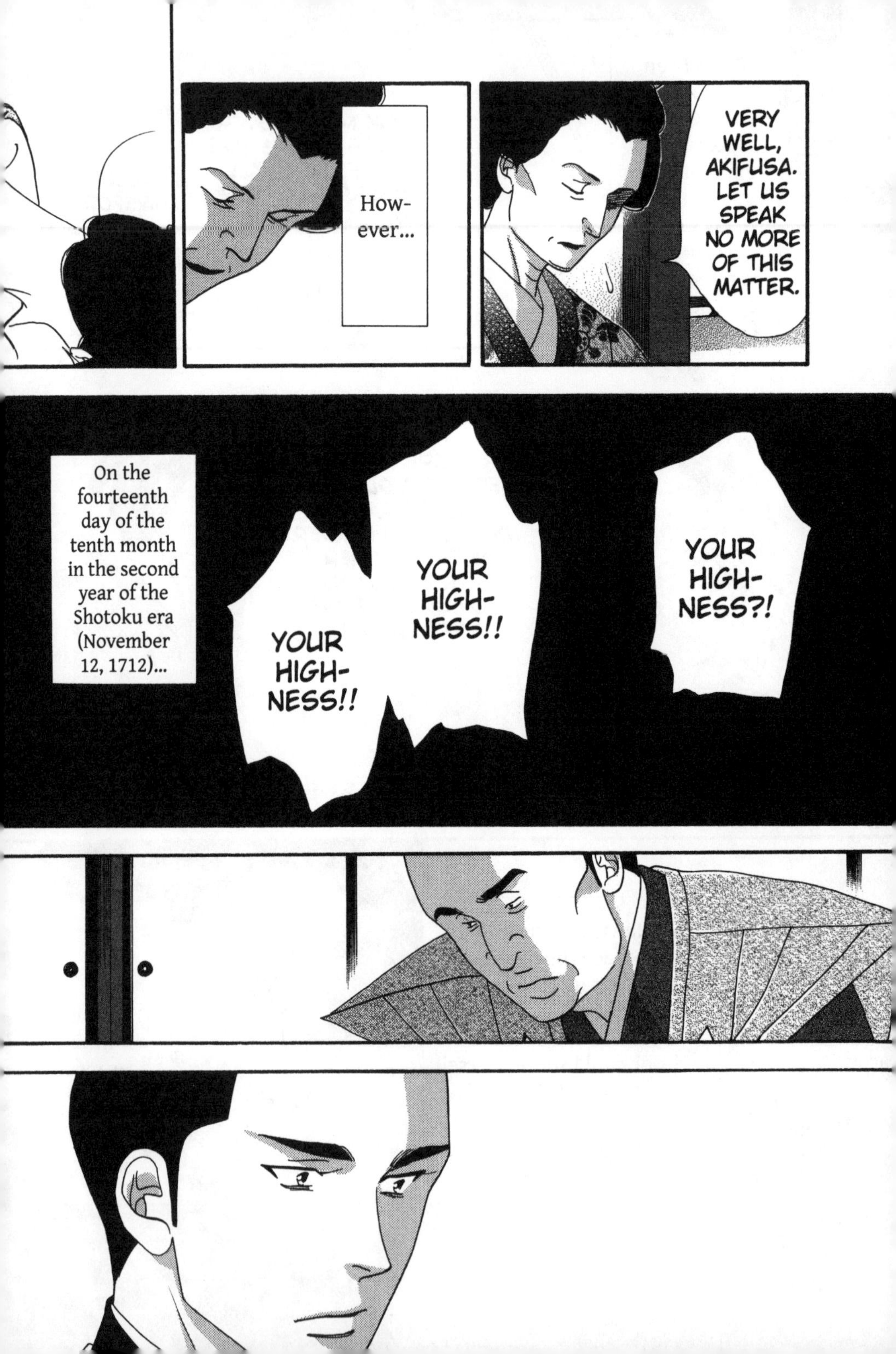
VERY WELL, AKIFUSA. LET US SPEAK NO MORE OF THIS MATTER.
However...
YOUR HIGHNESS?!
YOUR HIGHNESS!!
YOUR HIGHNESS!!
On the fourteenth day of the tenth month in the second year of the Shotoku era (November 12, 1712)...

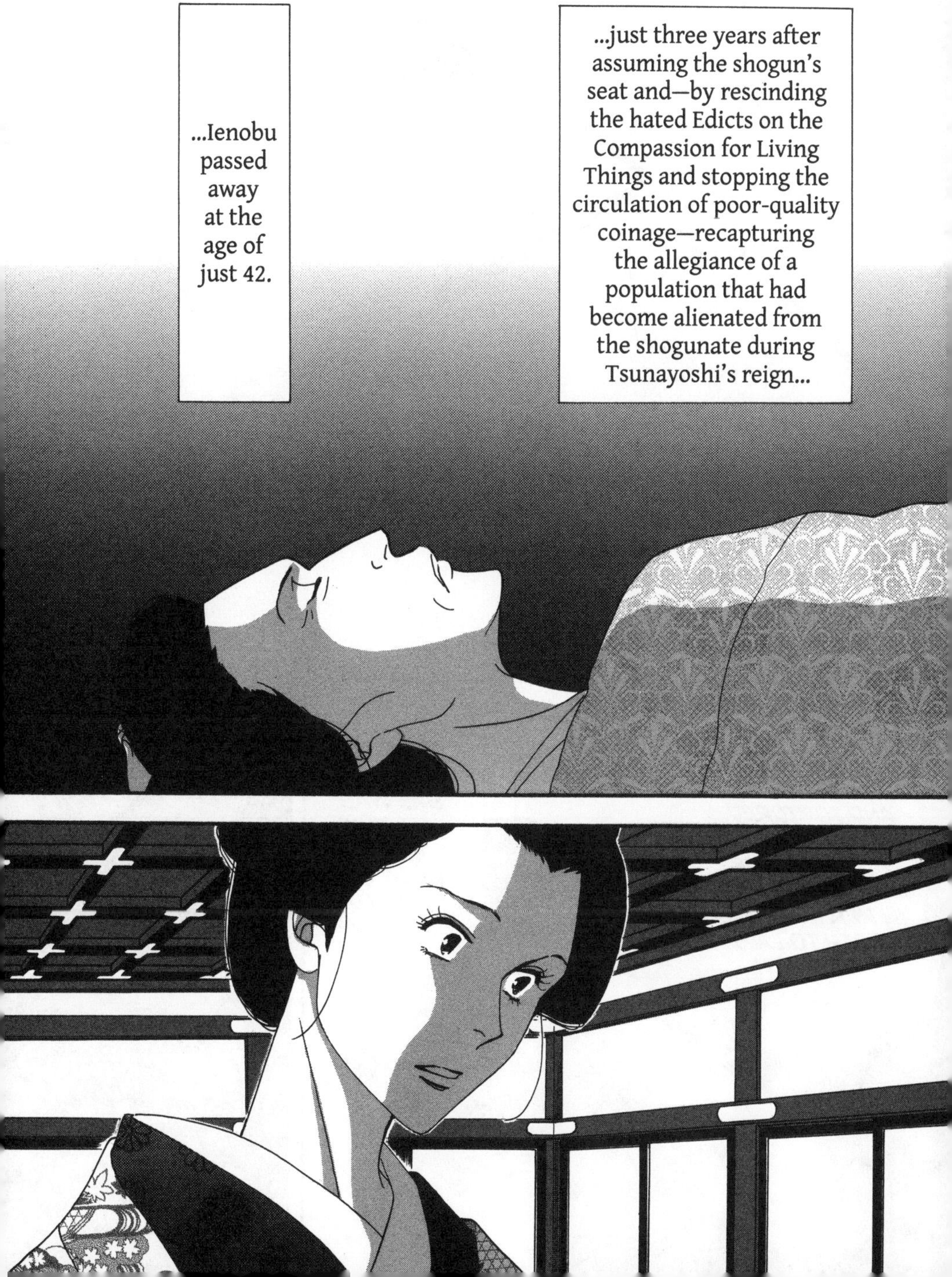
...just three years after assuming the shogun's seat and—by rescinding the hated Edicts on the Compassion for Living Things and stopping the circulation of poor-quality coinage—recapturing the allegiance of a population that had become alienated from the shogunate during Tsunayoshi's reign...
...Ienobu passed away at the age of just 42.

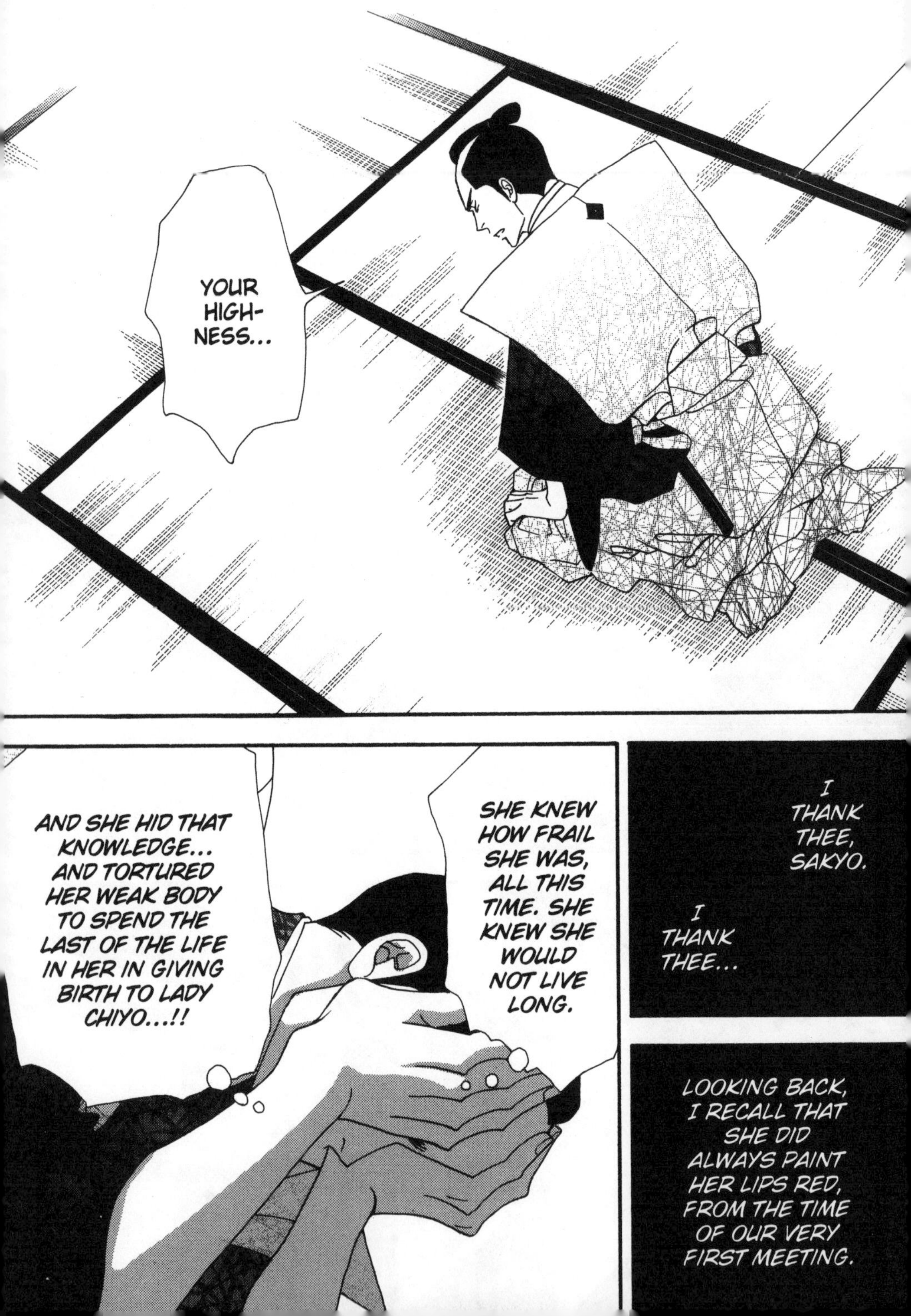
YOUR HIGH-NESS...
I THANK THEE, SAKYO.
I THANK THEE...
LOOKING BACK, I RECALL THAT SHE DID ALWAYS PAINT HER LIPS RED, FROM THE TIME OF OUR VERY FIRST MEETING.
SHE KNEW HOW FRAIL SHE WAS, ALL THIS TIME. SHE KNEW SHE WOULD NOT LIVE LONG.
AND SHE HID THAT KNOWLEDGE... AND TORTURED HER WEAK BODY TO SPEND THE LAST OF THE LIFE IN HER IN GIVING BIRTH TO LADY CHIYO...!!

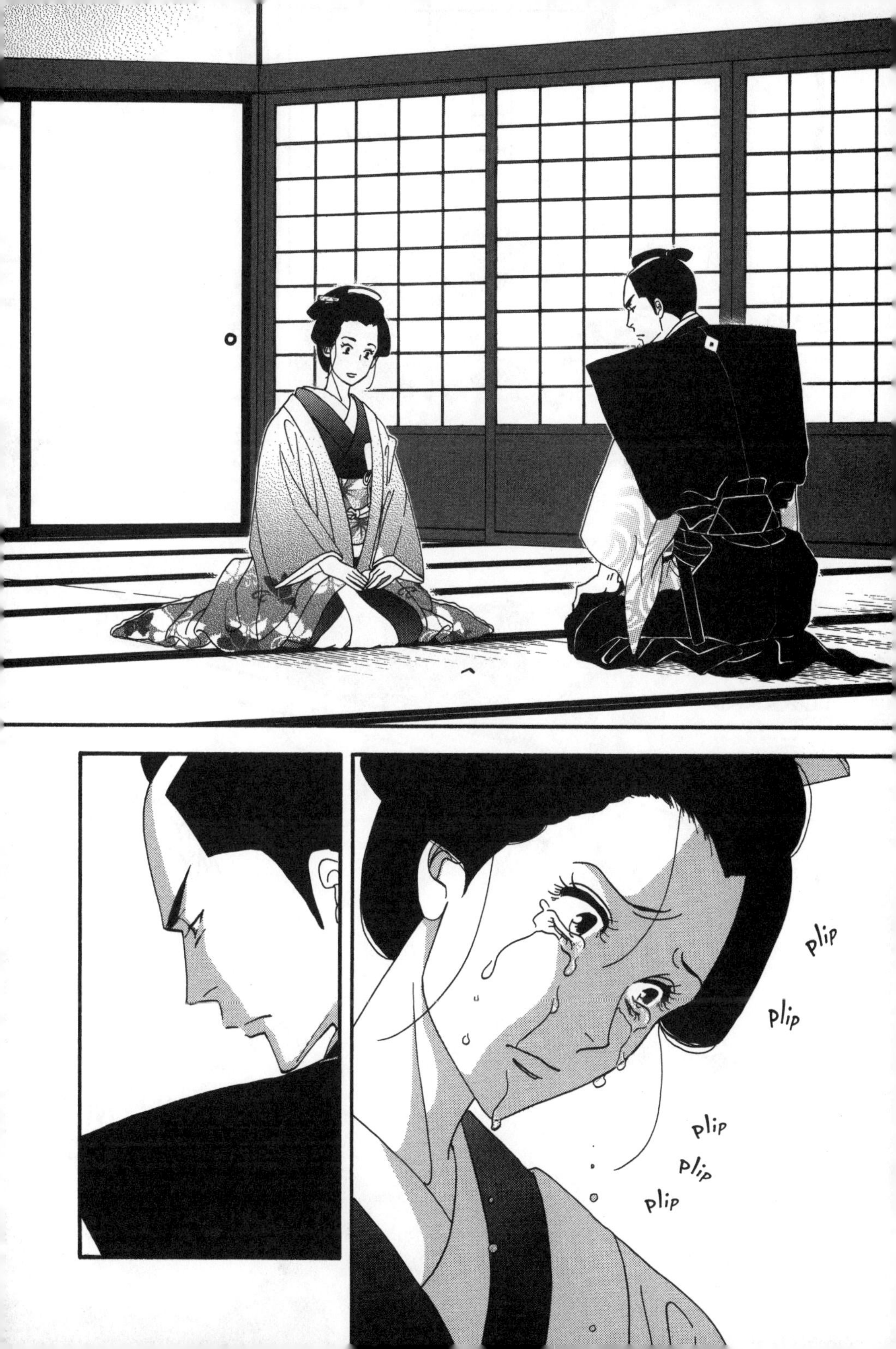
plip
plip
plip
plip
plip

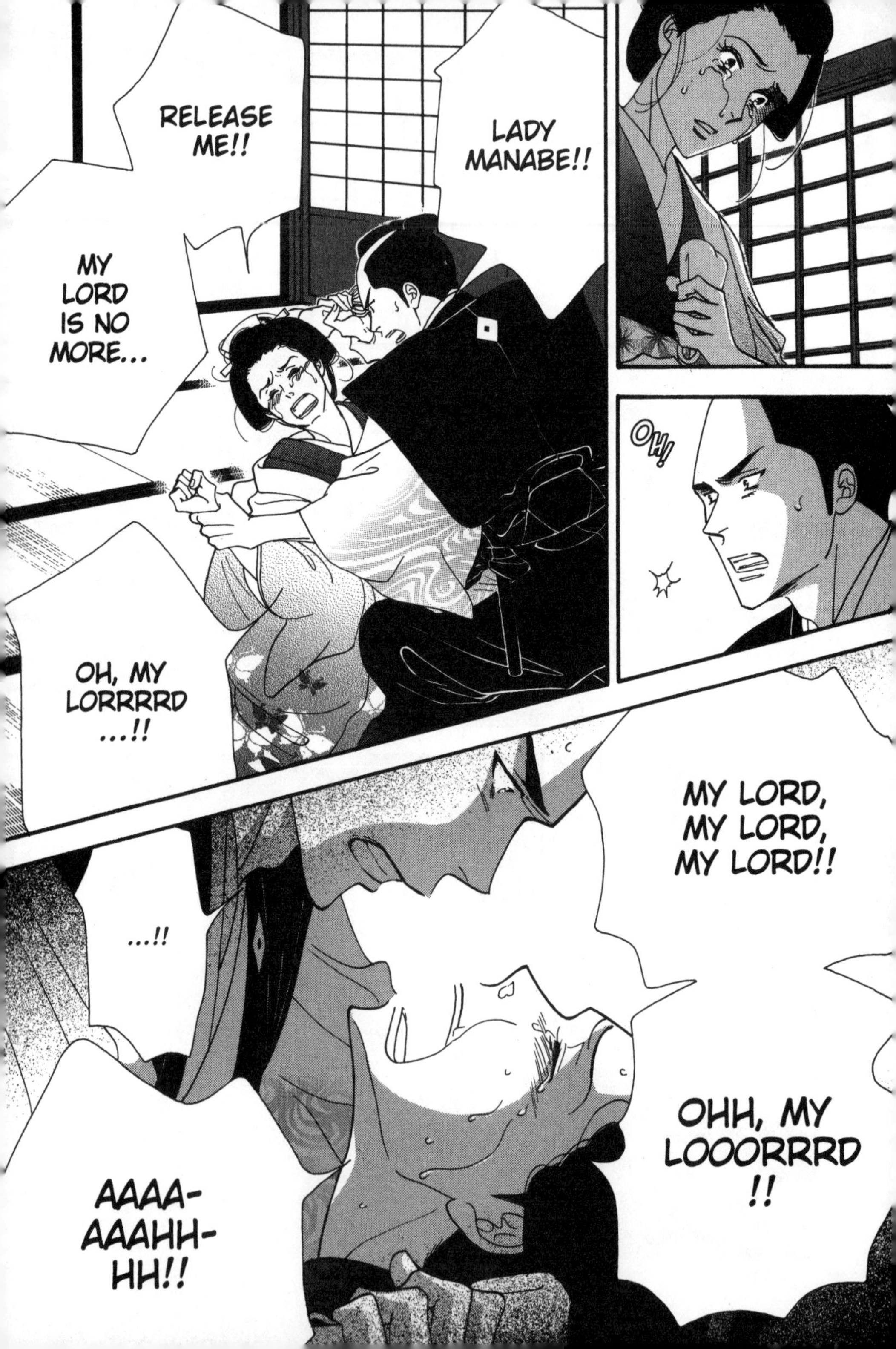
OH!
LADY MANABE!!
RELEASE ME!!
MY LORD IS NO MORE...
OH, MY LORRRRD ...!!
MY LORD, MY LORD, MY LORD!!
...!!
OHH, MY LOOORRRD !!
AAAA-AAAHH-HH!!

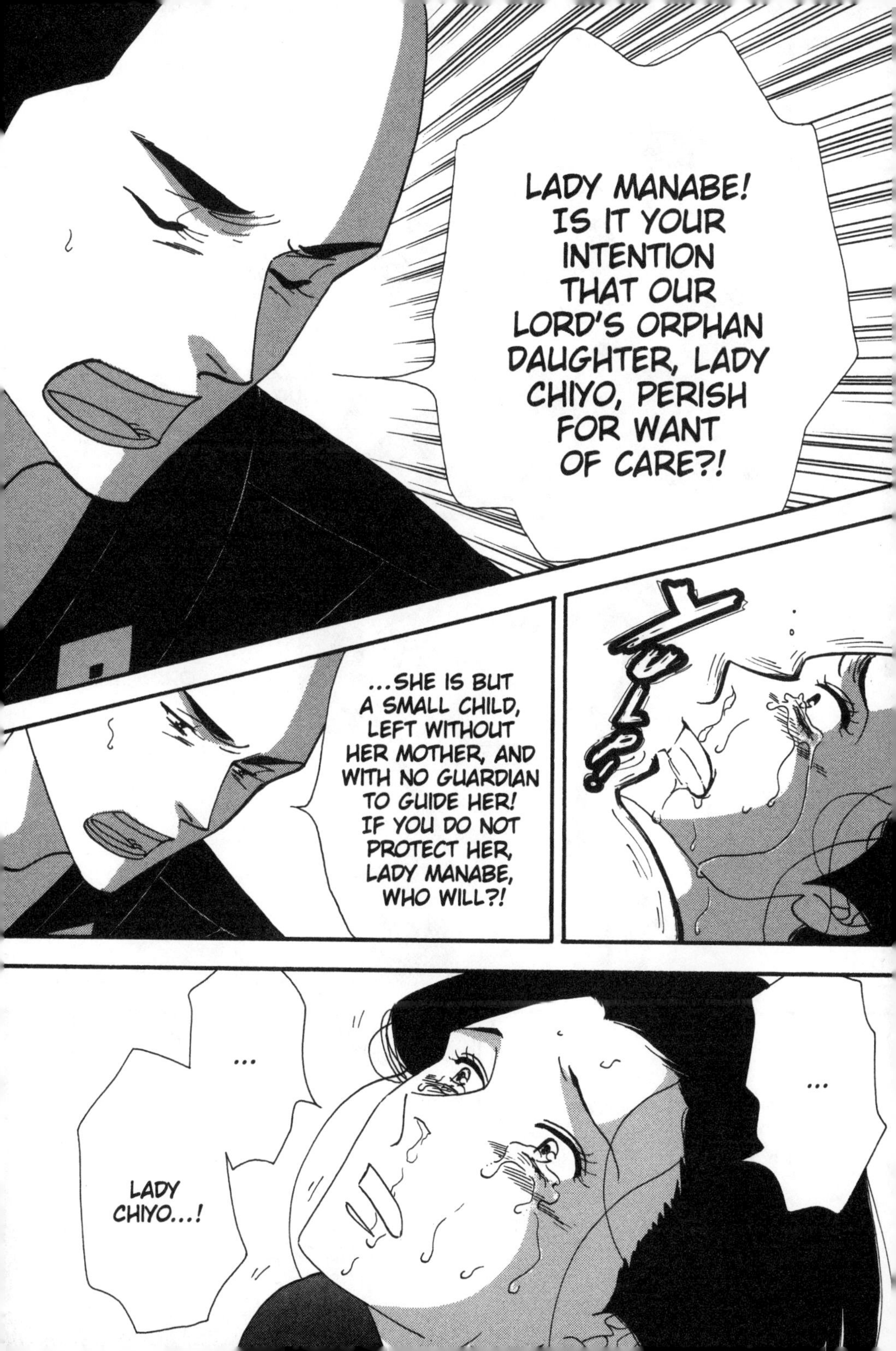
LADY MANABE! IS IT YOUR INTENTION THAT OUR LORD'S ORPHAN DAUGHTER, LADY CHIYO, PERISH FOR WANT OF CARE?!
...SHE IS BUT A SMALL CHILD, LEFT WITHOUT HER MOTHER, AND WITH NO GUARDIAN TO GUIDE HER! IF YOU DO NOT PROTECT HER, LADY MANABE, WHO WILL?!
...
...
LADY CHIYO...!

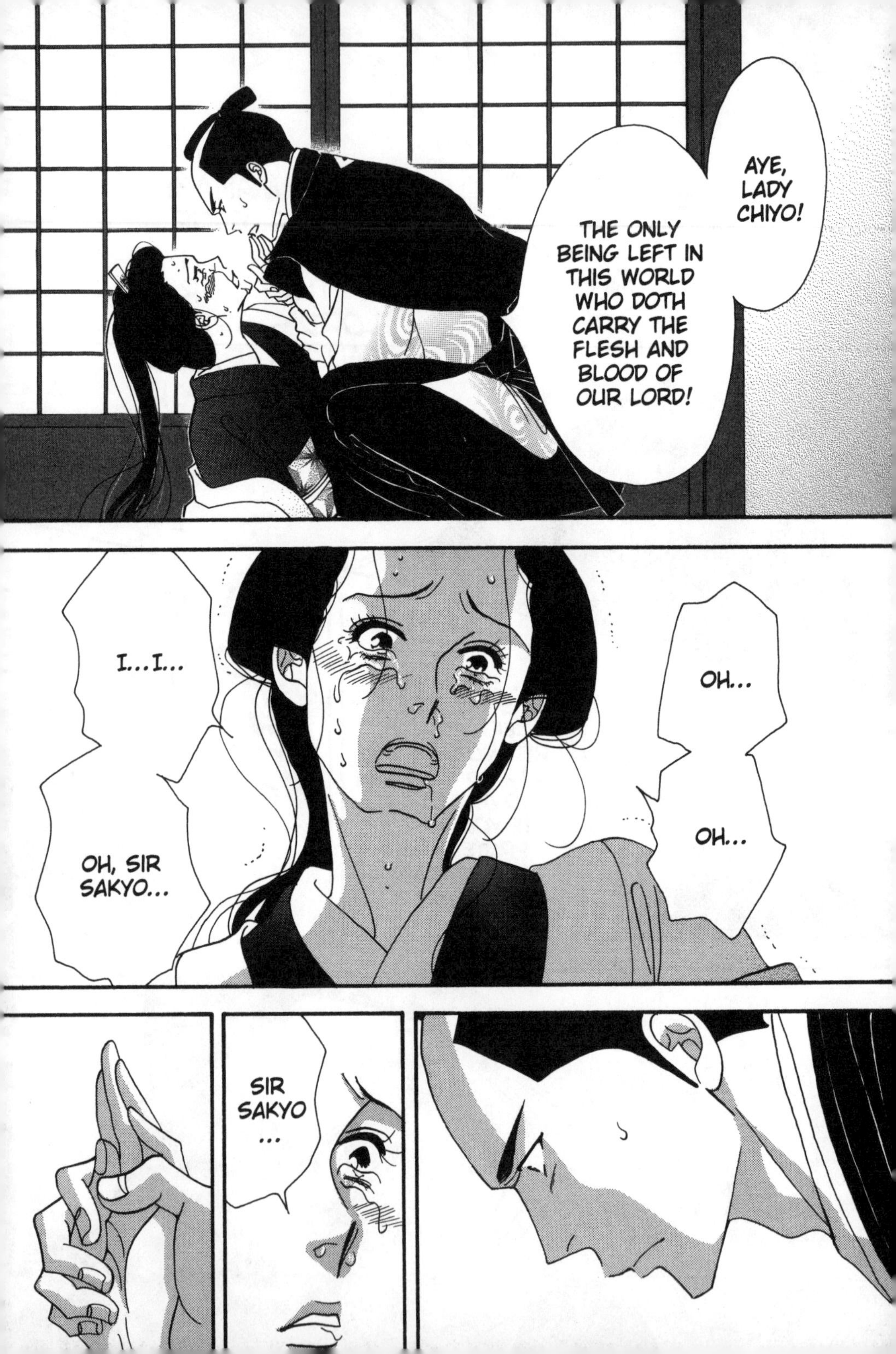
AYE, LADY CHIYO!
THE ONLY BEING LEFT IN THIS WORLD WHO DOTH CARRY THE FLESH AND BLOOD OF OUR LORD!
OH...
OH...
I...I...
OH, SIR SAKYO...
SIR SAKYO ...

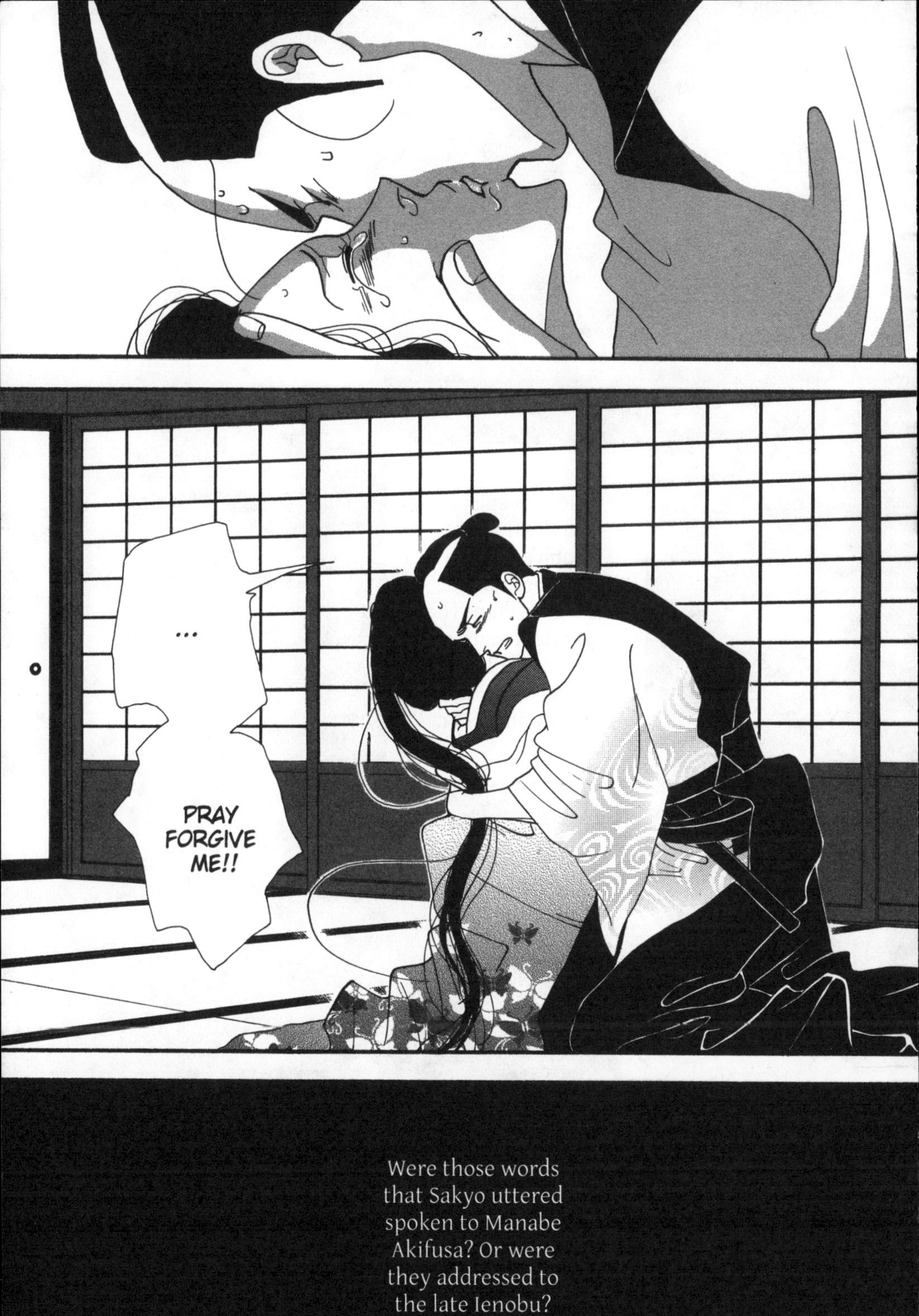
...
PRAY FORGIVE ME!!
Were those words that Sakyo uttered spoken to Manabe Akifusa? Or were they addressed to the late Ienobu?

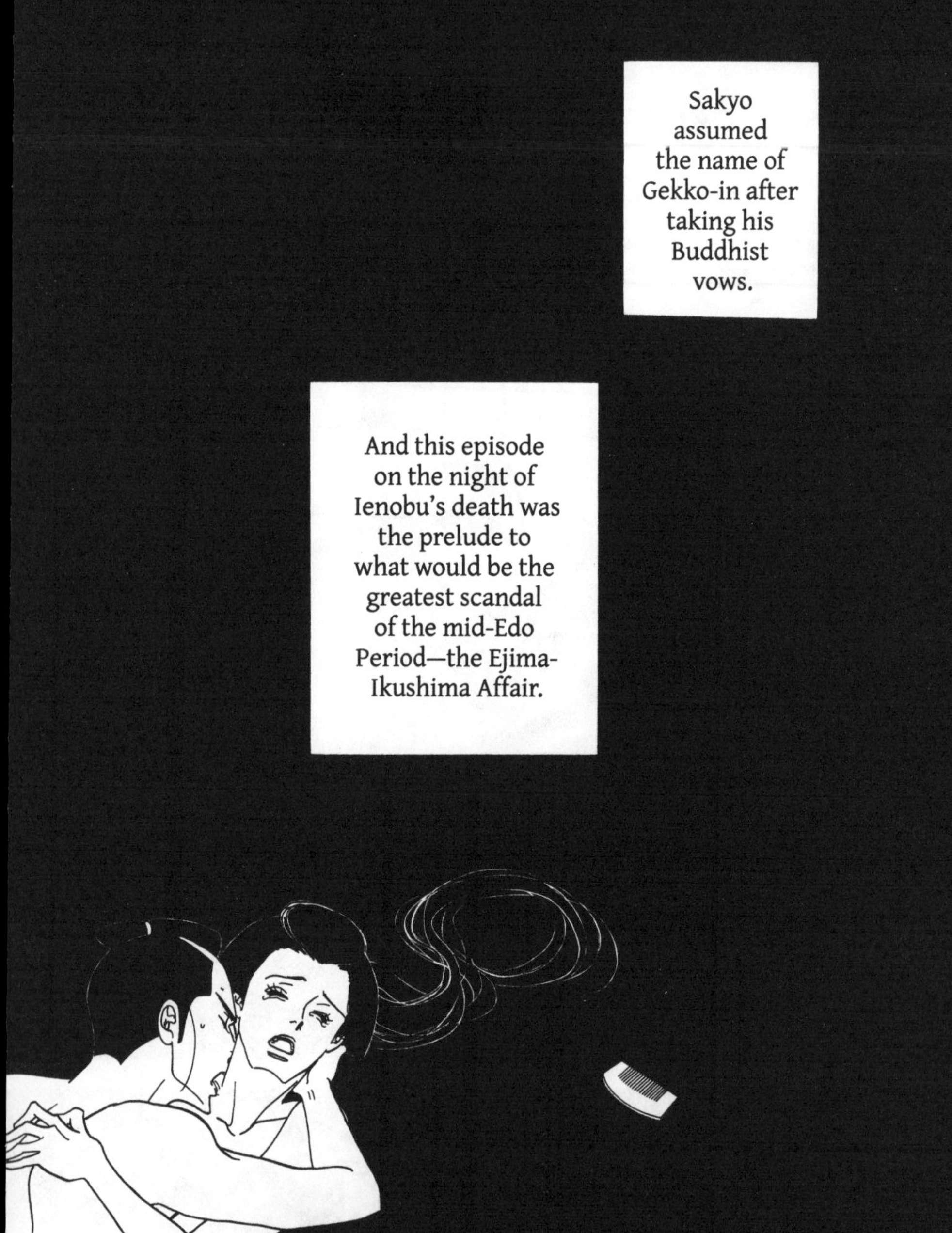
Sakyo assumed the name of Gekko-in after taking his Buddhist vows.
And this episode on the night of Ienobu's death was the prelude to what would be the greatest scandal of the mid-Edo Period—the Ejima-Ikushima Affair.

Ōoku
● THE INNER CHAMBERS

Ōoku: The Inner Chambers

VOLUME 6 · END NOTES

by Akemi Wegmüller

Page 8, panel 1 · Kii branch

The three Tokugawa branches (*gosanke*) descended from three of the historical Ieyasu's sons. The branches are the Owari, Mito, and Kii.

Page 8, panel 1 · Retirement

In Japan an aristocrat could retire and pass the title to his heir.

Page 34, panel 1 · Yokan

Candy made from sweet bean paste jellied with agar (a seaweed that acts like gelatin).

Page 129, panel 3 · Okada-ya

The paneled curtain over the door is called a *noren*, which serves the same function as a signboard does in the West.

Page 131, panel 1 · Yoshiwara

The pleasure quarters, originally located near what is today Nihonbashi in central Tokyo and eventually moved to the outskirts of the city. The area was walled off from the rest of the city and the courtesans were restricted to its confines.

Page 155, panel 1 · Zhu Xi

An influential Confucian scholar from 10th century China.

Page 163, panel 2 · Hatamoto

Hatamoto belong to the samurai class and are direct retainers of the shogunate. The term literally means "at the base of the flag," and refers to the position of military commander in charge of defending the army camp and flag.

Page 181, panel 1 · Yuzen fabrics

A type of resist-dyeing, similar to batik.

Creator Biography

Fumi Yoshinaga

Fumi Yoshinaga is a Tokyo-born manga creator who debuted in 1994 with *Tsuki to Sandaru* (*The Moon and the Sandals*). Yoshinaga has won numerous awards, including the 2009 Osamu Tezuka Cultural Prize for *Ōoku*, the 2002 Kodansha Manga Award for her series *Antique Bakery* and the 2006 Japan Media Arts Festival Excellence Award for *Ōoku*. She was also nominated for the 2008 Eisner Award for Best Writer/Artist.

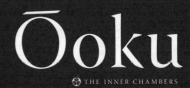

Ōoku

THE INNER CHAMBERS

Ōoku: The Inner Chambers
Vol. 6

VIZ Signature Edition

Story and Art by Fumi Yoshinaga

Translation & Adaptation/Akemi Wegmüller
Touch-up Art & Lettering/Monalisa De Asis
Design/Fawn Lau
Editor/Pancha Diaz

Printed in Canada

Published by VIZ Media, LLC
P.O. Box 77010
San Francisco, CA 94107

10 9 8 7 6 5 4 3 2 1
First printing, July 2011

www.viz.com

VIZ SIGNATURE
www.vizsignature.com

RATED M FOR MATURE

PARENTAL ADVISORY
ŌOKU: THE INNER CHAMBERS is rated M for Mature and is recommended for ages 18 and up. Contains violence and sexual situations.
ratings.viz.com

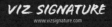

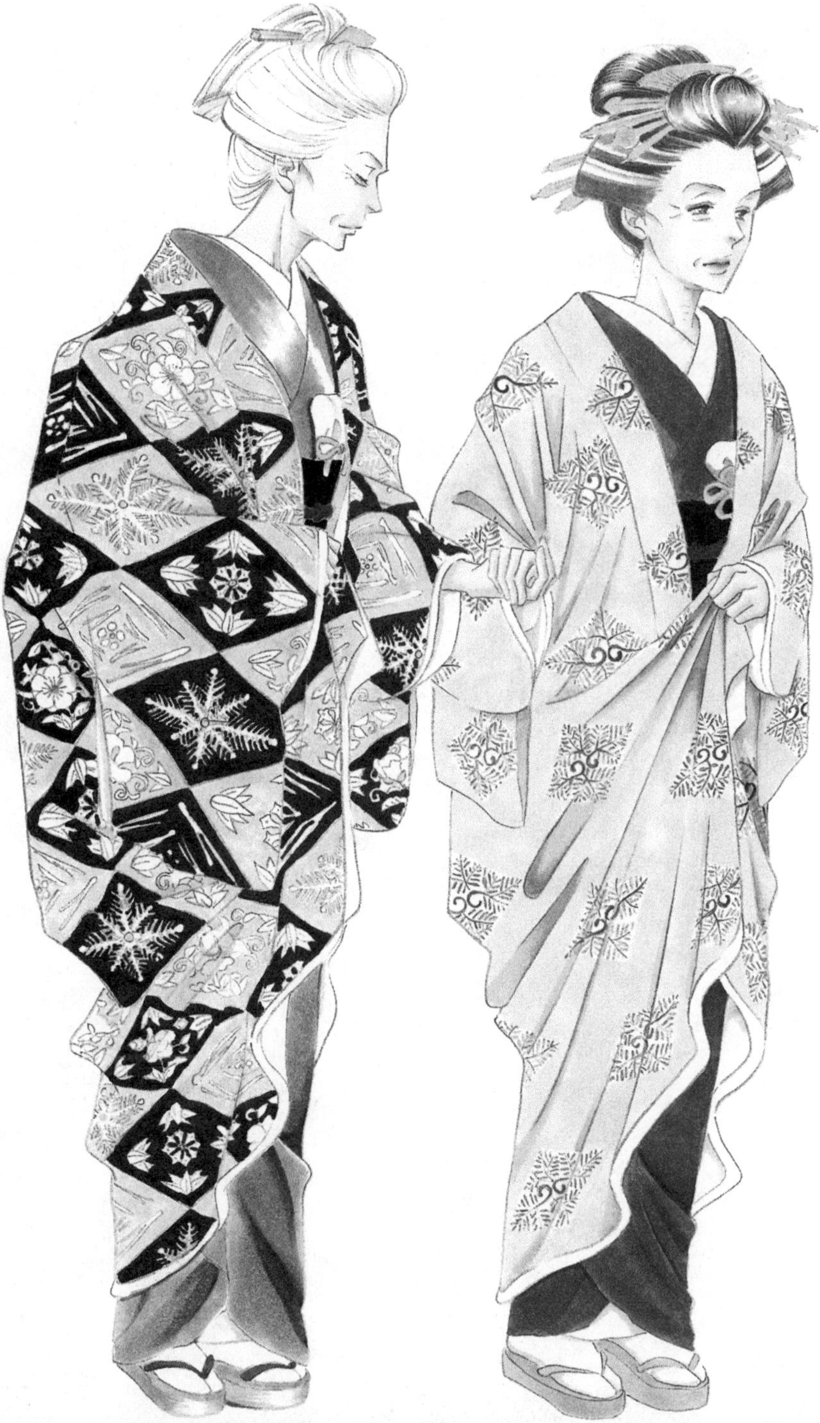

THIS IS THE LAST PAGE.

Ooku: The Inner Chambers has been printed in the original Japanese format in order to preserve the orientation of the original artwork.

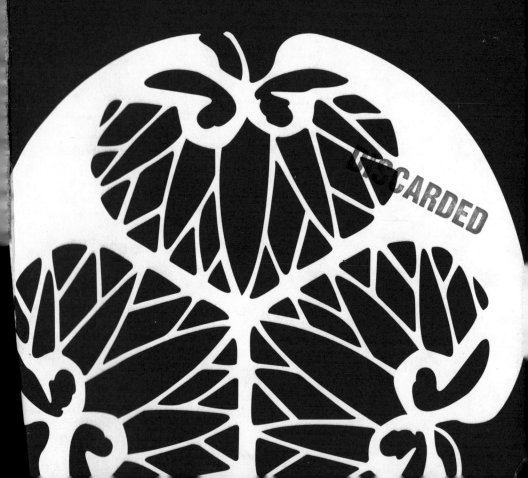